# COMMUNITY PROPERTY

## IN A NUTSHELL®

### FOURTH EDITION

JO CARRILLO
Professor of Law,
University of California
Hastings College of the Law

WEST
ACADEMIC
PUBLISHING

*For*
CLCM (1955–2017)
and
EJH (1935–2017)
*of blessed memory.*

# PREFACE TO THE FOURTH EDITION

A community property system is a public institution for administering property rights between married persons. The premise of a community property system is that spouses are partners, and as such they should share ownership of property that they acquire during marriage by effort. The legal idea of intimate partners who work together is one whose time has come. And yet, only a minority of U.S. states allow for community property between married persons.

COMMUNITY PROPERTY IN A NUTSHELL, 4th EDITION offers an updated roadmap to the law of the nine U.S. community property jurisdictions: Arizona, California, Idaho, Louisiana, Nevada, New Mexico, Texas, Washington, and Wisconsin. I also include, where relevant, information about Alaska and Tennessee, two states that offer married persons an option to adopt community property by private document.

The audience for this work is students and state legislators. Students because they will be the lawyers and judges of the future. And state legislators because the community property terrain is ever-changing, and law practice (which is often discretionary and oral) too often contradicts the written rules of legal doctrine and policy. It seems useful, therefore, to provide a handy reference to the written law for state legislators who seek to modernize the legal institutions of marriage and divorce.

Each chapter is divided into three parts. Part A overviews the chapter topic. Part B details the law. Part C presents specific statutes and cases from each of the nine U.S. community property jurisdictions.

I wish to thank the University of Michigan Law Library for the hospitable and extended use of its on-site collection. A special thanks to RCV, MCO, LJO, and KBV.

JO CARRILLO

February 23, 2018

# OUTLINE

PREFACE TO THE FOURTH EDITION ............................. V
TABLE OF CASES ...................................................... XXI

### PART 1. PRELIMINARY MATTERS

**Chapter 1. Preliminary Matters** ........................... 3
A. Overview ................................................................ 3
   1. Basic Definitions ............................................... 5
      a. Property ...................................................... 6
      b. Acquired ..................................................... 7
      c. Onerously .................................................... 7
      d. Married ....................................................... 8
      e. Domiciled .................................................. 10
      f. Apportionment ......................................... 10
   2. Implications of Characterization .................. 11
   3. Rationale for the Community Property
      System ............................................................. 12
   4. Types of Community Property Systems ....... 14
B. History: Common Law versus Community
   Property .................................................................. 16
C. Individual Community Property States ............. 18
   1. Common Threads ............................................. 18
   2. Some (Current) Uncommon Threads ........... 20
   3. Historical Differences Among the U.S.
      Community Property States ......................... 22

**Chapter 2. Contractual Modification** ............... 27
A. Overview ................................................................ 27
B. Detail .................................................................... 29
   1. Premarital Agreements Before 1983 ........... 29

2. The Uniform Premarital Agreement Act of
   1983 ................................................................ 33
3. The Uniform Premarital and Marital
   Agreement Act of 2012 ................................... 36
4. Transmutations ............................................... 38
   a. Formalities: Writing and Express
      Declaration Requirements ....................... 41
   b. Transmutation by Deed ............................ 42
   c. Interspousal Obligations Implicit in a
      Transmutation: Voluntariness and
      Financial Disclosure ................................ 47
   d. Exempt Property ....................................... 49
   e. Transmutation by Operation of Law ....... 50
C. Individual States ................................................ 50
   1. Arizona ........................................................... 50
   2. California ....................................................... 55
   3. Idaho .............................................................. 67
   4. Louisiana ....................................................... 71
   5. Nevada ............................................................ 78
   6. New Mexico .................................................... 83
   7. Texas .............................................................. 87
   8. Washington .................................................... 90
   9. Wisconsin (WUMPA) ..................................... 94

**PART 2. CHARACTERIZATION**

**Chapter 3. Community Property** .................... **101**
A. Overview ............................................................ 101
B. Detail ................................................................. 101
   1. Types of Community Property Systems ..... 101
   2. The Community Property Sharing
      Principle ........................................................ 103
   3. The General Community Property
      Presumption ................................................. 105

4. Special Community Property
   Presumptions ................................................. 111
   a. The Joint Form Title Community
      Property Presumption ............................. 111
   b. A Special Presumption for Sums on
      Deposit in Any Demand Deposit
      Account of a Married Person ................... 114
5. Miscellaneous Statutory Provisions That
   Can Affect Characterization ........................ 121
   a. The (Now Obsolete) Married Woman's
      Separate Property Presumption ............. 121
   b. Preserving the Community Property
      Character of Property in a Revocable
      Trust ......................................................... 123
   c. Asset Appreciation versus Rents,
      Issues, and Profits ................................... 123
6. Statutes Protecting Third Parties ............... 124
7. Miscellaneous Statutory Provisions ........... 127
8. Alaska, Tennessee and Puerto Rico ............. 128
   a. Alaska ..................................................... 128
   b. Tennessee ................................................. 131
   c. Puerto Rico .............................................. 131
C. Individual States ............................................... 132
   1. Arizona ......................................................... 132
   2. California ...................................................... 137
   3. Idaho ............................................................. 142
   4. Louisiana ...................................................... 143
   5. Nevada .......................................................... 151
   6. New Mexico ................................................... 152
   7. Texas ............................................................. 154
   8. Washington ................................................... 158
   9. Wisconsin ..................................................... 159

**Chapter 4. Separate Property** ......................... **163**
A. Overview ............................................................... 163
B. Detail .................................................................... 164
   1. "Acquired": Timing and Effort ..................... 164
   2. When: Before Marriage ............................... 167
   3. When: After a Date of Separation .............. 170
   4. How: By Gift ................................................ 172
   5. How: Rents, Issues, and Profits from
      Separate Property ....................................... 174
   6. How: Personal Injury Recoveries ................. 177
      a. Proper Party to Bring the Action ........... 178
      b. Spousal Immunity ................................... 178
      c. The Community Property Defense ........ 180
      d. Reasons for Apportioning Personal
         Injury Settlements .................................. 182
      e. Elements of a Personal Injury
         Settlement .............................................. 185
      f. Problems with Apportioning Personal
         Injury Settlements .................................. 186
   7. Historic (Transitional) Forms of Separate
      Property ......................................................... 188
   8. Summing up: Acquisition Before
      Marriage, During Separation, and
      After Divorce ................................................ 192
C. Individual States ................................................. 192
   1. Arizona ........................................................ 192
   2. California ...................................................... 194
   3. Idaho ............................................................ 197
   4. Louisiana ..................................................... 199
   5. Nevada ......................................................... 203
   6. New Mexico ................................................. 206
   7. Texas ............................................................ 208
   8. Washington .................................................. 212

9. Wisconsin .......................................... 215
D. Question and Answer................................ 220

**Chapter 5. Joint Tenancy Meets
Community Property** ............................... 225
A. Overview............................................... 225
  1. Types of Joint Form Titles ....................... 225
    a. Tenancy in Common.......................... 226
    b. Joint Tenancy with the Right of
      Survivorship.................................... 226
    c. Tenancy by the Entirety..................... 227
    d. Community Property........................... 228
    e. Community Property with the Right of
      Survivorship.................................... 229
    f. Homestead Rights ............................ 230
  2. Common Law Concurrent Titles in a
    Community Property System..................... 231
B. Detail .................................................. 234
  1. Prevalence of the Joint Tenancy Title
    Form ................................................ 234
  2. Joint Tenancy Compared with
    Community Property.............................. 236
    a. Dissolution Proceedings ..................... 238
    b. Severance ..................................... 238
    c. Probate Law Interaction ..................... 239
    d. Tax Consequences of a Sale After
      Death........................................... 240
  3. Creating the Joint Tenancy ..................... 245
    a. "Joint"......................................... 245
    b. "Joint Tenancy"............................... 245
    c. "Joint Tenancy with the Right of
      Survivorship" ................................. 246

       d. Deed Declarations and Extrinsic
          Evidence to Hold the Property as
          Separate Property ................................... 246
   4. The Special Joint Form Title Community
     Property Presumption ............................... 246
   5. Nominal Title, "For Convenience" .............. 251
   6. Joint Bank Accounts ................................... 252
   7. Joint Safe-Deposit Boxes ........................... 254
   8. Summing up: Joint Form Titles at
     Dissolution and Death ............................... 255
C. Individual States ............................................. 256
   1. Arizona ....................................................... 256
   2. California ..................................................... 261
   3. Idaho ........................................................... 265
   4. Louisiana .................................................... 266
   5. Nevada ........................................................ 266
   6. New Mexico ................................................ 267
   7. Texas ........................................................... 270
   8. Washington ................................................. 273
   9. Wisconsin ................................................... 278

**Chapter 6. Characterization Problems** ......... 281
A. Overview ......................................................... 281
   1. Approach .................................................... 281
     a. Before .................................................... 281
     b. After ..................................................... 281
   2. Commingling .............................................. 284
     a. Complete Ownership .............................. 285
     b. Pro Tanto (Pro Rata) Ownership ........... 286
     c. Credit Acquisitions ............................... 287
     d. Transmutations by Operation of Law .... 290
   3. Tracing Records .......................................... 291

4. Inception of Title versus Pro Tanto
   Ownership ...................................................... 292
B. Detail ................................................................. 296
1. Tracing to and Through Commingled
   Bank Accounts ............................................. 296
   a. Techniques and Options ........................... 297
   b. Common Law Equitable Claims .............. 300
   c. Conversion Damages ................................ 302
2. Community Labor in a Separate Property
   Business ......................................................... 304
   a. The Civil Law Approach versus the
      American Law Approach ......................... 306
   b. *Pereira* Apportionment versus
      *Van Camp* Reimbursement ..................... 307
      i.   The Apportionment Approach .......... 307
      ii.  The Reimbursement Approach ........ 308
      iii. *Pereira* .................................................... 309
      iv.  *Van Camp* ............................................. 311
      v.   Excess Profits or
           Reimbursement? ............................... 312
   c. Extent of the Gain ................................... 313
   d. Type of Business Organization .............. 314
   e. Contrasts to Community Property
      Doctrines .................................................... 315
3. Credit Acquisitions ...................................... 316
   a. General Principles ................................... 316
   b. Character of Loan Proceeds (Borrowed
      Funds) ......................................................... 316
   c. Community Property Contributions to
      the Purchase of Separate Property ........ 317
   d. A General Approach ................................. 318
4. Deferred Compensation ................................ 321
   a. Types of Deferred Compensation ........... 321

b. Severance, Death, Disability, and
Retirement Benefits ............................... 323
c. Division upon Divorce of Retirement
and Disability Benefits........................... 328
d. Government Retirement Plans.............. 330
C. Individual States.................................................. 334
1. Arizona ........................................................ 334
2. California..................................................... 340
3. Idaho............................................................ 358
4. Louisiana..................................................... 363
5. Nevada......................................................... 367
6. New Mexico ................................................. 369
7. Texas............................................................ 371
8. Washington ................................................. 375
9. Wisconsin .................................................... 380

## PART 3. MANAGEMENT AND CONTROL

**Chapter 7. Management and Control** ............ **385**
A. Overview............................................................... 385
B. Detail .................................................................. 385
1. Management and Control............................. 385
a. Community Property in General............ 387
b. Community Personal Property .............. 389
c. Community Real Property ...................... 389
d. Separate Property .................................. 390
e. Commingled Property ............................ 390
f. Partnership Fiduciary Duties................ 390
2. The Partnership Fiduciary Standard ......... 391
3. Time Frames ............................................... 395
4. Gifts ............................................................ 396
a. Gifts of Community Property Made by
One Spouse to the Other Spouse .......... 397

    b. Gifts or Low Value Transfers of Community Personal Property Made by One Spouse to a Third Party ............ 398
    c. Portion of the Gift That Is Set Aside..... 401
    d. Gifts Made by One Spouse to a Nonspousal POD Beneficiary in a Term Life Insurance Policy..................... 404
C. Individual States................................................ 408
  1. Arizona .......................................................... 408
  2. California........................................................ 409
  3. Idaho.............................................................. 414
  4. Louisiana....................................................... 415
  5. Nevada........................................................... 418
  6. New Mexico ................................................... 421
  7. Texas.............................................................. 423
  8. Washington ................................................... 426
  9. Wisconsin ...................................................... 428

**Chapter 8. Liabilities** ....................................... **433**
A. Overview............................................................. 433
B. Detail ................................................................. 436
  1. Liability of Community Property................. 439
    a. For Contract Obligations Incurred During Marriage...................................... 439
    b. For Obligations Incurred Before Marriage...................................................... 443
    c. For Other Obligations ............................ 447
    d. For Tort Liability Adjudged Against One Spouse................................................ 447
    e. Liability of One-Half of the Community............................................... 449

2. Liability of Separate Property ..................... 451
   a. For One Spouse's Individual Debts
      During Marriage...................................... 454
   b. For Debts Incurred During Marriage
      as a Community Manager...................... 455
C. Individual States................................................ 457
   1. Arizona ............................................................ 457
   2. California........................................................ 461
   3. Idaho................................................................ 466
   4. Louisiana........................................................ 470
   5. Nevada............................................................ 473
   6. New Mexico .................................................. 474
   7. Texas................................................................ 479
   8. Washington .................................................. 481
   9. Wisconsin ...................................................... 488

## PART 4. END OF MARRIAGE

**Chapter 9. Divorce**................................................ **497**
A. Overview................................................................ 497
B. Detail .................................................................... 498
   1. Ending the Community ............................... 498
   2. Annulment, Legal Separation,
      Dissolution ..................................................... 500
      a. Annulment ................................................ 501
      b. Legal Separation...................................... 501
      c. (Absolute) Divorce ................................. 502
   3. Dissolution of Property............................... 503
      a. The Theoretical Ideal ............................ 503
      b. Separate Property.................................... 507
      c. Community Property............................... 507
   4. Complications................................................ 508
      a. Concealed Assets ..................................... 508
      b. Omitted Assets......................................... 510

     c. Difficult to Divide Assets ........................ 511
     d. Conflict of Laws ..................................... 515
     e. Separation ............................................... 516
  5. Spousal Support ............................................. 517
C. Individual States .............................................. 520
  1. Arizona ......................................................... 520
  2. California ...................................................... 521
  3. Idaho ............................................................. 529
  4. Louisiana ...................................................... 531
  5. Nevada .......................................................... 532
  6. New Mexico .................................................. 534
  7. Texas ............................................................. 535
  8. Washington ................................................... 537
  9. Wisconsin ..................................................... 538

**Chapter 10. Death** .............................................**543**
A. Overview ......................................................... 543
  1. The Decedent's Estate ................................. 543
  2. Community Property Variations ................ 545
B. Detail ............................................................... 547
  1. Probate Administration of Community
    Property ........................................................ 547
     a. Administration of Community
       Property ................................................... 549
     b. Present Rules for the Administration
       of Community Property ........................... 549
  2. Forced Elections and Family
    Protections ................................................... 549
     a. Taking Under the Decedent's Will ........ 550
     b. Taking Against the Decedent's Will ...... 551
  3. Intestacy Statutes ....................................... 552
  4. Individual Retirement Account Assets ........ 555

C. Individual States..............................................557
   1. Arizona ............................................557
   2. California.........................................558
   3. Idaho...............................................563
   4. Louisiana.........................................564
   5. Nevada............................................569
   6. New Mexico .....................................570
   7. Texas...............................................572
   8. Washington .....................................574
   9. Wisconsin .......................................577

## PART 5. SPECIAL PROBLEMS

**Chapter 11. Nonmarital Relationships**..........**583**
A. Overview..............................................................583
B. Detail ................................................................584
   1. The Putative Spouse and the Division of
      Property...........................................584
   2. Nonmarried Cohabitants............................587
     a. Contract......................................589
     b. Implied Contract.....................................589
     c. Partnership .............................................591
     d. Form of Title ...........................................591
     e. Unjust Enrichment..................................592
     f. Constructive Trust...................................593
     g. Resulting Trust.......................................594
     h. General Equitable Principles..................594
C. Individual States..............................................594
   1. Arizona ............................................594
   2. California.........................................595
   3. Idaho...............................................599
   4. Louisiana.........................................601
   5. Nevada............................................604
   6. New Mexico .....................................605

7.  Texas....................................................... 606
8.  Washington ............................................. 609
9.  Wisconsin ............................................... 610

**Chapter 12. Federal Problems** ......................... **613**
A.  Federal Supremacy ...................................... 613
    1.  Overview of the Federal System ................. 613
    2.  Federal Pre-Emption ................................ 615
B.  State Constitutional Provisions ...................... 618
    1.  Overview: Federal and State
        Constitutions....................................... 618
    2.  State Constitutional Definitions of
        Separate Property ................................. 621
    3.  Retroactive Changes in Community
        Property Laws ...................................... 623
        a.  Retroactivity ................................. 623
        b.  Vested Rights ................................. 625
        c.  Texas Due Course ............................ 627
C.  Conflict of Laws......................................... 629
    1.  Choice of Law ...................................... 629
        a.  Forum ......................................... 629
        b.  Domicile....................................... 630
        c.  Situs........................................... 633
        d.  Place Where Tort Committed ............... 633
    2.  Moving to a Community Property State .... 634
        a.  Multistate Problems ......................... 634
        b.  Retiring in a Community Property
            State .......................................... 634
        c.  Privileges and Immunities Problems .... 635
        d.  The Concept of Quasi-Community
            Property....................................... 636
        e.  Emigration from a Community
            Property State................................ 637

D. The Internal Revenue Service ........................... 638
E. A Concluding Thought ....................................... 638

INDEX ........................................................................ 641

# TABLE OF CASES

### References are to Pages

Acurio v. Acurio, 72, 74
Addison v. Addison, 636
Aetna Life Ins. Co. v. Wadsworth, 379
Alsenz v. Alsenz, 156
Amason v. Franklin Life Ins. Co., 374
Anderson v. Anderson, 82
Armer v. Armer, 54
Arnett v. Reade, 13
Arnold v. Department of Retirement Systems, 379
Arnold v. Leonard, 175, 209, 622
Aufmuth, Marriage of, 347
Aufrichtig v. Aufrichtig, 75, 200
Baca v. Baca, 208
Baldwin's Estate, In re, 261
Banner Life Insurance v. The Mark Wallace Dixson
   Irrevocable Trust, 362
Barber v. Barber, 75
Barlow v. Barlow, 378
Barnett v. Jedynak, 337
Barrett v. Barrett, 69
Baruch v. Clark, 469
Battiste v. Battiste, 335
Beals v. Ares, 86
Beam v. Bank of America, 312, 345, 368
Becker, Succession of, 566
Bell v. Bell, 198
Bell-Kilbourn v. Bell-Kilbourn, 340
Bender v. Bender, 46, 51
Benedetto v. Benedetto, 72
Benoit v. Benoit, 568
Bergen v. Wood, 599
Bergman, Marriage of, 357
Betz v. Riviere, 365
Bibb, Estate of, 46
Blackledge v. Schwegmann, 603

Blethen v. Pacific Mutual Life Ins. Co. of Cal., 354
Bliss v. Bliss, 470
Bolster, Marriage of, 90
Bonds, Marriage of, 56, 61
Bordelon v. Bordelon, 364
Boudreaux v. Boudreaux, 76
Bouquet, Marriage of, 627
Bowart v. Bowart, 335
Brenchley's Estate, In re, 610
Brouillette v. Brouillette, 367
Brown v. Brown, 179
Brown, Marriage of, 214
Buol, Marriage of, 188, 264
Burkle, Marriage of, 66
Burney v. Burney, 536
Byrne v. Laura, 598
Cameron v. Cameron, 536
Campbell v. Sandy, 93
Cargill v. Hancock, 360
Castleberry, Estate of, 158
Ceja v. Rudolph & Sletten, Inc., 596
Central Adjustment Bureau, Inc. v. Thevenet, 479
Chance v. Kitchell, 370
Chavez v. Chavez, 269
Claveria v. Claveria's Estate, 608
Claveria's Estate v. Claveria, 608
Cockrill v. Cockrill, 336
Coffey's Estate, In re, 379
Connell v. Connell, 366
Cooper v. Cooper, 334
Cottone v. Cottone, 211
Creasman v. Boyle, 609
Credit Bureau of Eastern Idaho, Inc. v. Lecheminant, 361,
    467
Cross v. Cross, 595
Curtis v. Curtis, 87, 365
Czerneski, In re, 217
Dahle-Fenske, In re, 490
Davis, Marriage of, 195
deElche v. Jacobsen, 438, 484
Dell v. Heard, 479
Deshotels v. Deshotels, 72

Devlin, Marriage of, 196
Devries v. Gallio, 368
Dorbin v. Dorbin, 370
Downer v. Bramet, 165
Drahos v. Drahos, 337
Duberstein, Commissioner v., 165
Dué v. Dué, 144
Dunagan v. Dunagan, 67
Egelhoff v. Egelhoff, 329
Eggemeyer v. Eggemeyer, 628
Elia v. Pifer, 459
Eshom v. Eshom, 409
Ettefagh, Marriage of, 140
Evans v. Evans, 335
Everson v. Everson, 340
Faget, In re Succession of, 73
Farver v. Department of Retirement Systems of State of
    Washington, 379
Federal Deposit Ins. Corp v. Martinez Almodovar, 132
Fernandez v. Romo, 193
Fidelity & Casualty Co. v. Mahoney, 108
Fisch v. Marler, 483
Fletcher's Estate v. Jackson, 270
Flores v. Flores, 207
Flower, Marriage of, 259
Forrest v. Forrest, 204
Fox v. Fox, 527
Fox, Estate of, 611
Free v. Bland, 613
Freeburn, Estate of, 360
Freehe v. Freehe, 179
Friedlander v. Friedlander, 30, 90
Fruth v. Divito, 51
Gapsch v. Gapsch, 358
Gardner v. Gardner, 97
Geise, Matter of, 96
George v. Ransom, 167, 174
Gonzalez, Marriage of, 355
Goodloe v. Williams, 372
Gorden v. Gorden, 80
Graffeo v. Graffeo, 364
Graham v. Franco, 211

Gram, Marriage of, 356
Graves v. Beutler, 277
Green, Marriage of, 358
Greenwald v. Greenwald, 94
Griggs v. Griggs, 362, 363
Grigsby v. Reib, 607
Grinius, Marriage of, 316, 349
Grost v. Grost, 375
Guadagni, State v., 594
Gudelj v. Gudelj, 316
Haley v. Highland, 482
Hall v. Hall, 69
Harrell v. Hochderffer, 211
Hatcher v. Hatcher, 193
Havins, Marriage of, 356
Hawkins v. Front St. Cable Ry. Co., 213
Hay v. Hay, 605
Hedtke v. Hedtke, 536
Heikes, Marriage of, 264, 352
Hilley v. Hilley, 271
Hirsch, Marriage of, 465
Hisquierdo v. Hisquierdo, 363, 615
Hodges v. Hodges, 595
Holliday v. Holliday, 76
Holmes v. Beatty, 272
Holohan v. Melville, 278
Horn, Marriage of, 356
Horton v. Horton, 52
Howe v. Haught, 460
Howell v. Howell, 331
Howell, In re Marriage of, 58, 332, 618
Hrudka v. Hrudka, 51
Hug, Marriage of, 356
Hughes v. Hughes, 86
Hunt v. Campbell, 51
Imperato, Marriage of, 346
Jacobs, Marriage of, 379
Johnson v. Johnson, 368
Johnson, Marriage of, 378
Jones v. Ridgon, 173
Jones v. State, 530
Jones v. Weaver, 136

Joplin v. Borusheski, 607
Josephson v. Josephson, 198
Jurek v. Jurek, 193
Keene v. Edie, 484
Kelley v. Kelley, 568
Kennedy v. Kennedy, 367
Kennedy v. Plan Adm'r for Dupont Sav. & Inv. Plan, 357
Kerley v. Kerley, 80
Klein v. Klein, 179
Koester, Marriage of, 346
Lake v. Lake, 622
Lamb, Estate of, 605
Lambert v. Peoples National Bank of Washington, 277
Langston v. Langston, 373
Laughlin v. Laughlin, 369
Lawlis v. Thompson, 611
LeClert v. LeClert, 371
Lehman, Marriage of, 356
Lezine v. Security Pacific Financial Services, 411
Lindsey, Matter of Marriage of, 609
Littleton v. Prange, 606
Logan, Estate of, 355
Lorenz, Marriage of, 355
Los Angeles & S.L.R.R. v. Umbaugh, 204
Lucas v. Earl, 47
Lucas, Marriage of, 264, 352
Luna v. Luna, 339
MacDonald, Estate of, 42
Mahone, Marriage of, 465
Malmquist v. Malmquist, 367, 368
Malone v. Cannon, 566
Manfer, Marriage of, 171
Mansell v. Mansell, 331
Marsal, Succession of, 568
Marsden, Marriage of, 317, 348
Marvin v. Marvin, 597, 605
Matson, Marriage of, 90
McAlpine v. McAlpine, 76
McCarty v. McCarty, 331, 615
McClary v. Thompson, 88
McDonald v. Senn, 13
McKissick v. McKissick, 267

McTiernan & Dubrow, Marriage of, 353
Medlin v. Medlin, 595
Melissa, Marriage of, 58
Melton v. State, 608
Merkel v. Merkel, 378
Meyer v. Meyer, 94
Michelson v. Michelson, 534
Milling v. Collector of Revenue, 149
Milton v. Milton, 149
Mix, Marriage of, 343
Moore v. Moore, 568
Moore, Marriage of, 317, 347
Morales, Succession of v. Kieckoefer, 132
Motley v. Motley, 536
Muckle v. Superior Court, 523
Muller v. Muller, 72
Munguia, Marriage of, 465
Murphy, Estate of, 344
Musker v. Gil Haskins Auto Leasing, Inc., 52
Neely v. Neely, 52
New Phase Invs., LLC v. Jarvis, 467
Newberry v. Newberry, 375
Nguyen v. Nguyen, 607, 608
Nichols Hills Bank v. McCool, 483
Nikiporez, Estate of, 213
Norris v. Norris, 274
Norris v. Vaughan, 155
Northern Bank & Trust Co. v. Graves, 488
O'Krepki, In re Succession of, 72
Obergefell v. Hodges, 8
Oil Heat Co. of Port Angeles v. Sweeney, 213
Olson, Estate of, 276
Orta v. Arzuaga, 132
Padgett, Marriage of, 357
Passmore, In re, 489
Pearson v. Fillingim, 372, 375
Pendleton & Fireman, Marriage of, 57
Pennington, Marriage of, 610
Pepper, Estate of, 370
Pereira v. Pereira, 309, 344
Pestrikoff v. Hoff, 128
Phillips v. Wellborn, 371

Pinto, Marriage of, 196
Poe v. Seaborn, 614
Poppe, Marriage of, 358
Porter v. Porter, 52
Potthoff v. Potthoff, 52, 336
Prince v. Freeman, 605
Quiring v. Quiring, 70
Radermacher v. Radermacher, 530
Ramsey v. Ramsey, 362
Rau v. Rau, 135
Reed Tool Co. v. Copelin, 211
Reed v. Reed, 68, 619
Regents of the University of California v. Benford, 357
Reichert v. Sunshine Mining Co., 600
Rice v. Rice, 362
Ricks v. Smith, 271
Riddle v. Harmon, 262
Rivera v. Rivera, 83
Robison v. Robison, 368
Rogers v. Yellowstone Park Co., 198
Rogers Walla Walla, Inc. v. Ballard, 277
Rosan, In re Marriage of, 503
Rossin, Marriage of, 356
Rothman v. Rumbeck, 340
Rueschenberg v. Rueschenberg, 335
Runcorn v. Shearer Lumber Products, Inc., 199
Sanchez v. Sanchez, 85
Schilling v. Embree, 459
Schlaefer v. Financial Management Service, 51
Schmanski v. Schmanski, 80
Schreiber v. Schreiber, 82
Schwegmann v. Schwegmann, 603
Schwingle v. Keifer, 607
Scott v. Scott, 367
Seaton, Marriage of, 605
See v. See, 340
Selby v. Savard, 461
Self v. Self, 179
Shaheen v. Khan, 72
Shaw v. Greer, 460
Sherman, Marriage of, 348
Simplot v. Simplot, 359

Sims v. Sims, 366
Sims' Estate, In re, 53
Skadden, Marriage of, 356
Skarda, Marriage of, 374
Small v. Bartyzel, 379
Small v. McMaster, 607
Smith v. Capital One Bank (USA) N.A., 490
Smith v. Dalton, 484
Smith v. Deneve, 607
Sogg v. Nevada State Bank, 79
Soto v. Vandeventer, 208
Speer v. Quinlan, 359
Spengler, Marriage of, 355
Sprague v. Sprague, 372
Spreckels v. Spreckels, 399, 624
Stallworth, Marriage of, 526
Steinberger, Marriage of, 356
Stephen v. Stephen, 134
Stephenson, Marriage of, 357
Stevens v. Anderson, 595
Stevens v. Stevens, 70
Stewart v. Stewart, 13
Stitt, Marriage of, 465
Stockdale v. Stockdale, 68
Suter v. Suter, 143, 198, 619
Swink v. Fingado, 268
Swink v. Sunwest Bank, 268
Swope v. Swope, 359
Talbot v. Talbot, 145
Texas Employers' Ins. Ass'n v. Borum, 607
Theriot v. Theriot, 418
Thompson and Thompson, In re, 361
Thornton, Estate of, 635
Travelers Insurance Company v. Johnson, 361
Trierweiler, Estate of, 379
Trimble's Estate, In re, 86, 269
Vaiaud, Succession of, 568
Valento v. Valento, 173, 337
Van Camp v. Van Camp, 311
Van Maren v. Johnson, 13
Vanwassenhove v. Vanwassenhove, 469
Vardilos v. Vardilos, 372

Vasquez v. Hawthorne, 610
Verneuille, Succession of, 366
Vieux v. Vieux, 317, 347
Vivaldi v. Mariani, 132
Walker, Marriage of, 390
Walrath, Marriage of, 352
Watts v. Watts, 611
Westcott v. Westcott, 366
White's Estate, In re, 371
Whittlesey v. Miller, 211
Whorton v. Dillingham, 599
Wiley's Estate v. Commissioner, 158
Wilkerson v. Aven, 360
Williams v. McKnight, 271
Williams v. Paxton, 143, 469
Williams v. Williams, 51, 76, 605
Wilson v. Wilson, 211
Windauer v. O'Connor, 193
Windsor, United States v., 620
Winsberg v. Winsberg, 266
Wissner v. Wissner, 325, 615
Wolford v. Wolford, 68
Zier, Marriage of, 90

# COMMUNITY PROPERTY

## IN A NUTSHELL®

FOURTH EDITION

# PART 1
# PRELIMINARY MATTERS

# CHAPTER 1
# PRELIMINARY MATTERS

## A. OVERVIEW

A community property system is a default marital property system that applies to married persons domiciled in the state.

Community property systems exist in nine U.S. jurisdictions: Arizona, California, Idaho, Louisiana, Nevada, New Mexico, Texas, Washington, and Wisconsin (by statute).

The commonwealth of Puerto Rico allows for community property.

Alaska and Tennessee are separate property states that allow married persons to opt into community property by contract or trust.

The Internal Revenue Service, where relevant, determines and collects tax in accordance with the taxpayer's community property domicile.

Generally, there are two types, or characters, of property in a community property system: community property and separate property.

The community property systems in the U.S. share common patterns, but each state has developed its own variations.

The following principles generally hold in all community property jurisdictions. Ownership of community property by spouses is by halves. Record title does not necessarily control the character of an asset. The character of an asset determines corollary rights related to management and control, disposition at dissolution or death, and federal income tax liability.

Community property states differ on important points. Three examples follow.

*The character of separate property rents, issues, and profits during the continuance of the marriage.* A majority of U.S. community property states follow the rule that separate property rents, issues, and profits are separate property, by application of the (common law) tracing rule. A minority of U.S. community property states continue the civil law approach, which characterizes all rents, issues, and profits received during marriage as community property.

*The enablement of superseding community property presumptions.* All states apply a general community property presumption. Some states have enacted superseding community property presumptions that apply to joint form titles or to sums on deposit in a demand deposit account.

*The characterization of property during a period of separation.* A majority of states characterize earnings and accumulations during a period of separation as separate property. A minority characterize the same as community in character.

## THE COMMUNITY PROPERTY STATES

**By default: Arizona, California, Idaho, Louisiana, Nevada, New Mexico, Texas, Washington and Wisconsin.**

By option only: Alaska and Tennessee.

U.S. Community Property States

## 1.   BASIC DEFINITIONS

"Characterization" describes the process by which property is classified either as community property or the separate property of a spouse. Quasi-community property and quasi-marital property are additional classifications that can be used, depending on the state.

Terminology varies from state to state.

The more popular term community property is used in this Nutshell, however, Wisconsin uses the term "marital property" to describe property owned by a married couple (as opposed to a larger community, such as the entire family).

The term separate property is used in this Nutshell, but Wisconsin uses the term "individual property." The terms used by Wisconsin derive from its adoption of the Uniform Marital Property Act.

Here is a working definition of community property:

*Community property is property acquired onerously by a married couple during the marriage while domiciled in the community property state.*

This definition is subject to enough exceptions that it serves only as a guide. Five of the key words— "property," "acquired," "onerously," "married" and "domiciled"—require pages of explanation. A summary of these major considerations follows:

## a. Property

Whether tangible or intangible, real or personal, vested or contingent, the community property asset in question must be something capable of being transferred. Employment earnings, real estate, contract rights, shares of stock, stock dividends, sums on deposit in a bank account, business accounts, computer hardware, software, data, an automobile, a patent, a copyright, a trademark, a professional practice, business goodwill, celebrity identity. Each of these "things" is capable of being transferred and therefore capable of ownership as property.

The marriage itself is not property.

Some assets may be exempt from the community property system by statute or case law. For example, a professional degree might be excluded from the community property system.

## b. Acquired

The character of an asset is fixed at the time that it is originally acquired. The point of acquisition is the point at which the owner's legal rights come into existence.

Property acquired *before* marriage comes into the marriage as the separate property of the acquiring spouse. Property acquired *during* marriage is presumed to be community property unless proven otherwise.

The character of an asset can be established by the character of its purchase funds. The general rule is that community property funds purchase community assets, and separate property funds purchase separate property assets.

## c. Onerously

Property obtained through the labor or industry, or talent of either spouse during the marriage is community property.

Talent is regarded as highly personal to its holder and therefore not transferable. But property derived from the exercise of talent is transferable. Earnings are acquired through labor. Contract rights, patents, copyrights are all examples of accumulations that also are acquired through labor, industry, or talent.

Onerous title is a labor-based benefit or right. The opposite of onerous title in a traditional community property system is lucrative title. Lucrative title is acquired by gift or windfall. The concept of gift is broad. A gift can be acquired by inter vivos transfer, by devise, or by descent. Gifts made in trust fall into the category of inter vivos transfers.

### d. Married

The right to marry is constitutionally protected. All states are thus required to license a marriage regardless of the applicants' genders. *Obergefell v. Hodges*, 576 U.S. ___, 135 S.Ct. 2584, 192 L.Ed.2d 609 (2015).

A lawful marriage comes into existence at the time that statutory formalities are met by a couple who is domiciled in the state. Among the U.S. community property states, informal marriage (sometimes mistakenly called "common law marriage") is only permitted in the state of Texas.

Formal alternatives to marriage continue to exist. Registered Domestic Partners (RDP) status is offered in several states. RDPs may have all the rights and obligations of spouses, depending on state law.

A *void* marriage is not a valid marriage. A void marriage never comes into legal existence. Even so, states require a void marriage to be annulled by court judgment so as to provide notice to third parties. A void marriage remains void at the death of one of the partners.

A *voidable* marriage is presumed valid until annulled or dissolved. At the death of one of the partners, a voidable marriage becomes valid.

A *putative* marriage is one in which one or both partners believe, in good faith, that their otherwise void or voidable marriage is valid. Many states adopt the equitable putative spouse doctrine so as to confer the rights and obligations of marriage on the putative spouse or spouses. In such a case, rights and obligations flow not from marriage, since the marriage is not valid, but from equitable norms.

*Nonmarried cohabitants* do not have the same rights and obligations as married persons. In a state that follows the equitable marriage doctrine, as Washington does, one or both unmarried cohabitants can petition to use the state family code to determine rights of property and support. Most U.S. community property states, California being a prime example, steer clear of the equitable marriage doctrine. Although no cases have been found that explicitly support the following claim, the doctrine of equitable marriage is constitutionally problematic for how it forces one of the litigants into the consequences of marriage by judicial action.

### e. Domiciled

Domicile (often confused with or substituted for residence) is a legal conclusion based on presence and intent. In brief, legal domicile is established in one state at a time, by an intentional act to make the state one's home for personal legal matters.

### f. Apportionment

Every marriage has a possibility of three estates:

- The community estate;

- The separate property estate of one spouse; and

- The separate property estate of the other spouse.

A person must be married in order to acquire community property, but not all property of married persons must be community property.

Community property is owned by the spouses in equal shares and subject to division as marital property.

Separate property is individually owned by one spouse.

As a point of logic, during marriage, property can be concurrently owned by character specific pro rata shares. Concurrently owned property is owned by two or more estates, not by the individuals per se. Thus, one asset can be owned by:

- One spouse's separate property estate and the community estate; or

- Both spouses' separate property estates; or

- Both spouses' separate property estate(s) and the community estate.

In the event of dissolution, the modern trend is to encourage the parties to negotiate a partition through bargain and exchange. If the parties cannot agree on an outcome, state statutes typically require a family court to step in so as to partition the community property, or any community property share of an asset that is concurrently owned by the community and one or both separate property estates. Some states mandate the family court to partition community property in equal, fifty-fifty shares. Other states allow the family court discretion to divide community property equitably, depending on the circumstances of the case.

## 2.   IMPLICATIONS OF CHARACTERIZATION

In a community property system, issues routinely arise over acquisition, apportionment, control, dissolution, succession, and taxation. Issues include:

- Management and control rights to sell, lease, encumber, give, and transfer.

- Disclosure and financial transparency rights and obligations.

- Creditors' rights.

- Tort awards and liability.

- Tax determinations and liens.

Dissolution (divorce) or death terminates a marriage, and prevents further acquisition of community property.

Dissolution, as discussed above, requires the parties to agree to a partition of community assets.

The death of a spouse triggers the transfer of property to the decedent spouse's intestate heirs or will beneficiaries. Since no person has the right to devise property belonging to another, each spouse's testamentary rights extend only to a one-half interest in the community property. With respect to statutory rights of inheritance, a surviving spouse has a clear right to the decedent's community property.

In addition to the major problems that occur during and at the end of a marriage, issues may arise under particular state law provisions, federal constitutional or statutory provisions, or conflict of laws areas.

### 3. RATIONALE FOR THE COMMUNITY PROPERTY SYSTEM

The community property system favors the family. Such a system conclusively presumes that a spouse's labor contributes to the acquisition of family wealth in the form of community property.

There are types of onerously acquired community property where the labor involved in acquisition may be slight (unearned income, rents, dividends) or where it may be entirely borne by one spouse with varying degrees of support, from the other. In a community property system, it doesn't matter what a spouse actually does to assist in (or to detract from) the acquisition of an asset during marriage. If the asset is community property, then both spouses are vested in that asset as of the time of acquisition.

The language of equality in the community property system preceded actual equality in many cases. For example, California used the term "community property" as early as 1849, but under the ruling in *Van Maren v. Johnson*, 15 Cal. 308 (1860), a wife had (only) a contingent interest in community property that vested at divorce or death. It was not until 1927, following litigation in *Stewart v. Stewart*, 199 Cal. 318, 249 P. 197 (1926), that the state enacted legislation to recognize a wife as having a vested interested in community property as of the date of acquisition. Today that legislation is found in gender-neutral form at Cal.Fam.Code § 751.

The change between recognizing community property as vested rather than contingent was one that permeated the jurisprudence of the U.S. community property states. See for example, *Arnett v. Reade*, 220 U.S. 311, 31 S.Ct. 425, 55 L.Ed. 477 (1911) and *McDonald v. Senn*, 53 N.M. 198, 204 P.2d 990 (1949), discussed below.

Additionally, until the mid-1970s, the legal management and control of community property was given to the husband. Today, every community property jurisdiction follows gender-neutral management rules. See Chapter 7.

## 4. TYPES OF COMMUNITY PROPERTY SYSTEMS

Common to the concept of community property is that each spouse enjoys present, vested, and equal (or equitable) rights in community property. But there is no single community property system. There are several systems, each with its commonalities and differences. Some big picture differences are discussed next.

The term *matrimonial regime* indicates that the system characterizes both assets and liabilities. The regime approach is accurate to the civil law origins of community property law; this system is maintained in Louisiana.

*Universal, middle* and *ganancial* approaches exist in deciding which assets of the married couple will be shared under the community property system. Here the question is what, if any, parts of the premarital property should be converted into community property by virtue of the marriage.

The universal, or Roman-Dutch, form of community property changed all premarital property into community property upon marriage.

Among middle approaches between including and excluding all premarital property from the community was that found in France between 1804 and 1965. Under that approach, the community included all immovable property acquired during marriage (similar to the ganancial system) and all movables, whenever acquired (similar to the universal system). Modifications were also made for dowry and for gifts to the married couple. In 1965, France adopted a ganancial system.

The Spanish form of community property is the parent ganancial system of the U.S. states. It derives from the Visigoths. In a ganancial system, premarital property remains the separate property (*bienes propios*) of its individual owner, while property acquired during marriage by labor is characterized as community property (*bienes gananciales*). Today the ganancial system or a variant thereof operates in many countries around the world.

Within the U.S., ganancial systems divide along the line of how permeable they are to civil and common law marital property concepts. Louisiana is closer to its civil law origins than are the other U.S. community property states. California has strong ties to the common law tradition, brought by the '49ers, and thus it actively used and still uses the case law method to define, interpret, and amend its family law statutes. New Mexico relied on California statutes in setting up its community property statutes, but then looked to the law of Spain and Mexico to define and interpret those statutes.

All U.S. community property states characterize the property that either spouse brings to the marriage as separate in character. This legal outcome derives from the ganancial nature of the state's community property system. A minority of states characterize separate property rents, issues and profits as community property during the marriage by a civil law rationale called usufruct. A majority characterize the same as separate property during marriage. Here, the rationale derives from the common law, and it has to with trust law, which permits tracing and accounting as an ordinary part of ongoing property management.

## B.   HISTORY: COMMON LAW VERSUS COMMUNITY PROPERTY

The first written recognition of community property appeared in the year 693 CE in the Visigothic Code; it was restated in the Fuero Juzgo of 1241 CE. The Visigoths, nomadic Germanic tribes, had been driven across the Danube River into the Roman Empire in 376 CE by the Huns. In their migrations from Scandinavia first southeast and then west, the Visigoths left a heritage of community property. For example, community property appeared in Sweden as early as 1200 C.E. in the Law of West Goths, according to the Manuscript of Aeskil or Eskil.

Under the community property ganancial system, which pre-dates the common law system, the wife retained her legal identity, even in marriage. By contrast, under the English common law system, upon marriage, the wife's legal identity merged into that of her husband's; no longer possessing a legal identity of her own, the married women could not acquire, manage, or control property in marriage.

Additionally, under the common law of England (before the passage of the Married Woman's Property Act), the married woman did not acquire a share in her husband's earnings, accumulations, or property, as did her counterpart in the ganancial system. And though the married woman had common law dower rights, she was excluded from intestate succession under the law of primogeniture, which favored her husband's male heirs. Dower gave the surviving wife (only) a life estate in one-third of the realty of which the husband owned in fee simple absolute during the marriage. Not permitted to enter into contracts, a married woman in the common law system was effectively barred from the institution of property as a matter of law. The husband's legal dominion over the property of the marriage gave life and death power over the person of the wife.

In the U.S., community property doctrines were historically litigated and decided upon by common law trained lawyers and judges. Given their training, these 19th century legal actors saw it "logical" to develop subsidiary rules that restricted the wife's powers of management, control, and devise in much in the same way that the English common law system, unmodified by the Married Women's Property Act, had done.

In the last half of the 20th century, common law title jurisdictions in the U.S. passed statutes to achieve greater equality between the marital partners during and at the end of marriage. The Uniform Martial Property Act (UMPA for short) (see also the Model Marital Property Act (MMPA)) was adopted by Wisconsin. The Uniform Marriage and Divorce Act (UMDA), which depending on what provisions are adopted can create results similar to community property states at divorce, was entirely enacted by Kentucky (the first), then partially by Colorado, and most recently by Montana.

Despite major trends toward divorce reform in the U.S., misunderstandings about the community property system versus the common law system are widespread and continue to persist. Prior to 1948, for example, acquirers and possessors of community property had federal income, estate, and gift tax advantages that did not exist for a domiciliary of a common law (separate property title) state. In order to gain those same advantages, the states of Michigan, Nebraska, Oklahoma, Oregon and Pennsylvania and the (then) Territory of Hawaii adopted community property systems. In Pennsylvania, the community property statute was declared unconstitutional. In the other states and in Hawaii the community property system was repealed shortly after the 1948 amendments to the Internal Revenue Code (I.R.C.) eliminated the tax advantages that the adoption of community property had meant to address by permitting joint income tax returns, a marital deduction for both gift and estate taxes, and the gift-splitting provisions of the gift tax.

## C. INDIVIDUAL COMMUNITY PROPERTY STATES

### 1. COMMON THREADS

The common threads of the community property systems rest in a major premise and its underlying principles.

The premise is that marriage creates an economic partnership in which both partners (the spouses) are vested. Three common subprinciples are contractual modification, equality of interest, and tracing.

The *contractual modification principle* enables the spouses to alter some or all of the default community property rules by enforceable private contract. Spouses can contract between themselves or, acting together or alone, with a third party. See Chapter 2.

The *equality of interest principle* recognizes that spouses obtain equal vested shares in community property as of the date of acquisition or accumulation. See Chapter 3 and 4.

The *tracing principle* characterizes an asset acquired during marriage identically with the labor or funds that were used to acquire a legal right to the property. As noted above, the general rule is that community property gives rise to community property and separate property gives rise to separate property. See Chapter 5 and 6.

These three principles provide the broad outlines of a default community property system that is strong enough to protect individuals within a marriage and yet flexible enough to allow them to manage and pledge community property. See Chapters 7 and 8.

Additionally, historical cases must be analyzed against the backdrop of the law under which they were decided. Prior to 1927, it was common for community property states to (unfairly) hold that the community property interest for the female spouse was contingent rather than vested. And prior to 1975, the male spouse alone (unfairly) had the legal right to manage and control community personal property, making financial decisions skewed in a gender-specific way. Therefore, cases that predate 1927 and 1975 are gender biased. Most have been superseded by statute.

## 2.    SOME (CURRENT) UNCOMMON THREADS

Each state balances the above three common principles differently. This could create instances of what might be called local peculiarities were it not for the fact that each state's system is one of local peculiarities.

For example:

- Arizona and Texas have adopted the Uniform Premarital Agreement Act (the UPAA for short). Louisiana and Washington have not. California has adopted and so significantly amended the UPAA that the California Premarital Agreement Act (the CPAA for short), is considered sui generis.

- Among U.S. community property states, only Texas continues to permit informal marriage. No community property state recognizes informal divorce; and all community property states define a bigamous marriage as void.

- A minority of states characterize the rents, issues, and profits of separate property as community property, in line with the civil law. A majority of states recognize the same as separate property, in line with the American rule that permits tracing.

- All states characterize property at inception of title. A minority of states reimburse an estate of a different character that helps buy a disputed asset. A majority of states give the contributing estate a pro tanto ownership percentage in line with (what is sometimes also called) the American rule on apportionment.

In general, when an approach is called "American" it is relative to an approach called "the civil law." American modifications to the parent system rely on the concept of the trust, which identifies ownership interests by tracing assets back to their source.

Be aware that legislatures are reluctant to retroactively change vested community property interests. In states where community property is protected by the state constitution, a legislature lacks authority to retroactively change property rights. But even in states where the community property system is entirely or primarily legislative, retroactive changes can cause characterization disputes between the spouses and between the spouses and third party purchasers and creditors. The practical result of retroactive change is that each change in the definition of community property may create a new category of community property that gets added on to the categories that existed before. Thus, historical analysis is often a tool in community property law.

### 3.   HISTORICAL DIFFERENCES AMONG THE U.S. COMMUNITY PROPERTY STATES

The history of statehood and adoption of the community property system in each of the states also has both common threads and individual variations:

Arizona, California, Nevada, and part of New Mexico were acquired by the U.S. in 1848 by the Treaty of Guadalupe Hidalgo which terminated the Mexican-American War. The Treaty ceded vast western territories to the U.S. Utah, Colorado and Wyoming did not adopt community property. It is often said that the practical difficulty of adopting community property in pre-statehood polygamous Utah can be readily seen, and yet community property was adopted in Idaho, also a state with a distinct Mormon history.

From at least since 1865, the community property system was recognized by the Arizona Territory. Since statehood, Arizona has tended to follow decisions of California and Texas, with some early leanings towards the laws of Washington, which itself has looked to California. THE RECORDS OF THE ARIZONA CONSTITUTIONAL CONVENTION OF 1910 (John S. Goff ed.) confirms that Arizona delegates voted to indefinitely postpone a restatement of community property law in the constitution because they regarded community property as purely legislative in character.

California adopted the community property system by a general state constitutional provision. Over its history, the state has developed a community property system that is more than the sum total of its hyper-specific parts. The system is meticulously maintained by the California Legislature, which is aided, through litigation, by the California courts of appeal. Consequently the California system can be fairly characterized as either a sui generis system or as a hybrid civil law/common law system. Today, California, being one of largest and most diverse U.S. community property, is an influential workshop for the other U.S. states.

Idaho was originally included in the Oregon Territory and was added to the Washington Territory in two parts, one in 1853 and the other in 1859. Idaho existed from 1863 until 1867 as a territory without the community property system. The community property system was added in 1867. It continued from that date to and through statehood in 1890 and into the present. When Idaho became a state in 1890 it had already developed its own body of community property law, one not influenced by a Spanish-Mexican heritage.

Louisiana is the state that nurtures the legal traditions of the civil law in its matrimonial regime. The present state of Louisiana bears only a slight resemblance to the vast territory which was named after Louis XIV of France. The shifting ownership of the mouth of the Mississippi River during the 17th and 18th centuries is a history in miniature of alternating Spanish and French colonial influence. The Custom of Paris prevailed in Louisiana until 1769; after which the Spanish ganancial system took effect. When Napoleon put a stop to alternating ownership by selling the Louisiana Territory to the U.S. in 1803, the community property system was already well established in the territory. But, of all the territory acquired in that vast purchase only the land south of the 33d parallel (called by Congress the Territory of Orleans, and now the state of Louisiana) retained community property. The balance of the states which were formed from the Louisiana Purchase (like the territory of East and West Florida) did not, even though community property is part of their legal history.

Nevada, acquired from Mexico along with California, was originally part of the Utah Territory. Since admission to the Union in 1864, Nevada has had a constitutional provision recognizing community property. Nevada tends to look to California or Washington law in developing its law.

New Mexico, consisted partly of land from the Republic of Texas and partly of land acquired by the Treaty of Guadalupe Hidalgo, and it included the present state of Arizona until 1863. New Mexico's borders between Texas and California were subject to change from time to time. Historians differ as to whether Spanish to Mexican to New Mexican community property rules continue in an unbroken chain, although case law holds that it does. In 1876, the common law was adopted in the New Mexico Territory and the civil law was repealed, except where adopted by statutes or required by Treaty. Otherwise, a military code (the Kearny Code) went into effect until 1907. When the New Mexico Act was passed, it largely adopted California community property statutes. In 1912, when New Mexico become a state, its courts began to look to the law of Spain and Mexico to interpret the community property system, thus officially recognizing the civil law origin of the New Mexico system. *McDonald*, supra.

Texas, an independent republic from 1836, joined the Union on December 29, 1845. An original Texas Constitution of 1869 was formed but it was replaced in its entirety with the Texas Constitution of 1876, which remains the organic law of Texas today. Texas was formerly a part of Mexico and subject to the laws of Spain. When the state became a Republic and later joined the Union it not only carried over a Spanish-Mexican heritage of the community property system, it enshrined that system in the Constitution of 1876, thus placing community property above the reach of any particular legislature. Part of the legal history of Texas is the low regard in which decisions of the post-Civil War Reconstruction period courts are held. For more on the Texas community property system, see JEAN A. STUNTZ, HERS, HIS, AND THEIRS: COMMUNITY PROPERTY LAW IN SPAIN AND EARLY TEXAS (2005).

Washington, originally part of the Oregon Territory, entered the union as a constitutional dependency in 1853. Washington did not have a strong French, Spanish, or Mexican tradition, much like Idaho, and the common law was prevalent in the state through the 1870s. But Washington had a progressive start as a territory where settlers (individually and collectively) homesteaded geographies divided by the sometimes impassable

Cascade Mountains. Washington adopted its first community property statute in 1869, a statute modeled on the community property provision in the 1850 California Organic Act. The statute was updated in 1873 and codified in 1881 in a form that remained in force up to and after statehood in 1889. For more on early Washington legal history, see SANDRA F. VANBURKLEO, GENDER REMADE: CITIZENSHIP, SUFFRAGE, AND PUBLIC POWER IN THE NEW NORTHWEST, 1879–1912 (2015).

Wisconsin attained statehood in 1848 and had a common law regime through 1985. On January 1, 1986, Wisconsin became the first state to adopt a shared marital property system, the Uniform Marital Property Act (called WUMPA for short).

Alaska adopted the Alaska Community Property Act in 1998. The Act offers an elective system for married persons who want to opt into community property by use of a contract or an Alaska trust.

Tennessee enables married residents to use a private contract to opt into community property.

Proposals have been made for New Hampshire to enable a community property option. See Calvin Massey, *Why New Hampshire Should Permit Married Couples to Choose Community Property*, 13 U.N.H. L. REV. 35 (2015) and Jo Carrillo, *Liberty and Community in Marriage: Expanding on Massey's Proposal for a Community Property Option in New Hampshire,* 15 U.N.H. L. REV. 289 (2017).

# CHAPTER 2

# CONTRACTUAL MODIFICATION

## A.  OVERVIEW

The contractual modification principle permits parties to alter default community property rules by contract.

How does a contract work in the context of marriage in a community property state?

*Timing.* A contract can be executed before, during, or at the end of marriage. Premarital agreements are executed before marriage. Marital agreements are executed during marriage. Transmutations take place during marriage. Marriage settlement agreements are executed at the end of marriage.

*Formalities.* States enact statutes that set out contract enforceability rules. These statutes guide parties through the contracting process. Sometimes parties enter into an informal agreement between themselves about property matters or personal rights and obligations during marriage. Informal agreements raise enforceability problems.

A premarital contract generally must be in writing and signed by the parties to be married. Consideration likely will not be required; the purpose of such a rule being to invalidate any argument that the marriage itself was consideration for the contract. Some states additionally require that premarital and marital contracts be acknowledged by witnesses or even notarized.

*Disclosure and voluntariness.* Even if a contract meets the state formalities requirements, the contract (or a contract term or fragment) may be subject to nullification for substantive reasons. Community property states typically nullify a contract (or a contract term) if there is no legal basis upon which to find it enforceable. *Unfair* contracts fall into this category. (Unfair in this context typically means undisclosed.) *Coerced* contracts fall into this category. (Coerced in this context typically means involuntary.)

When premarital agreements are analyzed under different legal standards than are marital agreements it is because the parties were not be in a confidential relationship, as a matter of law when they executed the contract. During marriage the parties are in a confidential relationship as a matter of law; before marriage, in most states, they are not.

*Substantive terms.* Parties can seek to modify property rights and personal rights and obligations by contract.

*Spousal support modifications or waivers* are terms by which the parties waive or alter the right to postdissolution spousal support. The right to support during a marriage is generally not waivable by contract, whereas the right to postdissolution support generally is.

What is the legal justification for distinguishing between spousal support rights during marriage as opposed to after dissolution?

One answer is that a married person's right to support from a spouse during marriage is considered a key component of the institution of marriage, whereas the right to postdissolution support is not considered a key component of the institution of divorce. Another answer is that the right to petition for postdissolution support is a private right that can be knowingly and intelligently waived, subject to judicial oversight. Yet another answer is that the public interest is implicated anytime a court adjudges spousal support to be necessary. Here, the argument is that it is fairer to the public for a judge to order a financially able ex-spouse to pay postdissolution support than it is to enforce a contract term that will result in the needy ex-spouse's public assistance eligibility.

## B.   DETAIL

### 1.   PREMARITAL AGREEMENTS BEFORE 1983

A premarital contract is an agreement made between prospective spouses in contemplation of their impending marriage. A premarital contract becomes legally effective upon the date of marriage. It is presumed to be enforceable when the marriage ends by dissolution or death unless it is proved to have been the product of coercion or deceit.

Under the Spanish system premarital contracts were enforceable from the date of the marriage forward. Mutual consent to the marriage was sufficient consideration to support the contract. But proof of fraud, duress, or undue influence—offered at the time of enforcement (typically the end of the marriage)—formed the basis for voiding the contract. Early U.S. community property states followed these aspects of Spanish law by permitting married persons to enter into private contracts between themselves so as to modify or even waive certain of the obligations and rights of marriage.

Spanish law regarded the parties to the contract as being in a confidential relationship. The confidential relationship commenced, as a matter of law, from the date of the engagement; it continued on until the end of the marriage. The law of some U.S. jurisdictions continues with this approach. In these states, prospective spouses are deemed to be in a confidential relationship from the time of their engagement onward. See e.g. *Friedlander v. Friedlander*, 80 Wash.2d 293, 494 P.2d 208 (1972) (*en banc*). In other states, prospective spouses contract at arm's length. Only on the date of marriage do they enter into a confidential relationship as a matter of law. See e.g. Cal.Fam.Code 721.

The legal consequence of when a confidential relationship comes into existence is a matter of analytic significance. This is because once the parties are in a confidential relationship—whether by operation of law or fact—any contract term that disproportionately benefits one party at the expense of the other can be challenged in court. Confidants enjoy a relationship of trust with each other. As such the law requires that they not take unfair advantage of the trust placed in them by the other.

When a contract enriches one confidant at the expense of the other, the enrichment is scrutinized as having been obtained without a legal basis. Proof that the adversely affected party voluntarily entered into the contract despite knowing all the relevant facts surrounding the enrichment may help to neutralize concerns about fairness.

As noted above, a minority of U.S. community property states place the parties in a relationship of confidence as a matter of law (not fact) at the start of the parties' engagement. A majority of states draw a bright line before and after the date of marriage such that before marriage the parties are not in a confidential relationship (absent factual proof to the contrary) whereas from the date of marriage on they are.

Therefore, in a majority of states premarital agreements are negotiated as arm's length transactions. Enforceability depends on meeting state formalities, not on substantive fairness. Wisconsin is an exception; Washington may be one as well. In states that have enacted the UPAA, voluntariness and fairness are also factors in determining enforceability.

When one party is enriched at the expense of the other, the question becomes whether that enrichment is just or unjust. The civil law answer to this question places the problem more squarely in the realm of contract with an approach known as the "no legal ground approach." Here, the idea is that unjust enrichment is based on a single principle, namely that where there is no legal basis for the enrichment, restitution is in order.[1] The common law answer to the question of unjust enrichment is more in line with tort law, however, in that recovery is based on the incremental enumeration of wrongful acts in the case at hand.

Prior to adopting the UPAA, and absent a statute to the contrary, a U.S. community property state could potentially adopt the (civil law) no legal ground approach or the (common law) unjust factor approach or a hybrid of the two approaches. Only a careful reading of case law would determine the state's approach.

After adoption of the UPAA, a state seemingly commits to the no legal ground approach for these reasons. One, intimate partners have the right to contract, before marriage, over property rights and liabilities. Two, when a contract enriches one party at the expense of the other, the enrichment is acceptable as being within the benefitted party's freedom of contract rights. Three, the benefitted party's enrichment can be legally challenged, however, if it can be shown to have been the consequence of deceit or coercion. Deceit or coercion are defined within the terms of the UPAA. Deceit typically means the absence of financial disclosure. Coercion can mean any act that substitutes the will of the benefitted party for that of the adversely affected party. Upon proof of either deceit or coercion, the contract becomes unenforceable.

---

[1]     See for example, Peter Birks, UNJUST ENRICHMENT 2d EDITION (2005).

By contrast, prior to adoption of the UPAA or in those states that have not adopted the UPAA, contract enforceability does or may focus less on formalities and more on two recurring policy issues. Are the contract terms void for public policy? Do the rights and duties affected by the contract further a public interest (leaning them toward being nonwaivable) or are they private (and thus waivable)?

## 2.    THE UNIFORM PREMARITAL AGREEMENT ACT OF 1983

In 1983, the National Conference of Commissioners on Uniform State Laws promulgated the Uniform Premarital Agreement Act (the UPAA 1983 for short).

As of this printing, the UPAA has been adopted by twenty-six U.S. jurisdictions and the District of Columbia. Seven of the adopting jurisdictions are community property states: Arizona, California, Idaho, Nevada, New Mexico, Texas, and Wisconsin. California adopted the UPAA in 1985, but then amplified and modified it to such an extent that the resulting statute—called the California Premarital Agreement Act (or CPAA for short)—is considered so far a departure from the original UPAA 1983 as to be sui generis. New Mexico adopted UPAA formalities for contract enforceability (a writing signed by both parties), but then added the additional requirement of formal acknowledgment. Wisconsin adopted a version of the UPAA 1983 that is also a departure from the original.

Louisiana and Washington, have not adopted the UPAA 1983. Louisiana has statutory provisions of its own. Washington relies on decisional law.

The UPAA 1983 clarifies the issue of baseline enforceability. A **"[p]remarital agreement"** is defined as **"an agreement between prospective spouses made in contemplation of marriage and to be effective upon marriage."** UPAA §§ 1 and 4 (1983). Property is defined as **"an interest, present or future, legal or equitable, vested or contingent, in real or personal property, including income and earnings."** *Id.* Enforceability of any premarital agreement is premised on proof of a **"writing . . . signed by both parties."** UPAA § 2 (1983). Consideration is not required to avoid the following arguments from being raised. One is that the marriage itself constitutes sufficient consideration as a matter of law. Another is that mutual consent to reciprocal terms constitutes sufficient consideration as a matter of law. *Id.*

The UPAA § 3(a)(4) permits parties to contract over a broad scope of property matters, **"the modification or elimination of spousal support[,]"** choice of law to govern the construction of the agreement, and **"any other matter, including [the parties'] personal rights and obligations, not in violation of public policy or a statute imposing a criminal penalty."** UPAA § 3(a)(8) 1985 (1983).

Contract enforceability is additionally a function of voluntariness and the disclosure of property and financial obligations. UPAA § 6(a) 1985 (1983). The absence of disclosure is a basis for alleging contract unconscionability as a matter of law. UPAA § 6(c) 1985 (1983). The test for unconscionability derives from the Uniform Marriage and Divorce Act of 1970 [UMDA 1970], which provides that the terms of a separation agreement are legally binding on a court **"unless it finds, after considering the economic circumstances of the parties and any other relevant evidence produced by the parties ... that the separation agreement is unconscionable."** UMDA § 306 (1970).

Following the UMDA (1970), UPAA § 6(b) links spousal support provisions with eligibility for public assistance. The consequence is that upon proof that the lack of spousal support could cause the party against whom enforcement is sought to be eligible for public assistance, a court **"notwithstanding the terms of the agreement, may require the other party to provide support to the extent necessary to avoid that eligibility."** In effect, UPAA § 6(b) operates by giving a court discretion to modify an unconscionable spousal support provision in the interest of protecting the public fisc.

To sum up, under the UPAA 1983, a premarital contract must be in writing and signed by both parties to the marriage to be enforceable. If it meets these basic formalities, it is presumed enforceable. Rebuttal rests with the party against whom enforcement is sought, meaning with the party who challenges a provision in the contract or the contract itself. Contract challenges can be made on one or both of two grounds: unjust enrichment or involuntariness. To establish unjust enrichment proof of a lack of disclosure is key. To establish involuntariness, proof of an impaired decision-making or negotiation process is required. Evidence of pressure, relational dependence, power imbalances, abuse, mistake, domestic violence at the time of the contract are examples of circumstances that can nullify an adversely affected party's intent to contract.

Otherwise, only Washington and Wisconsin requires that substantive contract terms be fair to each party. In the other eight states, because the parties negotiate at arm's length, substantively unfair provisions may nevertheless be enforceable.

### 3.   THE UNIFORM PREMARITAL AND MARITAL AGREEMENT ACT OF 2012

The Uniform Premarital and Marital Agreement Act (the UPMAA 2012 for short) was promulgated by the National Conference of Commissioners of Uniform State Laws in 2012. The UPMAA 2012 has been adopted by Colorado and North Dakota. No community property state has adopted the UPMAA 2012.

The UPMAA § 6 relies on the UPAA 1983 formation requirements. It then complicates the definition of a premarital agreement from an agreement made in contemplation of marriage (the original UPAA 1983 definition set out above) to an agreement that is **"between individuals who intend to marry which affirms, modifies, or waives a marital right or obligation during**

**marriage or at separation, marital dissolution, death of one of the spouses, or the occurrence or nonoccurrence of any other event."** UPMAA § 2(5).

Comments to the UPMAA (2012) indicate that the expanded definition of a premarital agreement is not intended to encompass "cohabitation agreements" or contracts "not intended to affect the parties' existing legal rights and obligations upon divorce or death." The example given for the latter is "Islamic marriage contracts with their deferred Mahr payment provisions." UPMAA § 2, Comment. The National Conference of Commissioners gives no further clarification on its decision to draw a bright line between premarital agreements and cohabitation agreements, or alternatively between premarital agreements and Islamic marriage contracts (Mahr).

Litigation over the enforceability of intimate partner agreements illustrates that the UPMAA language is potentially problematic for at least two reasons. One, the social terrain from contemplating marriage, to intending to marry, to contracting for a valid marriage is not necessarily characterized by bright line dates or even by publicly recognizable moments. All too often, these transitions are traversed, if they are, in private moments. Two, expressly excluding Islamic marriage contracts from the reach of legislation intended to protect intimate partners who enter into legally binding agreements with each other may be constitutionally unjustified. Given these two gaps, the expanded definition of a premarital contract in the UPMMA 2012 falls short of its aim to protect intimate partners who contract or transact with each other over property or personal rights and obligations or both.

## 4. TRANSMUTATIONS

A transmutation changes the character of property, and thus alters the spouses' marital property rights as between themselves and, sometimes, third parties. Changes from community property to separate property, separate property to community property, or the separate property of one spouse to the separate property of the other spouse are all possible. Check to determine whether one or all of the three possible types of transmutations are allowed in the jurisdiction.

A transmutation can be effected in one of several ways: by a written agreement, by a written declaration made by one spouse alone, and, in some states, by the delivery of a deed.

A *transmutation by agreement* becomes effective when both spouses sign a written agreement to transmute one or more assets. Typically the agreement is based on a bargained for exchange between the spouses.

A *transmutation by declaration* occurs when one spouse, acting alone, transmutes one or more assets so as to benefit the other spouse. It is not uncommon for a declared transmutation to be gratuitous (not the result of an exchange of value and thus not supported by consideration).

In some states, the *delivery of a valid deed* can effect a transmutation of the titled asset.

Finally, a spouse who manages a community property business may have the legal authority, even if acting alone, to effect a transmutation on behalf of the business entity.

The following principles apply to transmutations in most U.S. community property states.

- A valid transmutation becomes effective on the date it is made.

- Most contemporary state codes mandate that a transmutation must be in writing to be valid.

  o A transmutation agreement, to be valid, must comply with state statutory formalities, be the result of voluntarily action, and be based upon disclosure. State formalities are found in the state family code or in case law.

  o Some states go further to mandate that any such writing contain an express declaration made or joined in by the adversely affected spouse.

- A valid transmutation can only be reversed by a subsequent (also valid) transmutation. The physical destruction of a written transmutation document does not invalidate a prior transaction.

- In most U.S. community property states oral
  transmutation are no longer valid.

A transmutation may relate to property that
already exists. It may relate to contract rights in
property that does not yet exist (like royalties, future
earnings, or future contract proceeds). By corollary,
any property interest, present or future, legal or
equitable, vested or contingent, real or personal,
because it can be characterized as community
property, may be the subject of a transmutation. A
transmutation may be made on an asset-by-asset
basis, or on an estate-wide basis. And as noted above,
a transmutation may be effected with or without
consideration.

*Interspousal gifts of a personal nature* are, in some
states, categorically exempt from statutory
formalities. If so, covered gifts can be transmuted by
a physical act of delivery. Gifts of real estate are not
exempt from transmutation formalities; and even if,
hypothetically, they were, compliance with the state
statute of frauds would be necessary in order to effect
a valid conveyance.

Transmutation formality exemptions may be
subject to a value limitation. Property that exceeds
the limitation must be transmuted in accordance
with transmutation formalities. The policy behind a
value limitation is to protect the donor spouse and
third-party creditors from dissipation of the
community estate by the act of one spouse making a
gift to the other.

Finally, a transmutation can be effected by operation of law. Commingling can result in a transmutation if the assets of different characters (community and separate) are mixed together— *commingled*—to such a degree that their component parts became untraceable. The rationale for such an outcome is gift based; the law presumes that a spouse who permits separate property to be commingled with community property to the point of confusion intends to make a gift of the commingled property to the community. The act of allowing the confusion to occur, while not an express declaration per se, meets the present intent element for a valid inter vivos gift. The act of commingling the property meets the delivery requirement. Acceptance is presumed.

## a. Formalities: Writing and Express Declaration Requirements

Prior to the 1980s, U.S. community property states permitted oral and even tacit transmutations.

Since the 1980s, the trend is to require that transmutations be in writing unless the property being transmuted is exempt from the writing formality either by a statute or a court ruling. For example, California enacted legislation, effective on January 1, 1985, requiring that a transmutation, to be valid, must be **"made in writing by an express declaration that is made, joined in, consented to, or accepted by the spouse whose interest in the property is adversely affected."** Cal.Fam.Code § 852(a).

The concept of the *express declaration* is at the core of most transmutation formalities, whether a statute so provides or not. The reason is that a transmutation is a transfer of property, and as such the evidence must show that the adversely affected spouse had the present intent to divest him or herself of title or interest by changing the character of the asset or assets. A written express declaration, whether it appears in an agreement or in a unilateral transfer, is documentary proof of a present intent ("I transmute X" as opposed to "I will transmute X") to change the character of the property at issue. *Estate of MacDonald*, 51 Cal.3d 262, 272 Cal.Rptr. 153, 794 P.2d 911 (1990).

An express declaration can be the subject of a contract agreement, or it can appear within a contract term or fragment. It can be also made within a deed, or an informal writing, like a card, or a letter, or a text or email.

## b. Transmutation by Deed

Whether a deed alone can transmute an asset depends on both a close reading of state law and of the facts of the case. Every U.S. community property state relies on community property presumptions that are raised depending on whether and, if so, how the asset is titled. The key issue in determining the character of an asset, therefore, is time of acquisition.

In all U.S. community property states, an asset acquired during marriage no matter whether it is titled in both spouses' names, untitled or titled in one spouse's name alone is nonconclusively presumed to be community property in character. For a titled asset, changing the form of the titled asset by deed (say, for example, from joint title to sole title or vice versa), without more, may not necessarily effect a transmutation of the asset, depending on state law.

*Illustration 2.1:* At Time 1, B and C buy a house during marriage. They take title to the house in joint tenancy. The house is acquired while B and C are married, making it presumptively community in character. At Time 2, still during marriage, B and C use a quitclaim deed to convey the house to B in sole title. The change in title from joint title (title in the name of "B and C") to sole title (title in the name of "B" alone) may or may not constitute a transmutation depending on the law of the jurisdiction.

The rule on deeds varies.

In some states, a change in title form (joint title to sole title) does not automatically effect a transmutation of the titled asset. More evidence than just the deed itself is required.

In other states, a deed can be sufficient documentary evidence of a transmutation. Some states rationalize this outcome based on whether the word "grant" or the phrase "hereby grants" is interpreted by a judge to be an express declaration. Other states rationalize it based on the presence or absence of conflicting documents such as separate property inventories. Still others rationalize it based on compliance or noncompliance with additional formalities (the deed is acknowledged or notarized) that are required so as to distinguish a deed that is intended to transmute the titled asset from one that is not.

Despite the differences in state laws, if B and C petition for dissolution, here is the process for analysis. First, the house in Illustration 2.1 above will be inventoried as a presumptively community property asset—because it was acquired during marriage—notwithstanding the change in title. Second, if B wants to claim that the delivery of the deed transmuted the house, then B needs to prove that delivery of the deed, without more, was sufficient to meet state transmutation formalities.

*Illustration 2.2:* At Time 1 before marriage B owns a house with a mortgage. At Time 2, during marriage, B conveys title jointly to B and C ("to B and C as joint tenants"). Assume that B's purpose in creating a joint tenancy is to refinance the mortgage on the house by using C's income. At inception of title, the house is B's separate property because it was acquired before marriage. Did B's conveyance to "B and C as joint tenants" change the character of the house from separate to community property?

Here, the answer is likely yes under a series of rationales. Some states have a special joint form title community property presumption that may apply. Other states might consider the deed, with its granting language, to be an express declaration of B's intent to change the character of the house from separate to community property. Still other states may consider both the conveyance and its purpose, which is to obtain borrowed funds from a lender by representing that C's income is reachable in the event of default.

With Illustration 2.2 (as with Illustration 2.1), despite differences in state laws, if B and C petition for dissolution, the process of analysis likely proceeds as follows.

- Step one: the house is inventoried as a presumptively community property asset—either because it is in joint title when the parties seek dissolution, or because the community of B and C can be said to have acquired an interest in the house on the day B changed the title from sole to joint form. Either of these rationales includes the house in the definition of community property, the former by use of a presumption, and the latter by application of the inception of title rule.

- Step two: B has the burden of rebuttal. Therefore, if B wants to claim that the house is separate property, B will need to prove that B lacked the requisite present intent to transmute the house from separate property to community property on the date that B executed the joint form deed.

How clear does the language in the deed need to be in order to transmute an asset? Is the word "grant" enough? If not, what more is required?

Whenever a deed is clear and ambiguous, California, Arizona, and Idaho exclude extrinsic evidence of intent. In such a situation, a court may look only to the deed itself for evidence of the adversely affected spouse's present intent to transmute the asset.

*Estate of Bibb*, 87 Cal.App.4th 461, 104 Cal.Rptr.2d 415 (2001) illustrates the point. In *Bibb*, supra, the single word *"grant"* in a deed was held to meet the express declaration requirement where the grantor owned the property in sole title before marriage and then conveyed it to himself and his wife during marriage in order to refinance the property (the facts of Illustration 2.2 above). In *Bender v. Bender*, 123 Ariz. 90, 597 P.2d 993, 997 (1979), the benefitted spouse asked the adversely affected spouse to sign a lengthy deed that included clear language of disclaimer. The court labeled the deed a "disclaimer deed," and deemed the language of disclaimer sufficient evidence of the adversely affected party's present intent to give up any interest in the property. The court explained in dicta that had the adversely affected party signed a quitclaim deed instead of the disclaimer deed, the quitclaim would have been too bare in its recitations to prove a present intent to transmute.

*Present intent versus future intent.* A transmutation requires a present intent to transfer or divest oneself of the affected property or interest. A statement in the valid will of a still-living testator is a declaration of future intent. As such, the wills of living persons are inadmissible on the issue of present intent to transfer. The rationale is that a will is ambulatory (subject to change or revocation during the testator's lifetime). See e.g. Cal.Fam.Code § 853.

Federal law prohibits or restricts the transmutation of federal obligations from separate property into community property. In such a case, a transmutation might comply with state law, clearly contain an express declaration, and yet still be invalid for federal law purposes. See Chapter 12.

Relatedly, efforts to transmute property can be effective between the spouses but ineffective against third parties, like creditors. See, for example, *Lucas v. Earl*, 281 U.S. 111, 50 S.Ct. 241, 74 L.Ed. 731 (1930), a case in which a transmutation agreement was valid as between the spouses under state law, but void for purposes of shifting an income tax burden under federal law.

## c. Interspousal Obligations Implicit in a Transmutation: Voluntariness and Financial Disclosure

Colonial Spanish law provided that a wife's renunciation of existing property was voidable in cases of fraud, deceit, duress, or undue influence. If a husband gained any advantage in a transaction with the wife, a constructive fraud was presumed. The burden then fell to the husband to rebut the presumption with evidence of "full and fair disclosure or explanation to the wife ... that she understood fully the effect [of the transmutation] upon her." deFuniak and Vaughn, PRINCIPLES OF COMMUNITY PROPERTY (2nd ed. 1971), § 138.

California legislation parallels the Spanish concept by how it incorporates nonmarital business partnership rules into the family code. Cal.Fam.Code

§ 721(b), in particular, provides that spouses occupy **"confidential relations with each other"** and, therefore, ***"any unfair advantage"*** that one spouse obtains in an advantage with the other gives rise to an evidentiary presumption of undue influence. (Italics added.) The initial burden is on the adversely affected spouse to show any unfair advantage. Once shown, the presumption of undue influence is raised. That presumption clearly favors the adversely affected spouse, meaning the spouse whose net worth is diminished by the transmutation. Once the presumption is raised, rebuttal rests with the benefitted spouse, meaning the spouse whose net worth is enhanced by the transmutation.

A transmutation is best understood as a transaction between the spouses who have rights and obligations relative to each other that arise out of their status as married persons. If one spouse is adversely affected by a gratuitous transaction, historically and modernly, there has been a process for reviewing that transaction at the end of the marriage. The process turns on whether the benefitted spouse used deceit or coercion to obtain an unfair advantage against the other spouse.

Spouses can effect a transmutation relative to each other without recording the same in the public record. However, when a transmutation affects the rights of a third party, like a creditor, most states require that the spouses give third parties constructive notice of the change in character. Failure to do so leaves the third party's rights unchanged by the transmutation. See for example,

Cal.Fam.Code § 852(b). In other words, recordation does not decide the validity of the transmutation as between the spouses themselves, but recordation all too often does decide the rights of third parties.

A transmutation of personal property generally need not be recorded. But here again, if the rights of a third party are affected by the transmutation, then recordation may be necessary to preserve a spouse's rights relative to a bona fide purchaser or creditor.

All transmutations are potentially subject to the laws governing fraudulent transfers. Arizona (1989), California (1990), Idaho (1987), Nevada (1987), New Mexico (1989), Texas (1987), Washington (1987), and Wisconsin (1987) adopted the Uniform Fraudulent Transfer Act (the UFTA for short); Louisiana is the sole holdout.

The UFTA is derived from the 1571 Statute of 13 Elizabeth c. 5. Today, however, the UFTA is superseded by the Uniform Voidable Transactions Act U.L.A. (2014), (the UVTA for short). California, Idaho and New Mexico repealed the UFTA and replaced it the UVTA. See e.g., Cal.Fam.Code § 851, Cal.Civ.Code § 3439, and Cal.Civ.Code § 2429.14, effective January 1, 2016. See Chapter 8 for more on liabilities and creditors' rights.

### d. Exempt Property

Certain types of property may be categorically exempt from transmutation formality requirements, as discussed above.

Cal.Fam.Code § 852(c), for is an example of a statute that clearly exempts interspousal gifts of a tangible, personal nature that are intended to be used solely or primarily by the donee spouse so long as they are not **"substantial in value taking into account the circumstances of the marriage."**

Exempt property is transmuted upon delivery of the asset.

### e. Transmutation by Operation of Law

Transmutation by operation of law occurs when property is commingled to the point of confusion, as discussed above. The doctrine of confusion is sometimes codified or alluded to as a rationale for an outcome. See for example, Cal.Fam.Code § 852(d).

## C.  INDIVIDUAL STATES

### 1.  ARIZONA

Arizona adopted the UPAA, effective September 21, 1991. Ariz.Rev.Stat.Ann. § 25–201 to § 25–205. From that date forward, premarital agreements must be in writing and signed by both of the parties contemplating marriage.

If the above factors are established the premarital agreement is enforceable unless the party against whom enforcement is sought proves either (i) that the agreement was not voluntarily executed or (ii) that the agreement was unconscionable and the party lacked fair and reasonable disclosure of the property involved.

The issue of unconscionability must be affirmatively raised by the party against whom enforcement is sought; a trial court does not have the power to raise the issue on its own initiative (sua sponte). *Schlaefer v. Financial Management Service*, 196 Ariz. 336, 996 P.2d 745 (Ariz. App. 2000). Likewise, fraud and mistake must be affirmatively raised, even if the parties are married. *Bender v. Bender*, 123 Ariz. 90, 597 P.2d 993, 997 (1979), citing *Hunt v. Campbell*, 19 Ariz. 254, 169 P. 596 (1917) as to fraud and *Fruth v. Divito*, 26 Ariz.App. 154, 546 P.2d 1163 (1976) as to mistake.

State public policy does not prohibit provisions that modify or eliminate postdissolution spousal support. Ariz.Rev.Stat.Ann. § 25–203(A)(4). But, if there is such a provision and it **"causes one party to the agreement to be eligible for [public] support. . . ."** a court has the discretion to award spousal support notwithstanding the existence of the contract. Ariz.Rev.Stat.Ann. § 25–202(D). In disputes about spousal support modification or waiver clauses, the standard of proof is clear and convincing evidence. *Hrudka v. Hrudka*, 186 Ariz. 84, 919 P.2d 179 (Ariz. App. 1995), citing *Williams v. Williams*, 166 Ariz. 260, 801 P.2d 495, 497 (Ariz. App. 1990).

Premarital agreements executed *before* 1991 (the effective date of Arizona's UPAA) follow a reverse presumption than those that are executed after the state's adoption of the UPAA. The standard for *pre-*UPAA premarital agreements places the burden of proof on the spouse who seeks enforcement of the agreement. That spouse—the contract proponent—must prove by clear and convincing evidence that the spouse opposing the contract nevertheless executed the agreement voluntarily and received adequate disclosure.

Arizona has no statutory transmutation provision. Instead, for proof of transmutation, Arizona relies on the inception of title rule unless modified by an agreement between the spouses. Inception of title refers to the time the property right comes into existence, not to the time that legal title to the asset is originally conveyed. *Potthoff v. Potthoff*, 128 Ariz. 557, 627 P.2d 708 (1981). The initial character of the property is determined by the inception of title rule. See *Musker v. Gil Haskins Auto Leasing, Inc.*, 18 Ariz.App. 104, 500 P.2d 635 (Ariz. App. 1972); see also inception of title cases tracing back to *Horton v. Horton*, 35 Ariz. 378, 278 P. 370 (1929). Once the character of an asset is set, it does not change except by agreement between the spouses or by operation of law. *Bender,* supra, *Porter v. Porter*, 67 Ariz. 273, 195 P.2d 132 (1948). When a transmutation agreement is offered to rebut the general community property presumption, the standard of proof is clear and convincing evidence, a topic discussed more fully in Chapter 3. *Neely v. Neely*, 115 Ariz. 47, 563 P.2d 302 (1977).

A transmutation agreement, to be valid, must be in writing. A contract or a deed will suffice if there is also evidence of conduct undertaken contemporaneously with the agreement that indicates an intent on the adversely affected spouse's part that the benefitted spouse should have rights to the property. *In re Sims' Estate*, 13 Ariz. App. 215, 475 P.2d 505 (Ariz. App. 1970). *Bender,* supra applies the test to a deed.

In *Bender*, supra, the wife signed what the court labeled a "disclaimer deed" for Arizona real estate that had been purchased by the husband with funds that he earned during marriage, while domiciled in Canada (a noncommunity property jurisdiction). The disclaimer deed recited the source and character of the real estate purchase funds as the husband's separate property; it included language that read: "[t]he undersigned [wife] has no past or present right, title, interest, claim or lien of any kind or nature whatsoever in, to or against said property;" and it was signed by the adversely affected wife. *Id.* at 996. First, the court deemed the disclaimer deed to be clear and unambiguous on its face, thus excluding extrinsic evidence about the backstory to the deed's execution. Next, the court deemed the recitation in the deed sufficient to meet the clear and convincing evidence standard for purposes of proving the wife's intent, on the date she signed the disclaimer deed, to deny any interest in the Arizona trailer park.

*Bender* distinguishes in dicta between the use of a disclaimer deed and a quitclaim deed. A disclaimer deed contains recitations that the court categorized as "contractual." Whereas a quitclaim is a bare grant. As the court explained, "there is no denial of interest made" in a quitclaim deed, as there is in a disclaimer deed. Instead, a quitclaim deed is "solely the relinquishment (or gift) of any possible interest one has in certain property." *Id.* 997.

This leads to the question of the character of gifts. Ariz.Rev.Stat.Ann. 25–211, discussed in Chapter 4, presumptively excludes from the definition of community property any asset acquired by one spouse by gift, devise, or descent. When property is acquired during marriage by both spouses from a third party donor, however, the property is presumptively community property. Likewise when property is acquired during marriage as a gift by one spouse from the other spouse. Rebuttal is by clear and convincing evidence. *Hrudka*, supra at 186.

Regarding interspousal gifts of a personal nature, one spouse's possession of the property is not enough to prove that it was transmuted to the separate property of the possessor. Instead, the possessor must prove (i) donative intent on the part of the donor spouse, (ii) delivery of the gifted property, and (iii) a vesting of irrevocable title in the donee on delivery. *Armer v. Armer*, 105 Ariz. 284, 289, 463 P.2d 818, 823 (1970)(in banc). There does not appear to be an explicitly followed value limitation in Arizona for interspousal gifts. But the equities are with the community as, here again, the gift of a personal item acquired or purchased during marriage remains community property unless the donee spouse proves otherwise by clear and convincing evidence. *Id.*

Generally, changes in form are not enough to transmute property, nor is the act of commingling one character of property with another character. As with the other U.S. community property states,

Arizona follows the general rule that community and separate property can be commingled without losing their character. The doctrine of confusion provides a limit to this rule: at the point that the separate property component in commingled property can no longer be identified, the entire property becomes community by operation of law. *Potthoff*, supra, at 711.

## 2.     CALIFORNIA

California passed the California Premarital Agreement Act in 1985, effective January 1, 1986 (the CPAA 1986 for short). The CPAA 1986 was modeled on the UPAA, with important differences discussed below. California amended the CPAA in 2001, effective January 1, 2002 (the CPAA 2002 for short). The amended CPAA 2002 can be found at Cal.Fam.Code §§ 1500 through 1620.

Premarital contract enforceability is determined by the law that was in force at the time the contract was executed. Thus, a brief historical analysis of California law is necessary to understanding the law. Contracts executed before or on December 31, 1985 are governed by case law of the same period. Contracts executed between January 1, 1986 and December 31, 2001 are governed by the CPAA 1986 and relevant case law commencing on 1986. Contracts entered into from January 1, 2002 forward are governed by the CPAA 2002 and any relevant case law.

Formalities for executing a premarital contract are consistent in the CPAA 1986 and 2002. Both versions of the CPAA require that a premarital agreement be in writing and signed by the parties to be married. Consideration is not required. Like the UPAA, the CPAA 1986 and 2002 place the burden of proof on **"the party against whom enforcement is sought . . . ."** The CPAA mandates that the burden placement does not change even if fraud, undue influence, coercion, or other factors relevant to the judge are alleged as the basis for not enforcing a contract, an interpretation confirmed in. *Marriage of Bonds*, 24 Cal.4th 1, 99 Cal.Rptr.2d 252, 5 P.3d 815 (2000).

Parties may contract with respect to a broad array of property issues and personal rights and obligations. Cal.Fam.Code § 1612(a)(1) through (a)(7). They cannot, however, use a premarital contract to adversely affect the right of child to support, circumvent state public policy, or agree to terms that are illegal when the contract is signed. Cal.Fam.Code § 1612(a)(7) and (b). The waiver of spousal support during marriage is an example of a term that would be against state public policy.

Parties retain the right to modify or waive the right to postdissolution spousal support by premarital or marital contract. Here again, an historical framework is relevant. Prior to 1986, post-dissolution spousal support waivers were unenforceable as a matter of law. The CPAA 1986 adopted the UPAA but omitted the specific UPAA provision that expressly permits the modification or elimination of spousal support by premarital contract. Thus, the CPAA 1986 expressly authorizes prospective spouses to contract over provisions altering **"personal rights and obligations,** *not in violation of public policy* **or a statute imposing a criminal penalty"** during and at the end of marriage, but (unlike the UPAA § 3) the CPAA 1986 makes no specific mention of whether modifying or waiving postdissolution spousal support is in violation of public policy (italics added). See Cal.Fam.Code § 1612(a)(7).

In *Marriage of Pendleton & Fireman*, 24 Cal.4th 39, 99 Cal.Rptr.2d 278, 5 P.3d 839 (2000), the California Supreme Court held that a postdissolution spousal support waiver in a premarital agreement executed after January 1, 1986 was not per se unenforceable (despite the prior law and the deliberate omission in the CPAA 1986 of the UPAA "modification or elimination of spousal support" clause). The court reasoned that because spousal support is a personal right and obligation, spousal support modifications and waivers are implicitly authorized by the phrase in the CPAA 1986 that allows parties to alter their **"personal rights and obligations . . . ."** Cal.Fam.Code § 1612(a)(7). The court then turned to the issue of whether the spousal support waiver in dispute was **"in violation of public policy"** under Cal.Fam.Code § 1612(a)(7). On this issue, it ruled that the support waiver entered into between Pendleton and Fireman did not offend public policy because when the contract was signed the prospective spouses were mature, self-sufficient in property, relatively equal in education, and represented by independent counsel. The party against whom contract enforcement was sought argued that she was harmed by not being permitted to petition for postdissolution spousal support so as to maintain her marital standard of living. The court rejected that argument noting that the party against whom enforcement was sought had the same resources at the end of the marriage as she had enjoyed at its beginning (approximately $2.5 million in invested assets). If the contract term were enforced, said the court, that party still would in no way be eligible for public aid. See *Marriage of Howell*, 195 Cal.App.4th 1062, 126 Cal.Rptr.3d 539 (2011) and *Marriage of Melissa*, 112 Cal.App.4th 598, 151 Cal.Rptr.3d 608 (2012) for a continuation of the public policy discussion in the CPAA 2002 era.

*Pendleton and Fireman*, supra, led to the passage of Cal.Fam.Code § 1612(c), a section added to the CPAA in 2002, effective January 1, 2002. Cal.Fam.Code § 1612(c) explicitly addresses the enforceability of postdissolution spousal support waivers by building on the court ruling that a spousal support waiver falls within the statutory phrase **"personal rights and obligations, not in violation of public policy ...",** which is found in Cal.Fam.Code § 1612(a)(7).

Under the newly added Cal.Fam.Code § 1612(c) **"[a]ny provision in a premarital agreement regarding spousal support, including but not limited to, a waiver of it, is not enforceable if the party against whom enforcement ... is sought was not represented by independent counsel at the time the agreement ... was signed, or if the provision regarding spousal** support is unconscionable at the time of enforcement. An otherwise unenforceable provision ... may not become enforceable solely because the party against whom enforcement is sought was represented by independent counsel."

Summing up postdissolution spousal support waivers. Prior to January 1, 1986, postdissolution spousal support modifications and waivers are void as against public policy. From January 1, 1986 to December 31, 2001, *Pendleton and Fireman*, supra, applies. From January 1, 2002 forward, Cal.Fam.Code § 1612(c) applies, and it provide a litmus test for enforceability of a postdissolution spousal support modification or waiver. Such a provision **"is not enforceable"** as a matter of law if the party against whom enforcement will be sought was not represented by independent counsel when the contract was executed (signed). But even if a party was represented by independent counsel when the contract was signed, Cal.Fam.Code § 1612(c) gives a court discretion to sever any postdissolution spousal support provision that the court deems to be **"unconscionable at the time of enforcement."** A postdissolution spousal support waiver is unconscionable if its enforcement would leave the spouse who waived spousal support rights eligible for public assistance.

For purposes of spousal support modifications and waivers, the UPAA § 6(b) links unconscionability with the need for seeking public assistance; it also gives a court discretion to modify an offending spousal support waiver. By contrast, the CPAA 2002, does not explicitly adopt the UPAA definition for unconscionability. Nor does it adopt the remedy of contract modification. Instead, the CPAA 2002 authorizes the court to sever any unconscionable spousal support provision from the otherwise (potentially) enforceable premarital agreement. Once an unconscionable spousal support provision is severed from the rest of the premarital contract, the affected party's statutory right to petition for spousal support is reinstated in furtherance of the public interest.

For purposes of general contract enforceability, the concept of unconscionability is defined differently than it is for purposes of postdissolution spousal support waivers. In the above postdissolution spousal support waiver analysis, unconscionability is defined in terms of need (eligibility for public assistance). In the general contract enforceability, analysis, unconscionability is defined in terms of financial disclosure. Cal.Fam.Code § 1615(a)(1) and (2), both of which went into effect on January 1, 1986, provide that **"[a] premarital agreement is not enforceable if the party against whom enforcement is sought provides either of the following: (1) That party did not execute the agreement voluntarily. (2) The agreement was unconscionable when it was executed . . ."**

The original UPAA treats voluntariness as a question of fact and unconscionability as a question of law. California follows this approach. Both CPAA 1986 and 2002 underscore that the definition of unconscionability **"shall be decided by the court as a matter of law."** Cal.Fam.Code § 1615(b).

The legal definition of unconscionability, for purposes of assessing general contract enforceability under Cal.Fam.Code § 1615(a)(2)(A)–(C), turns on financial disclosure received by the party against whom enforcement is sought. The statute thus provides that an agreement is unconscionable if before execution **"all of the following applied to [the] party [against whom enforcement is sought]"**:

- **"That party was not provided a fair, reasonable, and full disclosure of the property or financial obligations of the other party."** Cal.Fam.Code § 1615(a)(2)(A).

- **"That party did not voluntarily and expressly waive, in writing, any right to disclosure ... beyond the disclosure provided."** Cal.Fam.Code § 1615(a)(2)(B).

- **"That party did not have, or reasonably could not have had, an adequate knowledge of the property or financial obligations of the other party."** Cal.Fam.Code § 1615(a)(2)(C).

The above sections of Cal.Fam.Code § 1615 codify the widely cited case of *Marriage of Bonds*, supra. In that case, the parties signed a premarital agreement containing reciprocal clauses providing that all property earned during the marriage would be the separate property of the earning spouse. The young Barry Bonds, who went on to be a high earning baseball star, was represented by counsel when he signed the premarital contract; Sun Bonds, the bride, was not. Nearly a decade after the marriage, the parties sought dissolution. Sun alleged that she did not sign the contract voluntarily and was, in fact, coerced by the circumstances surrounding the signing of the contract into waiving her statutory rights to community property. Sun argued that since she signed the contract without the assistance of an attorney, the court should deem coercion as a matter of general law and thus shift the burden of proof from her to Barry. The effect of Sun's proposed (and ultimately rejected) shift would be that rather than require Sun (the party against whom contract enforcement was sought) to prove that the contract was the result of coercion or undue influence, as the CPAA 1986 mandates, Barry (the party seeking to enforce the contract) would be required to prove that the contract was voluntarily entered into, as general law provides. In a lengthy opinion, the California Supreme Court upheld the placement of the burden of proof under the CPAA 1986. The court reasoned that CPAA 1986 mandates that the burden of proof fall on the party who challenges the enforceability of a premarital contract (**"the party against whom enforcement is sought"**), and that there it should remain.

The question of voluntariness is a question of fact. Cal.Fam.Code § 1615(c) appeared for the first time in the CPAA 2002. It attempts to list *Marriage of Bonds*, supra, factors by providing: **"it shall be deemed that a premarital agreement was not executed** voluntarily unless the court finds in writing or on the record all of the following:"

- "The party against whom enforcement is sought was represented by independent legal counsel at the time of signing the agreement . . . " or else waived the right to be represented by counsel in writing, (§ 1615(c)(1) and (3)); and

- The party against whom enforcement is sought had "not less than seven calendar days" between the signing of the agreement and "the time that party was first presented with the agreement and advised to seek independent legal counsel," (§ 1615(c)(2)); and

- If unrepresented by counsel, the party against whom enforcement is sought was "fully informed of the terms and basic effect of the agreement as well as the rights and obligations he or she was giving up" in a language in which he or she was "proficient," and did receive a memorialized version of the required information, and did "execute a document declaring that he or she received the information required . . ." (§ 1615(c)(3)); and

- The agreement and any other writings "were not executed under duress, fraud, or undue influence," or without "capacity to enter into the agreement." (§ 1615(c)(4)); and

- There is an absence of **"[a]ny other factors the court deems relevant."** (§ 1615(c)(5)). Domestic violence can be a considered factor.

Premarital contract amendments and revocations (as opposed to the premarital agreements themselves) are executed during, not before, marriage. During marriage the spouses are in a confidential relationship with each other as a matter of law. Additionally, the spouses are held to fiduciary duties set forth in Cal.Fam.Code § 721(b), discussed briefly below and again in more detail in Chapter 7.

Transmutations can be effected by agreement, by express declaration, or operation of law. Parties are statutorily permitted to transmute property from community to separate, from separate to community, or from the separate property of one spouse to the separate property of the other spouse. A transmutation is valid if it meets the statutory formalities discussed below *and* if it complies with the partnership fiduciary standards set forth in Cal.Fam.Code § 721(b). Some interspousal gifts are exempt from the writing requirement, but no transmutation is exempt from the application of Cal.Fam.Code § 721(b).

On January 1, 1985, California took the lead in requiring that transmutations be made in writing by an **"express declaration"** that is **"made, joined in, consented to, or accepted by the spouse whose interest in the property is adversely affected."** Cal.Fam.Code § 852(a). An express declaration is the present intent to effect a transmutation. It can appear in a contract, a deed, or even in a birthday card, an email, or a text. There is no requirement that the written instrument be formal, only that it contain an **"express declaration."**

Generally, a transmutation is offered as proof to rebut one or more of the general community property presumptions. In California, rebuttal is by preponderance of the evidence. In other states (Arizona is an example) rebuttal is by clear and convincing evidence. See, Section C, Arizona.

Cal.Fam.Code § 721(b) provides that spouses are in a confidential relationship to each other and thus that **"neither shall take any unfair advantage of the other."** Unless the transmutation is a product of a bargained for exchange, proof that the transmutation was gratuitous (meaning a gift) raises a presumption of undue influence in favor of the adversely affected party. So too might a bargained for exchange raise the presumption of undue influence, especially if the adversely affected party was not represented by independent counsel. The presumption of undue influence arises out of the spouses' confidential relationship. The burden of rebuttal is on the benefitted spouse to show that he, she or they did not take any unfair advantage of the adversely affected spouse's trust or vulnerabilities. Or, stated positively, that the transmutation was voluntary and based on disclosure.

**"Any unfair advantage"** is a question of fact. So, does mere arithmetic inequality raise the presumption of undue influence? More specifically, if the transmutation is the result of a bargained for exchange, must the outcome be arithmetically equal?

*Marriage of Burkle,* 139 Cal.App.4th 712, 43 Cal.Rptr.3d 181 (2006), answered no. In that case the parties transmuted property by contract during a period of separation, a time when parties are still in a confidential relationship as a matter of law. Each was represented in the contract negotiation phase by a teams of attorneys (plural). The parties reconciled, but eventually filed for dissolution a few years later. At dissolution, the wife contended that because she was walking away from the marriage with a significantly lower net worth than she would have otherwise enjoyed had she not signed the reconciliation contract the presumption of undue influence should be raised. The court of appeal disagreed. Key to the court's holding was that both parties had negotiated and executed the reconciliation agreement with attorneys whose duty it was to ensure that the contract was entered into voluntarily and with the necessary disclosure.

Cal.Fam.Code § 852(c) identifies property that is exempt from the written transmutation formalities as a **"gift between spouses of clothing, wearing apparel, jewelry, or other tangible articles of a personal nature that is used solely or principally by the spouse to whom the gift is made and that is not substantial in value taking into account the circumstances of the marriage."** For an eligible interspousal gift, the change in character is effected when the gift is delivered.

### 3.   IDAHO

Idaho adopted the UPPA 1983 in Idaho Code §§ 32–921 to 32–929, effective July 1, 1986. Idaho Code § 32–922 was added in 1995; it provides that a premarital agreement **"must be in writing signed by both parties."** Consideration is not required.

Enforceability of the written contract also requires compliance with Idaho Code § 32–917, which mandates that such contracts must, in addition to being in writing, be **"executed and acknowledged or proved"** in the same way that is required for conveyances of land.

The statute was interpreted in *Dunagan v. Dunagan*, 147 Idaho 599, 213 P.3d 384 (2009), a case in which the parties orally agreed before marriage to keep their finances separate during marriage. At dissolution, the separate property proponent offered evidence of partial performance (the parties had maintained separate accounts) that the judge declined to consider. On appeal the Supreme Court of Idaho upheld the trial court's decision to exclude such evidence as a matter of law; its rationale was that Idaho courts will recognize and enforce only those premarital agreements that comply with Idaho Code § 32–917, which is to say only those premarital agreements that are in writing and properly executed and acknowledged, and not otherwise illegal. *Id.* at 387.

In terms of the scope of what parties can contract over, Idaho Code § 32–923(d) explicitly permits the

modification or elimination of postdissolution
spousal support.

Spousal support provisions are excepted under
Idaho Code § 32–925(2), which provides that a
spousal support provision is **"not enforceable"** if it
**"causes one party to the agreement to be
eligible for support under a program for public
assistance at the time of separation or
dissolution."** Upon proof of causation **"a court,
notwithstanding the terms of the agreement,
may require the other party to provide support
to the extent necessary to avoid [public
assistance] eligibility."** The burden of proof is on
the party against whom enforcement is sought. *Id.*

Transmutations can be of community property to
separate property, separate property to community
property, or the separate property of one spouse to
the separate property of the other spouse. A
transmutation can be effected any time during
marriage. But to be deemed valid, a transmutation,
whether of personal or real property, must comply
with the statutory formalities discussed above.
*Stockdale v. Stockdale*, 102 Idaho 870, 643 P.2d 82
(1982), *Reed v. Reed*, 137 Idaho 53, 44 P.3d 1108,
1114 (2002), citing *Wolford v. Wolford*, 117 Idaho 61,
785 P.2d 625, 630 (1990). The party alleging the
validity of the transmutation has the burden of proof.
*Wolford*, supra at 630.

Transmutations by deed are permitted. Idaho Code
§ 32–906(2) provides that **"[p]roperty conveyed by
one spouse to the other shall be presumed to be
the sole and separate estate of the grantee and**

**only the grantor spouse need execute and acknowledge the deed or other instrument of conveyance . . ."** notwithstanding the provisions on equal management and control of community property found at Idaho Code 32–912. The transmutation is limited to the base property, not to any rents, issues, and profits derived therefrom. If the parties seek to transmute both the base property and its rents, issues, and profits, they must specifically state their intention in the instrument of conveyance.

Although conveyances typically involve a deed, a conveyance could arguably by effected by an agreement or other type of written instrument. Idaho Code § 32–912, at the very least, presumes the admission of a written instrument into evidence, but there is no explicit language otherwise limiting the form that the conveying instrument must take. Nevertheless, when the conveyance is by deed, case law conflicts on whether parol evidence should be admissible for purposes of explaining deed language that a judge otherwise deems plain and unambiguous. See e.g. *Hall v. Hall*, 116 Idaho 483, 777 P.2d 255 (1989) and *Barrett v. Barrett*, 149 Idaho 21, 232 P.3d 799 (2010).

Idaho Code § 32–916 states generally that statutory law governing domestic relations (Idaho Code, Title 32), which is to say the state community property system, applies unless there is **"a marriage settlement agreement entered into during marriage containing stipulations contrary thereto."** Idaho Code § 32–917, discussed above applies such that the agreement **"must be in writing, and executed and acknowledged or proved in like manner as conveyances of land are required to be executed and acknowledged or proved."** As discussed above, agreements concerning rights and obligations during marriage, whether executed before or during marriage, are enforceable only if they are in writing and not against public policy or illegal. *Wolford*, supra, *Stevens v. Stevens*, 135 Idaho 224, 16 P.3d 900 (2000), *Dunagan*, supra.

An illegal contract is void for public policy. In *Quiring v. Quiring*, 130 Idaho 560, 944 P.2d 695 (1997), wife induced husband to sign a quitclaim deed of his interest in the community property home in exchange for promises to refrain from informing law enforcement about alleged acts of sexual abuse by husband against the wife's minor child and to refrain from informing husband's employer about a criminal indictment against him for charges that were ultimately dropped. The family court awarded the house to the wife as her sole property. On appeal, the Idaho Supreme Court reversed, calling the underlying agreement that led to the delivery of the quitclaim deed to wife illegal and void. The rationale given was twofold. One, a party cannot contract to refrain from reporting sexual abuse of a child. Two, obtaining a contract benefit (in this case the quitclaim deed) by threat of "arrest or exposure to hatred, contempt or ridicule is theft by extortion and violates Idaho criminal law." *Id.* at 702.

## 4.   LOUISIANA

Louisiana has not adopted the UPPA 1983. The Louisiana Civil Code relies instead on the concept of the matrimonial regime, while at the same time further distinguishing between legal and contractual matrimonial regimes. LSA–C.C. Arts. 1734 and 1755 deal with matrimonial contracts (called matrimonial agreements in the state) made in contemplation of marriage.

A legal matrimonial regime is defined as the default system of principles and rules that govern the ownership and management of the property of a married person. LSA–C.C. Art. 2325. By statute, a matrimonial regime may be legal (called a community of acquets and gains as established by LSA–C.C., Book 3, Title VI), contractual (the result of the parties efforts to waive the default rules of the state community property system by an enforceable contract), or hybrid (meaning a modified regime that is partly legal and partly contractual). LSA–C.C. Art. 2326.

If the parties enter into a contractual matrimonial regime, they do so by a matrimonial agreement. **"A matrimonial agreement is a contract establishing a regime of separation of property or modifying or terminating the legal regime as provided by law."** LSA–C.C. Art. 2328. Any provisions of the legal regime that "have not been excluded, limited, or modified by contract retain their force and effect." Revision Comments, 1979, LSA–C.C. Art. 2325.

The terms of a matrimonial agreement determine how the parties have contracted to characterize property and future acquisitions obtained during marriage. *Shaheen v. Khan*, 142 So.3d 257 (2014); *In re Succession of O'Krepki*, 193 So.3d 574 (2016). LSA–C.C. Art. 2329 expresses a strong legislative policy against signing away community property rights during marriage without court approval. This policy is upheld time and again by the courts. *Acurio v. Acurio*, 2017 WL 1709823 states the policy in the positive: "the legal regime of community property is presumed and the state has a long legislative policy favoring community rights. Whether the policy is expressed in negative or positive terms, the consequence is that statutes governing matrimonial agreements are read in context with each other and construed strictly as a matter of law." See for example: *Muller v. Muller*, 72 So.3d 364, 367 (2011), distinguished by *Benedetto v. Benedetto*, 182 So.3d 344 (2015); *Deshotels v. Deshotels*, 150 So.3d 541 (2014), which is disagreed with by *Acurio*, supra.

LSA–C.C. Art. 2329 lifts incapacities to contract based on marital status that were part of the 1870 Code. Today, married persons in Louisiana have the right to enter into a contractual matrimonial regime with each other **"before or during marriage as to all matters that are not prohibited by public policy."** They may contract with each other, sell or lease property to each other, employ each other, enter into compromise agreements with each other, and so on.

It makes sense that married persons may agree to establish a legal matrimonial regime between them (meaning to abide by the community property system) without court approval. It is only when married persons seek to modify or terminate the legal matrimonial regime between them that they must obtain court approval. LSA–C.C. Art. 2329 thus also mandates the court approval process as a **"joint petition and a finding by the court that [the agreement] serves their best interests and that they understand the governing principles and rules."** Not all agreements between the parties constitute a modification or termination of the legal matrimonial regime, but generally agreements that purport to modify and terminate the legal matrimonial regime do need court approval. So do agreements that would govern future acquisitions if enforced. *In re Succession of Faget*, 53 So.3d 414 (2010).

New Louisiana domiciliaries are temporarily exempt from the court approval requirement. **"During the first year after moving into and acquiring a domicile in [Louisiana], spouses may enter into a matrimonial agreement without court approval."** LSA–C.C. Art. 2329.

LSA–C.C. Art. 2331 prescribes formalities. A matrimonial contract **"shall be made by authentic act or by an act under private signature duly acknowledged by the spouses."** An authentic act requires that a party execute the agreement before two witnesses. An act under private signature duly acknowledged requires that the parties sign before a notary. Either are acceptable under the governing LSA–C.C. Art. 1836.

Should private acknowledgment be before or during marriage? LSA–C.C. Art. 2331 places no explicit time requirement on privately acknowledged signatures. Recently, *Acurio v. Acurio*, 2017 WL 1709823 reversed see *Acurio v. Acurio*, 197 So.3d 253 (Ct. App. 2016). In that case, the state Supreme Court invalidated a marital agreement that had been made before marriage, but not duly acknowledged until after the date of the marriage. Reversal was on the ground that LSA–C.C. Art. 2331 (a marital agreement must be executed by authentic act or under private signature duly acknowledge) should be read in the context of other family law, and specifically in the context of LSA–C.C. Art. 2329, with the outcome being that court approval is required for marital agreements for which the formalities component is completed during marriage.

To sum up, LSA–C.C. Art. 2329 requires court approval for substantive terms and LSA–C.C. Art. 2331 sets out the formalities for executing a matrimonial agreement. The penalty for not complying with these applicable statutes is that the contract is deemed unenforceable. *Deshotels*, supra at 544 and *Acurio*, supra. In the absence of a legal matrimonial agreement (the community property system) comes back into effect by operation of law. LSA–C.C. Art. 2325, Revision Comments, 1979.

In terms of scope, prospective spouses and spouses have the right to enter into a matrimonial agreement "as to all matters that are not prohibited by public policy." *Barber v. Barber,* 38 So.3d 1046 (La.App. 2010) held that Louisiana legislative policy expressly prohibits, as a matter of public policy, agreements that **"renounce or alter the marital portion or the established order of succession."** Any attempt to alter these rights by contract is void ab initio, the justification being that testamentary rights are rules of public order. LSA–C.C. Art. 7 and LSA–C.C. Art. 2330.

Louisiana legislative and case law specifically prohibits modifications and waivers of spousal support during marriage. Marriage includes any period of separation. *Barber,* supra at 1049, citing LSA–C.C. Art. 98. Case law defines the start and end date of a period of separation. *Aufrichtig v. Aufrichtig,* 796 So.2d 57 (2001) reviews relevant cases and factual distinctions between marriage, separation, and termination.

Spousal support during a period of separation is called alimony *pendente lite* in Louisiana case law. Any attempt to use a contract to alter the right of support during marriage or during a period of separation, defined as a time when the marriage has not yet irretrievably and irreparably broken down, is void as against public policy. *Barber,* supra. The rationale relates back to statutory duties of support that exist during marriage.

LSA–C.C. Art. 98 further provides that **"[m]arried persons owe each other fidelity, support, and assistance."** Comment (e) explains that **"[t]he spouses' duties under this Article, as a general rule, are matters of public order from**

**which they may not derogate by contract."**
*Barber*, supra at 1049, citing *Holliday v. Holliday*,
358 So.2d 618, 620 (La. 1978). Offending spousal
support provisions are stricken from an otherwise
(potentially) enforceable matrimonial agreement.
LSA–C.C. Art. 2034.

In short, Louisiana case law voids contracts that
attempt to modify or eliminate support during
marriage and alimony *pendente lite* (spousal support
during a period of separation). Separation
nonconclusively presumes that the marriage may be
repaired. That said, alimony contracts may be
recognized as valid if they are executed after the
marriage has irretrievably and irreparably broken
down but before the start of a divorce proceeding.
*Boudreaux v. Boudreaux*, 745 So.2d 61, 62 (1999),
*Williams v. Williams,* 760 So.2d 469, 474 (2000).

Contracts that attempt to modify or eliminate
permanent alimony (spousal support after the
parties file for dissolution) are not per se against
public policy. The Louisiana Supreme Court decided
as much in the rehearing decision of *McAlpine v.
McAlpine*, 679 So.2d 85, 90 (La. 1996). The rationale
was that the right to petition for permanent post-
divorce alimony is a private right and thus it is not
against public policy to modify or waive it by contract.

Offending clauses are null (stricken) and rescission
is the remedy. *McAlpine*, supra at 90, citing *Holliday*,
supra, 620. Nullifying an offending term of a
matrimonial agreement does not necessarily nullify
the remaining provisions. LSA–C.C. Art. 2034.

Matrimonial agreements can affect the rights of third parties as well as the rights the spouses themselves. Thus a creditor is permitted to challenge the enforceability of a matrimonial agreement that is in fraud of the creditor's rights. See LSA–C.C. Arts. 2036–2044. To protect creditors' rights, Louisiana law advises that matrimonial agreements be recorded. A matrimonial contract is **"effective toward third persons as to immovable property, when filed for registry in the conveyance records of the parish in which the property is situated and as to movables when filed for registry in the parish or parishes in which the spouses are domiciled."** LSA–C.C. Art. 2332.

A gift of community property by one spouse to the other is called a donation. Community property donations are governed by LSA–C.C. Art. 1744. The rule is that **"[t]he donation of a spouse to the other spouse"** of an undivided community property interest **"transforms that interest into separate property of the donee . . . [and] an equal interest of the donee is also transformed into separate property. . . ."** LSA–C.C. Art. 2343.

A gift of separate property made by one spouse to the community is also called a donation. The rule for separate property donations is LSA–C.C. Art. 2343.1: **"[t]he transfer by one spouse to the other . . ."** of separate property **"with the stipulation that it shall be part of the community, transforms the thing into community property."**

Louisiana law incorporates the civil law distinction between gratuitous (lucrative) and onerous title. A donation can be either gratuitous or onerous. Gifts from employers are remunerative and, therefore, onerous. Under LSA–C.C. Art. 2343.1 **"a transfer by onerous title must be made in writing and a transfer by gratuitous title must be made by authentic act."**

## 5.  NEVADA

Nevada adopted the UPAA 1983 in 1989. The Nevada UPAA applies to all premarital contracts executed on or after Oct. 1, 1989. See Nev.Rev.Stat. § 123A.010 through § 123A.100. Premarital contracts are required to be in writing and signed by both parties. Nev.Rev.Stat. § 123A.040. Consideration is not required. Nev.Rev.Stat. § 123A.050. A premarital contract is not enforceable unless the party against whom enforcement is sought proves that he or she did not execute the agreement voluntarily; the agreement was unconscionable when it was executed; or disclosure was lacking or inadequate. Nev.Rev.Stat. § 123A.080(1).

Parties are permitted to contract for **"[t]he modification or elimination of alimony or support or maintenance of a spouse ...."** Nev.Rev.Stat. § 123A.050.1.(d). The legal definition of unconscionability is a question of law and it conforms to the definition used in the UPAA 1983 discussed in Section B above. Nev.Rev.Stat. § 123A.080.2. provides: if a premarital agreement modifies or eliminates **"alimony or support** maintenance of a spouse, and that modification or elimination causes one party to the agreement to be eligible for support under a program of public assistance at the time of separation or marital dissolution, a court, notwithstanding the terms of the agreement, may require the other party to provide support to the extent necessary to avoid that eligibility."

If a pre-1989 agreement complies with the Nevada UPAA—and no case has so held—it is presumed enforceable. If not, then the agreement will be adjudicated under the common law of contracts. *Sogg v. Nevada State Bank*, 832 P.2d 781 (Nev. 1992). The Nevada Supreme Court has the power to review the validity of a premarital contract de novo. *Id.*

Nev.Rev.Stat. § 123.070 permits spouses to enter into **"any contract, engagement or transaction with the other . . . respecting property . . . "** This code section is silent about whether any such contract, engagement or transaction must be in writing. However, the code section does specify that in any such transaction the spouses are subject **"to the general rules which control the actions of persons occupying relations of confidence and trust toward each other."** The remedy for breach is restoration of the property.

Specifically, with respect to transmutations, married persons cannot alter their legal relations by contract except as to (i) property, (ii) an agreement to separate, or (iii) support rights and obligations during any such period of separation.

Nevada law covers interspousal gifts by reference to the general definition of separate property found at Nev.Rev.Stat. § 123 and § 130. Thus, when one spouse obtains property by gift from the other spouse during marriage, that property falls out of the community property presumption absent clear and convincing evidence to the contrary. *Kerley v. Kerley*, 910 P.2d 279 (1996). Whereas when one spouse conveys or places separate property in joint title during marriage, the titled asset is presumed a gift to the community absent clear and convincing evidence to the contrary. *Schmanski v. Schmanski*, 984 P.2d 752 (1999), citing *Gorden v. Gorden*, 569 P.2d 397, 398 (1977).

The *Kerly*, supra, rule is broad enough to cover spouse to spouse conveyances of real property, so long as they are gifts (gratuitous transfers) made to the donee spouse alone. In *Kerley*, supra, for example, husband conveyed property to himself and wife as joint tenants, and later the husband and wife jointly reconveyed by quitclaim deed to husband alone. At dissolution, an issue of apportionment arose. The district court applied the community property presumption. Husband appealed. The Supreme Court of Nevada granted a rehearing and remanded with instructions to presume the spouses' delivery of the quitclaim deed to the husband to be a gift from the wife to the husband of her interest in the property. Such a presumption shifts the burden of proof to the community property proponent to prove by clear and convincing evidence that the conveyance was not a gift. *Id*. at 280. *Schmanksi*, supra, involved community personal property (sums on deposit in a joint tenancy investment account). There, the Nevada Supreme Court clarified that the act of transferring separate property from a sole account into joint tenancy investment account presumed a gift from the grantor (the donor spouse) to the community.

Several Nevada statutes explicitly contemplate or outright require that agreements between spouses be in writing to be enforceable. And yet, none of the statutes listed below specifically address the question of whether a transmutation must be in writing to be valid under Nevada law. The statutory gap leaves open the possibility that an oral transmutation may still be valid in Nevada.

- Nev.Rev.Stat. §§ 123.140, 123.150 and § 123.160 contemplate a written inventory of separate property assets. The inventory is required by Nev.Rev.Stat. § 123.140 to be **"made out and signed ... acknowledged or proved in a manner required for the acknowledgment of proof of a conveyance of real property, and may be recorded, if such person is a resident of this State ...."**

- Nev.Rev.Stat. § 125.150.2 mandates a court to dispose of property held by the spouses in joint tenancy at divorce in equal shares unless justice requires otherwise.

- Nev.Rev.Stat. § 123.220 is the general definition of community property; it permits spouses to exclude assets from its reach by

"[a]n agreement in writing between the
spouses." This same provision does not
explicitly refer to transmutations.

• Nev.Rev.Stat. § 123.270 speaks to marriage
settlement agreements executed near or at
dissolution. The statute mandates that "[a]ll
marriage contracts or settlements must
be in writing, and executed and
acknowledged or proved in like manner
as a conveyance of land is required to be
executed and acknowledged or proved."

In *Anderson v. Anderson*, 107 Nev. 570, 816 P.2d
463 (1991), the spouses signed the requisite
withdrawal slips, and closed a joint bank account. At
that time, they divided what were community
property sums on deposit between them in unequal
shares. The husband later challenged the unequal
distribution, relying on *Schreiber v. Schreiber*, 99
Nev. 453, 663 P.2d 1189 (1983), which upheld an oral
transmutation agreement already performed. The
Nevada Supreme Court ruled that, even if part
performance were available as a defense, the
husband was equitably estopped from challenging
the unequal distribution. The court declined to rule
on the peripheral question of whether
transmutations must be in writing, leaving it instead
to the Nevada legislature to clarify. In the opinion of
the court: "The important principle to be gleaned
from the California experience is that the task of
creating requirements that depart from prevailing
common-law norms is one better left to the
legislature." *Id.* at 574.

Nevada case law confirms that common law contract defenses are available, including those of part performance and estoppel. See for example, *Schreiber*, supra. As between the spouses and a third party (like for instance the Internal Revenue Service and other creditors), however, a transmutation must be in writing to be valid.

## 6.   NEW MEXICO

New Mexico adopted the UPAA 1983, effective July 1, 1995. See N.M.Stat.Ann. § 40–3A–1 to § 40–3A–10 (1978). In that adoption, the UPAA 1983 formalities were amplified so that to be enforceable under New Mexico law, a premarital agreement must be in writing, signed by both parties, *and* acknowledged while in the state of New Mexico. N.M.Stat.Ann. § 40–3A–4.B (1978). That same code section amplifies the UPAA 1983 in yet another key way. The UPAA 1983 disallows only provisions that affect the right of a child to support, whereas the New Mexico version of the UPAA disallows any provisions that **"adversely affect the right of a child *or spouse* to support, . . . ."** Both unconscionability and voluntariness are issues of law in New Mexico (unlike in, for example, California, where unconscionability is a question of law but voluntariness one of fact).

*Rivera v. Rivera*, 149 N.M. 66, 243 P.3d 1148 (Ct. App. 2010), adjudicated the relationship between contract enforceability and adverse effect on the spousal support right. In that case, the parties signed a premarital agreement that waived spousal support rights. No disclosure was provided. The enforceability of the contract was taken up by the appellate court, which ruled that, in the absence of disclosure, a waiver of postdissolution spousal support is unconscionable as a matter of public policy. Additionally, the absence of a severability clause in the premarital contract or of any other evidence that "the waiver of spousal support [was] in exchange for other benefits or concessions," left the court "unable to conclude that any portion of the agreement was valid without the unconscionable provisions." *Id.* at 1154.

New Mexico permits transmutations per N.M.Stat.Ann. § 40–2–2 (1978): **"Either husband or wife may enter into any engagement or transaction with the other, or with any other person respecting property, which either might, if unmarried; subject, in transactions between themselves, to the general rules of common law which control the actions of persons occupying confidential relations with each other."** In New Mexico, as in Nevada, the code section is silent about whether any such engagement or transaction must be in writing.

The validity of an oral transmutation contract between married persons appears to remain unsettled. An early case notes that joinder (which presumes the existence of a written document) is required for community real estate. See *McDonald*, supra, discussed in Chapter 1. But that same case makes no mention of an historical writing requirement for transmutations of community personal property. Instead of a bright line rule imposing a writing requirement for valid transmutations, any gap in the above statute (N.M.Stat.Ann. § 40–2–2 (1978) is filled by cases that invoke the law of confidential relationships.

That said, N.M.Stat.Ann. § 40–3–14 (1978), the management and control statute discussed in Chapter 7, creates exceptions to the equal management and control rule for community personal property titled in one spouse's name alone or that the spouses have **"designated in a written agreement"** to be under the sole authority of one spouse. (Title documents are written documents.)

This statute (N.M.Stat.Ann. § 40–3–14 (1978) arguably could be interpreted to effect a transmutation by law, especially in light of case law indicating that an asset title in one spouse's name alone raises a separate property presumption as to that asset. *Sanchez v. Sanchez*, 106 N.M. 648, 748 P.2d 21 (Ct. App.), cert. denied, 106 N.M. 627, 747 P.2d 922 (1987). But at least three strong policy arguments push against such an interpretation. One, community property states generally require that transmutations be intentional, not accidental. Two, community property codes employ community property presumptions, not separate property presumptions. Three, community property systems are primarily organized to protect the community. For the above reasons, New Mexico would be well served by a statutory provision abrogating *Sanchez*, supra.

New Mexico case law on confidential relationships includes at least four widely followed lines of precedent with which to analyze a contested transmutation. Any one line could be applied depending on the facts of the case. For this reason, much of the precedent is yellow flagged.

Here are four reported options for analyzing undue influence within the confidential relationship of marriage:

- One option invokes a high standard of proof per the *Trimble* Rule, which holds that a "transmutation must be established by clear, strong and convincing proof—more than a mere preponderance of evidence" so as to "preserve the virility of our indigenous form of marital property ownership." *In re Trimble's Estate*, 57 N.M. 51, 253 P.2d 805 (1953). A clear, strong, and convincing proof standard might not require a written transmutation, but it would certainly privilege a written transmutation document relative to any circumstantial evidence offered to prove an oral transmutation.

- Another option raises a presumption of undue influence to protect the adversely affected spouse. *Hughes v. Hughes*, 96 N.M. 719, 634 P.2d 1271 (1981).

- A third option relies on equitable trust principles. *Beals v. Ares*, 25 N.M. 459, 185 P. 780 (1919)(fraud), discussed in *McDonald*, supra, at 201; and *Curtis v. Curtis*, 56 N.M. 695, 248 P.2d 683 (1952)(presumptive fraud).

- A fourth option mandates full and fair disclosure as to the property that is the subject of the transmutation. *Beals*, supra.

## 7.   TEXAS

Texas adopted the UPAA 1983 effective April 17, 1997. The Texas provisions appear at V.T.C.A.Fam.Code §§ 4.001–4.010. A premarital agreement must be in writing and signed by both prospective spouses; consideration is not necessary. V.T.C.A.Fam.Code § 4.002.

Parties may contract for the modification or elimination of postdissolution spousal support per V.T.C.A.Fam.Code § 4.003(4). Like California, Texas has omitted the UPAA language that grants a court the power to modify an unconscionable spousal support provision at enforcement. The omission is significant because V.T.C.A.Fam.Code § 4.006(c) provides that **"[t]he remedies and defenses in this section are the exclusive remedies or defenses, including common law remedies or defenses."**

The Texas Constitution of 1876 was silent on the issue of transmutation. Still, that constitution enshrines a married person's right to partition or exchange community property for separate property.

In 1949, Tex. Const. Art. XVI § 15 was amended to permit spouses to **"partition between themselves in severalty or into equal undivided interests** all or any part of their existing community property, or exchange between themselves the community interest of one spouse in any property for the community interest of the other spouse in other property, whereupon the portion or interest set aside to each spouse shall be and constitute a part of the separate property of each spouse." The amendment also enabled the legislature to pass statutes governing formalities for the partition and exchange process.

Among those legislative formalities, V.T.C.A.Fam.Code § 4.102 clarifies what proof is required for enforcing **"partition or exchange."** (The partition and exchange maneuver requires what is known as the "Texas two-step," a transmutation strategy discussed in Chapter 5). Partition and exchange agreements must be in writing and signed by both parties. V.T.C.A.Fam.Code § 4.104. They presumably can be challenged on the same grounds as premarital contracts, which is to say for failure to meet formalities or for lack of voluntariness or disclosure. *McClary v. Thompson*, 65 S.W.3d 829 (2002).

Amendments to the Tex. Const. Art. XVI § 15 in 1949, 1980, 1987 and 1999 were necessary to allow for spouses to convert separate property to community property. Texas law now provides that **"[a]t any time, spouses may agree that all or part of the separate property owned by either or both spouses is converted to community property."** V.T.C.A.Fam.Code § 4.202. Statutory provisions further require that such agreement **"(a)**

**. . . to convert separate property to community property (1) must be in writing and: (A) be signed by the spouses; (B) identify the property being converted; and (C) specify that the property is being converted to the spouses' community property; . . . ."** Importantly: **"(b) The mere transfer of a spouse's separate property to the name of the other spouse or to the name of both spouses is not sufficient to convert the property to community property . . . ."** V.T.C.A.Fam.Code § 4.203. To ensure enforcement of an agreement to convert separate property to community property, V.T.C.A.Fam.Code § 4.205 provides example language that if **"prominently displayed in bold-faced type, capital letters, or underlined, is rebuttably presumed to provide a fair and reasonable disclosure of the legal effect of converting property to community property: . . . "**

Texas follows the civil law rule that characterizes the rents, issues, and profits of separate property as community property during the continuance of the marriage. The Texas approach can be inferred from Tex. Const. Art. XVI § 15.

Nevertheless, spouses have the statutory right to opt for the American rule. V.T.C.A.Fam.Code § 4.103 provides that **"[a]t any time, the spouses may agree that the income or property arising from the separate property that is then owned by one of them, or that may thereafter be acquired, shall be the separate property of the owner."** The statutory rule applies to income earned from the date of the agreement forward, not to the base property itself, or to income earned from the base property prior to the agreement.

## 8. WASHINGTON

Washington case law governs premarital agreements, since Washington has not adopted the UPAA 1983. Two salient themes of Washington case law are these. One, when should a confidential relationship arises between intimate partners as a matter of law? Two, what standard of proof should apply?

In Washington, prospective spouses are in a confidential relationship as of the date of their engagement. As a result, the party who seeks to enforce a premarital contract has the burden of showing that the contract was fair and fairly made. A premarital contract is deemed substantively fair if it makes a meaningful provision for the spouse against whom enforcement is sought. A meaningful provision is the consequence of full disclosure as to the "amount, character and value" of the property involved. A contract entered into voluntarily is one for which each contracting party had knowledge of his or her rights. *Friedlander v. Friedlander*, 80 Wash.2d 293, 494 P.2d 208 (1972) and *Marriage of Matson*, 107 Wash.2d 479, 730 P.2d 668 (1986) set forth the basic doctrine. *Marriage of Zier*, 136 Wash.App. 40, 147 P.3d 624 (App.Div. 3 2006) and *Marriage of Bolster*, 146 Wash.App. 1042 (App.Div. 1. 2008) split on its application.

Separate property agreements can be used to determine ownership rights upon the death of either spouse. Wash.Rev.Code § 26.16.120. Such an agreement is defined by statute as a contract, not a will. The rationale for labeling separate property agreements nontestamentary is that the agreement functions as a nonprobate device. A separate property agreement conveys property to the surviving spouse upon the death of the first spouse to die, whereas a will becomes irrevocable at death but does not otherwise result in an automatic conveyance of title at death. Separate property agreements must meet statutory requirements (writing and acknowledgment) in order to be valid.

Real property can be transmuted by one spouse's gift, conveyance, or sale to the other spouse. Wash.Rev.Code § 26.16.050 allows spouses and registered domestic partners to **"give, grant, sell or convey directly to the other spouse or other domestic partner his or her community right, title, interest or estate in all or any portion of their community real property. . . ."** Statutory formalities serve as proof of the grantor-spouse's intention to transmute the property. Those formalities provide that the deed or transfer from the grantor-spouse (meaning the spouse who is releasing any community property interest in the property) **"shall sign, seal, execute and acknowledge the deed as a single person . . . ."** The benefitted spouse need not also sign the deed. Noncompliance with statutory formalities supports a legal conclusion that the grantor's intent was not to release any community property interest in the titled asset.

When a release of one spouse's community property interest in community property real estate affects the rights of a third party grantee or transferee, Wash.Rev.Code § 26.16.095 comes into play. The statute deems as a bona fide purchaser any third party who can prove that (i) the purchase was for value and (ii) title to the asset, on the date of purchase, was clear on its face. The spouse who continues to claim a community property interest in the disputed property bears the burden of rebuttal.

What can a spouse whose name does not appear on a title document do to protect a community property interest in real estate relative to third parties? This is potential trap for the unwary since married persons can and do take title to community property in one spouse's name alone.

Wash.Rev.Code § 26.16.100 gives a spouse whose name is not on a deed ninety (90) days after the original deed to the property has been recorded to set forth the nature of his or her claim to the property in a subsequent instrument. That instrument must be recorded in the auditor's office in the county where the land is located in order to affect the rights of third party conveyees. Recordation puts subsequent conveyees on notice of the existence of a marital relationship between the spouse in whose name title appears to be vested (the spouse whose name is on title) and the spouse whose name does not appear on the deed (but whose marital claim is nevertheless recorded in the chain of title). Failure to record a statement of claim in the allotted time period results in a mandate to a judge that a bona fide purchaser

**"shall be deemed and held to have received the full legal and equitable title to such real estate free and clear of all claim of the other spouse or other domestic partner."** In such a case, the bona fide purchaser for value would take the grantor-spouse's community property interest by conveyance and the other spouse's community property interest by operation of Wash.Rev.Code § 26.16.100.

A recorded claim not only gives third parties constructive notice of the marital relationship, it also acts as a cloud on title to the property for the bona fide purchaser. The cloud on title can be released by compliance with Wash.Rev.Code § 26.16.100 or with proof that the property is **"the separate property of the person in whose name the title to the said real estate, or any part thereof . . . ."** Proof is by examination of the public record, specifically meaning the **"conveyances on record in the office of the auditor of the county . . ."** where the land is located. Wash.Rev.Code § 26.16.110.

To sum up, Wash.Rev.Code § 26.16.100 protects the bona fide purchaser for value who transacts with a married grantor. But the statute does not necessarily protect a purchaser from the claims of the grantor's spouse. Protection will depend on whether the third party exercised reasonable diligence to obtain knowledge of the existence of a marital relationship within the state of Washington. This issue can be litigated only if the grantor's spouse files a timely claim of interest. See *Campbell v. Sandy*, 190 Wash. 528, 69 P.2d 808 (1937).

### 9. WISCONSIN (WUMPA)

Wisconsin adopted the Uniform Marital Property Act (UMPA 1983), referred to as WUMPA, effective January 1, 1986. Legislative Counsel Committee Notes appears at the start of Chapter 766. Premarital and marital agreements are discussed in general terms under a section labeled "Nontax Provisions." W.S.A. 2009, Chapter 766, at 39–40.

Generally, marital property agreements are made between the spouses and comply with Wis.Stat. § 766.58(6). The codal rule includes provisions on procedural and substantive fairness; indicating that three elements of proof are necessary for an equitable marital property agreement: (i) the agreement was voluntarily entered into; (ii) the agreement was entered into based on fair and reasonable disclosure given by each spouse of his or her financial information; and (iii) the substantive provisions dividing the property are fair to each party. See e.g., *Greenwald v. Greenwald*, 154 Wis.2d 767, 779–80, 454 N.W.2d 34, 38 (Ct. App. 1990), disagreed with by *Meyer v. Meyer*, 239 Wis.2d 231, 620 N.W.2d 382 (2000) on a different issue. Additionally, spouses are held to a duty of good faith in matters involving **"marital property or other property of the other spouse. This obligation may not be varied by a marital property agreement."** Wis.Stat. § 766.15.

**"Agreements executed before marriage"** (called premarital agreements in other states) if **"intended to apply only after [the parties'] determination date"** are treated as marital property agreements per Wis.Stat. § 766.585. (The parties' determination date, defined more fully in Chapter 4, is the last of these events to occur: marriage; domicile in the state; or 12:01 a.m., January 1, 1986 (the date that WUMPA became effective)). This same statute does not govern agreements signed before the determination date **"except as provided otherwise in a marital property agreement made after the determination date."** Wis.Stat. § 766.58(12). But Wis.Stat. § 766.588, discussed below, does. Finally, the law on the date that the agreement applies (meaning the date that the agreement comes into legal existence), not the law on the date the agreement was signed, governs, here again by the authority of Wis.Stat. § 766.585.

Spousal support modification and waiver provisions are enforceable so long as they do not result **"in a spouse having less than necessary and adequate support, taking into consideration all sources of support."** Wis.Stat. § 766.58(9)(a). (Waiver becomes "elimination" under WUMPA.) If a spousal support provision makes **"one spouse eligible for public assistance at the time of dissolution of the marriage or termination of the marriage by death, the court may require the other spouse or the other spouse's estate to provide support necessary to avoid that eligibility, notwithstanding the marital property agreement."** Wis.Stat. § 766.58(9)(b). Here, to rephrase, the statutory remedy is judicial modification of the waiver.

Among the permitted methods of transmutation (called classification or reclassification under WUMPA) are deeds signed by both spouses, gifts, bilateral written marital property agreements, and written consents regarding life insurance premiums and proceeds.

Wisconsin allows parties to identify separate property by use of an individual property classification agreement. Wis.Stat. § 766.587. Separate property agreements determine the property rights of the parties at the end of the marriage, but in relation to creditors, they are only effective against those creditors who were given a copy of the document before extending credit. *Matter of Geise*, 132 B.R. 908 (Bkrtcy. E.D. Wis. 1991), citing Wis.Stat. § 766.587.

Parties can reclassify separate property so that it becomes marital property on the date of marriage. To effect such an agreement, parties are directed to use a statutory terminable marital property classification agreement (STMPCA for short), details for which are set out at Wis.Stat. § 766.588. A STMPCA is terminable, meaning that the STMPCA either ends automatically 3 years after it is entered into (in the absence of disclosure) or it ends 30-days after one spouse delivers a signed notice of termination to the other spouse (with adequate disclosure). And the 30-day notice termination is unilateral, meaning that one spouse acting alone can affect the termination. A signed notice of termination by one spouse to the other can be personally delivered or sent by certified mail to a last known address.

Wis.Stat. § 766.588, Schedule A is a form that noninclusively lists general asset and liability categories that, if disclosed, could avoid an automatic termination of the STMPCA after three years.

STMPCA termination is prospective, not retrospective. Only property rights from the date of the termination forward are affected by a STMPCA termination. Property rights obtained under the terms of the STMPCA are not reclassified on the date of termination. Ordinary contract defenses are not ruled out when it comes to a STMPCA; here, the rationale is that a sole owner is reclassifying his or her sole property as marital property and therefore, contract defenses (in particular the defense of lack of consideration) should remain available. Legislative Counsel Committee Notes—1987 Act 393, W.S.A. 2009 at 111.

Like separate property agreements, discussed above, a STMPCA is only effective against those creditors who were given a copy of the document before extending credit

Otherwise, marital property agreements are presumptively equitable; the burden of rebuttal is on the party who challenges the agreement at the end of the marriage. *Gardner v. Gardner*, 527 N.W.2d 701, 190 Wis.2d 216 (1994), rev. denied 531 N.W.2d 327 (1995).

# PART 2
# CHARACTERIZATION

# CHAPTER 3
# COMMUNITY PROPERTY

## A. OVERVIEW

There are only two types of marital property in a community property system: community property and separate property.

Every U.S. community property jurisdiction defines community property by a broad, flexible principle called the sharing principle. Characterization of property can be by proof or by the use of general or special community property presumptions. The spouse who seeks to establish a separate property interest bears the burden of rebuttal.

## B. DETAIL

Every U.S. state employs traditional community property principles in one form or another.

### 1. TYPES OF COMMUNITY PROPERTY SYSTEMS

Forty-one states are common law separate property title states; and two of these—Alaska and Tennessee—are community property option states. Nine states are ganancial community property states.

A *ganancial* community property system distinguishes between community and separate property.

A *universal* marital property system characterizes all property as community property, no matter how or when it was acquired. Wisconsin tends toward this direction without going all the way. See Section 3, Wisconsin.

A *deferred* community property system relies on title as evidence of ownership during marriage. At divorce, a community estate comes into existence (hence it is deferred until divorce) as authorized by statute or decisional law.

An *equitable division* state is a common law title state that replicates community property outcomes in the case of dissolution or death. In a dissolution proceeding, common law equitable division states follow the equitable division doctrine, either as codified by statute or by judicial decision. Of the forty-one U.S. common law equitable division states, forty have adopted equitable division by statute; only one, Mississippi, relies on a judicial version of the doctrine.

One meaningful difference between the forty-one separate title states and the nine community property states has to do with vesting. In the forty-one U.S. common law states, a nonearning spouse's rights in property acquired during marriage are contingent until confirmed by a court judgment at the end of marriage. In the nine U.S. community property states, community property rights in an asset vest upon acquisition.

## 2.  THE COMMUNITY PROPERTY SHARING PRINCIPLE

The cornerstone of a community property system is the sharing principle. All U.S. community property statutes employ it in an "all property except . . . " form. By this principle, any property acquired during marriage while domiciled in the state is community property.

Marriage and domicile can be called into question of course. But, by and large, proof of marriage and domicile are established by documentation.

Proof of date of date of acquisition may be harder to establish. Records can be lost, parties memories can falter, and so on. Therefore, each U.S. community property state employs a general community property presumption.

Sometimes, even with the use of an evidentiary presumption (discussed next), it may still be difficult to determine the character of an asset. In such a case, the civil law doctrine of onerous title is used. That doctrine holds that property acquired during marriage by the effort of one or both spouses is an onerous— labor based—acquisition that falls within the community property sharing principle. By contrast, property acquired by windfall or gift is a lucrative acquisition, and as such it falls within the definition of separate property.

Typically, the way a general community property presumption works is that upon proof of acquisition during marriage while domiciled in the state, the property is characterized as community property unless proven to be separate property.

The community property principle covers all types of property, leaving it to the courts to analogize to settled law when litigation over a contested category of assets ensues.

Characterizing an asset in a ganancial system raises issues of domicile, timing, and validity of marriage.

- *Domicile:* Only property acquired while the acquiring spouse is domiciled in the state can be community property within that state's community property system. It is domicile in the state not location of the asset that matters for purposes of characterization.

- *Timing:* Any property acquired during marriage, while domiciled in the state, can be community property so long as it acquired by onerous means. Onerous acquisition implies labor, and earnings are an artifact of labor.

- *Validity of marriage:* Only a valid marriage produces community property.

How does unpaid housekeeping, as a form of labor, fit into the sharing principle? Every community property system relies on a housekeeper's presumption as a matter of state policy. Each spouse's labor, whether paid or unpaid, is characterized and thus produces community property. The housekeeper's presumption is significant for how it treats a non-wage labor contribution to the family as the equivalent of a monetary or wage-based contribution.

In U.S. community property jurisdictions, the housekeeper's presumption is conclusive, meaning it is irrebuttable as a matter of policy. The housekeeper's presumption is operationalized in the equality of interest principle, which holds that the spouses' equal rights in a community property asset are vested as of the date of that asset's acquisition.

### 3. THE GENERAL COMMUNITY PROPERTY PRESUMPTION

Upon proof of acquisition during marriage, a general community property presumption can be raised.

The general community property presumption applies to any property not otherwise governed by a special community property presumption. A special presumption, whether statutorily enacted or judicially created, applies to specific types or titled assets. Special presumptions are discussed below.

A majority of states imply a general community property presumption from the basic community property statute. A minority codify the general presumption.

California and New Mexico make the general community property presumption acquisition-based. Rebuttal is by tracing the acquisition back to a separate property source or by producing an enforceable agreement between the parties that the asset is to be all or part separate property.

In these states the standard of rebuttal is the low preponderance of the evidence standard, while in other states, rebuttal must be made by the higher clear and convincing evidence standard. One rationale for using the low evidentiary standard is to spread the risk of judicial error in a dissolution proceeding equally between the parties. See Cal.Fam.Code § 760 and N.M.Stat.Ann. § 40–3–8 (1978). Another is that a low burden of proof guards against inadvertent divisions based on notions of fault that might result from use of a high clear and convincing standard of proof. Divorce in all U.S. community property states is either pure no-fault or no-fault by option of the petitioner. (No fault option means that the jurisdiction is fault-based, but it allows parties to adopt no-fault principles for their dissolution). When a community property state commits to no-fault dissolution, evidence of fault should be inadmissible for purposes of dividing community property.

Louisiana and Texas also have enacted a possession-based general community property presumption. A possession-based presumption considers only the mere fact of possession at the end of the marriage. Because proof of acquisition is more precise an indicator than proof of possession, Texas raises the standard of proof to clear and convincing evidence for its possession-based presumption. See LSA–C.C. Art. 2340 and V.C.T.A. Fam.Code § 3.003.

Differences exist among the nine U.S. community property states as to what type of evidence is admissible to rebut a presumption. Generally, tracing is sufficient, but an agreement may be needed in some situations.

Rebuttal of any community property presumption confirms the disputed asset as all or part separate property in character. Proportional ownership between the community estate and one spouse's or both spouses' separate property estates is permitted.

The following illustrations apply a general community property presumption. Illustrations 3.1 through 3.3 below involve an untitled asset. Illustration 3.4 below involves an asset titled in one spouse's name alone.

*Illustration 3.1:* During marriage the spouses purchase an untitled work of art at a fair. In all states proof that the artwork was acquired during marriage raises an acquisition-based general community property presumption. Assume one spouse concedes that the artwork was acquired during marriage but nevertheless seeks to confirm a separate property interest. That spouse—called the separate property proponent—can rebut the general community property presumption either by tracing the purchase back to a provable separate property source or by producing an enforceable agreement between the spouses that the artwork is not to be community property. The separate property claimant bears the burden of rebuttal by preponderance of the evidence.

*Illustration 3.2:* During marriage a spouse possesses an untitled artwork whose date of acquisition is unknown. In a state without a possession-based community property presumption, a community property proponent would need proof of date of acquisition to convince a court to raise the presumption. While the length of the marriage arguably could be considered a proxy for acquisition during marriage, proof of possession and of acquisition are not necessarily the same. By comparison, in a state with both an acquisition and a possession-based general community property presumption, proof of possession alone would be a sufficient legal basis for a court to raise a general presumption of community property as to the artwork.

*Illustration 3.3:* During marriage, Driver, uses $25,000 of provable separate property bank deposits from Account A and $25,000 of community property bank deposits from Account B to purchase a $50,000 collectible (appreciating) sports car. Title to the car is in Driver's name alone. At dissolution, the acquisition-based general presumption can be appropriately raised because the car was acquired during marriage while domiciled in the state in Driver's name alone, as the vehicle title record will prove. If Driver seeks to confirm a separate property interest in the sports car, Driver can rebut the general community property presumption by tracing $25,000 of the $50,000 purchase to Driver's separate property contribution.

*Fidelity & Casualty Co. v. Mahoney*, 161 P.2d 944 (Cal. Ct. App. 1945) helps distinguish between the concept of acquisition and possession. The case also gives insight into the discretion available to the fact finder in deciding whether to raise the general community property presumption in the first place.

In *Fidelity*, a newlywed spouse used out of pocket cash (which the court deemed to be $1) to buy an airplane accident insurance policy just before boarding a plane. The insured spouse named his son from a prior marriage as the sole pay-on-death (POD) beneficiary. The plane crashed. The insured was killed. The insurer delivered the insurance premium of $5,000 to the court. The insured's son argued that the $5,000 insurance proceeds were separate property and thus belonged entirely to him by contractual designation (the insurance POD). The insured's surviving spouse contended that the proceeds were community property, and therefore that she was entitled to a one-half share ($2,500) of the insurance proceeds. The surviving spouse also argued that because the decedent spouse was in possession of the $1 used to buy the accident policy, he must have acquired the $1 during the (brief) marriage. The judge ruled in favor of the decedent's son, the separate property claimant.

On appeal the question was whether the trial court had erred in declining to raise the general community property presumption as to the $1 on the basis of possession alone. The court of appeal affirmed the trial court's decision. It explained that California law does not presume when property was acquired; it only presumes that property is community property if it is shown to have been acquired during the marriage while domiciled in the state. Therefore, given the short term nature of the marriage, the burden of establishing that the $1 was acquired during marriage fell to the surviving spouse. The court went so far as to suggest that had the wife introduced evidence about the decedent's financial information (like "whether [the decedent's] bank account was large or small or whether the bank account had been in existence a long or short time . . . [or] whether his monthly salary was large or small") there would have been a legal basis upon which to raise the general community property presumption. But without such evidence, the general community property presumption could not properly be raised, meaning that the court was required to distribute the accident insurance proceeds entirely to the decedent's son in accordance with contract POD.

Had *Fidelity* been decided in Texas, the acquisition-based general community presumption might have been raised by evidence that the decedent spouse possessed the $1 during his short marriage. It would then be up to the separate property claimant, the son, to rebut that presumption by clear and convincing evidence. V.T.C.A.Fam.Code § 3.003.

The difference between the two outcomes is procedural as well as practical. In a state with an acquisition-based community property presumption, such as California, the community property claimant bears the burden of proving acquisition during marriage. Only after that initial hurdle is cleared can the judge raise the general community property presumption within the bounds of the law. Whereas in a state with both an acquisition-based and a possession-based community property presumption, such as Texas, the community property claimant has an option to move for one or the other community property presumption.

## 4.   SPECIAL COMMUNITY
## PROPERTY PRESUMPTIONS

Special community property presumptions supersede the general community property presumption.

In a few states, special presumptions provide, within the context of the enabling statute itself, the exact parameters for rebuttal. But in most states this is not the case.

The legal (as opposed to the policy or social) rationale for enabling a special presumption is key to how it functions. For example, some state statutes are based on a contract-based community property presumption for joint form titles, whereas other state statutes steer clear of contract theory when assessing the character of joint titles. And some states employ a presumption as to sums on deposit in an account to prevent the impairment of community property by the simple movement of funds, whereas others do not.

### a. The Joint Form Title Community Property Presumption

In the context of marriage, title in "joint form" means that the asset in question is titled in both spouses' names. An examination of the title record would show both spouses' names: "*Spouse One and Spouse Two*" or "*Bip and Bop*".

There are two clear trends with respect to applying a community property presumption to joint form titles.

One trend is to enact a contract-based statute that allows the fact finder to raise an evidentiary presumption that a jointly titled asset, if acquired during marriage, is community property in the context of a dissolution proceeding. California follows this approach by a legal rationale that rests in contract law. A joint title represents a first agreement between the title holders to characterize the titled asset as community property in the event of dissolution. Rebuttal is upon proof of a subsequent (second) contract amending the first. The amending second agreement must specifically modify or nullify the first agreement by providing that the property is to be all or part separate property in the event of dissolution.

Other states, New Mexico is the example, have enacted a special joint form title community property presumption without tying rebuttal to contract theories.

Still other states divide joint titles as if they were community property. Washington and Arizona follow this approach. Here, no special presumption is involved. Moreover, since a contract rationale is not employed, rebuttal evidence of an intention to hold a separate property interest can come from any number of possible sources.

Precedent decides whether a special presumption can apply retroactively or not. In California, retroactive application of the special joint form title community property presumption is constitutional. The rationale is that the use of an evidentiary presumption merely starts the analysis, it does not disrupt either party's vested property rights. Whether rebuttal requires a written second agreement does, however, raise constitutional issues. This topic is discussed in Chapters 5 and 12. ·

*Illustration 3.4:* The spouses purchase a house during marriage. At that time they take title in both of their names as joint tenants. The spouses reach no other agreement as to the character of the house. Subsequently, the spouses file for dissolution. Assume the jurisdiction has a contract-based statutory joint form title community property presumption. For purposes of the dissolution proceeding, upon proof of acquisition during marriage, the house is presumed to be community property. Rebuttal requires that the separate property proponent produce a second written contract, the terms of which demonstrate that, notwithstanding the use of a joint title, the house was to be all or part separate property in the event of dissolution.

*Illustration 3.5:* Same facts as Illustration 3.4 above except that the jurisdiction does not have a statutory joint form title presumption. Rather it treats property in joint title as community property for purposes of division in a dissolution proceeding. Here, the property is treated as community property absent any evidence, contract-based or not, that the parties intended otherwise. See Section C, Nevada and Washington.

## b. A Special Presumption for Sums on Deposit in Any Demand Deposit Account of a Married Person

Three of the nine U.S. community property states—Arizona, California, and New Mexico—have adopted the Uniform Multiple-Person Accounts Act (UMPAA for short) as part of their probate code. Of the two states that allow married persons to choose community property by contract or trust, only Alaska has adopted the UMPAA.

The National Conference of Commissioners on Uniform State Laws approved the UMPAA in 1989 so as to address three issues that come up in relation to demand deposit accounts:

- Ownership rights between owners;

- The existence, validity, and revocability or survivors' benefits; and

- Financial institution protection.

UMPAA covers bank, savings and loan association, and credit union accounts.

Every covered account is made up of two distinct assets: (i) the account contract and (ii) the sums on deposit in the account.

The bank contract determines who has legal access to and liability for the account. Access to the sums on deposit in an account is a distinct issue from ownership of sums on deposit on any given date.

A sole account is an account for which the bank contract is in one party's name alone. A joint account is an account for which the bank account is in two or more parties' names.

A sole account gives only the named party access to the account.

A joint account gives two or more parties access to the account.

In the context of marriage, a sole account gives one spouse access to the account, whereas a joint account gives both spouses access to the account.

Generally, absent proof otherwise, sums on deposit are owned by the party or parties who have access to the account. Of the community property states that have adopted UMPAA, the trend is to modify this UMPAA general rule with a special community property presumption that applies to depositors who are married to each other. This special presumption is discussed in more detail below.

Despite its application to multiple-party accounts, UMPAA is not limited to joint bank accounts. The definition of account makes clear that a covered account is one that is either in sole or joint form.

The traditional phrase "joint account" is an imprecise label. Too imprecise to identify how two or more persons might come to desire legal access to a single demand deposit account. In the context of marriage, more specifically, depositors who are married to each other may want access to a particular account for any number of reasons. A married couple may want to add both of their names to an account because they genuinely regard themselves as co-owners of the sums on deposit in that account. Or, they may hold the view the sums on deposit in the joint account are owned relative to whichever spouse makes an actual deposit. Or, they might believe that only one of them is the true owner of the sums on deposit in the account, but that the other should be able to access the account as an agent with authority to withdraw funds in case of the owning spouse's illness or death.

In light of the many reasons for opening a joint account, it is not difficult to understand why a joint account set up for one purpose, in the words of UMPAA, **"may yield unwanted consequences for other purposes."** Uniform Multiple-Person Accounts Act, 8B U.L.A. 3, 5 (2014). Therefore, to better protect account depositors and financial institutions the UMPAA proposes these rules for all joint accounts, no matter whether the depositors are married to each other or not.

- The ownership of sums on deposit in a joint account is determined by the named depositors' net contributions to the account.

- Joint account balances transfer on the death of a depositor to account survivors, unless the contract expressly negates survivorship rights.

- Financial institutions may pay out the withdrawal demands of one joint account depositor without exposing itself to liability from the other joint account depositors.

- Financial institutions are not responsible for keeping records of the joint depositors' net contributions.

These rules distinguish between the rights of (i) joint depositors, (ii) creditors, and (iii) the financial institution that maintains the deposit account. Moreover these rules, as promulgated, apply to unmarried and married depositors.

In a community property state, because the deposit of joint depositors who are married to each other could be community or separate in character, a superseding community property presumption for sums on deposit in a demand deposit account resolves what could be vexing ownership issues.

Without the special presumption the multiple outcomes in a community property state are as follows. There is typically a line of cases holding that sums on deposit in the account of a married person are presumed to be community property. All U.S. community property systems acknowledge as much, especially when it comes to joint accounts, meaning accounts to which both spouses have contractual rights to withdraw sums on deposit. There can be a contrary line of precedent that the title to the account (sole or joint) determines the character (community or separate) of the sums on deposit in that account. And there can be a line of precedent holding that only the tracing rule (not account title) ultimately determines the character of sums on deposit in the account of a married person.

To address these potentially time-consuming litigations, the clear trend among community property states is to enact, within their UMPAA law, a superseding community property presumption for sums on deposit in any demand deposit account of a married person. Typically, this presumption is found in the same code in which UMPAA is enacted. In most states, UMPAA is enacted as part of the state probate code. The four states that have enacted UMPAA in the community property context (Alaska, Arizona, California, and New Mexico) also have enacted a special community property presumption for sums on deposit in any demand deposit account of a married person.

The California presumption is possession-based. Cal.Prob.Code § 5305(a) nonconclusively presumes that sums on deposit in any account of a married person are community property unless proven otherwise. The separate property claimant bears the burden of rebuttal. Rebuttal is by (i) tracing specifically identified net deposits back to separate property or (ii) by producing an enforceable written agreement between the spouses that certain deposits in a disputed account are not to be community property. Commingled accounts require the use of specialized records, the details of which are set out in the California Multiple-Parties Account Law (CAMPAL for short). A successful rebuttal determines only the character of net sums on deposit, not the character of any purchases that were made with sums withdrawn from the disputed account. Purchases from the account are analyzed separately. Here, "net" means any sums remaining after family expenses have been paid from the account. All of these issues are discussed in more detail in Chapter 6.

The special presumption for sums on deposit in an account also can be adopted as part of a state's domestic violence prevention efforts, as in California. If so, the rationale for the possession-based presumption is to neutralize bad faith and negligent attempts by one spouse to impair the other spouse's community property rights in sums on deposit by the act of moving money from one account to another.

One final note, not many courts, practitioners, or commentators appear to be familiar with the UMPAA or, as in California, with the state modifications to UMPAA.

*Illustration 3.6:* During marriage to each other, W and H maintain three bank accounts. Account 1 is in W's name alone. Account 2 is in H's name alone. Account 3 is a joint tenancy account in both W's and H's names.

Who can access Accounts 1, 2, and 3?

On the issue of account access:

- Account 1 is W's sole account. Only W can access (withdraw) funds.

- Account 2 is H's sole account. Only H can access (withdraw) funds.

- Account 3 is W's and H's joint account. Either spouse can access (withdraw) funds.

Who owns the sums on deposit in Accounts 1, 2, and 3?

The answer to this distinct question depends on state law. Assume that the state in question has enacted a superseding community property presumption identical to the one found at Cal.Prob.Code 5305(a).

- All sums on deposit in Account 1, W's sole account, are presumed community property absent proof to the contrary.

- All sums on deposit in Account 2, H's sole account, are presumed community property absent proof to the contrary.

- All sums on deposit in Account 3, W's and H's joint account, are presumed community property absent proof to the contrary.

Benefits of a superseding community property presumption for sums on deposit in any account of a married person are many. Two follow. One, the special presumption strikes a balance between simplifying account issues and recognizing community and separate property ownership interests (once established). Two, the special presumption prevents community property from being impaired by the movement of sums from a joint account to a sole account or vice versa.

A special community property presumption for sums on deposit in an account only addresses ownership of the sums on deposit. It does not address access or succession issues. Access and succession continue to be manipulable by one spouse acting alone. Manipulations, whether bad faith or not, create many possible impairments, including but certainly not limited to:

- One spouse's right of access to sums on deposit, as when money is moved from a joint account to one spouse's sole account;

- Cancellation of a right of survivorship as to sums moved from a joint tenancy account to a sole account (or a tenancy in common account, or a community property account);

- Waiver of the right to devise as to sums moved from a sole account (or a tenancy in common account, or a community property account) to a joint tenancy account.

In short, community property states can facilitate important public policies by enacting a special possession-based community property presumption for sums on deposit in any account of a married person. At the very least, the special presumption can make dissolution more efficient by simplifying litigable issues that can arise over bank accounts. More compellingly, the special presumption can further domestic violence prevention efforts.

## 5. MISCELLANEOUS STATUTORY PROVISIONS THAT CAN AFFECT CHARACTERIZATION

### a. The (Now Obsolete) Married Woman's Separate Property Presumption

In the context of U.S. community property systems, a married woman's separate property presumption was used in a minority of states up until the mid-1970s, an era known as the male management era.

This presumption, typically the only separate property presumption in any given jurisdiction, was rationalized as protection for married women who otherwise were statutorily divested of legal rights to manage and control community property.

The presumption confirmed as the wife's separate property any titled asset that the married woman's husband had transferred to her during their marriage in her name alone. The rationale was gift based: since the husband had the legal right to manage and control the community property estate, it was deemed more likely than not that when the husband transferred property out of that estate to the wife in her name alone he did so with donative intent. Rebuttal required proof of the absence of husband's donative intent as to the transferred asset(s).

All U.S. community property states have transitioned from male management to equal or dual management systems. For that reason the gender specific married woman's separate property presumption is now obsolete.

California and New Mexico codified the married woman's separate property presumption. But after the transition to equal management and control, each state non-retroactively repealed it. In California, the presumption is repealed for all property acquired by a married woman in her name alone on or after January 1, 1975. In New Mexico, the cutoff date for application of the married woman's presumption is on or after January 1, 1973. Cal.Fam.Code § 803; N.M.Stat.Ann. § 40–3–12(B) (1978).

## b. Preserving the Community Property Character of Property in a Revocable Trust

The trust is a product of the British common law. Still, its use has been adapted to community property systems.

California, Idaho, and Wisconsin have specific statutes to preserve the community property character of property held in a revocable trust. The statutes are consistent with estate planning efforts to preserve a stepped-up basis for the survivor's one-half of community property, as provided by I.R.C. § 1014(b)(6).

## c. Asset Appreciation versus Rents, Issues, and Profits

When an asset grows more valuable over time, it appreciates.

Appreciation remains bundled with the asset until the point of severance. As to character, the unsevered appreciation of community property is community property, the unsevered appreciation of separate property is separate property.

Once severed, appreciation becomes realized. The same presumption that governs the underlying asset governs the severed appreciation. Here again the principle is that community property produces community property, whereas separate property produces separate property.

Appreciation is not the same as an asset income stream.

When an asset produces an income stream it produces, in the parlance of the community property system, rents, issues, and profits. (The traditional ganancial system referred to income streams as "fruits and profits" as discussed above).

Among U.S. community property states there is a split in outcome as to separate property rents, issues, and profits.

A minority of U.S. community property states (Idaho, Louisiana, Texas and Wisconsin) follow the civil law approach on separate property rents, issues, and profits. The civil law approach holds that separate property income streams are characterized as community property during the marriage, historically by usufruct. In minority-view states, the parties can reach a contrary agreement as to separate property rents, issues, and profits, but their agreement must expressly transmute the income stream of the underlying separate property asset.

A majority of states (Arizona, California, the innovator of the rule, New Mexico, Nevada, and Washington) follow the American-rule approach on separate property rents, issues, and profits. The American approach holds that separate property income streams, because they trace back to a separate property source, are also separate property.

## 6.    STATUTES PROTECTING THIRD PARTIES

Spouses have rights and duties relative to each other. They also have rights and liabilities relative to third parties. For that reason, states enact notice laws that are intended to give third parties confidence in transacting with married persons. Creditors' rights are discussed in Chapter 8.

Some third-party protection statutes, like the UMPAA discussed above, are designed to protect banks and other financial institutions as well as spouses. Others are designed to permit creditors to transact with one or the other spouse knowing that the acts of one spouse will bind the community.

Despite the existence of statutes to protect third parties, transactions between a spouse and a third party do not determine the character of property. Nor do transactions between a spouse and a third party necessarily limit the other spouse's right to manage and control the property. State community property laws govern questions about the spouses' rights and duties between themselves, notwithstanding any statutory provisions that are otherwise intended to protect third parties.

Some third-party protection statutes retain former (rescinded or amended) statutory rights or methods of characterizing assets. The constitutional necessity for retaining such statutes is seldom litigated. Perhaps this is due to the practical need of preserving the stability of public title records.

More generally, most states require joinder (meaning both spouses' signatures on consequential documents) in the real estate context.

California balances the need to protect a nonjoining spouse's rights to community real property with the need to encourage third parties to transact with married persons. The California statute does this by putting third parties on notice that both spouses must join in executing any consequential real estate instrument delivered by a married person. Consequential instruments are defined as those relating to the sale, conveyance, encumbrance, or long term lease (one year or longer) of the property. See Chapter 7.

When both spouses sign a consequential instrument, a purchaser or encumbrancer of community property real estate who takes "in good faith, without knowledge of the marriage relation" takes free of the claims of a spouse who later moves to avoid (rescind) the transaction. If only one spouse signs a consequential real estate document, the burden of proof falls to the third party to show that inquiries were made into the marital status of the person whose name appears on the document. In other words, in California, third parties are protected by how the law incentivizes them to obtain both spouses' signatures on any consequential real estate transaction. Cal.Fam.Code § 1102.

Other states have different or additional third party protections when it comes to real estate.

Texas protects a bona fide purchaser who acquires property from a married person without knowledge of the marriage. V.C.T.A. Fam. Code § 5.24(b). The protection comes into play only if the property is presumed to be subject to the sole management, control and disposition of the transacting spouse. This rule comports with the more general Texas rules on community property dual management and control.

Washington provides that a bona fide purchaser takes real property clear of the community property claim of a spouse whose name does not appear on record title or on a recorded community property claim. Thus the bona fide purchaser of Washington real estate titled in one spouse's name alone takes over the spouse whose name is not on the record title. But Washington law also gives the spouse whose name is not on the title a short period of time to file (and thus litigate) a claim of interest in the real property. A recorded claim of interest is a challenge to the bona fide purchaser's priority position. See Wash.Rev.Code § 26.16.095, discussed in Chapter 2.

## 7. MISCELLANEOUS STATUTORY PROVISIONS

Before marriage, compiling an inventory of the property that one owns is a practical way to identify (and later prove) a separate property interest in the listed assets.

Some states have adopted provisions that authorize a prospective spouse to record any such inventory. California, Idaho, Nevada and Texas permit a married person to create evidence of the separate character of property by filing and recording an inventory of the property at the time of the marriage.

Nevada provides a way for parties to record a supplemental inventory during the marriage. The Nevada statute delineates the technique for creating an asset-specific separate property inventory and for establishing its authenticity.

Louisiana permits a **"declaration in an act of acquisition that things are acquired with separate funds."** LSA–C.C. Art. § 2342. The Louisiana declaration is like an inventory in that it can be created unilaterally by one spouse. It is unlike an inventory in that declarations are made on an asset-by-asset basis, at the time an asset is acquired.

In the absence of statutory direction, the time to record a separate property inventory is at or reasonably near the date of marriage.

Inventories become relevant at the end of a marriage by dissolution or by death. Some states (California is one) encourage parties to inventory their assets at dissolution, by using a form provided by the state's Judicial Council. See Appendix A.

The inventory is most persuasive when it is current. But even a current (recently compiled) inventory will not immunize assets from ambiguity, commingling, fungibility, transmutation, change of form, the claims of third parties, or the like.

## 8.    ALASKA, TENNESSEE, AND PUERTO RICO

Alaska and Tennessee do not have default community property systems. However, each state is briefly mentioned here because each allows married persons to opt into community property.

### a. Alaska

Alaska is a common law equitable distribution state, not a community property state. *Pestrikoff v. Hoff*, 278 P.3d 281 (Alaska 2012). However, Alaska allows married persons to opt into community property ownership as to one, some, or all assets.

The Alaska Community Property Act, found at Alaska Stat.Ann. § 34.77.010 through § 34.77.995 (2014) covers various issues including the classification of property, management and control, transactions between spouses, obligations of spouses, bona fide purchaser protection, community property agreements, life insurance proceeds, and community property agreements and trusts.

For married persons who choose community property, the general rule, found at Alaska Stat.Ann. § 34.77.030 (2014) is as follows: **"Except for property that is classified otherwise in this chapter, property of spouses is community property under [Alaska law] only to the extent provided in a community property agreement or community property trust."**

As to a community property agreement: unless the terms of the community property agreement provide otherwise, management and control is title-based under Alaska Stat.Ann. § 34.77.040 (2014). The terms of the community property trust govern management and control issues of property in the trust.

Formalities for setting up a community property agreement are set out at Alaska Stat.Ann. § 34.77.090 (2014). A community property agreement governs property acquisition while both spouses are domiciled in the state. Alaska Stat.Ann. § 34.77.060 (2014).

As to a community property trust, these specifics apply. The terms of the community property trust govern assets transferred to the trust. Formalities for setting up a community property trust are found at Alaska Stat.Ann. § 34.77.100 (2014). A community property trust may be settled by one spouse or both spouses even if neither is domiciled in the state so long as **"[a]t least one trustee is a 'qualified person . . .' "** A qualified person is defined as an individual person who resides in Alaska, an Alaska trust company, or a bank that is organized under Alaska law. Either or both spouses can serve as a qualified trustee so long the fiduciary spouse (or, if both spouses are fiduciaries, at least one spouse) is: **"(1) an individual (A) who . . . resides in this state; (B) whose true and permanent home is in this state; (C) who does not have a present intention of moving from this state; and (D) who intends to return to this state when away."** Alaska Stat.Ann. § 34.77.100(a) (2014).

A community property agreement must be identified as such with a standard notice **"in capital letters"** prominently placed at the head of the agreement. Alaska Stat.Ann. § 34.77.90. A community property trust must be identified in the same way. Alaska Stat.Ann. § 34.77.030.100(b) (2014).

The purpose of the capitalized notice requirement is to protect third parties who transact with one or both spouses.

Alaska has adopted the UMPAA, as discussed above.

## b. Tennessee

Tennessee is a common law equitable distribution state. As of 2010, pursuant to Tenn. Code Ann. § 35.17.101–35.17.108 (2015), married persons can opt into a Tennessee community property trust.

There is no requirement that the parties be domiciled in the state. The only requirement is that a qualified trustee manage the trust. A qualified trustee is defined as either a Tennessee resident or a company authorized by state law to act as a fiduciary.

Management and control rights must be set forth in the terms of the trust.

Dissolution occurs when an asset is distributed from the trust.

## c. Puerto Rico

The Puerto Rico community property system derives from articles found in such sources as the Civil Code of Puerto Rico (1902), the Spanish Civil Code (1889), and the Civil Code of Louisiana (1870). Puerto Rico primarily differs from other U.S. community property states in how it uses liquidation rather than dissolution rules.

In Puerto Rico, a conjugal partnership is formed by the act of marriage. The purpose of a conjugal partnership is to acquire property and to meet the spouses' financial obligations during marriage.

At divorce, a conjugal partnership is liquidated as if it were a commercial partnership. P.R. Laws Ann.

Title 31, § 381 (1993). It is not dissolved as it is in the other U.S. states.

Puerto Rican decisional law underscores the liquidation approach by holding that the determination of property at the end of a marriage cannot be made by the individual spouses. Rather property must be liquidated to pay off the debts, charges, and obligations of the conjugal partnership. Surplus community property shall be divided between the parties if and only if there is property remaining after the liquidation process is over. Often cited foundational cases are *Vivaldi v. Mariani*, 10 D.P.R. 444 (1906) *Sucesion of Morales v. Kieckoefer*, 17 D.P.R. 304 (1911), and *Orta v. Arzuaga*, 23 D.P.R. 259, 268 (1915).

A federal case that discusses Puerto Rican conjugal partnership law is *Federal Deposit Ins. Corp v. Martinez Almodovar*, 671 F. Supp. 851 (D. Puerto Rico 1987).

## C.  INDIVIDUAL STATES

### 1.  ARIZONA

Ariz.Rev.Stat.Ann. § 25–211(A) states the basic community property principle found in the Uniform Marriage and Divorce Act Section 307 Alternative B. The relevant text provides:

**"All property acquired by either husband or wife during the marriage is the community property of the husband and wife except for property that is:**

**1. Acquired by gift, devise or descent.**

**2. Acquired after service of a petition for dissolution of marriage, legal separation or annulment if the petition results in a decree of dissolution of marriage, legal separation or annulment."**

The Arizona statute implies an acquisition-based general community property presumption.

Ariz.Rev.Stat.Ann. § 25–318 reads:

**"In a proceeding for dissolution . . . or for legal separation, or in a proceeding for disposition of property following dissolution of the marriage . . . [the court] shall also divide the community, joint tenancy and other property held in common equitably, though not necessarily in kind, without regard to marital misconduct."**

The language explicitly mandates a court to divide joint tenancy and tenancy in common titles as community property is divided, which is to say equitably without regard to fault. But the statute does not as explicitly identify whether it is intended to enable (or not) a special community property presumption, which would be raised only upon proof of acquisition during marriage. Nor does the statute restrict the evidence that can be presented as the basis for recognizing a separate property interest in a jointly titled asset.

Ariz.Rev.Stat.Ann. § 25–318(A) (2015–2016) turns on a concept of quasi-community property, without using that label.

> **"In a proceeding for dissolution . . . or for legal separation, or in a proceeding for disposition of property following dissolution of the marriage . . . [p]roperty acquired by either spouse outside this state shall be deemed to be community property if the property would have been community property if acquired in this state."**

But the statute has been interpreted in line with *Stephen v. Stephen*, 284 P. 158 (Ariz. 1930), which holds that the character of movable property (bank deposits, cash, businesses are movable personal property) acquired during marriage is determined by the law of the married person's domicile at the time of acquisition. A corollary of this rule is that such out-of-state property, if later exchanged for Arizona property, would determine the character of the Arizona property.

Ariz.Rev.Stat.Ann. § 25–217 (2007) is an important notice for married persons moving to Arizona. It is especially important for retirees.

> **"Marital rights in *property which is acquired in this state* during marriage by persons married without the state who move into the state shall be controlled by the laws of this state."** (Italics added.)

Together, the above statutes and decisional interpretations suggest that the Arizona law, in its sensitivity to conflict of laws problems, governs the categorization of a limited pool of property as limited by the ruling in *Stephens*, supra. One, property onerously acquired in the state during marriage while domiciled in the state is clearly Arizona community property, unless separate property was used to purchase it. Two, property in joint title is divided as if it were Arizona community property, as discussed above. But otherwise, point three prevails: only movable (personal) property acquired while the married person is domiciled in the state is squarely included within the definition of Arizona community property. Movable property acquired elsewhere is characterized by the law of the married person's domicile at the time of its acquisition. The implication of these rules for retirees requires careful analysis of conflict of laws issues.

Also, note that characterization and division are separate issues. Characterization of personal property acquired in another state, may nevertheless be divided equally or equitably depending on the law of the other jurisdiction. In that case, the outcome that would have prevailed in the parties' previous domicile might be identical to the outcome the parties' reach in Arizona notwithstanding any holding about the Arizona character of the property. See e.g. *Rau v. Rau*, 6 Ariz. App. 362, 432 P.2d 910 (1967), citing *Stephen*, supra.

Conflict of laws issues may also extend to management and control rights during marriage. For example, if a married person were to move to Arizona from a common law title state owning a movable asset titled in his or her name alone, that asset would be characterized according to the law of the domicile where it was acquired. If the same married person were to sell that out-of-state asset and use the sale proceeds, after moving to Arizona, to buy Arizona property titled in his or her name alone, the new purchase might likely be characterized as separate property by tracing. In Arizona each spouse has the exclusive right to manage, control and dispose of his or her separate property; therefore, during marriage, the new purchase would be subject to the sole management and control of the acquiring spouse. For more on management and control, see Chapter 7.

On the community property side of the conflict of laws spectrum, if a married person domiciled in California were to sell California community personal property titled in her or his name alone before moving to Arizona, and then, after reestablishing domicile in Arizona, use the sale proceeds to buy property in Arizona, that property—by application of the tracing rule—might arguably be controlled by California law, not Arizona law. See *Jones v. Weaver*, 123 F.2d 403 (9th Cir. 1941).

Conflict of laws issues in a dissolution proceeding can be complex. They are raised here only because of Arizona's reputation as a retirement destination. See Chapter 12 for more on conflict of laws.

If a marriage ends by the death of a spouse, the Revised Arizona Probate Code uses a different statute, Ariz.Rev.Stat.Ann. § 25–211 (2015–2016), to define community property.

Retirees who move to Arizona face additional issues than those discussed above. At the end of marriage, whether a non-owning spouse is protected or not depends upon how the marriage ends. In a dissolution, Arizona, being a community property state, does not have an equitable division statute. Even if *Stephens*, supra, serves as a doctrinal rebuttal mechanism for the quasi-community property concept, in a dissolution, a non-owning retiree can rely on the quasi-community property concept to argue for equitable division without regard to fault.

At death, Arizona law is potentially far less protective for a retiree who did not earn an income during marriage. Similar to what happens at dissolution, because Arizona is a community property state it does not have a forced share statute. In the case of the owning spouse's death, the non-owning surviving spouse's financial future will depend largely on the decedent spouse's estate plan. Rights of survivorship will transfer property to the survivor outside of probate, of course. But otherwise, for retirees whose work life was in another state, there may be little or no Arizona community personal property from which the non-owning surviving spouse can draw on for support.

## 2. CALIFORNIA

Cal.Fam.Code § 760 states the basic community property principle: **"Except as otherwise provided by statute, all property, real or personal, wherever situated, acquired by a married**

**person during the marriage while domiciled in this state is community property."**

The equality of interest principle is stated at Cal.Fam.Code § 751: community property rights **"[d]uring continuance of the marriage relation are present, existing, and equal . . . ."** Each spouse acquires a one-half interest in a community property asset upon its acquisition. At dissolution, the spouses can agree to trade or offset their rights as they see fit. If they cannot reach an agreement, a factfinder shall dissolve their estate on an asset-by-asset basis in accordance with the equal division rule set out in statutes governing dissolution.

California recognizes quasi-community property. For purposes of a dissolution proceeding, quasi-community property is defined by Cal.Fam.Code § 125(a) as property acquired: **"By either spouse while domiciled elsewhere which would have been community property if the spouse who acquired the property had been domiciled in [California] at the time of its acquisition."**

Quasi-community property does not come into existence when one or both spouses establish a domicile in California. To the contrary, any property that one or both spouses own when they move into the state continues to be characterized by the laws of the acquiring spouse's former domicile. It is only when a petition for dissolution is filed in a California superior court that one or both parties are deemed to grant a California Superior Court authority to characterize pre-domicile acquisitions either as quasi-community or as separate property.

In a probate proceeding Cal.Prob.Code § 66 uses a nearly identical definition of quasi-community property.

Property acquired by a person during a void marriage is not within the California community property system; rather, it is individual property, acquired by a single person. A voidable marriage does acquire community property or quasi-marital property unless annulled (see statute below). However, a person who in good faith believes that their otherwise void or voidable marriage was valid can obtain a judicial declaration of putative spouse status. Once declared a putative spouse, that person has an option to use the state's quasi-*marital* property system or its general laws. In California, the quasi-marital property system permits a putative spouse to access rules, rights, and obligations as set forth in family code.

Quasi-marital property is **"property acquired during the union which would have been community property or quasi-community property if the union had not been void or voidable."** Cal.Fam.Code § 2251(a)(2).

Case law interprets the community property statute, Cal.Fam.Code § 760, as including within its terms a general presumption that property acquired during a marriage while domiciled in the state is more likely than not community in character. The general community property presumption is raised on discretion of the court. Once raised, the covered asset is community property unless the separate property claimant can prove otherwise. Rebuttal of the general community property presumption is by tracing or by agreement. A low standard of proof—preponderance of the evidence—is adopted so as to equalize the risk of judicial error in applying the equal division principle. *Marriage of Ettefagh,* 150 Cal.App.4th 1578, 59 Cal.Rptr.3d 419 (Cal.Ct.App. 1st Dist. 2007).

California has enabled a statutory community property presumption for any property acquired during marriage in any joint form title. Cal. Fam.Code § 2581. Rebuttal is by a clear statement in the title document or by an enforceable written agreement that one or both spouses are to retain a separate property interest in the asset. The special joint form title community property presumption is discussed further in Chapter 5.

In 1990, effective 1991, California adopted into the Probate Code a statutory community property presumption that applies to sums on deposit in any account of a married person. CAMPAL Cal.Prob.Code § 5305(a) rebuttal is by tracing or by agreement that one or both spouses is to retain a separate property interest in specific sums on deposit in a specific account. The policy behind this special community property presumption is to prevent the impairment of either spouse's community property interest in the sums on deposit in an account by the movement of money, meaning by the transfer of funds from one account to another. CAMPAL is discussed further in Chapter 6.

The general community property presumption is applicable after the death of former spouse for a limited period of time. However, Cal.Fam.Code § 802 exempts from the general community property presumption **"any property to which legal or equitable title is held by a person at the time of the person's death if the marriage during which the property was acquired was terminated by dissolution of marriage more than four years before the death."**

Cal.Fam.Code § 780 creates a special category of community property for money and property received in settlement of a personal injury claim that arose during marriage. Otherwise, the personal injury claim itself is not proprietary (on the theory that a personal injury claim is not transferable on a market) and therefore not subject to characterization even if the claim arose during marriage. Special community property, unlike ordinary community property, is subject to a mandatory assignment rule, found at Cal.Fam.Code § 2603, that favors the injured person. The statute has two nullifying exceptions. One is where **"commingling with other assets of the community estate"** has occurred. The other is where **"the interests of justice require another disposition."** For the second exception, no more than one-half of the settlement shall be awarded to the non-injured spouse.

Money and property received as satisfaction for personal injury claims that arose before marriage or after separation are received by the injured spouse as separate property. Money and property received as a settlement for personal injury claims against the other spouse are also received by the injured spouse as separate property, no matter when received. Money and settlements received for personal injury claims are discussed further in Chapter 4.

Statutory rights and obligations regarding the management and control of community property come into existence on the date of marriage and continue through dissolution. Cal. Fam. Code § 721, § 1100 (e), and § 1102, all of which are discussed further in Chapter 7. The characterization of property determines legal management and control rights.

The Judicial Council provides standardized forms to the public that may be used to inventory assets upon dissolution. The standardized forms list each asset, date acquired, gross fair market value, amount of debt, net fair market value and the petitioner's and respondent's proposal for division of the asset. Separate property claims and potentially commingled property are also noted as such.

### 3.   IDAHO

Idaho Code § 32–906 is the basic statute. It provides, in part that **"[a]ll other property acquired after marriage by either husband or wife is community property."** This statute implies, rather than directly states, that property acquired after (meaning during) marriage by both of the spouses, as for example with a jointly titled asset, is also community property, a standard discussed further below.

By the same provision Idaho adopts the civil law rule on separate property rents, issues, and profits. **"The income, including the rents, issues and**

**profits, of all other property, separate or community,"** is community property, unless it has been specifically transmuted by an agreement between the parties. The phrase **"all other property"** refers to Idaho Code § 32–903 and § 32–904, both of which define separate property.

Property acquired during marriage in both spouses' names (joint form title) is community property unless the spouses agree otherwise. See Chapter 5.

Idaho Code § 32–907 and § 32–908 allow for the filing of a separate property inventory. The statutory provisions are gender specific, but by the holding in *Suter v. Suter*, 546 P.2d 1169 (Idaho 1976), the statute now applies on a gender neutral basis. Cases decided prior to *Williams v. Paxton*, 559 P.2d 1123 (Idaho 1976) may be outdated under current principles of equal protection law.

Idaho law, like California law, preserves the community property character of property held in a revocable trust, per Idaho Code § 32–906A.

### 4.   LOUISIANA

Community property is **"property acquired during the existence of the legal regime through the effort, skill, or industry of either spouse; property acquired with community things or with community and separate things, unless classified as separate property . . .; property donated to the spouses jointly; natural and civil fruits of community property; damages awarded for loss or injury to a thing**

**belonging to the community; and all other property not classified by law as separate property."** LSA–C.C. Art. 2338.

Louisiana strongly discourages the creation of joint tenancy titles, as discussed in Chapter 5. Property acquired during marriage in joint form title is community property.

According to the Civil Code of 1870, the word property is a translation of the civil code concept of patrimony, which breaks property down into *propriete* and *biens*. *Dué v. Dué*, 342 So.2d 161, 165 (La. 1977)(characterizing attorney contingency fee contracts as community property). Other community property states do not rely on the concept of patrimony. The concept has a long history in Louisiana law, but it is unclear how closely courts in the state rely on the patrimony concept today.

One consequence of relying on the civil law concept of patrimony is that in Louisiana, both assets *and* obligations are characterized as community or separate LSA–C.C. Art. 2361 thus obligations **"incurred by a spouse during the existence of a community property regime are presumed to be community obligations."** Obligations that do not benefit the spouses, the family, or the other spouse are not. LSA–C.C. Art. 2363. In the other U.S. community property states, by comparison, the clear trend is that only the individual spouses—not the marriage as an entity—assume obligations. See Chapter 8.

Louisiana adopts a possession-based general community property presumption limited in application to "things." Set out in LSA–C.C. Art. 2340 and Art. 2342, the presumption states: **"[t]hings in the possession of a spouse during the existence of a regime of community of acquets and gains are presumed to be community, but either spouse may prove that they are separate property."** The word "things" has historically been defined to mean all property (as complicated by the concept of patrimony discussed above) acquired during the marriage. "Possession" in the Louisiana community property system has a narrower definition than one might find in general property law: possession, in the context of a marriage, indicates that the spouse holds the property as an owner, not as a caretaker or bailee.

LSA–C.C. Art. 2342, discussed in the previous paragraph, is a gender-neutral update of the declaration rule. Today, either spouse has a right to declare **"[i]n an act of acquisition"** that the asset is **"[a]cquired with separate funds as . . . separate property. . . ."** The non-acquiring spouse may concur in the declaration, making it a double-declaration. The **"either spouse may prove"** language is a response to equal protection concerns, as explained by LSA–C.C. Art. 2340 Comment (b). Thus, either one or the other spouse may controvert a declaration with what seems under *Talbot v. Talbot,* 864 So.2d 590, 600 (La. 2003) to be a rebuttal standard that can consider any manner of proof:

> "As a matter of policy and in the interest of fairness, we find that the community presumption contained in article 2340 is

rebuttable by either spouse upon a showing by a preponderance of the evidence the separate nature of property brought into the community."

A spouse's intestate heirs and the creditors also have a right to controvert a declaration, regardless of whether or not the surviving spouse concurred at acquisition. Time limits apply. However, once an asset has been alienated, encumbered, or leased for consideration, a declaration of separate property stands so as to protect third parties who transact with a married person.

Louisiana is in the distinct minority of U.S. community property states on the issue of how best to characterize gifts made by a third party to the spouses jointly. Donations are defined by LSA–C.C. Art. 1468 and Art. 1469 as transfers made **"merely from liberality."** Donations are discussed further in Chapter 4.

Otherwise, the basic Louisiana community property statute codifies the rule that donations (gifts) made to the spouses jointly are community property in character. (See the LSA–C.C. Art. 2338 phrase: **"property donated to the spouses jointly; . . ."**). In other community property states a gift made by a third party to one spouse alone before or during marriage is the donee-spouse's separate property; and in a clear majority of U.S. community property states a gift made jointly to both spouses during marriage falls under the definition of separate property, even if owned concurrently, unless the donor intended to make a gift to the community or there is a statute or court case indicating otherwise. In the states that have a special joint form title presumption (California) or, alternatively, a rule that jointly titled property is divided as if it were community property (Arizona), a gift made to the spouses in joint title during marriage would effectively replicate the Louisiana rule that jointly titled donations acquired during marriage are presumptively community property.

The benefit of the Louisiana rule on donations is that it cuts through legalistic circumventions about timing, title form, and third-party donative intent by recognizing that the donor who makes a gift to a married couple in joint title probably does so with the intention of benefiting the spouses as a community, not as individuals. There is an exception to this rule: Revision Comments from 1979 indicate, if the spouses **"do not live in community,"** i.e., if they have agreed to live in a contractual matrimonial regime in lieu of the legal one, then **"the donor may not create a community regime for the spouses. In such a case, the property given to them is separate property held in indivision."** Separate property is discussed in Chapter 4.

Louisiana follows the general civil law ganancial separate property income rule.

LSA–C.C. Art. 2339 provides in a general statute titled **"Fruits and revenues of separate property . . ."** that the receipts (rents, issues, profits, and other revenues) of separate property obtained during marriage are community property, unless the owner reserves them as separate property by a declaration that is executed and recorded. Recordation is intended to protect the adversely affected spouse by providing proof, as between the spouses, of the declaration as it was made on a set and certain date. The rights of third parties are of secondary concern. A more specific standard applies to minerals and oil and gas revenues. **"[M]inerals produced from or attributable to a separate asset, and bonuses, delay rentals, royalties, and shut-in payments arising from mineral leases are community property."**

The difference between a general declaration and one for mineral extractions is this. Generally, separate property fruits are community during the marriage by usufruct, but then returned to their separate property owner at the end of marriage. Extracted mineral products, on the other hand are exempt from the usufruct rule. LSA–C.C. Art. 2339 bases that exemption on revision comments 1976 of LSA–C.C. Art. 551 which excludes mineral production from the definition of fruits and revenues. The theory behind the exemption is that mineral substances extracted from the ground are not fruits because their extraction depletes the underlying property, whereas the harvesting of fruits does not.

The community owns (rather than just enjoys by usufruct) extracted mineral products. Thus any *income* derived from a mineral lease, community or separate, during marriage is outright community property. The dominant rationale evokes management and control rights. There also appears to be an implicit acquisition-based rationale at work in the case law. The justification given is that a mineral lease relates to rights in the underlying real estate, but the extraction of a mineral (oil or gas, for example) requires labor, which belongs to the community. Therefore, a person can own mineral lease rights prior to marriage, making the lease a separate property asset. But any development of the lease during marriage, if it is the consequence of community expenditure or labor, would bring the extracted mineral product within the labor principle of community property. The Louisiana rationale contrasts with the Texas rationale on extracted mineral products, as discussed below.

Fruits are produced periodically by a thing without a diminution of its substance. Fruits can be natural or civil. Natural fruits are the product of the earth or of animals. Civil fruits are revenues like rents, issues, and certain corporate distributions. Louisiana abandoned the term "profits" (previously found in the English-language version of its Civil Code) as an erroneous translation of the French word for "fruits." An extended explanation of the change is provided in LSA–C.C. Art. 551.

*Milling v. Collector of Revenue*, 57 So.2d 679 (La. 1952), a state tax case, suggests that "bonuses, delay rentals, royalties, and shut-in payments from separate property fall into the community though they are not [explicitly] classified as fruits under Article 551." Here again, the rationale would be that the above assets produce income without diminishing their source. In *Milton v. Milton*, 71 So.3d 326 (La.Ct.App. 2011), writ denied 69 So.3d 1150 (La. 2011) the separate property owner of cows petitioned for a reimbursement from the community for income produced during marriage in the form of milk. In denying the separate property owner's reimbursement request, the court characterized the milk as a fruit to which the community was entitled to, by right of usufruct, during the marriage.

Usufruct is a civil law concept. It is defined as **"[a] real right of limited duration on the property of another."** LSA–C.C. Art. 535. As a personal servitude, usufruct benefits a party in his or her enjoyment. The benefitted party is called the "usufructuary;" the burdened party is called the "naked owner." In the marriage context, usufruct creates a nonreimbursable right to a separate property income stream for the duration of the marriage. Cases sometimes make an analogy between usufruct and beneficial ownership, but any similarity in the context of marriage is superficial. Usufruct gives the community a terminable right to use, but not to sue for partition. Whereas beneficial ownership, once confirmed by a court judgment, is outright ownership that supports an action for partition.

Louisiana has the most extensive statutory pattern, outside of the uniform principal and income acts, for defining usufruct. LSA–C.C. Art. 535 and Art. 629 deal extensively with the relationship between the usufructuary and the naked owner as to different types of property. As usufructuary, the community has the right to possess and enjoy separate property fruits for the duration of the community regime. This right is free from the interference of the naked owner (the spouse who owns the separate property asset). Additionally, absent a contrary testamentary disposition, the law recognizes a right of usufruct in a surviving spouse over the half of the community inherited by the decedent spouse's descendants. See Chapter 10.

## 5. NEVADA

Nev.Rev.Stat. § 123.220 is the basic statute: **"All property, other than that stated in NRS 123.130, acquired after marriage by either husband or wife, or both, is community property unless otherwise provided by:**

**1. An agreement in writing between the spouses.**

**2. A decree of separate maintenance issued by a court of competent jurisdiction.**

**3. NRS 123.190** [NRS 123.190 governs appropriated separate property earnings, discussed below.

**4. A decree issued or agreement in writing entered pursuant to NRS 123.259."** [NRS 123.259 refers to the division of the community estate in cases where one spouse is institutionalized.]

Nev.Rev.Stat. § 123.190 above reveals the concept of appropriated earnings. The statute deems as a gift one spouse's written permission to allow the other spouse to **"appropriate"** his or her earnings. Appropriated earnings, **"[w]ith such issues and profits,"** become **"[s]eparate property."** This unusual statute crosses the line from the earner's exclusive management and control of uncommingled community property earnings (as in Texas) to the donee's outright ownership and exclusive control of the gifted earnings. See Chapter 4.

Nevada allows for a general community property presumption but not for a special joint form title presumption. The general community property presumption is supplemented by extensive legislation concerning the procedure for and effect of recording a written inventory of the separate property of a married person. The applicable statutes include Nev.Rev.Stat. §§ 123.130 through 123.170, and the following language of Nev.Rev.Stat. § 123.160:

> **"[t]he failure to file for record an inventory of [the] . . . separate property [of a married person resident in Nevada] . . . or the omission from the inventory, . . . of any part of such property, . . . is prima facie evidence, as between such married person and purchasers in good faith and for a valuable consideration from the other spouse, that the property of which no inventory has been so filed, or which has been omitted from the inventory, is not the separate property of such person . . . ."**

Nev.Rev.Stat. § 123.140 permits the recording of **"[a] further and supplemental inventory. . . "** during marriage.

## 6.    NEW MEXICO

N.M.Stat.Ann.    § 40–3–8(B)    (1978)    defines community property as **"[p]roperty acquired by either or both spouses during marriage which is**

**not separate property. . . .**" The spouses' respective interests in community property are present and vested. Quasi-community property is defined by the same statutory provision.

The general acquisition-based community property presumption is modeled on California's implied presumption, but the New Mexico presumption is codified. The general community property presumption arises from the fact of acquisition during marriage. N.M.Stat.Ann. § 40–3–12(A) (1978) provides: **"Property acquired during marriage by either husband or wife, or both, is presumed to be community property."** The spouse who asserts that the property is all or part separate in character bears the burden of rebuttal.

In 1984, New Mexico adopted a special joint form title community property presumption. N.M.Stat.Ann. § 40–3–8(B) (1978) reads in relevant part: **"[C]ommunity property means property acquired by either or both spouses during marriage which is not separate property. Property acquired by a husband and wife by an instrument in writing whether as tenants in common or as joint tenants or otherwise shall be presumed to be held as community property unless such property is separate property within the meaning of subsection A of this section."** This joint title form presumption is not limited to a dissolution proceeding, thus indicating that it can be raised in a probate proceeding.

Rebuttal of the joint form title community property presumption is by proof of one the elements listed in

N.M.Stat.Ann. § 40–3–8(A) (1978). Generally, if the jointly titled asset is proved to have been acquired before marriage, acquired by gift during marriage, or subject to a separate property agreement between the spouses, the special joint form title presumption is rebutted.

N.M.Stat.Ann. § 40–3–8(A)(5) (1978) provides that the special community property presumption is rebutted for **"property designated as separate property by a written agreement between the spouses, including a deed or other written agreement concerning property held by the spouses as joint tenants or tenants in common in which the property is designated as separate property."**

## 7.   TEXAS

The basic community property statute in Texas is V.T.C.A.Fam. Code § 3.002 and § 3.003 (a). The statute is acquisition-based. It provides that **"[c]ommunity property consists of the property, other than separate property, *acquired* by either spouse during marriage."** (Italics added.) Rebuttal is by preponderance of the evidence.

Texas also has a possession-based general community property presumption found at V.T.C.A.Fam. Code § 3.003 (West 2006). This statute provides: **"Property *possessed* by either spouse during or on dissolution of marriage is presumed to be community property."** (Italics added.) Rebuttal requires clear and convincing evidence.

Texas originated the homestead concept. Homestead property is a community property title. And because state formalities ensure that joint tenancy is intentionally, not accidentally, used, there is little need for a family code joint form title community property presumption.

Texas follows the civil law rule on separate property rents, issues, and profits. During marriage the community is entitled to any income derived from a separate property asset. Texas does not explain the rule by reference to usufruct, at least not in its statutes or recent case law.

Texas differs from the Louisiana when it comes to extracted mineral products. The Louisiana rationale appears in Section C, Louisiana above.

The Texas rule, by comparison, as stated in *Norris v. Vaughan*, 260 S.W.2d 676, 681 (Tex. 1953), adapts the labor principle, in a possibly diluted form, for gas leases that are acquired before but developed during marriage. For such a lease the labor principle is restricted to proof, offered by the community property proponent (who may be a spouse or an heir in a probate proceeding), that there was "an expenditure of community funds or effort as to impress community character on the gas produced." Absent such proof, the sale proceeds of a separate property mineral lease (i.e. any extracted mineral products) remain separate property. If the lease interest is acquired during, rather than before, marriage with separate property capital, then the profits, gas produced, and sale proceeds are community property outright subject to a reimbursement right for the lease owner.

Arguments have been made to extend *Norris*, supra, to intellectual property. *Alsenz v. Alsenz*, 101 S.W.3d 648 (Tex.App. 2003), a patent case, considered this argument as a matter of first impression. The court noted that the character of the patents was not at issue, only the income received from the patents during marriage was. Building on this premise, the court went on to issue a two-part holding: (i) "a spouse is entitled to an interest during marriage in the revenue stream from intellectual property that was created by the other spouse before marriage" (*Id.* at 654) and (ii) the income stream generated during the marriage from a patent obtained by a spouse prior to marriage is a "revenue" and a "fruit" of separate property; as such, the income stream is community property under Texas law. *Id.* at 654.

At first glance, one practical difference between the *Norris* and the *Alsenz* approaches seems negligible, but may in fact be material. The cases, read together, illustrate the salient difference between usufruct rights and outright ownership.

Under *Norris* the oil-and-gas profits, products and sale proceeds are characterized depending on the inception of the lease rights and on proof of a community expenditure. If inception of right to a mineral lease is before marriage, the products of the lease are owned as separate property absent a showing of a community expenditure or effort to develop the lease. But if inception of right to the oil-and-gas lease occurs during marriage, no matter the source of purchase funds, the products of the lease are owned entirely as community property, subject to a

capital reimbursement for the spouse who invests any
separate property purchase capital.

Under the rule in *Alsenz*, the income from a patent
that was issued before marriage is viewed as a
secondary income stream generated by the underlying
separate property asset (the patent). As such the
community has the right to enjoy, but not to own,
patent income during the marriage even absent proof
of a community expenditure or effort to develop the
patent. The community's usufruct right ends at
dissolution, at which time the patent income is
returned to the inventor spouse as her separate
property. This approach as applied to patents is novel
and subject to change.

Texas has one of the broadest statutory
authorizations designed to protect third persons.
V.T.C.A.Fam. Code § 3.104(b) provides, among other
things, that a third person dealing with a married
person is entitled to rely on the authority of that
married person to deal with the community property.
This rule is nullified by the third party's fraud. It is
also nullified by the third party's actual or
constructive knowledge of the transacting spouse's
lack of authority to deal. Despite third-party
entitlement, it may be factually difficult in any state
for a third party to meet the definition of a bona fide
purchaser who was unaware of a transferor's marital
relationship.

Recording of an inventory of the separate property
of a married person is permitted by V.T.C.A.Fam.
Code § 3.004, but not required to preserve and prove a
separate character claim (as it is in Nevada).

The 1980 amendment to TEX. CONST. ART. XVI, § 15, provides, in part: **"[i]f one spouse makes a gift of property to the other that gift is presumed to include all the income or property which might arise from that gift of property; . . .".** This clause creates a new presumption in Texas (which, being a civil rule state, would otherwise deem the income from separate property to be community property if received during marriage). The new presumption is that a gift from one spouse to the other of separate property is presumed to be a gift of the future income of that property as well. This provision was probably aimed at federal estate tax questions raised by *Estate of Castleberry v. C.I.R.*, 68 T.C. 682 (1977), which was subsequently reversed by *Wiley's Estate v. C.I.R.*, 610 F.2d 1282 (5th Cir. 1980). Texas law continues to develop on this point. See Chapter 4.

## 8. WASHINGTON

Washington's basic community property statute is Wash.Rev.Code § 26.16.030 (West 2016), a provision that both describes the attributes of community property and defines the term.

**"Property not acquired or owned, as prescribed in RCW 26.16.010** ["Separate property of husband"] **and 26.16.020** ["Separate property of wife"]**, acquired after marriage or after registration of a state registered domestic partnership by either domestic partner or either husband or wife or both, is community property."** Oddly, for such a large community property state, the Washington Legislature has not yet amended applicable codes to be gender neutral.

Washington characterizes joint tenancy titles as community property in character absent proof that both spouses declared contrary intentions. The state approach calls for enhanced joint tenancy creation formalities so as to steer married persons toward community property titles. See Chapter 5.

But even where the parties use a joint tenancy title with the idea of creating separate property interests, there may be litigation over characterization. During marriage, a joint tenancy title between married persons defaults to community property upon severance. At dissolution, the joint tenancy property is characterized as community property. See Chapter 5.

## 9.    WISCONSIN

Wisconsin adopted the Uniform Marital Property Act in 1983 (WUMPA) by Act 186, Sec. 47, which became effective on January 1, 1986.

Wis.Stat. § 766.001(2) (2009) states: **"It is the intent of the legislature that marital property is a form of community property."** The Wisconsin marital property system applies to spouses upon their determination date, which in most cases is the same as the date of marriage. Wis.Stat. § 766.31(6). See Chapter 4 for a definition of determination date.

Wis.Stat.  § 766.31(1)–(4) is the basic statute. Subsection (1) states the general provision: **"(1) General. All property of spouses . . ."** and not just the property acquired during the marriage **"[i]s**

**marital property except that which is classified otherwise by this chapter and that which is described in sub. (8)."**

Subsection (2) states a general marital property presumption. **"(2) <u>Presumption</u>. All property"** not just property acquired during the marriage, **"[i]s presumed to be marital property."**

However, Subsection (3) states the equality of interest principle: **"(3) <u>Spouse's interest in marital property</u>. Each spouse has a present undivided one-half interest in each item of marital property . . . ."** This clause appears to necessitate an item-by-item characterization at dissolution.

Subsection (3) carves out two clear exemptions, both of which apply when a marriage ends by death and both of which allow for an aggregated value division rather than an asset-by-asset division. The first exemption is a nonemployee spouse's terminable interest in a deferred employment benefit plan or individual retirement plan (if it is traceable to the rollover of an earlier retirement plan). See Chapter 6. The second exemption is a decedent-spouse's estate if, by enforceable marital agreement, the spouses opted for an aggregate value division of marital assets (i.e. the division of a hotchpot marital property estate) at the death of one of them rather than for the item-by-item division envisioned by the statute.

As for separate (individual) property streams of income, Subsection (4) adopts, with articulated exceptions, the rule that all income earned or received from *individual* property during marriage is community property. **"(4) Classification of Income. [i]ncome earned or accrued by a spouse or attributable to property of a spouse during marriage and after the determination date is marital property."** As discussed below, this subsection amplifies the civil law ganancial separate property income rule.

The classification of income rule is subject to two major qualifications, both listed in the basic statute. Subsection (8) states that property exchanged for or with the proceeds of individual property is individual property. Subsection (9) states: **"The interest of a spouse in property owned immediately before the determination date is treated as if it were individual property."** Individual property is defined at and discussed in Chapter 4.

Referring back to the types of community property systems discussed above, WUMPA and Subsections (1) and (2) in particular make Wisconsin as close to a universal marital property system as exists in the U.S today, while Subsections (8) and (9) steer it toward the ganancial fold that prevails in the U.S. community property states. Moreover, Wisconsin amplifies the civil law rule on separate property rents, issues, and profits by making the community the owner of those streams of income, rather than merely a user entitled to those streams of income during the continuance of the marriage.

Wisconsin has no need for a special joint form title presumption because marital title may be held in common law joint tenancy form.

# CHAPTER 4
# SEPARATE PROPERTY

## A.  OVERVIEW

Separate property is defined by state statute to include property acquired before marriage; gifts received by a spouse during marriage; and (in some states) the rents, issues, and profits of either.

Generally, gifts received by one spouse during marriage are defined as the donee spouse's separate property. States can differ with respect to how a gift to both spouses is characterized. Variations in law depend primarily on statutory presumptions (as in Louisiana) and on case law regarding the role of donor intent in gift characterization. The state community property system is overlaid onto the common law of gifts.

As discussed in Chapter 3, U.S. community property states split on how to characterize separate property revenues, often referred to as "rents, issues, and profits." A minority of states—Idaho, Louisiana, Texas and Wisconsin—characterize such income as community property during the continuance of the marriage. A majority of states—Arizona, California, Nevada, New Mexico, and Washington—characterize the same as separate property during the marriage.

States split on how to characterize money and property received by a spouse during marriage in settlement of a personal injury claim. Some states characterize all or some personal injury awards as separate property. Others characterize the same as community property or special community property. Special community property is assignable to the injured spouse in a dissolution unlike ordinary community property which is divided in half.

## B.  DETAIL

### 1.  "ACQUIRED": TIMING AND EFFORT

The word "acquired" has a precise meaning both in the statutory definition of community property and in the civil law. But the term differs in usage as discussed below.

Statutory definitions of community property put a focus on *when* property is acquired. All property acquired during marriage by a couple domiciled in a community property state is presumed community, as discussed in Chapter 3. All other property is separate property by definition. Statutory variations are discussed below, but generally property owned before marriage is separate property by virtue of its having been acquired before marriage (timing).

Classic civil law definitions of community property put a focus on *how* property is acquired (effort). Property acquired during marriage through personal labor or work earnings is "onerously" acquired. Property acquired without personal effort is "lucratively" obtained. The distinction between onerous and lucrative acquisitions is discussed in Chapter 3.

Onerous is a broad term that covers earnings and accumulations. Lucrative is also a broad term that covers gifts and windfalls.

For example, a "business gift" can become disputed at dissolution because of the ambiguity of the context in which it was received. Often a business gift is exchanged in lieu of earnings; at the same time it is (often) labeled a tip or gratuity, or it is somehow understood (even if only implicitly) as an exchange for services rendered. Cases treat this type of accumulation as onerously acquired on the theory that a true gift is something transferred for no consideration whatsoever whereas a business gift is property exchanged for something of value often in the form of labor or time thus making it onerously acquired. Some analogies are possible to federal income tax cases like *Commissioner v. Duberstein*, 363 U.S. 278 (1960), which treats the "business gift" as taxable income. Gambling proceeds could be understood as onerous or lucrative depending on the skill involved, but they are more typically characterized by tracing the winnings to their source.

In *Downer v. Bramet*, 152 Cal.App.3d 837, 199 Cal.Rptr. 830 (Cal.App.Ct. 4th Dist. 1984) an employer labeled a transfer of an interest in a ranch (real estate) to an employee-spouse a "gift". Contending that the ranch was separate property, the donee spouse chose not to disclose the "gift" to his spouse in their dissolution proceeding. Years after the dissolution, the ranch was sold. Upon learning of the sale, the former wife sued the employee spouse to establish a community property interest in the ranch sale proceeds. The claimant relied on the following facts: the ranch was given in lieu of pension benefits; the employee spouse had no social relationship with the employer; and the employer had made identical gifts to other employees in lieu of pension benefits. The trial court dismissed the ex-wife's claim. She appealed. The court of appeal reversed and remanded with the instruction to treat the ranch as community property upon proof of its onerous acquisition.

The importance of *Downer* is that the donor's label (this is a "gift"), without more, did not necessarily determine the character of the gifted property as between the spouses. Instead, the analysis turned to the timing (when) and effort (how) of acquisition.

Appreciation of an asset is characterized according to its source. This is the rule in all community property states, despite a split in authority on how to actually characterize separate property rents, issues, and profits. The states that follow the American rule characterize the rents, issues and profits of separate property as separate property. The states that follow the civil law ganancial rule characterize the same as community property during marriage.

*Illustration 4.1:* A spouse owns an unencumbered separate property rental unit. What is the character of the rents received? In a civil law state (Idaho, Louisiana, Texas, and Wisconsin), the rents are community property during the marriage. In an American rule jurisdiction (Arizona, California, Nevada, New Mexico, and Washington) the rents are characterized as separate property during the marriage.

States that follow the American rule for rents, issues, and profits might explain the break from the civil law ganancial rule differently, depending on their unique histories. Louisiana justifies its decision to by reference to the civil law concept of usufruct. Most other states reference their state constitutions, which, because they protect the right to own separate property during marriage, permit tracing.

In states that constitutionally protect a spouse's right to own separate property during marriage, changes in that property's form are also protected by case precedent, which might reject the outcome of the original ganancial rule altogether, as in *George v. Ransom*, 15 Cal. 322, 76 Am.Dec. 490 (Cal. 1860).

As an aside, the civil law permitted tracing, but only as to land-for-land exchanges and reinvestments of separate property land sale proceeds in land. See e.g. William O. Huie, "Some Principles of Texas Community Property," COMPARATIVE STUDIES IN COMMUNITY PROPERTY LAW 116–117, Jan. P Charmatz and Harriet S. Daggett eds. (1955), citing Law, William Q. de Funiak, PRINCIPLES OF COMMUNITY PROPERTY 2ND 142 (1943) and translations of Spanish commentaries like Gutierrez and Matienzo. The common law permitted tracing to all property.

## 2.   WHEN: BEFORE MARRIAGE

The greatest category of separate property— ignored by statutory schemes (except in Louisiana and Wisconsin) yet completely recognized by judicial decisions—is property received in exchange for separate property.

All U.S. community property jurisdictions, statutes (and, in some instances, state constitutional provisions) specifically dictate that property owned before marriage is separate property. By this rule, selling property owned before marriage and using the sale proceeds to purchase property during marriage makes the purchased property separate property, by operation of the tracing principle.

*Illustration 4.2:* A spouse owns an unencumbered rental unit as separate property. If the spouse sells the rental unit for $x and uses the proceeds to buy a boat for $x, what is the character of the boat? In all jurisdictions the boat is separate property by the tracing principle.

*Illustration 4.3:* A spouse owns an unencumbered rental unit as separate property. The unit is sold for $x. The owning spouse deposits the sale proceeds ($x) into a joint bank account shared with the other spouse. What is the character of the deposited $x? Here, a jurisdictional split arises depending on whether the jurisdiction has adopted UMPAA with a community property presumption for sums on deposit in any account of a married person (California falls into this category). In a state with such a presumption, the sale proceeds become presumptively community property upon their deposit into any bank account; this leaves it to the separate property owner to rebut the presumption. In the other states, the sale proceeds remain separate property. There is no presumption, but practically speaking, it is still up to the separate property owner to prove the character of the deposit.

*Illustration 4.4:* A spouse owns an unencumbered rental unit as separate property. She uses rents to buy a second rental unit. What is the character of the second rental unit? A jurisdictional split arises. In a majority of community property states (the American rule jurisdictions), the rents are separate property, and anything purchased with those rents also will be separate property by tracing. In a minority of community property states (the civil law jurisdictions), the rents are community property, making any purchases from them also community property in character.

Any or all of the above outcomes can be altered by a premarital agreement or by a valid transmutation.

Thus, in the above examples, if the owning spouse validly transmutes the rent producing real estate into community property, the character of the real estate will change notwithstanding its acquisition prior to marriage. In some states, transmutation of the underlying property (rental real estate in the example under consideration) implicitly transmutes that property's rents, issues and profits. But in other jurisdictions, rents, issues, and profits must be expressly identified and transmuted in order to effect a valid change in their character.

Additionally, the general rule is that the mere act of commingling separate property with community property does not change the character of the commingled property, absent confusion. If the spouse, in the rental unit example above, commingles rent deposits with community property earnings in an American rule jurisdiction, the separate property rents retain their character. If the same events occur in a civil law state where rents are community property by law, commingling does not occur when rents are deposited with community property earnings.

### 3.   WHEN: AFTER A DATE OF SEPARATION

Legal separation and divorce uniformly terminate the marriage.

In a majority of states a date of separation ends the community estate's ability not to hold property but to earn and accumulate it. (The Louisiana rule covers all property.) Separation must be delineated. States can require formal separation (as with a court order or a formal contract). Some recognize informal separation (as when a spouse leaves the family home or otherwise communicates an intent to end the marriage).

In states that require a legal separation or divorce to end a marriage, the spouses' earnings and accumulations continue to be characterized as community property during periods of (informal) physical separation. In states that permit physical (informal) separation as a method for ending the community, post-separation earnings and accumulations become separate property notwithstanding the absence of a formal petition for separation.

In California, physically separated spouses arc still subject to the community property system, but their earnings and accumulations during separation are characterized as the accumulating spouse's separate property. Cal.Fam.Code § 771. In Washington, where spouses can enter into a separation agreement and where courts have declined to apply the community property laws to a defunct marriage, accumulations not provided for in a separation contract seemingly continue to be characterized as community property even during periods of physical separation.

Timing may be critical to litigating the character of property earned or accumulated after a date of separation. California statutory law recognizes the act of living separate and apart as sufficient to effect a date of separation, a term defined in a new code section. Cal.Fam.Code § 90. The new definition incorporates case law precedents holding that an informal period of separation starts when at least one of the spouses intends to end the marriage *and* takes action (independently or mutually) to further that intent. In *Marriage of Manfer*, 144 Cal.App.4th 925, 50 Cal.Rptr.3d 785 (2006), for example, the spouses decided to end the marriage in 2004, but family and friends did not find out about the breakup until 2005. The court of appeal ruled that a subjective date of separation test applies. Subjective in this context means the intention of a spouse or the spouses (if they are in agreement about the separation) determines when the community ends, not the objective perceptions of third parties (family and friends).

### 4. HOW: BY GIFT

Property received by gift is ordinarily the separate property of the donee spouse. As discussed in Chapter 3, Louisiana modifies this rule by characterizing as community property **"property donated to the spouses jointly."** LSA–C.C. Art. 2338. So does Wisconsin, as also discussed in Chapter 3.

A gift is defined in the common law as a gratuitous transfer. But, courts have declined to follow the rigid definition of a gift as being totally without consideration and a sale as being for any consideration. A transaction can be partly a sale (in which case the purchase takes the character of the property for which it was exchanged) and partly a gift (in which case the gift becomes separate property). The purchase for $100 of a racing bicycle with a fair market value of $10,000 is an example of a transfer for which the boundary between sale (onerous exchange for consideration) and gift (lucrative exchange for no consideration) might be litigated.

Wedding gifts to the married couple are often received before marriage. This makes such gifts separate property by timing. It was once possible for a court to hold that wedding gifts were community property by virtue of an oral or implicit transmutation that occurred on the date of marriage. However, today, because most states require written express declarations for a transmutation to be valid, the oral or implied transmutation rationale is no longer determinative. Therefore, if parties want their wedding gifts to be community property they can effect that outcome with an agreement or a formal transmutation, as discussed in Chapter 2.

An alternative rationale for characterizing wedding gifts as community property is to focus on the third party donor's intent in making the gift. In Louisiana, a premarital (engagement) gift could be construed as property donated to the prospective spouses jointly upon condition of marriage; if so, the gift would (hypothetically) vest in the community upon marriage. LSA–C.C. Art. 2338. *Jones v. Ridgon*, 32 Ariz. 286, 257 P. 639 (1927) indicates that Arizona would go in the same direction as Louisiana; however, the recent case of *Valento v. Valento*, 225 Ariz. 477 240 P.3d 1239 (Ct.App. 2010) signals otherwise. Wisconsin, in the default WUMPA provision, characterizes third party gifts made during marriage to both spouses as marital (community) property unless the third party donor expresses a contrary intent. Wis.Stat. § 766.31(7)(a).

Texas characterizes gifts (including wedding gifts) as the separate property of the recipients by constitutional provision and by statute. V.T.C.A. Fam.Code § 3.001(a)(2).

California statutory law is silent on the wedding gift issue. Cal.Fam.Code § 770 provides that **"all property acquired by the person after marriage by gift, bequest, devise, or descent"** is separate property. This suggests that, regardless of the donor's intent, a wedding gift made before or after marriage falls within the definition of separate property. If the donor intends a gift to both spouses, he or she can wait until the marriage takes place and make the transfer to the spouses in joint form title. A gift received during marriage in joint form title, in California, would raise the special joint form title community property presumption, but only in the context of a dissolution proceeding. The separate property proponent would then bear the burden of rebuttal. The California presumption is found at Cal.Fam.Code § 2581. See Chapter 2 and Chapter 5.

## 5.   HOW: RENTS, ISSUES, AND PROFITS FROM SEPARATE PROPERTY

This section builds on Illustrations 4.1 through 4.4 above.

Income streams from separate property are uniformly identified in statutes as "rents, issues and profits" or "fruits and revenues" (in Louisiana). As discussed above, Idaho, Louisiana (by usufruct), Texas and Wisconsin, characterize the income of separate property obtained during marriage as community property during the continuance of the marriage.

An early California case started a contrary trend that gave rise to the American rule. In *George v. Ransom*, supra, the California Supreme Court interpreted a provision of the California Constitution that all property owned by the wife prior to marriage shall be her separate property to include the capital gains of that property. Cal.Fam.Code § 770(a)(3) codifies the holding by providing that "separate property of a married person includes . . . the rents, issues, and profits" of separate property. Today, the American rule is embedded in the community property systems of Arizona, California, Nevada, New

Mexico, and Washington. It is not likely to be changed in these states.

The Texas Supreme Court, construing an identical clause in the Texas Constitution in *Arnold v. Leonard*, 114 Tex. 535, 273 S.W. 799 (1925), reached an exactly opposite conclusion. The Texas Supreme Court held that the Texas legislature was constitutionally prohibited from characterizing the rents, issues and profits accrued during marriage by the wife's separate property. Thus, in Texas, property owned before marriage includes only the base property, not the capital accumulations of that property.

The American rule/ civil law rule split is only over the character of separate property rents, issues and profits obtained during marriage. There is no disagreement among the community property jurisdictions as to the character of the separate property rents, issues, and profits obtained prior to or after the termination of the community: that income is clearly separate property. Likewise, there is no disagreement among the jurisdictions as to the character of rents, issues, and profits obtained from community property during marriage: that income is clearly community.

Rents and interest payments for the use of property, or money and other items that are renewable, recurrent and non-consuming are definitely classified as rents, issues and profits. Stock or cash dividends are too.

The civil law definition of fruits, and how that term differs from the concept of rents, issues, and profits is discussed in Chapter 3.

Profits are capital gains produced by separate property. In Arizona, California, Nevada, New Mexico and Washington, separate property livestock, separate property businesses, separate property non-tax deferred investment accounts, and separate property crops can give rise to profits during marriage. Increase in the value of these base assets due to market rises or inflation is not defined as rents, issues, or profits. Thus, as discussed in Chapters 3 and 6, the law distinguishes between income streams and property appreciation.

Depreciating or depleting items produce receipts which are often, but not always, classified as rents, issues, or profits. Among these items are timber, coal, stone, and mineral extraction. Three of the major oil and gas producing states—California, Louisiana and Texas—are community property states. For more on extracted mineral products, see Chapter 3, Section 3, Louisiana and Texas.

Complete consumption of the item that produced receipts, such as a legal or equitable life estate or an annuity, poses problems in the states which follow the civil law rule on separate property rents, issues, and profits. If such receipts are deemed to be separate property rents, issues, or profits, a total conversion of separate property into community property could result. Conversely, if those receipts are not separate property rents, issues, or profits, there would be no allocation to the community of the income produced by holding wealth for a period of time and the civil law rule would be circumvented. While a proportionate allocation between separate and community is possible, civil law states treat the receipts of such assets as being similar to a liquidating dividend from a corporation, i.e., as a receipt of capital as opposed to a rent, issue, or profit.

Community property states generally decline to apply many common accounting and economic concepts of income. Thus, adjustments are seldom made for depletion, depreciation, or the diminished purchasing power of the dollar.

Dividing separate property rents, issues, and profits from property appreciation can raise problems in all jurisdictions. In Idaho, Louisiana, Texas and Wisconsin the dividing line is between income, which belongs to the community, and natural increases, which belong to the separate property owner. Except in Arizona, increases in size or bulk do not give rise to separate property; the underlying property simply retains its separate property character. Likewise, increases in market value due to market conditions, including inflation, should not change the character of the property. Accessions and accretions normally have the same character as the original property

## 6.   HOW: PERSONAL INJURY RECOVERIES

Personal injury recoveries raise unique issues because a personal injury claim, although not itself property, can result in a settlement of money and property.

### a. Proper Party to Bring the Action

In the 1970s, male management was replaced with equal management and control. The transition required reconsideration of the necessary party issue. For personal injury claims, the injured party is the proper party to maintain the action. When a jurisdiction apportions personal injury recoveries into community and separate elements (some, but not all do), it may be possible that both spouses will be necessary parties to an action.

The spouse to whom separate property belongs is the proper party to maintain an action at law concerning that asset.

### b. Spousal Immunity

This ancient common law doctrine forbade certain (or all) types of law suits between spouses in their status as spouses. The doctrine that barred one spouse from suing another during the marriage was rooted in several systemic concerns expressed in the so-called "unity of husband and wife" rationale. According to that rationale, the public policy of preserving peace and tranquility in the home (regrettably this policy covers up rather than prevents domestic violence); the supposed adequacy of criminal and divorce law; the fear of a flood of social matrimonial disputes in the courts; the fear of false testimony, and collusion; and the risk of insurance fraud were regarded as legitimate policy justifications upon which to preclude, as a matter of law, one spouse from suing the other spouse during the continuance of the marriage for a personal injury.

The majority of states have abolished the doctrine of interspousal tort immunity, as has the Restatement. See e.g. *Freehe v. Freehe*, 81 Wash.2d 183, 500 P.2d 771 (1972), *Self v. Self*, 58 Cal.2d 683, 26 Cal.Rptr. 97, 376 P.2d 65 (1962) and *Klein v. Klein*, 58 Cal.2d 692, 26 Cal.Rptr. 102, 376 P.2d 70 (1962). In Wisconsin (and under WUMPA), interspousal immunity is explicitly eliminated in several situations.

(*Freehe*, supra, was overruled by *Brown v. Brown*, 100 Wash.2d 729, 675 P.2d 1207 (1984)(en banc) on different grounds. *Freehe*, supra, characterized as community property a recovery for injuries to a married person by a third party tortfeasor. *Brown*, supra, characterized the same as separate property except to the extent that the recovery compensated for lost wages which would have been community property but for the injury.

Immunities do not apply in domestic violence situations. Where one spouse intentionally injures the other, some states provide that damages are the separate property of the injured spouse whether the settlement is received during or after the marriage. In these states, the injured spouse's action for intentional tort can be brought against the other spouse during marriage, or upon separation or divorce. Other states require that an action by one spouse against the other for an intentional tort committed during marriage (or by extension during a period of separation) be brought after divorce, as a subsequent action. Not all states distinguish between intentional and negligent harms when it comes to permitting one spouse to sue the other in tort.

Immunities no longer apply in actions by one spouse against another for property and economic torts. To allow spouses to protect their vested property rights in marital property, equitable and partnership related actions between spouses are permitted, often by statue. These can include an action for damages for breach of the spousal fiduciary duty; an action for an accounting of the property; an action to determine the rights and obligations of the spouses; an action for adding a spouse's name to the title of certain marital property or to bank accounts titled solely in the other spouse's name; and claims for impairment of a community property interest (economic torts). See for example Cal.Fam.Code § 1101.

## c. The Community Property Defense

Imputed contributory negligence in the context of marriage was sometimes referred to as the community property defense. The community property defense became available when one spouse's personal injuries were caused by a third party and the other spouse's contributory negligence. The defense worked like this. If one spouse was injured in an accident in which the other spouse was adjudged contributorily negligent, the community property defense barred the community estate from recovering damages. The policy underlying the community property defense was that a negligent spouse should not benefit from his or her own negligence.

Some states, California being one, abrogated the imputed contributory negligence theory as a matter of law, and instead adopted a contribution system. Under the contribution system, if an injured spouse sues a third party but chooses not to name the other spouse as a defendant, the third party can counter-claim against the unnamed spouse for an adjudication on whether the unnamed spouse was a contributing proximate cause of the plaintiff spouse's injury. If the answer is yes, then the third party can seek a contribution from the contributorily negligent spouse.

In the case of couples who are intentionally or unintentionally not married, different outcomes result. For nonmarried cohabitants, because they cannot acquire community property, the community property defense is not applicable absent an equitable alteration of the ordinary rules. For putative marriages, it is possible to be deemed by law to have come into ownership of community property or community property analogies (like, for example, California's concept of quasi-marital property); such a result could also produce an analogy to the community property defense. The different outcomes turn on marriage validity doctrines, which of course differ from state to state. Even so, a trend is emerging in light of declining marriage rates. In a community property defense jurisdiction, the more lawful the marriage, the more the community property defense applies. The unmarried couple avoids the defense to which a putatively married couple is perhaps subject, and to which a lawfully married couple is certainly subject.

It is possible that these types of litigation-related problems were responsible for any (past) trend toward apportioning personal injury recoveries into their separate and community property elements. In the typical automobile accident case, however, case law in every jurisdiction illustrates how the community property defense could be and was invoked by and for a casualty insurance company to avoid liability, rather than by and for a spouse personally.

## d. Reasons for Apportioning Personal Injury Settlements

A personal injury award has different components. Each component is discussed in the next section. Commentators have argued and judges have held that at least some of these components trace to separate property, and thus should be characterized as the separate property of the injured spouse.

Currently, three rationales for such an outcome prevail.

One, the onerous-lucrative rationale recognizes the personal injury cause of action and all recoveries received from third parties as community property, not because they are obtained through labor, but because they are not a gift. One possible limitation of this analysis is the approach taken by Nevada courts that a personal injury remedy is not within the definition of acquisition as set forth in the general community property statute.

Two, the private-slash-personal right rationale considers the personal injury recovery as a settlement of money for damage to a personal right, rather than to a property right. The rationale draws a sharp line between a property claim and a personal injury claim. In California, for example, a property claim can fall within the definition of accumulation but a personal injury claim cannot, because it is personal to its holder. Thus the personal injury claim is not subject to characterization; money or property received in settlement of the personal injury claim are. The theory is that only the settlement (not the underlying personal injury claim) represents a tradable "accumulation" for purposes of property characterization.

Commentators sometimes counter that a personal injury claim, because it can impact earnings, can or should be defined as an accumulation. These commentators focus on how to characterize disability payments made by an employer to an injured worker. Worker's compensation is derived from the employment, which sounds in community, but it is measured by the type of injury, which is said to be personal. Moreover, disability insurance is designed to replace future loss of income, which could be community or separate depending on the parties' marital status. From this perspective—the argument goes—depending on the facts of the case, a personal injury claim could be defined as an accumulation in one case but a non-accumulation in another.

Given the conceptual difficulty of breaking down personal injury settlements, including workers compensation, into components, the more accepted view is to name the injured spouse as the community agent for management and control of any personal injury action that arises during the marriage. If such an action is not brought before dissolution, the injured spouse continues as the exclusive manager of the personal injury action once the marriage is over. If the injured (now-former) spouse decides, after divorce, to pursue the personal injury claim that arose during the prior marriage, any settlement received would be outside of the community property system. Some U.S. community property states, again California being one, have precedent that disallows placing a claim that arose during a dissolving marriage into trust with the intention of designing a pro rata division should a settlement be won after the final judgment of dissolution is issued.

The above theories do not acknowledge the argument that pain and suffering are a form of labor by the injured party. Nor do they fully address that the care of an injured spouse by the other spouse is a form of labor.

Finally, statutory reimbursements tend to be the systematic way to address the above issues. Thus if the community or the other spouse's separate property estate contribute to care and medical expenses of an spouse who was injured during the marriage, a reimbursement may be due in the event of dissolution.

## e. Elements of a Personal Injury Settlement

Most jurisdictions have viewed a recovery for personal injury as containing the following elements (excluding attorney fees):

(i) *Compensation for future earnings:* During the marriage, compensation for future earnings is deemed to be community property. Dissolution could make a portion of the future earnings separate. The courts have not been uniform in considering the risk of how a dissolution would impact the character of the future earnings portion of a settlement, or in allocating a portion to earnings while married and the balance to earnings after divorce.

(ii) *Reimbursement for past medical expenses:* During the marriage this reimbursement is often given to the community on the rationale that the medical expenses have been paid from community property funds. The better rule appears to require an examination of the character of funds that actually were used to pay the medical expenses, and to direct the recovery accordingly so as to effect a complete reimbursement. If this latter approach is followed, than any estate, whether the community estate or the separate property of the non-injured spouse, can request a reimbursement.

(iii) *Compensation for pain, suffering and disfigurement:* Money received for pain, suffering and disfigurement is generally regarded as the separate property of the injured spouse. Jurisdictions differ on the character of money received for loss of consortium, and for loss of whose consortium.

(iv) *Payments for loss of body parts:* Money received for lost (meaning severed) body parts is generally treated as separate property, especially when the injury is not related to a job. If the injury is both job related and measured by the injury to the worker, some states hold the award to be community.

(v) *Disability payments:* Compensation for disabilities poses special problems when combined or taken in lieu of retirement benefits. In some cases, a worker has been entitled to either retirement or disability payments, but not both. The rationale focuses on whether an election by an injured spouse to take disability payments impairs the non-injured spouse's right to one-half of community funds in an existing defined benefit (i.e. pension or pension-like) plan.

## f. Problems with Apportioning Personal Injury Settlements

One problem with apportioning personal injury recovery by the nature of the right that has been injured is that there is no certainty that the jury will accurately allocate the total award. For example, a jury may be aware that a plaintiff's fee for her lawyer will not be paid by direct court award; and knowing this, the jury might increase the amount of the recovery for pain and suffering (a separate property item) in order to reimburse amounts paid from the community to lawyers.

Apportionment problems arise in connection with the expenses and fees paid to personal injury attorneys. If the attorney's fee is deducted from the recovery, should it be allocated to one category or borne proportionately by all categories? If the attorney's fee is deducted proportionately from a recovery in which the jury increased the "pain and suffering" portion in contemplation of the fee, the medical expense reimbursement to the community will not recover one hundred cents on each dollar that the community paid, while the separate property will receive slightly larger payments for pain and suffering. Regardless of the conceptual support for apportioning personal injury money and property received in settlement of a personal injury claim against a third party, a disputed settlement can be deemed separate property, in whole or in part, by statutory default.

In the California community property system, money and property received during a marriage for a personal injury settlement that arose during marriage are entirely community property. But they are a special kind of community property that is assigned to the injured party in the event of a dissolution. The imputed negligence doctrine is abrogated except where an injured spouse sues a third party for personal injury but does not name the other spouse. In such a case, the third-party defendant has the right to cross-claim against the unnamed spouse. If the cross-claimed spouse is adjudged a proximate cause of the plaintiff spouse's injury, then the cross-claimed spouse owes a contribution to the third party. By this legal process, the third party and the spouse who has been adjudged a contributorily negligent party become jointly and severally liable to the plaintiff spouse. The pro rata share of the award received from the third party is characterized as special community property; the pro rata share received from the (now adjudged) contributorily negligent spouse is characterized as the plaintiff spouse's separate property. See Section C, California for relevant code citations.

## 7.    HISTORIC (TRANSITIONAL) FORMS OF SEPARATE PROPERTY

Because of constitutional problems, most statutory changes in the character of property operate prospectively. Thus, in each state, historic forms of separate and community property exist.

Statutory community property presumptions can be applied retroactively with no constitutional objections. For example, in a line of cases commencing with *Marriage of Buol*, 39 Cal.3d 751, 218 Cal.Rptr. 31, 705 P.2d 354 (1985), which is now superseded by statute, the California Supreme Court held that the retroactive application of Cal.Fam.Code § 2581 (the community property presumption that applies in a dissolution proceeding to assets titled in any joint form) neither impairs vested property interests nor violates due process of law. However, any and every change by statute (and many of the decisional changes) that affect a vested property right by requiring a written instrument for what previously could be accomplished without one may create a new class of historic property that maintains its now-outdated character going forward. See Chapter 2, Section C, California for examples.

Conflict of laws and legal transitions can create special categories of separate property within the confines of a state system, as discussed in Chapter 3, Section C, Arizona. Separate property often exists when acquired by a married person domiciled in a non-community property state and sometimes when domiciled in a different community property state than the one in which the dissolution or probate proceeding is taking place. Wisconsin places property acquired prior to its adoption of the community property system in an entirely different category called either "predetermination date" or "unclassified" property. This property is essentially individually owned separate property.

State transitions concerning the character of separate property rents, issues and profits may create historic forms of community or separate property.

The rule that character is determined at inception of title is uniformly followed by U.S. community property states, even though the jurisdictions split on how to account for post-acquisition commingling, especially in the form of labor and capital contributions. In American rule states, commingling can and likely will alter the character of an asset. In civil law rule jurisdictions, the character of the asset remains constant over time, but commingling gives rise to a reimbursement for the contributing estate. See Chapter 6.

The inception of title rule, at its core, describes the *original* acquisition. In the community property system, property is characterized at its wellspring, the point where the legal right is acquired. Exchanging one item of owned property for another is a trade or an exchange whose character is determined by the character of the original acquisition, meaning the wellspring.

The acquisition of property is usually the net effect of a series of acts undertaken over a period of time. An inventor may have an idea, research existing inventions, work upon and perfect her invention, seek a lawyer and apply for and receive a patent. Clearly the patent is property, and even a formal declaration of right (meaning a formal written title), but is the patent itself the wellspring? Or, was a property right acquired before the patent was granted?

By a legal fiction, all of the various acts and ceremonies necessary to complete a purchase, gift, or conveyance of title are generally deemed to be taken together as of the time of some substantial part. Thus the point of original acquisition is when the property right is first acquired. Later acts that ratify or confirm the property right are said to "relate back" to the point of original acquisition. The task often is to determine the substantial part that represents the act of "original acquisition" in what may be a series of acts that lead up to a secure legal right.

In the case of the inventor it is probable that the time of acquisition will precede the grant of, and even the application for, the patent. For an author, the time of acquisition might very well precede the negotiation of the book contract, or the publication of the book, or the transfer of royalties from publisher to writer. Somewhere around the time that a working model is made, or a book proposal or manuscript is presented for purposes of securing a publishing contract seems an early but still logical time to set as the date of original acquisition for this type of creative asset.

The marital status of the inventor or author at the time that the substantial part of acquisition occurs will determine the character of the property going forward for purposes of state law. To illustrate, an invention for which the substantial act of acquisition takes place during marriage is likely characterized as community property, whereas an invention for which the substantial act of acquisition takes place before marriage or during separation is likely characterized as separate property.

Examples of property acquired over time are deferred earnings and pension rights for labor exerted, earnings produced by writings, inventions and other artistic endeavors.

Celebrity status is characterized by this same analysis.

## 8. SUMMING UP: ACQUISITION BEFORE MARRIAGE, DURING SEPARATION, AND AFTER DIVORCE

The existence of a valid marriage is required for the creation and continuation of community property.

During marriage, only property acquired with labor can be community property.

Property acquired before marriage is separate property in all states, but there can be state law variation on the gift issue.

A majority of states characterize separate property rents, issues, and profits as separate property. A minority of states characterize the same as community property.

Earnings and accumulations acquired after a date of separation are separate property in most states.

## C. INDIVIDUAL STATES

### 1. ARIZONA

Ariz.Rev.Stat.Ann. § 25–213 defines separate property by restating the exceptions to community property listed in Arizona's basic community property statute Ariz.Rev.Stat.Ann. § 25–211. Separate property is **"real and personal property"** owned by a spouse **"before marriage, and that is acquired by that spouse during the marriage by gift, devise or descent, and the increase, rents, issues and profits of that property . . . ."** Ariz.Rev.Stat.Ann. § 25–213(A).

Separate property is also defined as property acquired after the separation or the filing of a petition to terminate the marriage: **"Property acquired after service of a petition for dissolution, legal separation, or annulment is also the separate property of that spouse if the petition results in a decree of dissolution of marriage, legal separation or annulment."** Ariz.Rev.Stat.Ann. § 25–213(B).

Until 1970, Arizona case law characterized recoveries for personal injuries as community property. In *Jurek v. Jurek*, 124 Ariz. 596, 606 P.2d 812 (1980)(In Banc), the Arizona Supreme Court followed the lead and logic of commentators and the courts of Nevada and New Mexico by characterizing the compensation for personal injuries caused by a third party as the separate property of the injured spouse, and the compensations for expenses incurred by the community for medical care and treatment and any loss of wages resulting from the personal injury as community property. Otherwise, the apportionment of a personal injury award into its component parts remains the rule in Arizona. *Hatcher v. Hatcher* 188 Ariz. 154, 933 P.2d 1222 (1996).

*Windauer v. O'Connor*, 107 Ariz. 267, 485 P.2d 1157 (1971)(In Banc), a domestic violence case, held that after divorce a spouse may sue a former spouse to recover damages for an intentional tort that occurred during the former marriage.

In *Fernandez v. Romo*, 132 Ariz. 447, 646 P.2d 878 (1982)(In Banc) the Arizona Supreme Court abolished the doctrine of spousal immunity in automobile accident cases.

## 2.   CALIFORNIA

California Constitution, Article 1, § 21 ensures that **"[p]roperty owned before marriage or acquired during marriage by gift, will, or inheritance is separate property."**

Cal.Fam.Code § 770 defines as separate property **"[a]ll property owned by the person before marriage; [a]ll property acquired by the person after marriage by gift, bequest, devise, or descent; and [t]he rents, issues, and profits of the property"** described in the statute. Indeed, the American rule requiring that separate property income streams be themselves characterized as separate property has its source in *George v. Ransom*, supra.

Cal.Fam.Code § 771, provides that the earnings of either spouse while **"living separate and apart"** are separate property; and, also during such a period, that the earnings and accumulations of **"the minor children living with, or in the custody of, the spouse ... are the separate property of the spouse."** The earnings and accumulations of **"an emancipated minor child"** continue to belong to the emancipated minor child.

Date of separation is defined in newly enacted Cal.Fam.Code § 70. Added in 2016, effective January 1, 2017, the provision defines date of separation as **"the date that a complete and final break in the** marital relationship has occurred, as evidenced by both of the following: (1) The spouse has expressed to the other spouse his or her intent to end the marriage. (2) The conduct of the spouse is consistent with his or her intent to end the marriage." The statute adopts a subjective standard (private intentions, communications, and actions between the spouses), but it also mandates that a judge take into consideration "all relevant" (objective) evidence. Importantly, the provision abrogates *Marriage of Davis*, 61 Cal.4th 846, 352 P.3d 401 (2015), a decision that required that one spouse establish a new domicile in order to mark a date of separation; the abrogation returns the issue to one determined by the Family Code.

Personal injury recoveries for a cause of action accrued during marriage have been community property except between 1957 and 1968, In 1968, California restored the community property character of the personal injury recovery, added the mandatory assignment rule, and attempted to eliminate imputed contributory negligence (the community property defense). Cal.Fam.Code §§ 780 and 783.

Currently, Cal.Fam.Code § 780 characterizes personal injury damages that are the result of causes of action that **"arose during the marriage"** as community property. Cal.Fam.Code § 781, on the other hand, characterizes as separate property damages from any cause of action that arose **"after the entry of judgment of dissolution ... or legal separation ... [or] while either spouse ... is living separate from the other spouse."**

Provisions to reimburse the non-injured spouse's separate property or the community property for any expenses paid **"by reason of the injury"** are set out in that section as well.

In a dissolution, a personal injury cause of action that arose during the marriage but had not yet been pursued or settled by the end of the marriage exits the marriage with the injured spouse. *Marriage of Pinto*, 28 Cal.App.3d 86, 104 Cal.Rptr. 371 (1972).

Money and property received during marriage in settlement of a personal injury claim that arose during the marriage is community property, as noted above, but it is subject to mandatory division pursuant to Cal.Fam.Code § 2603, which provides that Cal.Fam.Code § 780 personal injury money and settlements shall be assigned to the injured spouse unless economic conditions or the interests of justice require otherwise. But in no case shall the noninjured spouse's share exceed one-half of an apportioned personal injury settlement.

Certain purchases made from a personal injury recovery may be assigned to the injured spouse. *Marriage of Devlin*, 138 Cal.App.3d 804, 189 Cal.Rptr. 1 (1982) used the doctrine of tracing to set aside ordinary dissolution rules in favor of assigning to the injured spouse a residence that had been purchased with a personal injury settlement during marriage and modified for the injured spouse.

Cal.Fam.Code § 781 characterizes damages arising from a cause of action that one spouse has **"against the other spouse that arose during the**

**marriage"** as the separate property of the injured spouse. Likewise remedies for economic torts based on a breach of fiduciary duty are the separate property of the recovering spouse. Cal.Fam.Code § 1101(g) and (h). Conviction for the attempted murder of a spouse by the other spouse assigns to the injured spouse **"100 percent of the community property interest in the retirement and pension benefits of the injured spouse"** in addition to whatever other property the injured spouse is statutorily entitled to, and (by reference to other statutes) attorney fees and court costs. Cal.Fam.Code § 782.5. Other forfeiture statutes exist throughout the family code as a means to address interpersonal violence in the marital relationship. See a more detailed discussion, see Jo Carrillo, *Financial Intimate Partner Violence: When Assets and Transactions Become Weapons*, 9(4) FAMILY & INTIMATE PARTNER VIOLENCE QUARTERLY 67 (2017).

## 3.   IDAHO

Idaho Code § 32–903 provides that **"All property of either the husband or the wife owned by him or her before marriage, and that acquired afterward either by gift, bequest, devise or descent, or that which either he or she shall acquire with the proceeds of his or her separate property, by way of moneys or other property, shall remain his or her sole and separate property."**

Idaho is a civil law state. Idaho Code § 32–906, discussed in Chapter 3, the basic community property statute, characterizes **"[t]he income, including the rents, issues, and profits, of all property, separate or community"** as community property even if there is no dispute about the separate property character of the underlying asset. For discussion of this section, see *Josephson v. Josephson*, 115 Idaho 1142, 772 P.2d 1236 (Ct. App. 1989), abrogated (on other grounds) by *Bell v. Bell*, 122 Idaho 520, 835 P.2d 1331 (1992). Rents, issues, and profits may be transmuted from community to separate if **"both spouses, by written agreement specifically so providing, declare that . . . the income, including the rents, issues, and profits, from all or specifically designated separate property be the separate property of the spouse to whom the property belongs."** Transmutation is discussed in Chapter 2.

Idaho Code § 32–909 characterizes the earnings and accumulations of **"the wife . . . while she is living separate from her husband [as] the separate property of the wife."** The gender specific language is a remnant of the male-management era. Biased statutory language was held unconstitutional in *Suter v. Suter*, 97 Idaho 461, 546 P.2d 1169 (1976), which also declared earnings after a date of separation to be the community property of the spouses.

Idaho case law initially classified personal injury recoveries as entirely community property. However, *Rogers v. Yellowstone Park Co.*, 97 Idaho 14, 539 P.2d 566 (1974) allowed an Idaho spouse who was married to an employee of the corporate defendant to recover damages for her own pain and suffering as her separate property. The court based its characterization upon the nature of the right violated and the interest damaged (medical expenses paid, future earnings lost, pain and suffering). In the same decision, the Idaho Supreme Court abolished the doctrine of interspousal immunity.

In *Runcorn v. Shearer Lumber Products, Inc.*, 107 Idaho 389, 690 P.2d 324 (1984) a non-injured spouse was permitted to recover for the negligent loss of consortium in a worker's compensation case, reduced by the percentage of negligence attributable to the injured spouse.

## 4.   LOUISIANA

Louisiana defines separate property in LSA–C.C. Art. 2341 as property **". . . acquired by a spouse prior to the establishment of a community property regime; property acquired by a spouse with separate things or with separate and community things when the value of the community things is inconsequential in comparison with the value of the separate things used; property acquired by a spouse by inheritance or donation to him individually; damages awarded to a spouse in an action for breach of contract against the other spouse or for the loss sustained as a result of fraud or bad faith in the management of community property by the other spouse; damages or other indemnity awarded to a spouse in connection with the management of his separate property; and things acquired by a spouse as a result of a**

**voluntary partition of the community during the existence of a community property regime."**

**"The natural and civil fruits of the separate property of a spouse, . . ."** are community property, unless they are reserved under LSA–C.C. Art. 2339.

Under LSA–C.C. Art. 2356 **"The legal regime of community property is terminated by the death or judgment of declaration of death of a spouse, declaration of the nullity of the marriage, judgment of divorce or separation of property, . . ."** or, alternatively if there is a **"[m]atrimonial agreement that terminates the community."** Matrimonial agreements are discussed in Chapter 2.

In Louisiana, the community estate, and not just the marriage itself, is terminated rather than dissolved. In other states, the marriage is terminated but the community estate is dissolved. The practical effect of this linguistic distinction is that all property owned after the termination of the marriage (not just earnings and accumulations, as for example in California) is individually owned property. Thus, after the point deemed by a court to be the irretrievable and irreparable breakdown of the marriage, all property is individual property, meaning property not governed by the community property system. The closest equivalent of individually owned property in the matrimonial regime is separate property. See e.g., *Aufrichtig v. Aufrichtig*, 796 So.2d 57 (2001) for a review of relevant cases and distinctions between dates of marriage, separation, and termination. See also Chapter 2 for a discussion on how date of separation is determined.

**"[P]roperty acquired by a spouse by inheritance or donation to him individually; . . ."** is separate property, again, under LSA–C.C. Art. 2341 which is reproduced above. As discussed in Chapter 3, property jointly donated to both spouses by a third party is community property under LSA–C.C. Art. 2338, but as Revision Comments from 1979 indicate, if the spouses **"do not live in community,"** i.e., if they have agreed upon a contractual matrimonial regime in lieu of the legal one, then **"the donor may not create a community regime for the spouses. In such a case, the property given to them is separate property held in indivision."**

Generally, Louisiana adheres to many distinctions in the law of gifts. Gifts are labeled along a spectrum that ranges from gratuitous to remunerative. For purposes of determining whether a third party's gift to a donee spouse meets the definition of separate property, therefore, it may be necessary to analyze the factual context in which the gift was made. Other states include only gratuitous gifts in the definition of separate property; there is no case law indicating that Louisiana deviates from this approach.

Gifts between spouses are discussed in Chapter 2.

LSA–C.C. Art. 2343 provides that **"the donation of a spouse to the other spouse of his undivided interest in a thing forming part of the community transforms that interest into separate property of the donee. Unless**

**otherwise provided in the act of donation, an equal interest of the donee is also transformed into separate property ..."** as are any of the **"natural and civil fruits of the thing . . ."**

Louisiana has long recognized the distinctive elements of a personal injury action, and been willing to characterize each part in accordance with the right violated. The recognition was maintained and extended to either spouse in LSA–C.C. Art. 2344, effective January 1, 1980.

As a general rubric, the statutory default holds:

**"Damages due to personal injuries sustained during the existence of the community by a spouse are separate property."**

**"Nevertheless, the portion of the damages attributable to expenses incurred by the community as a result of the injury, or in compensation of the loss of community earnings, is community property. If the community regime is terminated otherwise than by the death of the injured spouse, the portion of the damages attributable to the loss of earnings that would have accrued after termination of the community property regime is the separate property of the injured spouse."** This statute is intended to encompass "injuries to the personality of the injured spouse" and "work[er's] compensation benefits." Revision Comments—1979.

## 5.   NEVADA

Nev. Const. Art. 4, § 31 provides, in part: **"All property, both real and personal, of a married person owned or claimed by such person before marriage, and that acquired afterward by gift, devise or descent, shall be the separate property of such person. . . ."**

The constitutional provision is amplified by Nev.Rev.Stat. § 123.130:

**"1. All property of the wife owned by her before marriage, and that acquired by her afterwards by gift, bequest, devise, descent or by an award for personal injury damages, with the rents, issues and profits thereof, is her separate property.**

**2. All property of the husband owned by him before marriage, and that acquired by him afterwards by gift, bequest, devise, descent or by an award for personal injury damages, with the rents, issues and profits thereof, is his separate property."**

Nev.Rev.Stat. § 123.180 provides that while the spouses are **"living separate and apart . . ."** the earnings of **"[a] minor child"** are the separate property of the custodial spouse. Nev.Rev.Stat. § 123.180, however, currently omits any reference to the earnings and accumulations of a spouse while living separate and apart from the other spouse. Nev.Rev.Stat. § 123.220, the general community property statute, fills the gap by providing that all property during the marriage is community property up until **"[a] decree of separate maintenance is issued . . . ."** *Forrest v. Forrest*, 99 Nev. 602, 668 P.2d 275 (1983) makes the same point.

Nevada has the most extensive legislation concerning the procedure for and effect of recording of a written inventory of the separate property of a married person. The applicable statutes include Nev.Rev.Stat. § 123.140 through Nev.Rev.Stat. § 123.160 (excerpted in Chapter 3 above).

Nevada's courts were among the first to judicially classify any part of a personal injury recovery as separate property, and among the first to judicially divide the recovery between separate and community in accordance with the right violated and the damage suffered. By stressing the onerous acquisitive character of community property, the rationale relied on was that personal injury recoveries are not necessarily community. So, for example, In *Los Angeles & S.L.R.R. v. Umbaugh*, 61 Nev. 214, 123 P.2d 224 (1942), the court ruled that the a monetary recovery for the wrongful death of a child by one spouse does not fall within the meaning of the word "acquired" as used in the general community property statute. By this rationale, during marriage, money and property obtained as a recovery for an injury to personal security is conceptualized as a replacement or exchange for loss rather than as an onerous acquisition.

However, the courts and the statutes concede that other aspects of a personal injury recovery are community in character. For example, in addition to

Nev.Rev.Stat. § 123.130 quoted above, Nev.Rev.Stat. § 123.121 provides:

"When a husband and wife sue jointly, any damages awarded shall be segregated as follows:

1. If the action is for personal injuries, damages assessed for:

   (a) Personal injuries and pain and suffering, to the injured spouse as his separate property.

   (b) Loss of comfort and society, to the spouse who suffers such loss.

   (c) Loss of services and hospital and medical expenses, to the spouses as community property.

2. If the action is for injury to property, damages shall be awarded according to the character of the injured property. Damages to separate property shall be awarded to the spouse owning such property, and damages to community property shall be awarded to the spouses as community property."

By this statute, damages are characterized by element for:

- Personal injury pain and suffering;

- Loss of consortium;

- Hospital and medical expenses;

- Loss of property.

## 6. NEW MEXICO

N.M.Stat.Ann. § 40–3–8(A) (1978) defines separate property in the usual way.

" 'Separate property' means:

**(1) property acquired by either spouse before marriage or after entry of a decree of dissolution or marriage;**

**(2) property acquired after entry of a decree entered pursuant to Section 40–4–3 NMSA 1978, unless the decree provides otherwise;**

**(3) property designated as separate property by a judgment or decree of any court having jurisdiction;**

**(4) property acquired by either spouse by gift, bequest, devise or descent; and**

**(5) property designated as separate property by a written agreement between the spouses, including a deed or other written agreement concerning property held by the spouses as joint tenants or tenants in common in which the property is designated as separate property."**

N.M.Stat.Ann. § 40–4–3, noted above, is the statute on court sanctioned separation. It reads: **"Whenever the [spouses] have permanently separated and no longer live or cohabit together as [spouses], either may institute proceedings in the district court for a division of property, disposition of children or alimony, without asking for or obtaining in the**

**proceedings, a dissolution of marriage."** Court sanctioned separation is the effectively the same as a legal separation.

Earnings after a date of separation but prior to a court sanctioned (legal) separation or divorce decree remain community property under general principles. New Mexico has no provision for the couple that is estranged but not yet legally separated. No-fault divorce was recognized as early as 1933, therefore the case law prohibits trial courts from considering fault when granting a divorce, dividing property, or awarding alimony.

New Mexico has a Family Violence Protection Act (the NMFVPA for short) found at N.M. Stat. Ann. § 40–13–1 through § 40–13–6 (1978). The NMFVPA was passed in 1987. In 2001, amendments allowed for financial remedies and counseling programs. See N.M. Stat. Ann. § 40–13–5 (1978). Otherwise, the no-fault principle prevails with respect to property matters between spouses.

Consistent with the no-fault divorce principle is *Flores v. Flores*, 84 N.M. 601, 506 P.2d 345 (1973), which held that one spouse has the legal right to sue the other spouse for an intentional tort that occurred during a period of separation. Or, an interspousal motion for a protective order can be brought during the divorce process, by way of a motion for debt classification, pursuant to N.M. Stat. Ann. § 40–13–5 (1978), or by way of a tort claim filed after the marriage is terminated, as in Arizona.

N.M. Stat. Ann. § 40–3–8E (1978) follows the American-rule that separate property rents, issues, and profits are also separate property.

New Mexico has a relatively unenhanced treatment of the character of personal injury recoveries compared to other community property states. In *Soto v. Vandeventer*, 56 N.M. 483, 245 P.2d 826 (1952), where the spouse obtained a tort judgment against a third party, the New Mexico Supreme Court followed Nevada law to characterize the injured spouse's compensation for pain and suffering as separate property, and the compensation for medical expenses, earnings, and loss of service to the community as community property. *Soto*, supra, does not apply, however, unless and until community indebtedness for medical expenses is established: see *Flores*, supra. Subsequent cases extend the *Soto*, supra, rule; see e.g. *Baca v. Baca*, 71 N.M.468, 379 P.2d 765 (1963) (recovery for the wrongful death of a child).

## 7. TEXAS

Tex. Const. Art. XVI, § 15, as amended in 1948, 1980, 1987, and 1999, defines separate property as **"All property, both real and personal, of a spouse owned or claimed before marriage, and that acquired afterward by gift, devise or descent, shall be the separate property of that spouse; . . ."**

V.T.C.A.Fam.Code § 3.001 further provides:

**"A spouse's separate property consists of:**

(1) **the property owned or claimed by the spouse before marriage;**

(2) **the property acquired by the spouse during marriage by gift, devise, or descent; and**

(3) **the recovery for personal injuries sustained by the spouse during marriage, except any recovery for loss of earning capacity during marriage."**

To date, Texas follows the civil law ganancial rule of declaring rents, issues, and profits of separate property to be community property during marriage. The key to this rule is the *absence* of the phrase "and rents, issues, and profits from separate property" in the constitutional provision that defines separate property. At this time, Texas has no statutory provision that clearly characterizes separate property income streams. However, case law has consistently interpreted the Texas Constitution to require that a community property character be given to the rents, issues, and profits of separate property obtained during marriage.

Texas has made various short-lived and unsuccessful efforts to transition toward the American rule, which recognizes separate property rents, issues, and profits as separate property. But *Arnold v. Leonard*, 114 Tex. 535, 273 S.W. 799 (1925) held unconstitutional two Texas statutes which attempted that transition. The court held that the Texas constitutional provisions describing the extent of a spouse's separate property contain an implied prohibition against the exercise of legislative power to change the specified circumstances in which property is defined as separate property. The rationale holds more generally as well. As discussed in Chapter 1, Texas enshrined the community property system in its state constitution so as to protect it from the acts of future legislatures. Over time other statutes have been enacted to move Texas toward into the American rule majority of U.S. community property states, but those statutes were eventually repealed, the result being that Texas continues in the civil law tradition as to separate property rents, issues, and profits.

A proposed constitutional amendment was recently in the works, but it did not pass. The amendment would have given courts discretion ("may") to partition the community property so that once partitioned "the future income from that property" could be characterized as the separate property of a spouse to whom it was assigned.

On a related point, Tex. Const. Art. XVI, § 15 currently permits that spouses may **"agree [in writing] between themselves that the income or property from all or part of the separate property then owned or which thereafter might be acquired by only one of them, shall be the separate property of that spouse."** Moreover, if a spouse makes a gift of separate property to the other spouse, **"that gift is presumed to include all the income or property which might arise from that gift of property."** Thus a transmutation of the underlying separate property will automatically include any future rents, issues, and profits that the property might produce. Transmutations are discussed further in Chapter 2.

Although V.T.C.A.Fam.Code § 3.001(a)(3), reproduced above, resolves the split character of two elements of a personal injury action, it does not mention reimbursements for proven medical expenses. Case law characterizes lost wages, medical expenses and other injury related community expenses as community property damages in a divorce action. *Cottone v. Cottone*, 122 S.W.3d 211 (2003), *Wilson v. Wilson*, 132 S.W.3d 533 (2004).

In *Graham v. Franco*, 488 S.W.2d 390 (1972), the Texas Supreme Court upheld the constitutionality of V.T.C.A.Fam.Code § 3.001(a)(3) while declining to define a tort cause of action as transferable property. There, the medical reimbursement element of the recovery was characterized as community in character, but the court also indicated, the pain, suffering and disfigurement elements of the recovery are the separate property of the injured spouse. This view has been followed recently by *Harrell v. Hochderffer*, 345 S.W.3d 652 (2011), where damages for disfigurement, past and future mental anguish, and past and future physical pain and suffering were characterized as separate property of the injured spouse.

In *Whittlesey v. Miller*, 572 S.W.2d 665 (1978), a wife's recovery for loss of consortium was held to result from her independent action, and thus separate in character. Also, such an action was permitted notwithstanding the husband's settlement with the tortfeasor. In *Reed Tool Co. v. Copelin*, 610 S.W.2d 736

(1980), even though the wife's claim against her husband's employer for the negligent loss of consortium was dismissed as derivative under the worker's compensation act, her claim for the *intentional* loss of consortium was allowed on the rationale that such a recovery would be separate property under V.T.C.A.Fam.Code § 3.001, subject to the wife's exclusive management and control, and thus non-derivative.

## 8.   WASHINGTON

Washington's statutes are distinctive in that they do not define separate property so much as they describe incidents of separateness. Wash.Rev.Code has distinct but identical provisions for spouses and domestic partners.

Wash.Rev.Code § 26.16.010 Separate property of a spouse provides:

**"Property and pecuniary rights owned by a spouse before marriage and that acquired by him or her afterwards by gift, bequest, devise, descent, or inheritance, with the rents, issues and profits thereof, shall not be subject to the debts or contracts of his or her spouse, and he or she may manage, lease, sell, convey, encumber or devise by will such property without his or her spouse joining in such management, alienation or encumbrance, as fully, and to the same extent or in the same manner as though he or she were unmarried."** This provision brings Washington into the majority of U.S. community property states that follow the

American rule characterizing separate property income streams as themselves separate.

Wash.Rev.Code § 26.16.020 extends this same language to domestic partners.

Wash.Rev.Code § 26.16.140 provides that if **"spouses or domestic partners"** are **"living separate and apart"** their respective earnings and accumulations are separate property. Relying on California decisional law, Washington courts have held that physical separation alone does not establish a date of separation. Rather, "the test is whether by the parties, in conduct have exhibited a decision to renounce the community, with no intention of ever resuming the marital relationship." *Oil Heat Co. of Port Angeles v. Sweeney*, 26 Wash.App. 351, 354, 613 P.2d 169 (1980). A date of separation does not hinge on proof of an intent to divorce; rather it hinges on far more qualitative proof that the parties no longer have "the will to union," a standard discussed in *Estate of Nikiporez*, 19 Wash.App. 231, 574 P.2d 1204, *rev. denied*, 90 Wash.2d 1013 (1978).

In Washington, a chose in action (the right to sue) was historically within the definition of property. *Hawkins v. Front St. Cable Ry. Co.*, 3 Wash. 592, 28 P. 1021 (1892), a case where a husband alone sued a streetcar company for damages suffered by his wife as a result of the streetcar driver's negligence. The defendant sought to amend the complaint to include the wife; it argued that husband had suffered no damages and could not recover for the wife's injuries. The trial court refused to include the wife; instead it instructed the jury that the husband could recover for the wife even if she was not a party to the action. The Supreme Court of Washington discussed the common law as it functions within the Washington community property system before holding that because *all* property acquired during marriage except by gift, bequest, or devise is community property, a chose in action acquired during marriage must fall within the definition of community property. The court supported its argument by reference to the (then) law of California. (Under current California law, a personal injury cause of action property is no longer regarded as transferable property, as discussed above.)

Later cases suggest a reform of the view expressed in *Hawkins*, supra. *Marriage of Brown*, 100 Wash.2d 729, 739, 675 P.2d 1207 (1984) ruled that because Wash.Rev.Code § 26.16.030 (the basic community property statute) applies only to onerous acquisitions of property during marriage; a chose in action for personal injury is not onerous. It is separate property, "except to the extent the recovery compensates the community for lost wages, which would have been community property or injury-related expenses, which the community incurred." *Id.* at 730.

A statutory change on the issue of interspousal immunity ensued after *Freehe*, supra. This happened when the state transitioned from contributory negligence to comparative negligence and abolished the community property defense by statutes that took effect in 1974. Wash.Rev.Code § 4.22.020 now provides that **"[t]he contributory fault of one spouse or one domestic partner shall not be imputed to the other spouse or other domestic**

**partner . . . to diminish recovery in an action by the other spouse or other domestic partner . . ., or his or her legal representative, to recover damages caused by fault resulting in death or in injury to the person or property, whether separate or community, of the spouse or domestic partner. In an action brought for wrongful death or loss of consortium, the contributory fault of the decedent or injured person shall be imputed to the claimant in that action."**

## 9.   WISCONSIN

Wis.Stat. § 766.31, titled **"Classification of Property of Spouses"** and discussed in Chapter 3 controls. The statute creates three basic property classifications: marital property (equivalent to community property); individual property (equivalent to separate property); and "predetermination date property" (also called "unclassified property"). All property of spouses is presumed to be marital unless classified otherwise by the spouses or by statute.

With respect to property rights Wis.Stat. § 766.31(8) provides that the basic rule **"does not alter the classification and ownership rights of property acquired before the determination date or . . . after the determination date in exchange for or with the proceeds of property acquired before the determination date."** Wis.Stat. § 766.31(9) provides that such property **"is treated as if it were individual property."**

Wis.Stat. § 766.31(7) defines individual, meaning separate, property as:

**"Property acquired by a spouse during marriage and after the determination date is individual property if acquired by any of the following means:**

(a) **By gift during lifetime or by a disposition at death by a 3rd person to that spouse and not to both spouses. A distribution of principal or income from a trust created by a 3rd person to one spouse is the individual property of that spouse unless the trust provides otherwise.**

(b) **In exchange for or with the proceeds of other individual property of the spouse.**

(c) **From appreciation of the spouse's individual property except to the extent that the appreciation is classified as marital property under s. 766.63.**

(d) **By a decree or marital property agreement or reclassification agreement under sub (10) designating it as the individual property of the spouse.**

(e) **As a recovery for damage to property under s. 766.70, except as specifically provided otherwise in a decree or marital property agreement.**

(f) **As a recovery for personal injury except for the amount of that recovery** attributable to expenses paid or otherwise satisfied from marital property and except for the amount attributable to loss of income during marriage. . . ."

Subsection (a) above makes a gift made by a third party to one spouse alone individual property. *In re Czerneski*, 330 B.R. 240 (Bkrtcy. E.D. Wis. 2005).

Subsection (b) classifies as individual property anything that is exchanged for or purchased with sales proceeds from individual property. Whether property can be traced back to individual property is a question of fact that will be upheld unless it is clearly erroneous. The issue here is one of identity: was the claimed property exchanged for or purchased with individual property? Once a factual finding is made through the use of tracing, the issue becomes a question of law about how to characterize the property.

Subsection (f) characterizes money and property received in settlement of a personal injury claim as individual property with exceptions for loss of income, as discussed below.

At a spouse's death **"[t]o the extent that marital property includes damages for loss of future income arising from a personal injury claim of a surviving spouse, the surviving spouse is entitled to receive as individual property that portion of the award that represents an income substitute after the death of the other spouse."** Wis.Stat. § 766.31(7m).

Wisconsin follows the civil law rule on separate property rents, issues, and profits, but with respect to interspousal gifts, **"[i]f a spouse gives property to the other spouse and intends at the time the gift is made that the property be the individual property of the donee spouse, the income from the property is the individual property of the donee spouse unless a contrary intent of the donor spouse regarding the classification of income is established."** Wis.Stat. § 766.31(10).

A Wisconsin married couple's "determination date" is the last date to occur of the following: marriage; establishment of a marital domicile in Wisconsin; or January 1, 1986.

"Predetermination date property" is property acquired by one or both spouses prior to their determination date (i.e., prior to the date on which the marital property law first applies to them). Wisconsin subdivides predetermination date property by the event which is the determination date. Thus, property owned at the determination date is either individual property or else it is treated as if it were individual property depending on whether facts of independent significance related to the timing of the marriage can be established.

Wis.Stat. § 766.31, parallels UMPA in its basic classification statute, and it adds important specifications:

**1. Trusts:** Wisconsin's statute specifies that a distribution of principal or income from a trust created by a third person to one spouse is the individual property of that spouse unless the trust provides otherwise. See Wis.Stat. § 766.31(7)(a) above.

**2. Personal injury recoveries:** Wisconsin treats as marital property any amount attributable to the loss of income during marriage. At the death of the injured spouse any such amounts become the individual property of the surviving spouse. These points are discussed above.

**3. Written consents:** Wisconsin sharply reduced the circumstances under which a "written consent" (a document signed by a person against whose interests it is sought to be enforced) may be used to reclassify marital property into individual property. Such a consent may be used only in relation to life insurance policies; and a written consent nevertheless remains a valuable planning device for insurance assets. Note however that Wisconsin does authorize marital property agreements, as discussed in Chapter 2.

**4. Unilateral statement for adopting the American rule for individual (separate) property rents, issues, and profits:** Wisconsin authorizes a legal document analogous to the Louisiana approach of allowing a naked owner to reserve, by written instrument, the right of usufruct to individual (separate) property rents, issues, and profits. The default rule in Wisconsin is that post-determination date rents, issues, and profits from either predetermination date property or individual property are characterized as marital (meaning community) property by default. However, the individual (meaning separate) character of rents, issues, and profits from individual property can be preserved. To do so, an owner must follow statutory formalities for producing a unilateral statement of intent specific to rents, issues, and profits. The statement must be signed, acknowledged before a notary public, and served by delivery or certified mail to the other spouse.

**5. Income from interspousal gifts:** Wis.Stat. § 766.31(10) attempts to avoid adverse death tax results.

## D.  QUESTION AND ANSWER

(1)  Before her marriage to H, W is an employee of ABC Corp., and W owns 100 shares of ABC Corp. stock.

(2)  During marriage, W receives 100 additional shares of ABC Corp. in a 2-for-1 split.

(3)  The next year, W receives 10 additional ABC Corp. shares as a 5% stock dividend.

(4)  Additionally, the value of ABC Corp. rose due to two factors: the intrinsic value of the business and inflation.

(5)  ABC Corp. declared cash dividends of $5,000 each in years 3, 4 and 5 of W's and H's marriage. In these same years, there were no stock splits or dividends.

(6)  W earned a salary for professional services in the amount of $100,000 for each of years 1 through 5.

(7) W earned pension benefits in the form of investments in a general account managed by ABC Corp., for each of years 1 through 5.

(8) During marriage, W is injured by a negligent driver. She settles her personal injury claim against that driver for $10,000.

Characterize each of the eight elements above as community (CP) or separate property (SP).

Assume:

General community property principles apply.

There are no marital agreements nor (where permitted) unilateral declarations between W and H as to the character of the above elements.

W and H are still married.

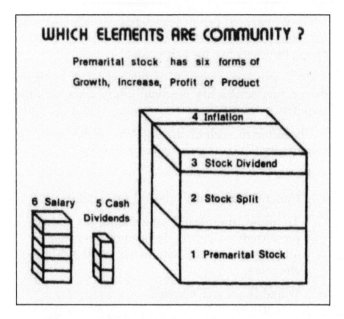

1. SP: The 100 shares of stock W owned before marriage are W's separate property.

2. SP: The 2-for-1 stock split is a "mere" change in form. Although the additional 100 shares are received during marriage, the additional 100 shares trace back to the original 100 shares of stock, which are separate property in character. Thus, the additional 100 shares of ABC Corp. stock are W's separate property.

3. SP: The stock dividend looks more like an income item (especially when cash dividends alternate with it), but stock dividends tend to be classified as a change in form rather than as rents, issues, or profits. Thus, the additional 10 shares that make up the stock

dividend trace back to W's separate property, making them separate property.

4. SP: The increase due to inflation is not a change in form. The principle is that a change in value does not alter the character of the property. The value of the shares fluctuate from market day to market day, but any fluctuation does not change the separate property character of the underlying shares. Thus W continues to own 210 shares of ABC Corp. stock as her separate property.

5. CHARACTERIZATION DEPENDS ON THE JURISDICTION: Cash dividends, once distributed, fall within the definition of rents, issues, and profits. Here, the income producing asset is W's separate property. In the American rule majority (Arizona, California, Nevada, New Mexico, and Washington), the cash dividends are the separate property income of W's 210 separate property shares of ABC Corp. stock; as such the dividends are characterized as W's separate property. In the minority civil law states (Idaho, Louisiana, Texas and Wisconsin) the cash dividends, although derived from W's separate property, are characterized as community property during the marriage.

6. CP: In all the community property states, income earned from any onerous source (salary, wages, tips, barter) is community property if acquired during the marriage while domiciled in the state.

7. COMMINGLED: In all community property states, deferred earnings, including pension rights, are community property if earned during marriage.

Here, because W was employed by ABC Corp. before and during marriage, her pension benefits are commingled and subject to apportionment. Apportionment will likely follow the time rule: W's separate property share of ABC Corp. pension benefits will be calculated by dividing the number of years W was employed before marriage by the total number of years she was employed by ABC Corp. The community property share of W's pension benefits will be calculated by dividing the number of years W was employed during marriage by the total number of years W was employed by ABC Corp. See Chapter 6.

8. CHARACTERIZATION DEPENDS ON THE JURISDICTION: In some states, W's personal injury settlement is her separate property. In other states, because the cause of action arose during the marriage and was obtained during the marriage, the personal injury settlement is community property. Among the former group of states, adjustments may be made for any part of the recovery that compensates for loss of income. Among the latter group of states, some may deem W's personal injury recovery a special type of community property for how it is subject to a mandatory assignment rule in the event of dissolution.

# CHAPTER 5

# JOINT TENANCY MEETS COMMUNITY PROPERTY

## A. OVERVIEW

Common law concurrent title forms—specifically the *joint tenancy with the right of survivorship* and the *tenancy in common*—are not part of the community property system. Even so, married persons in most U.S. community property states are not precluded from using either of these title forms.

Of specific interest is what happens when a marriage ends by dissolution or death, and the spouses own property that is titled in a common law joint title form.

But first, here is an inventory of concurrent title forms—also called joint form titles—and their origin.

## 1. TYPES OF JOINT FORM TITLES

**Concurrent titles and their origin:**

| Tenancy in common [TIC] | Common law origin |
|---|---|
| Joint tenancy [JTWROS] | Common law origin |
| Tenancy by the entirety [TBE] | Common law origin |
| Community property [CP] | Civil law origin |
| Community property with the right of survivorship [CPWROS] | A contemporary hybrid title |
| Homestead right [HR] | Texas community property origin |

### a. Tenancy in Common

*Tenancy in common* (TIC for short) is the default concurrent title form for real estate.

A TIC allows two or more persons—referred to herein as "joint tenants" or "tenants"—to own property together while still continuing to retain individual rights of devise and succession as to the titled asset. With a TIC, if one tenant dies his or her proportional share of the titled asset passes by devise or intestate succession.

*Illustration 5.1:* H and W acquire title to Blackacre during marriage in fee simple absolute as tenants in common (TIC). H devises Blackacre to C. Assume H dies before W. Upon H's death, H's one-half interest in Blackacre passes through H's estate to C. The consequence is that C and W own Blackacre as tenants in common.

### b. Joint Tenancy with the Right of Survivorship

*Joint tenancy with the right of survivorship* (JTWROS for short) is the opt-in common law concurrent title form for real estate.

A JTWROS allows two or more persons to concurrently own property under an agreement that each will waive his or her testamentary rights to the asset in exchange for a guaranteed right of survivorship.

The tenants' agreement is recited in the deed itself with whatever language the state law deems operative. In addition, the common law requires four unities be met in order to create the JTWROS: the unity of (1) time, (2) title, (3) interest, and (4) possession. Some states, like California, allow unilateral creation of the JTWROS; this rule relaxes the unity of time element by how it permits a sole owner to convey property she already owns to herself and another as JTWROS.

Assume two persons acquire property during marriage to each other. When the first joint tenant dies, his or her interest in the joint tenancy asset is removed. In the language of the common law, the deceased tenant's interest "vanishes," leaving the surviving tenant to step into ownership of the whole free of claims of the decedent's estate or heirs.

*Illustration 5.2:* H and W acquire Blackacre during marriage in fee simple absolute as JTWROS. Assume H dies before W. At H's death, H's interest is removed (it vanishes, in the language of the common law), and W becomes the sole owner of Blackacre by right of survivorship. As to Blackacre, H's estate or heirs have no claim against W for ownership of the property.

## c. Tenancy by the Entirety

*Tenancy by the entirety* (TBE for short) refers to a common law marital title form. The TBE is a unitary title, meaning that it is not a concurrent title with two owners, but rather a single title owned by the marital entity. The TBE can only be created in roughly half of the common law (separate property) marital property states, and then only by those married couples who opt into it.

Five unities are required to create a TBE: The unity of (1) title, (2) time, (3) interest, (4) possession, and (5) marriage.

A TBE cannot be created in any of the community property jurisdictions. However, once validly created in a state that allows its use, a TBE may be recognized as valid in the community property state, depending on countervailing state policies that protect creditors' rights.

The Texas homestead, discussed below, has been likened to a TBE because it (too) requires five unities. The Texas homestead is not a common law interest so much as it is a distinct interest created by the Texas Constitution.

### d. Community Property

*Community property* is a community property system default title form. The use of the *community property* title (CP title for short) is restricted to married persons (and, in some community property states, to registered domestic partners) who are domiciled in the state when the titled asset is acquired. With the traditional CP title, both spouses own the asset during their lifetimes; and at the death of one spouse, his or her one-half interest passes by devise or intestate succession.

*Illustration 5.3:* H and W are married and domiciled in a community property state. They acquire Blackacre (wherever situated) in fee simple absolute using a CP title. H later devises his CP title interest in Blackacre to a third party, D. Assume H dies before

W. Upon H's death, H's one-half CP interest in Blackacre passes to D. The consequence is that D and W own Blackacre in fee simple absolute, not in a CP title (since W and D are not married), but as tenants in common (TIC). (Spousal and family protections may delay D's rights to seek partition of the property.)

Only persons who are married to each other can use the CP title form.

### e. Community Property with the Right of Survivorship

*Community property with the right of survivorship* title (CPWROS for short) is restricted to those community property states that permit its creation by statute, and (within those states) to married couples and (in some states) registered domestic partners. See for example Cal.Civ.Code § 682.1.

The CPWROS is a hybrid title form insofar as it applies the right of survivorship to the traditional CP title. CPWROS allows spouses to waive testamentary rights with respect to the titled asset in exchange for a right of survivorship. At death, the property is characterized as community property, but the decedent spouse's interest vanishes, leaving the surviving spouse to step into ownership of the whole.

*Illustration 5.4:* H and W are married and domiciled in a community property state. They acquire title to Blackacre in fee simple absolute using a CPWROS title. Assume H dies before W. At H's death, H's interest is removed (it vanishes) and W becomes the sole owner of Blackacre by right of survivorship. W takes outside of probate, free of the claims of H's estate and heirs.

## f.  Homestead Rights

A *homestead right* allows a spouse to exempt certain property from forced sale for the payment of the other spouse's debts, typically those debts not related to a purchase money mortgage, taxes and some contractors liens.

Texas, Idaho, and Nevada create a homestead between the spouses from community property (or possibly even from the separate property).

Texas, by state constitutional provision, gives the surviving spouse the right to establish a homestead in community or (even) in separate property. The homestead right is a vested property right, not just a personal exemption, and as such its duration can be for the lifetime of the spouse who claims the exemption.

Tex. Const. Art XVI, § 16 states the parameters of the homestead right. Interpretive Commentary explains the purpose of the homestead right as being to preserve the integrity of the family as the basic unit of society; to provide the family with a home notwithstanding certain debts; and to allow "pioneers a sense of freedom and independence." *Id.*

The first Texas homestead exemption was passed with no debate in 1839. But the creditors' lobby quickly took notice and annulled the exemption in February 1840. By December 1840 the exemption was reenacted. When Texas was annexed by the U.S., the constitutional convention enshrined the homestead in the state's Constitution of 1845, Art. VII, § 22 (42 votes in favor; 14 votes against) to protect it from the vagaries of state politics.

Other states, like California, do not enshrine a homestead right in the state constitution. Instead, married couples can opt into one of the two available right of survivorship title forms (the JTWROS or the CPRWOS) if they want a titled asset to pass immediately on death to a spouse. California is a lien theory state, so the surviving spouse must assume any purchase money loans and taxes owed on exempt property, but otherwise the surviving spouse is statutorily protected from the decedent spouse's probate creditors because they cannot reach non-probate property, meaning property that passes by survivorship. All of the community property states employ probate code family protections that could be labeled homestead rights; however, most state protections are statutory, not constitutional (as in Texas).

Wisconsin, by statute, authorizes something similar to the Texas homestead right. Wisconsin calls its family protection survivorship marital property.

## 2. COMMON LAW CONCURRENT TITLES IN A COMMUNITY PROPERTY SYSTEM

Joint titles are the point at which the common law system routinely gets overlaid onto the community property system.

It is not uncommon for married persons to hold property using common law concurrent titles (the TIC and the JTWROS, assuming JTWROS title creation is permitted in the jurisdiction), or some combination thereof. (In fact, in vertically developed urban areas, like San Francisco, one building may be held in various forms of joint titles and sole titles, as supplemented by contracts).

Still, as discussed above, TIC and JTWROS have their historical origin in the English common law system, meaning that they are outside of any community property system. Technically, this makes these two common law concurrent titles separate in character.

The CP title form, by contrast, has its historical origin in the continental European community property system.

States have attempted to close the conceptual gap between the common law concurrent and community property title forms in at least four ways. The first is to enable married persons to use CPWROS. The second is to enable a special community property presumption that characterizes common law joint form titles as community property for purposes of a dissolution proceeding, a probate proceeding, or both. The third is to treat joint form titles (and especially the JTWROS) as community property in character absent evidence of a contrary intent. The fourth is to make it more difficult to effect a valid JTWROS, thus steering married property owners to the CP title form.

Most major assets like realty, stock certificates, automobiles and boats, have documents of title. Spouses commonly hold assets in joint form title, whether by deed, registration, or even by the will of a third party testator. Document recitals may be prima facie evidence of an agreement between the spouses to hold the property subject to a right of survivorship for purposes of death. But document recitals do not necessarily reflect that spouses' expectations as to the character of the titled asset in the event of dissolution.

Consider these scenarios.

- The spouses take title as JTWROS in order to avoid probate if one of them dies. But they are uninformed or misinformed as to how the title might function if the marriage ends by divorce.

- The spouses take title as JTWROS in order to avoid probate if one of them dies. But they have conflicting hidden intentions about what the character of the property should be if the marriage ends by divorce.

- The spouses take nominal title as JTWROS. But they believe the property is owned by one spouse because the other spouse is merely an agent.

The joint bank account, while not a true JTWROS can create additional problems.

- Community wealth flows to and through bank accounts, with each spouse being able to move sums on deposit.

- Sums on deposit in bank accounts are easily commingled.

- Assets are sometimes purchased with sums on deposit from bank accounts.

- A valid will could contradict the bank signature card instructions.

- The joint safe-deposit box signature card in some cases also may raise questions about the community or separate character of any property, but especially of untitled property (rings, heirlooms), stored in a jointly accessed safe-deposit box. This happens, for example, when a joint rental agreement declares that the box *and its contents* are held in "joint tenancy."

## B.   DETAIL

### 1.   PREVALENCE OF THE JOINT TENANCY TITLE FORM

With an expensive trust, parties can avoid the cost, delay, publicity, and inconvenience of probate administration with respect to the assets held in the trust. For relatively little expense, a JTWROS title can serve the same purpose of avoiding probate, but only as to the titled asset. For that reason, a JTWROS is considered a useful, albeit limited, estate planning tool.

In the typical situation, the family home is the married couple's single most valuable asset. Most often that asset has been purchased with a purchase money loan that is being repaid during marriage with community property earnings. Because of the importance of the asset to the family, the couple may be given to understand that they should take title to the asset in both of their names, "in case one of them dies." Their intentions are that if the marriage should terminate by the death of a spouse, the titled asset will fall outside of the decedent spouse's probate estate.

Normally the legal and tax ramifications of the choice between the JTWROS and CP title forms are not apparent to the parties at the time of the transaction, a time when they are married and (obviously) still alive. The ramifications (only) become clear later in time, if and when the marriage ends.

If the marriage ends by dissolution the issue will be whether the JTWROS asset is community or separate in character. One would assume that the value of the asset would be equally split between the spouses, but whether equal division is by default depends on state law. But take a state like Arizona: if the asset is deemed community in character, equitable division prevails; if it is deemed separate property JTWROS, equal division is the rule; and if the asset has been deemed to have defaulted to a TIC, ownership would be by pro rata contributions to purchase. Additionally, a JTWROS could raise management and control issues, as well as, in some states, questions about the family court's jurisdiction to partition the asset.

## 2.  JOINT TENANCY COMPARED
## WITH COMMUNITY PROPERTY

JTWROS, TIC, CP title and CPWROS may be regarded as distinct in a community property state for one purpose or another.

Some states, like California, give married couples the option to choose between JTWROS, TIC, CP title, or CPWROS for purposes of disposition at death. Other states, like Washington, use doctrinal crossover methods by which the severed JTWROS of two married persons defaults to CP title rather than to TIC (as was the case under the traditional common law).

Arizona, California, Idaho, Nevada, Washington permit the CPWROS title form or its equivalent if the spouses expressly opt into it. Wisconsin, with its concept of survivorship marital property, is the exception to the opt-in rule. Only the use of CPWROS or survivorship marital property makes clear that the spouses acquired the asset with the intention (i) that it be characterized as community at dissolution or death and (ii) that the survivor be guaranteed ownership of the whole by right of survivorship. Texas uses the homestead right to exempt property from the reach of the decedent spouse's conveyees and general creditors.

Moreover, on its face, a JTWROS recital in a deed may be interpreted to indicate that the spouses opted *for* the JTWROS form and *against* the (traditional) CP title form. But the face of a deed and the parties' intentions as to why they decided to use one deed form at Time 1 may be remembered quite differently at Time 2. For that reason, some states (Idaho) place very little trust in using deed recitation language as the basis for a default rule.

*At dissolution* a community property state can express and recognize a strong public policy interest in furthering equity between the spouses. If so, the state can enact rules to treat common law joint titles—the JTWROS and the TIC—as community in character for purposes of the *dissolution* proceeding.

*At the death of a spouse* a JTWROS recital better captures the parties' expectations if what the parties agreed to by taking title as JTWROS was that the survivor would take ownership by right of survivorship at the death of the first to die. (The non-hybrid traditional CP title does not transfer by right of survivorship.) Therefore the historical tendency has been to interpret JTWROS recitals as separate in character. This leaves it to the community property proponent to prove that notwithstanding the separate character of the JTWROS deed, the parties transmuted the asset from separate to community property. Transmutation formalities apply, meaning that any alleged rebuttal agreement would have to comply with the state transmutation rules, as discussed in Chapter 2.

But if the surviving spouse steps into ownership of the whole at the other spouse's death, what else would motivate a surviving spouse to argue that a JTWROS should be community in character?

One answer has to do with income tax valuation.

When a marriage ends by the death of a spouse, the surviving spouse may eventually sell the titled asset. The Internal Revenue Service rules for calculating the basis of an asset in the decedent's gross estate work out so that a JTWROS asset produces more income tax liability for the surviving spouse than does a CP titled asset. See Illustration 5.5 and 5.6 below.

Among the contexts in which there is a heightened risk of litigation over the characterization of a joint form titles are the following:

## a. Dissolution Proceedings

If state law allows a court to award the separate property of one party to the other; or if state law provides that the division of community property upon divorce shall be "equal" (50–50); or if fault has been eliminated as a basis for the apportionment or division of spouses' property, then whether a particular item is concurrently held separate property or community property is relatively less pressing than it is in states where the court does not have jurisdiction over JTWROS (on the basis of it being technically separate property character).

## b. Severance

A JTWROS can be severed (terminated) by one spouse who acts alone. Severing the JTWROS cancels the right of survivorship, but it does not necessarily end the concurrent ownership between the spouses unless the severance is by conveyance to a third party.

If one spouse severs a JTWROS title by conveying his or her interest to him or herself (through a straw person or directly if permitted by state law), then the two spouses continue on as concurrent owners, but without the right of survivorship. The severance means that the title form defaults to TIC, in most states. Or, as in Washington, to CP title. See Section C, Washington, Wash.Rev.Code § 64.28.040.

Severance is, therefore, consequential for how it restores each spouse's rights of devise and descent as to the titled asset.

## c. Probate Law Interaction

A salient difference between the four concurrent title forms becomes clear when a marriage ends by the death of one of the spouses.

Assets titled as JTWROS and CPWROS are owned by the surviving spouse without being subject to probate administration. For these titles, the right of survivorship ensures as much.

Assets titled in TIC or CP title are subject to the whole of probate administration unless a probate code statute provides the surviving spouse with an exception or exemption.

Probate assets are subject to the claims of the decedent spouse's creditors, beneficiaries, and nonspousal heirs.

## d. Tax Consequences of a Sale After Death

Another salient distinction between the types of joint form titles pertains to how the character of property owned by the first spouse to die can affect the income tax liability of the surviving spouse who sells the property.

Generally, the gain from the sale of property is computed by subtracting the seller's basis from the amount realized in the sale. I.R.C. § 1001. When property is acquired by a surviving spouse (the income taxpayer) from a decedent spouse, the taxpayer's adjusted basis in the property is **"the fair market value of the property at the date of the decedent's death."** 1. I.R.C. §§ 1014(a) and 1014(b)(6).

For the taxpayer, if his or her spouse holds JTWROS titles at death, those properties are subject to inclusion in the decedent's gross estate. The taxpayer "acquires" that property from the decedent only to the extent that the JTWROS property is included in the decedent's gross estate. As set forth in I.R.C. § 2040, the taxpayer's basis is equal to what the decedent claimed on the estate tax return. I.R.C. § 2040 labels a joint tenancy title where the decedent and the spouse are the only joint tenants, as a qualified joint interest. It further specifies that the value included in the gross estate for that property **"is one-half the value of the qualified joint interest."** *Id.* This means that the taxpayer is entitled to one-half of the fair market value of the qualified joint interest (the JTWROS) property as an adjusted basis in the property.

*Illustration 5.5:* During marriage B and C purchased a house for $100,000; they took title as JTWROS (Time 1). When B died the fair market value of the house was $500,000 (Time 2). Assume that at B's death, the house is characterized as concurrently owned separate property. Since the JTWROS is one in which B and spouse C were the only joint tenants, it meets the definition of a qualified joint interest under the I.R.C. 2040 (Time 3). In consequence of Time 1, Time 2, and Time 3, one-half of the house falls into the decedent's gross estate and gets a step-up in basis to $250,000 for B's federal estate tax purposes; and C is deemed to have acquired B's one-half interest by a transfer from B's estate. (Time 4). Assume C, in the same tax year, sells the house for $500,000 (Time 5). How much of a gain would the surviving spouse realize at the sale of the house for purposes of income tax liability?

The answer is $250,000.

To answer this question, (i) characterize the house, (ii) determine the step-up in basis, and (iii) calculate the taxpayer's gain when the house is sold.

- The house was purchased during marriage but titled in JTWROS (Time 1).

- At B's death the JTWROS was characterized as separate property (Time 2).

- The taxpayer acquired a one-half interest in the house ($250,000) by transfer from decedent's estate (Time 3).

- The taxpayer's basis is the other half ($250,000) of the $500,000 house that the taxpayer already owned as a joint tenant during the decedent's life (Time 4).

- The seller's gain from the sale of property is computed by subtracting the taxpayer's basis ($250,000) from the amount realized in the sale ($500,000). Using this I.R.C. formula, the taxpayer's gain is $250,000 of taxable income as a result of the sale, in the year of the sale. (Time 5).

What if the house had been held in CP or CPWROS title at the death of the first spouse to die? Or, what if the jurisdiction is one that treats JTWROS as community property? Would the surviving spouse have realized the same gain at the sale of the house for purposes of income tax liability?

*Illustration 5.6:* During marriage B and C purchased a house for $100,000; they took title in CP (Time 1). When B died the fair market value of the house was $500,000 (Time 2). Assume that the house is characterized as community property. The decedent's interest in the house, because it is community in character, is not included in the decedent's gross estate for federal estate tax purposes (Time 3). The rationale is that I.R.C. § 2056 contemplates that the house will be taxed when the surviving spouse dies. How much of a gain does the surviving spouse realize from the sale of the house in CP title for purposes of income tax liability?

The answer is $0.

- The house was purchased during marriage and titled in CP (Time 1).

- At B's death the house was characterized as a community property (Time 2).

- The taxpayer acquired no value from the decedent since the community property house was not included in the decedent's gross estate (Time 3).

- The taxpayer's basis is $500,000, the value of the house at B's death (Time 4).

- The taxpayer's gain from the sale of property is computed by subtracting the taxpayer's basis ($500,000) from the amount realized in the sale ($500,000). This leaves C with $0 of gain as a result of the sale, in the year of the sale.

Key differences between the JTWROS and the CP titles:

- A JTWROS title is includable in the gross estate of the decedent, the CP title is not. I.R.C. § 2040.

- Because the JTWROS was only between the spouses, one-half of the value of the house is included in the decedent's gross estate by federal statute. The surviving spouse acquires that one-half value from the decedent as a transfer. I.R.C. § 2040.

- A CP title is not includable in the decedent's gross estate and thus is not used to calculate the value of a transfer from the decedent to the surviving spouse. I.R.C. § 2040.

• The marital deduction was passed to address tax differences between JTWROS and CP.

To sum up, if the property in question is held as JTWROS, it may be deemed separate in character at the death of the first spouse to die, depending on state law. If property is held in CP title, it is community in character at the death of the first spouse to die.

Spouses who want the right of survivorship feature of the JTWROS with the federal estate and income tax savings feature of the CP title, can use a CPWROS, if allowed in the community property state where they are domiciled.

The above illustrations are intended to make a simple point: in the event of one spouse's death, different title forms may have unintended income tax consequences for the surviving spouse who must sell the property.

To address such consequences, at least one state— New Mexico—extends its statutory joint title form community property presumption to probate proceedings. Other states heighten JTWROS creation requirements so as to steer married persons toward using CP title. But in most states, the title of property at the death of a spouse determines its character, with JTWROS and TIC characterized as the decedent spouse's separate property absent evidence to the contrary.

## 3. CREATING THE JOINT TENANCY

JTWROS is an opt-in title form for real estate. For that reason the intention to create a JTWROS must be evident if not expressly stated in the conveyance (deed or will) by which the title is taken.

But what kind of language indicates an express statement that property be held as JTWROS?

### a. "Joint"

The word "joint" in a title document, without more, is insufficient to create a JTWROS.

The legal rationale is that the word "joint" is too general a word to capture the parties' agreement to waive rights of devise and succession as to the titled asset. Occasionally, courts will accept the word "joint" when used by a non-lawyer, but some supportive evidence that the parties' intended to create a JTWROS (or at least no contradictory evidence) also may be required.

### b. "Joint Tenancy"

Seemingly, the clearest minimum language recitation needed to create a JTWROS is the term "joint tenancy." California, for example, requires that a "joint tenancy" be expressly declared as such in the deed or will that creates it; but California law does not also require that the election "with a right of survivorship" be explicitly spelled out in the title document. Cal.Civ.Code § 683.

## c. "Joint Tenancy with the Right of Survivorship"

Texas requires that the right of survivorship (which is the main incident of the JTWROS) be spelled out in the conveyance (deed or will). Other formalities also apply.

## d. Deed Declarations and Extrinsic Evidence to Hold the Property as Separate Property

In some states, deed declarations of "joint tenancy" or "joint tenancy with the right of survivorship" are enough to create the JTWROS title.

But in other jurisdictions, a JTWROS cannot be created merely by recitations in a deed. Additional extrinsic formalities must be met, as in Texas and Washington. The legal rationale for such an outcome is that a title document is not reliable enough to indicate whether the spouses reached a specific agreement as to the character of the titled asset.

### 4.  THE SPECIAL JOINT FORM TITLE COMMUNITY PROPERTY PRESUMPTION

Prior to the mid-1980s, courts in community property states analyzed on a case-by-case basis the parties' intentions and expectations in choosing one joint form title form over another. The result was inconsistent precedents.

The problem (very simply stated) took this form: The couple used community property funds to purchase property that they then titled in JTWROS. Under general common law principles, the title form presumptively controlled its character; and thus rebuttal rested with the joint tenant—in this case the community property proponent—to show that the actual title was of a different character (community) notwithstanding the JTWROS title form. The historical rationale for placing the burden on the community property proponent was that community property purchase funds had been transmuted into separate property via the JTWROS deed. Additionally, the deed was said to represent a "first agreement" between the spouses to characterize the property as separate. The "first agreement" could be altered, but only by a subsequent agreement between the spouses. Such an agreement (the so called "second agreement") would need to specify that notwithstanding the use of a separate property title form (the first agreement) the property was to be community property in character.

In the pre-1980 era of easy transmutation, an oral or implied second agreement was sufficient to rebut the JTWROS title document. Agreement was defined as a bilateral communication between the spouses. An unexpressed belief ("I thought the house was 'ours' "), a unilaterally stated belief ("I often said that the house was 'ours' "), or a misunderstanding ("I thought that JTWROS was the same as community property") were not sufficient to prove that the parties replaced the first agreement (declared in the deed itself) with a subsequent contradictory agreement.

Today, easy transmutation is no longer the trend: Transmutations must be in writing. Some states require an express declaration by the adversely affected spouse. Plus, transmutations are scrutinized for voluntariness and the absence of unconscionability, as discussed in Chapter 2.

Nearly every community property jurisdiction has adopted an approach that works to characterize property acquired under *any* joint form title as community for purposes of a dissolution proceeding. (Among the U.S. community property states that permit joint tenancy titles, Nevada is the only holdout.) The rebuttal burden shifts to the separate property proponent to show a subsequent inconsistent agreement that the parties intended to characterize the property as separate in whole or part.

Some states allow the second (rebuttal) agreement to be established either by a clear statement in the title document or by an extrinsic agreement. Other states allow rebuttal by a broader range of evidence, including circumstantial evidence like tracing. Either way, the policy goal is to further the state's interest in equitable *and* consistent dissolution outcomes.

California explicitly asserts that its interest in the application of a special joint form title community property presumption is a compelling one. Cal.Fam.Code § 2581 further provides that an asset acquired during marriage in *any* joint title form (JTWROS, TIC, CP, or CPWROS) with funds of *either* character (community or separate) is presumptively community in a dissolution proceeding. Rebuttal rests with the separate property claimant. The range of rebuttal evidence is set forth (and thus limited) by statute. Additionally, rebuttal evidence is subject to other statutory tests for the absence of unconscionability and voluntariness.

*Illustration 5.7:* During marriage, H and W buy a house in California. They take title to the house as JTWROS. No other agreements are made between H and W as to the house. When H and W file for dissolution, what is the character of the house? Here, the house is presumptively community property by application of Cal.Fam.Code § 2581.

*Illustration 5.8:* Same facts as in Illustration 5.7 except that at purchase H and W also sign a written agreement (extrinsic to the deed) stating that H intends to keep a fifty-percent separate property interest in the house to reflect the percentage of H's separate property contribution to purchase. At dissolution, the community property presumption is raised by the joint form deed (the "first agreement"). H, as the separate property claimant, has the burden to rebut that presumption. H can do so by producing the subsequent contradictory agreement (the "second agreement"). Assuming the second agreement is enforceable, it will control the characterization of the house for purposes of the dissolution.

If the separate property contributor (i) cannot produce a rebuttal agreement and (ii) is also barred from tracing to separate property funds, then the separate property contributor can request a reimbursement. In some states, California again being the example, reimbursement is by statutory right, but it is without interest, payable upon partition, and limited by depreciation. (Not all community property states allow a statutory reimbursement in these circumstances.)

*Illustration 5.9:* During marriage, H and W buy a house in California for $100,000. They use $50,000 of community property and $50,000 of W's provable separate property funds to buy the house. H and W take title as JTWROS. They reach no other agreements about the character of the house. When H and W petition for dissolution, they sell the house for $500,000. By application of the statutory joint form title community property presumption the house is *entirely* (100%) community property in character. But W is statutorily entitled to a reimbursement of $50,000, without interest. At the sale of the house, the reimbursement to W must be paid off the top: $500,000 − $50,000 = $450,000. The remaining $450,000 is entirely community property, to be split equally ($225,000 − $225,000) between H and W.

Distinguishing between basis and appreciation is discussed further in Chapter 6.

*Illustration 5.10:* During marriage, H and W buy a house in California for $100,000. They use $50,000 of community property and $50,000 of W's provable separate property. They take title as joint tenants. At that time, W and H also sign a written agreement that W will keep a 50% separate property ownership interest in the house in the event of dissolution. When H and W dissolve their marriage, they sell the house for $500,000. The house is presumptively community property by application of the statutory community property presumption. But now W can rebut the presumption by producing the second agreement, which establishes that the house is concurrently owned by the community property estate (50%) and by W's separate property estate (50%). Note that the second rebuttal agreement controls pro rata shares of ownership. Moreover, because the terms of the rebuttal agreement mirror the actual net character contributions to purchase, no transmutation has occurred. The house is owned one-half by the community and one-half by W's separate property estate.

Chapter 6 covers these issues further.

## 5. NOMINAL TITLE, "FOR CONVENIENCE"

Why would a married couple specify "joint tenancy" if they did not intend to transmute their community property into separate property? Popular explanations include

- Statements that the form of title was "nominal," i.e., in name only. (The adhesion character of financial institution forms and practices makes such explanations reasonable.)

- The joint tenancy account was really intended as an agency account on which the names of both parties were listed "for convenience only."

These arguments have a reasonable ring and are often accepted by courts. The trier of fact has the last word in making such determinations. The trier is called upon to exercise its discretion based upon the often self-serving oral testimony of the parties (or one of them) that they intended exactly the opposite of what they previously signed a formal document saying they intended.

The "convenience" explanation is often used with nonspousal joint tenancies to indicate that the original depositor of the funds in a joint bank account did not intend to create a form of concurrent ownership, but only intended to create an agency so that the second person could withdraw the sums on deposit in the account for the benefit of the first person.

## 6. JOINT BANK ACCOUNTS

In many jurisdictions, special statutory rules exist for deposits of money in financial institutions, as discussed in Chapter 3. Although the term "bank account" is used in this book, each jurisdiction has a number of differing financial devices ("accounts," "shares," "certificates of deposit" and "money market certificates) and institutions (savings banks, credit unions, brokerage firms, whether brick-and-mortar or on-line). Precision is required in practice to determine which type of device, in which type of institution, is dealt with by a particular statute. Often a state will have two or more statutes dealing with "joint" bank accounts, as that term is used here.

For married persons, a "joint" bank account is created when the parties open an account in both of their names. A joint bank account can also be created when one spouse "adds" the other's name to a pre-existing account. Financial institutions generally have detailed provisions on preprinted cards or on-line forms that the parties must complete in order to open or modify a bank account. Generally, these forms are very specific in their "agreement" that the account is to be JTWROS and, more to the point, that either signatory has the contractual right to withdraw sums on deposit in the account in full and on demand during his or her life or upon death (as determined by a beneficial designation or a disposition).

Despite the bank signature card contract verbiage, bank accounts do not fall within traditional definitions of JTWROS. This is because of the statutory abrogation of the requirement of the four unities of time, title, interest, and possession. That is, in the context of a joint bank account, the parties (here we are assuming spouses) have full access to the joint bank account during their lives; this means that the bank can (without liability for misdelivery of funds) honor a request by either party, acting alone, to withdraw all of the sums on deposit from the account. Depending on the net character of the sums on deposit in the account, an excess withdrawal is conceptually contrary to the usual JTWROS rule that a joint tenant can, at severance, affect only his or her proportionate share of the total.

In the context of marriage, even join bank accounts predictably give rise to tracing issues because many acquisitions can be traced to or through a bank account. If the account is *un*commingled, then an asset purchased from the account takes on the character of sums on deposit that were used to make the purchase.

But what if the account is commingled?

If we assume that community property sums on deposit in a joint bank account are sufficient to make the purchase on the date in question, then even if separate property sums on deposit are (i) provable on the date of the purchase and (ii) sufficient to make the purchase, that purchase should be characterized as presumptively community in character, with rebuttal determined by state law.

Chapter 6 covers the characterization of accounts, sums on deposit in an account, and purchases made from commingled accounts.

## 7.   JOINT SAFE-DEPOSIT BOXES

Safe-deposit box agreements sometimes declare that all contents of the safe deposit box shall be joint tenancy between the co-tenants of the box. Such a declaration, if intended, can be binding upon the parties in the absence of a statute providing otherwise (such as exists in California or Nevada).

If one spouse predeceases the other, the legal issue becomes whether the joint tenancy rental agreement is sufficiently clear, specific, or fair enough to transmute the character of each and every community property asset or title stored in the box. In most states, the title to a safe-deposit box does not determine the title to the assets and titles stored in the box. However, control and possession can raise significant questions as to the disposition of an untitled asset in the box.

Even in the era of easy transmutation, reconciling a conflict between a safe-deposit signature card and a document in the safe-deposit box was uncertain, especially if the document was registered in the name of one or both spouses in a form of ownership other than joint tenancy, e.g., community property. The issue for courts in those cases was whether the safe-deposit signature card should prevail over the express registration of the particular asset.

In the era of formal transmutation, each asset, in theory, should be characterized independently. In other words, the simple act of placing an asset in a safe deposit box, should not effect a transmutation of the asset; nor should it create an exception to an asset-by-asset characterization rule. The best practice is to hold that a safe-deposit box signature card is not a title-changing transmutation with respect to the particular assets in the safe-deposit box unless it meets transmutation formalities.

If a deed or stock certificate is registered in one name but located within a safe-deposit box whose safe-deposit signature card declares that all contents of the box shall be joint tenancy, then the battle of paperwork probably should be resolved in favor of the express statement of title that is relatively more specific, i.e., the stock certificates rather than the safe-deposit box agreement.

Another method of resolving conflicting paper titles is to give effect to the later in time document. Formal transmutation rules diminish legal uncertainty in these cases.

## 8.   SUMMING UP: JOINT FORM TITLES AT DISSOLUTION AND DEATH

There are four concurrent title forms. They are the TIC, the JTWROS, the CP title and the CPWROS. The problem that JTWROS and TIC can cause in a community property system stems from the fact that those titles have their origin in the English common law, as such they are technically separate in character.

For purposes of a dissolution proceeding, most community property states presume or else treat property acquired during marriage in any joint title form as community in character. The special joint form title presumption allows for consistent dissolution judgments; so too does a rule that treats, rather than that evidentiarily presumes, all joint form titles as if they were CP titles. Both allow the parties and their advisors to better plan how to use a particular joint form title for a particular purpose (dissolution or death, probate avoidance or tax liability, and so forth).

## C.  INDIVIDUAL STATES

### 1.  ARIZONA

Under general law, the TIC is the default concurrent title for real estate, but parties can create a JTWROS by **"express words** [that] **vest the estate in the survivor on the death of a grantee or devisee."** Ariz.Rev.Stat.Ann. § 33–431(A) and (B).

Ariz.Rev.Stat.Ann. § 33–431(C) permits, in any deed recorded from or after December 31, 1994, the creation of **"[c]ommunity property with right of survivorship."** Spouses must opt into this title form with **"express words** [that] **vest the estate in the surviving spouse on the death of one of the spouses."**

Key to understanding joint tenancy title in particular is the inception of title rule. In Arizona, although the "marital rights" of married persons who move to Arizona are governed by Arizona law (see Ariz.Rev.Stat.Ann. § 25–217 discussed in Chapter 3), their "property rights" may ultimately be governed by another state's law. True, Arizona law employs a quasi-community property principle, but case law routinely applies the inception of title rule along with the tracing principle to analyze whether property acquired while domiciled in another state does or does not falls within the Arizona community property principle.

As a touch point, property acquired during marriage while domiciled in Arizona with Arizona community property labor or earnings is clearly Arizona community property. But property acquired otherwise may give rise to a characterization dispute. For Arizona community property, partition of the joint titles of parties who file a petition for dissolution in Arizona is equitable without regard to fault as set forth in Ariz.Rev.Stat.Ann. § 25–318(A): "**In a proceeding for dissolution of the marriage, or for legal separation ... [the court] shall assign each spouse's sole and separate property to such spouse. It shall also divide the *community*, joint tenancy and other property held in common equitably, though not necessarily in kind, without regard to marital misconduct.**" (Italics added.)

Implied in this language is the possibility, in the context of dissolution, that there exist joint tenancy titles that are separate in character (*separate* joint tenancy and other property held in common equitably) and those that are community in character (*community* joint tenancy and other property held in common equitably), depending on state law. These legal differences may be of consequence in the context of a dissolution proceeding for at least three reasons.

One, the difference between a community joint *tenancy* title and a separate property joint *tenancy* title is the difference between judicial discretion versus property right. Ariz.Rev.Stat.Ann. 25–318(A), above, mandates a judge to **"equitably"** divide community joint tenancy titles. The common law rules, by comparison, require that a joint tenancy title meet and maintain four unities (time, title, interest, and possession). Unity of interest means that the parties own equal shares of the property—this turns out to be simple math in the case of married joint tenants, since each spouse would, by right, own one-half of the whole. Therefore, the difference between a community joint tenancy and a separate property joint tenancy is in how each is divided at the end of the marriage. The joint tenancy characterized as community property gets an "equitable division" depending on how the judge analyzes the wide array of factors the statute allows her to consider. The joint tenancy characterized as separate property gets an "equal division" in accordance with general property doctrine.

Two, the difference between Arizona community property joint titles, more generally, and the joint titles of other community property states in the context of litigation comes down to rebuttal. Arizona follows the inception of title rule, which looks to when the original property right came into existence, not to the date the joint title was executed. If there is a discrepancy between the two dates, the inception of title rule encourages parties to produce evidence of intent as to character with respect to the earlier date.

In a dissolution proceeding, rebutting an Arizona joint title in a divorce proceeding could require an analysis of the following elements. Timing (when was the property in joint title acquired?); domicile (where did the parties live when the property was acquired?); source of funds (what is the character of the funds that contributed to the purchase of the property in the first place?)

If title was taken in joint title in a different community property state, standards for rebuttal might be more or less difficult to meet. In Arizona, for example, rebuttal turns on proof of the parties' intent, but no particular type of rebuttal evidence is required. In California, by contrast, joint form titles are presumed to be community property unless the parties can produce a clear statement in the deed or an extrinsic written agreement of a definite intent to keep a separate property interest.

Also in Arizona, *Marriage of Flower*, 223 Ariz. 531, 225 P.3d 588 (Ct. App. 2010) held that a court may consider statutory and non-statutory factors in assessing the equities of a particular case under Ariz.Rev.Stat.Ann. § 25–318. An analysis of joint title starts with the inception of title rule (what was the parties' intent as to character when the property was acquired?). From there it allows a judge to consider all other past, present, and implicitly future factors in making a decision. Relevant are factors casting light on whether the parties intended the property to be community or all or part separate in the context of a dissolution proceeding. Once these determinations are made, equitable division can ensue.

Of course, if the parties are indifferent to how the joint tenancy is ultimately characterized, then these legal differences are irrelevant to the outcome. But if the parties are in dispute, or if equitable turns out to be a far distant cry from equal, what appears to be a hair-line distinction between treating a joint title as community or separate can be material.

Three, community property not disposed of by a divorce decree is held thereafter by the parties as tenants in common. Here again, proportional ownership may become a post-dissolution issue to litigate. If one party made no significant financial contribution to the property, then the other party would have a basis upon which to argue that the noncontributor's share should be minimal.

In a dissolution proceeding, to sum up, joint titles might be divided equitably (for Arizona community property), equally (for common law joint tenancy), or according to proportional contributions to acquisition or purchase (for common law tenancy in common titles). In light of the above variations, and notwithstanding the habits of law practice, the Arizona statute is not as predictive as one might hope, especially given that Arizona has historically been a place where people choose to retire after a lifetime of working in another jurisdiction.

In the context of a marriage terminated by death, *Baldwin's Estate*, 50 Ariz. 265, 274–275, 71 P.2d 791, 795 (1937) affirms that community property is the preferred joint title form between Arizona spouses, but then recognizes that spouses domiciled in the state have a right to hold property as joint tenants with right of survivorship instead. Rebuttal occurs "only where it clearly appears that both spouses have agreed that the property should be taken [as joint tenants and not as community property]." Proof of a rebuttal is predicated on a showing that the disadvantaged spouse knew that the deed provided for a right of survivorship. Without evidence of specific knowledge concerning how the right of survivorship works, however, the mere insertion in the deed of right of survivorship language would not only defeat the community property law but also defeat the rights of the decedent's heirs.

## 2. CALIFORNIA

California permits the creation of community property with the right of survivorship when such is **"expressly declared in the transfer document . . ."** and **"[s]igned or initialed by the grantees."** Cal.Civ.Code § 682.1. The four unities are required to create a joint tenancy, but unilateral creation is also permitted by case law that relaxes the unity of time.

The creation of a joint tenancy is further permitted **"when expressly declared in the will or transfer to be a joint tenancy."** Cal.Civ.Code § 683.

As applied generally, *Riddle v. Harmon*, 102 Cal.App.3d 524, 162 Cal.Rptr. 530 (1980) permits unilateral severance of a joint tenancy. But *Riddle* was decided before the passage of Cal.Fam.Code § 2581, the special community property presumption for joint form titles obtained during marriage.

For that reason, it is likely that *Riddle*, supra, is or should be deemed superseded by statute in the case of a joint tenant who seeks to unilaterally and secretly sever a joint tenancy that he or she owns with a spouse. Plus, as part of ordinary management and control obligations, both spouses must join in any consequential transaction; arguably the severance of a right of survivorship is consequential. Spousal partnership duties set forth in Cal.Fam.Code § 721 are yet another basis for distinguishing *Riddle*, supra, in a contemporary case involving community real property. Finally, joinder (both spouses' signatures) is required for real property, even if either spouse acting alone has the right to manage and control personal property, including community sums on deposit in sole and joint bank accounts. Cal.Fam.Code § 1100(a) and Cal.Fam.Code § 1102.

Cal. Civ. Code § 683.2 counteracts *Riddle*, supra, by requiring that a deed affecting severance to a third party be recorded. Penalties apply as set forth in Cal.Civ.Code § 683.2(b), which acknowledges that a joint tenancy may be unilaterally severed, but also sets forth recording requirements to ensure that the severance is effective as to **"[t]he rights of a purchaser or encumbrancer for value in good faith and without knowledge of the written**

**agreement."** Subdivisions (a) and (b) waive joinder for purposes of severance. But those subdivisions apply to all joint tenancies in real property, not just to those that are held by married tenants. In other words, the joinder requirement in Cal.Fam.Code § 1102 is a more particular requirement than the joinder requirement in Cal.Civ.Code § 683.2, and therefore the Family Code likely supersedes the Civil Code as applied to spouses after January 1, 1985.

As explained above, an asset acquired during marriage in any joint form title is presumed to be community property in the context of a dissolution proceeding. California adopted a community property joint form title presumption in 1984. Cal.Fam.Code § 2580 and § 2581 state the policy and provide: **"For the purpose of division of property on dissolution of marriage or legal separation of the parties, property acquired by the parties during marriage in joint form, including property held in tenancy in common, joint tenancy, or tenancy by the entirety, or as community property, is presumed to be community property."** Rebuttal is by a clear statement in the title document, or by an (extrinsic written) agreement between the spouses that the titled asset is not to be community property in whole or part for purposes of a dissolution proceeding. See Chapter 3.

When a joint form title is adjudged entirely community in character, Cal.Fam.Code § 2640 applies to give a separate property contributor a reimbursement, without interest. **"Contributions to**

**the acquisition of property"** are defined under Cal.Fam.Code § 2640(a) as **"downpayments, payments for improvements, and payments that reduce the principal of a loan used to finance the purchase or improvement of the property but do not include payments of interest on the loan or payments made for maintenance, insurance, or taxation for the property."** Reimbursements are made without interest or adjustment for changes in monetary value and, under § 2640(b), **"may not exceed the net value of the property at the time of the division."**

Retroactive application of the Cal.Fam.Code § 2581 joint form community property presumption has been held to be constitutional. *Marriage of Buol*, 39 Cal.3d 751, 759, 218 Cal.Rptr. 31, 705 P.2d 354 (1985)(in bank). The rationale is that the use of an evidentiary presumption does not disturb vested property rights. Chapter 12 discusses California retroactivity.

Reimbursement under Cal.Fam.Code § 2640, on the other hand, is non-retroactive and applies only from January 1, 1984 forward. *Marriage of Heikes*, 10 Cal.4th 1211, 44 Cal.Rptr.2d 155, 899 P.2d 1349 (1995). By this case, a separate property contribution to the purchase of an entirely (100%) community property asset made before January 1, 1984 is a presumptive gift to the community under *Marriage of Lucas*, 27 Cal.3d 808, 166 Cal.Rptr. 853, 614 P.2d 285 (1980), which was superseded by Cal. Fam. Code § 2640 on this issue. That same contribution to purchase, if made on or after January 1, 1984, is a presumptive no-interest loan to the community, subject to the statutory reimbursement discussed above.

At the death of a spouse, decisional law controls such that joint form titles are characterized depending on whether they are common law title forms (JTWROS and TIC) or community property title forms (CP and CPWROS). Rebuttal is permitted.

Unique limitations on safe-deposit boxes are imposed by statute. Cal.Civ.Code § 683.1 states that safe-deposit box rental agreements shall not create a joint tenancy in the contents of the box, and **"[a]ny such contract or other arrangement purporting so to do shall be to such extent void and of no effect."**

Cal.Civ.Code § 682.1, which as discussed above permits the parties to declare a CPWROS, provides that CPWROS should be treated as JTWROS for purposes of passing property at death without the necessity of probate. Severance can be effected in the same way that severance of a JTWROS can be. However, as discussed above, spousal partnership fiduciary duties apply.

### 3.   IDAHO

In Idaho, a joint form deed is community property, unless there is clear and convincing evidence that the spouses intended to hold the property as joint tenants. Recitations in the deed itself (like for example a declaration of rights of survivorship) are not sufficient to meet the rebuttal standard. Therefore, in Idaho, the

CP title remains the default title in Idaho for married persons.

CPWROS is available to married persons who opt to use it. CPWROS can be created by grant, by transfer, or by devise to a husband and wife. See Idaho Code § 15–6–401. Divorce or annulment terminates a CPWROS per Idaho Code § 15–6–402.

### 4.   LOUISIANA

In Louisiana a joint form deed is characterized as community property. Louisiana has avoided much of the litigation concerning common law titles by disallowing the creation of the joint tenancy title form. *Winsberg v. Winsberg*, 56 So.2d 730 (La. 1952).

### 5.   NEVADA

Nev.Rev.Stat. § 111.064(2) recognizes both traditional community property and CPWROS: **"A right of survivorship does not arise when an estate in community property is created in a husband and wife, as such, unless the instrument creating the estate expressly declares that the husband and wife take the property as community property with a right of survivorship. This right of survivorship is extinguished whenever either spouse, during the marriage, transfers the spouse's interest in the community property."**

The distinction between community property and joint tenancy is highlighted by Nev.Rev.Stat. § 123.030: **"A husband and wife may hold real or**

**personal property as joint tenants, tenants in common, or as community property."**

Spouses must affirmatively opt into joint tenancy, however. The existence or non-existence of a joint tenancy must affirmatively appear in the deed per Nev.Rev.Stat. § 111.065(1), which has the effect of permitting spouse to transmute community property into joint tenancy **"[w]hen expressly declared in the transfer to be joint tenancy . . ."** Therefore, a deed reciting joint tenancy makes the titled asset concurrently held separate property unless the community property proponent proves otherwise. As to personal property, the same rule holds.

Additionally, Nev.Rev.Stat. § 111.065(2) provides: **"A joint tenancy . . . may be created by a written transfer, agreement, or instrument."** The word **"may"** was held to be mandatory in *McKissick v. McKissick*, 93 Nev. 139, 560 P.2d 1366 (1977).

Nevada recognizes a homestead (defined in Nev.Rev.Stat. § 115.010). When the homestead is declared upon community property it is deemed to be held as community property with right of survivorship, Nev.Rev.Stat. § 115.060.

### 6. NEW MEXICO

N.M.Stat.Ann. § 40–3–2 (1978) states: **"Husband and wife may hold property as joint tenants, tenants in common or as community property."**

A joint form title community property presumption was adopted in N.M.Stat.Ann. § 40–3–8(B) (1978). That presumption applies to **"[p]roperty acquired** by either or both spouses during marriage which is not separate property."

The presumption states that property "acquired by a husband and wife by an instrument in writing whether as tenants in common or as joint tenants . . . shall be presumed to be held as community property unless such property is separate property . . . ."

The New Mexico statutory presumption applies to acquisitions during marriage, but it is not on its face limited to a dissolution proceeding (as California). Plus, its application is retroactive (as in California). See *Swink v. Sunwest Bank*, 955 F.2d 31 (10th Cir. 1992) and *Swink v. Fingado*, 115 N.M. 275, 850 P.2d 978 (1993).

Additionally, N.M.Stat.Ann. § 47–1–16 (1978) does away with heightened proof requirements for the purposes of *establishing* a joint tenancy: "An instrument conveying or transferring title to real or personal property to two or more persons as joint tenants, to two or more persons and to the survivors of them and the heirs and assigns of the survivor, or to two or more persons with right of survivorship, shall be prima facie evidence that such property is held in a joint tenancy and shall be conclusive as to purchasers or encumbrancers for value. In any litigation involving the issue of such tenancy a preponderance of the evidence shall be sufficient to establish the same." Here, the preponderance of the evidence standard is used for rebuttal because the presumption effectively relates back to the point at which the interest was transferred to the spouses in joint title.

Rebuttal of the special joint form community presumption is by proof of any one of the following:

- Timing (acquisition before marriage).

- Gift (acquisition during marriage).

- Tracing (acquisition during marriage, but with separate property funds).

- Agreement (the parties executed a second agreement that the asset was all or part separate property).

If rebuttal is by tracing, the separate property proponent must show by a preponderance of the evidence that separate property was used to *acquire* the asset titled in tenancy in common or joint tenancy. See *Chavez v. Chavez*, 56 N.M. 393, 244 P.2d 781 (1952).

If rebuttal is by written agreement, the second agreement must, at least, identify the jointly titled property as separate in character.

Acquisitions and transmutations are treated differently. Under N.M.Stat.Ann. § 40–3–8(B) (1978), amended in 1990, *any subsequent change* during marriage in the *character* of a jointly titled asset (i.e. a transmutation) must "be established by clear, strong and convincing proof, which is a higher standard than a preponderance of evidence." *Trimble's Estate*, 57 N.M. 51, 253 P.2d 805 (1953). The *Trimble*, supra, is meant to "subject transactions between spouses to common law rules controlling actions of persons occupying confidential relations with each other." *Fletcher's Estate v. Jackson*, 94 N.M. 572, 579, 613 P.2d 714 (Ct. App. 1980). See Chapter 2 for more on the *Trimble* Rule.

N.M.Stat.Ann. § 45–2–804 (1978), amended in 2011 and effective January 1, 2012, governs revocations of probate and nonprobate transfers by divorce.

## 7. TEXAS

Holding title in JTWROS does not appear to be as commonly used in Texas as in other community property states (except Louisiana, which does not permit joint tenancies). Perhaps this is because Texas is the birthplace of the "homestead" concept, discussed in Section A.1 above.

Here is a description of the homestead right: Tex. Const. Art. XVI, § 52 provides: **"On the death of the husband or wife, or both, the homestead shall descend and vest in like manner as other real property of the deceased, and shall be governed by the same laws of descent and distribution, but it shall not be partitioned among the heirs of the deceased during the lifetime of the surviving husband or wife, or so long as the survivor may elect to use or occupy the same as a homestead, or so long as the guardian of the minor children of the deceased may be permitted, under the order of the proper court having the jurisdiction, to use and occupy the same."** Practitioner commentary suggests that the

homestead is akin to community property with the
right of survivorship.

In light of the homestead, as far as testamentary
rights go, there is little need for the JTWROS as
between married persons. The reason is that the
Texas homestead, makes community property
automatically with the right of survivorship.

Indeed, Texas has an inconsistent decisional
history of forbidding (or not) the creation of a
JTWROS from property that is community in
character. *Ricks v. Smith*, 159 Tex. 280, 318 S.W.2d
439 (1958), allowed the strategy; but *Ricks* was
overruled by *Hilley v. Hilley*, 161 Tex. 569, 342 S.W.2d
565 (1961), which held that the JTWROS argued for
could not be created from community property because
the acquisition during marriage was not by gift, but by
exchange of community property.

The Texas Legislature amended the predecessor of
V.T.C.A.Prob.Code § 46 by adding a final sentence
specifically" allowing "any husband and his wife . . .,
by written agreement, [to] create a joint estate out of
their community property, with rights of
survivorship." But the Texas Supreme Court declared
this quoted portion of the probate code
unconstitutional in *Williams v. McKnight*, 402 S.W.2d
505 (1966), citing *Hilley*. The Texas Legislature
subsequently deleted the overruled sentence from the
Probate Code, which has itself been repealed and
replaced with an Estates Code, effective January 1,
2014. See Chapter 10.

Nevertheless, if the married persons insist on placing community property into a JTWROS, Texas permits the use of a valid JTWROS so long as the married persons follow a process, known (at least in the far flung land of California) as the Texas two-step.

The Texas two-step turns on the rule that property purchased by Texas spouses with separate (as opposed to community) funds may be held as JTWROS, with the undivided one-half interest characterized as concurrently held separate property. Thus two-stepping spouses must first partition the community property into separate property (step 1), and then to execute written survivorship agreements for that separate property (step 2). *Holmes v. Beatty*, 290 S.W.3d 850, 855, 52 Tex.S.Ct.J.967 (2009). Together, the title (which ideally specifies a right of survivorship) and the written survivorship agreements (which also makes the right of survivorship explicit) serve as predictably solid proof of the spouses' intent to hold the property as JTWROS.

V.T.C.A.Prob.Code § 46, repealed effective Jan. 1, 2014 by the Texas Estates Code, is captioned **"Joint Tenancies."** The probate version of the Texas two-step permits parties to create a joint tenancy by a deed *plus* a written agreement **"[t]hat the interest of any joint owner who dies shall survive to the surviving joint owner or owners, . . . ."** A deed standing alone will not create a joint tenancy since **". . . no such agreement shall be inferred from the mere fact that the property is held in joint ownership."** This section does not apply to spouses regarding **"their community property . . . ".**

Through a series of amendments in 1948, 1980, 1987, and 1990, Tex. Const. Art. XVI, § 15 came to permit spouses to engage in more liberal transmutations, as discussed in Chapter 2. These amendments appear to give rise to the right to create a joint tenancy with the right of survivorship directly from community property. Evidence for this is in the following language: **"spouses may agree in writing that all or part of their community property becomes the property of the surviving spouse on the death of a spouse."**

## 8. WASHINGTON

As between nonmarried persons, Wash.Rev.Code § 64.28.010 sets out the requirements for creating a JTWROS: **"Joint tenancy shall be created only by written instrument, which instrument shall expressly declare the interest created to be a joint tenancy..."**

Wash.Rev.Code § 64.28.020. Subsection (1) makes the TIC the default joint title and allows for JTWROS: **"Every interest created in favor of two or more persons in their own right is an interest in common, unless acquired by them in partnership, for partnership purposes, or unless declared in its creation to be a joint tenancy, as provided in RCW 64.28.010, or unless acquired by executors or trustees...."**

However, Subsection (2) states that interests in common in the names of spouses or registered domestic partners are **"presumed to be community property."** In other words, even when Washington spouses set out to use the JTWROS deed form, the title presumptively defaults to CP title.

Wash.Rev.Code § 26.16.120 additionally allows spouses to enter into a community property agreement so as to dispose of community property by survivorship. **"Community property agreements"** are contractual, not testamentary, under the rationale of *Norris v. Norris*, 25 Wash.App. 290, 605 P.2d 1296 (1980). Any property subject to such an agreement is presumptively community property, unless established otherwise. Under the same code section, community property agreements must be made by the spouses **"by the execution of an instrument in writing under their hands and seals, and to be witnessed, acknowledged and certified in the same manner as deeds to real estate are required to be . . . ."**

For married persons and domestic partners, Washington courts have extended the requirements for the creation of a joint tenancy with the right of survivorship (the four unities) to also require clear and convincing evidence of the written intent of both spouses to convert a community property title into one with the right of survivorship. A community property agreement ensures that the specific property will pass by survivorship; it does not transmute that property into separate property.

A question sometimes raised about the Washington community property agreement system is whether the emphasis upon the formality of the agreement (written, signed, sealed, witnessed, acknowledged and certified) by which survivorship is affixed to community property may impose too high a standard for the layperson. One answer is that similar formalities for deeds (and the requirements for wills) have long served the dual function of, one, impressing parties with the importance of the act they undertake and, two, providing clear and convincing evidence of the parties' specific intent as to the asset.

Another answer is that since it appears under the law that a JTWROS title between married persons is presumptively community property both for purposes of dissolution and death, the Washington approach arguably simplifies, rather than complicates, the interface between the common law titles and the state community property system. In Washington, joint titles between spouses are presumed to be community in character. By executing a community property agreement the parties can opt for a right of survivorship as to any particular asset. The property covered by the community property agreement remains community in character, but it passes by survivorship. Thus, what the parties are agreeing to is analogous to CPWROS.

**(1) Joint tenancy interests held in the names of both spouses or both domestic partners, whether or not in conjunction with others, are presumed to be their community property, the same as other property held in the name of both spouses or both domestic partners. Any such interest passes to the survivor of the spouse or survivor of the domestic partner as provided for property held in joint tenancy, but in all**

other respects the interest is treated as community property.

(2) Either person in a marriage or either person in a state registered domestic partnership, or both, may sever a joint tenancy. When a joint tenancy is severed, the property, or proceeds of the property, shall be presumed to be their community property, whether it is held in the name of either spouse, or both, or in the name of either domestic partner, or both.

(3) This section applies as of January 1, 1985, to all existing or subsequently created joint tenancies.

The policy rationale, evident in Wash.Rev.Code § 64.28.040 (excerpted above), is that community property is the title form most protective of the marital estate.

Sometimes this question of which concurrent title the spouses' intended to use comes up even when a third party prepared or issued the disputed title. For example, in *Estate of Olson*, 87 Wash.2d 855, 557 P.2d 302 (1976), the court held that a separate property JTWROS is not established by one spouse's unilateral act of drafting and later executing a promissory note and real estate mortgage that referred to the property as joint tenancy with the right of survivorship. The court held that in the absence of an express written declaration by the marital community (i.e. both spouses) that the interest created was to be a joint tenancy (that is a common law title form), the property remained community property (albeit with the

Wash.Rev.Code 64.28.040(1) mandated right of survivorship). See also, *Rogers Walla Walla, Inc. v. Ballard,* 16 Wash.App.81, 553 P.2d 1372 (Ct.App. 1976), *review denied* 88 Wash.2d 1004 (1977) and *Graves v. Beutler,* 112 Wash.App. 1018 (2002). (*Graves* is not reported in P.3.)

*Lambert v. Peoples National Bank of Washington,* 89 Wash.2d 646, 574 P.2d 738 (1978)(en banc), involved a purchase of mutual fund certificates over a long period of time (1950 to 1972) by a wife who was acting as de facto manager during the male management era. At issue were the mutual fund certificates that she purchased with community property sums on deposit. Most of those certificates had been issued by the financial institution in a joint tenancy with the right of survivorship form; but some of them had been issued in tenancy in common. In an action between the husband's estate and the wife's conservator, the Washington Supreme Court upheld the characterization of the certificates as community property on the rationale that both spouses had not mutually consented to the change (from community property to JTWROS) as is required by Washington law. Dispositive were the following: the wife alone managed the community finances, the husband had limited English proficiency, and the parties were uninformed as to the different concurrent titles.

Written evidence of both spouses' intentions as to title form is often difficult to locate. Although banks retain signature cards, and vehicle registration records are centrally located, brokerage account records may be incomplete or prospective only.

Additionally, the background papers for deeds and promissory notes (as opposed to the deeds and notes themselves) may also be difficult to locate.

Of historical interest is that the JTWROS has had a difficult struggle for existence in Washington. Wash.Rev.Code § 64.28.010(1), above, which permits JTWROS for persons who are not married to each other dates back to a 1960 initiative. *Holohan v. Melville*, 41 Wash.2d 380, 249 P.2d 777 (1952)(en banc) is obsolete because of subsequent changes in the law, but it contains a useful history of joint tenancies in Washington.

### 9.   WISCONSIN

A joint tenancy deed executed on or after January 1, 1986 is characterized as survivorship marital property. A similar deed executed before January 1, 1986 remains joint tenancy.

Otherwise, Wisconsin blasts through the common law title interface with community property problem. Wis.Stat. § 766.60(4) by authorizing the holding of marital property in survivorship form:

**"(4)(a)   Spouses may hold property in any other form permitted by law, including but not limited to a concurrent form or a form that provides survivorship ownership. [T]o the extent the incidents of the tenancy in common or joint tenancy conflict with or differ from the incidents of [marital] property classification . . ., the incidents of the . . . joint tenancy, including the incident of survivorship, control."**

But Wis.Stat. § 766.60(5) authorizes a special form of marital property called **"survivorship marital property"**:

**"(5)(a) If the words "survivorship marital property" are used. . ., the marital property so held is survivorship marital property. On the death of a spouse, the ownership rights of that spouse in the property vest solely in the surviving spouse by nontestamentary disposition at death. . . ."**

The Legislative Council notes that the most significant differences between joint tenancy and survivorship marital property are the income tax treatment of basis at the death of a spouse and the right of a joint tenant to unilaterally destroy the right of survivorship.

Income tax basis at the death of the spouse differs depending on the character (individual or marital) of the property in question is discussed in Section B, above.

The ability to destroy the right of survivorship in survivorship marital property depends upon both the form in which the property is held and on whether the entire ownership interest or only a portion of it is transferred.

Wis.Stat. § 766.605 contains a rule covering the Wisconsin homestead: **"A homestead acquired after the determination date which, when acquired, is held exclusively between spouses with no 3rd party is survivorship marital property if no intent to the contrary is**

**expressed on the instrument of transfer . . . ."**
Under this statute, unless a contrary intent is shown,
a deed of realty to a husband and wife (and no other
person) as grantees creates survivorship marital
property if the realty is in fact a homestead. If the
deeded realty is not a homestead, the spouses have full
testamentary rights as to the property since the
property is marital property without a right of
survivorship.

Wis.Stat. § 766.60(4)(b)1 states that if **"a
document of title, instrument of transfer or bill
of sale"** after the determination date expresses an
intention to establish a joint tenancy or a tenancy in
common, the property is, respectively survivorship
marital property or marital property.

Similarly, Wis.Stat. § 766.60(4)(b)2 states:

**"A joint tenancy or tenancy in common
exclusively between spouses which is given to
the spouses by a 3rd party after the
determination date is survivorship marital
property or marital property, respectively,
unless the donor provides otherwise."** This
important provision clarifies situations were a third
party donor makes a gift to the spouses, of an asset
titled in both their names, during their marriage. The
Wisconsin rule is inclusive in its coverage and sensible
in its outcome.

# CHAPTER 6
# CHARACTERIZATION PROBLEMS

## A. OVERVIEW

This Chapter covers commingled bank accounts, separate property businesses, credit acquisitions, and work benefits.

### 1. APPROACH

#### a. Before

Before the material in this chapter applies, consider these important guidelines:

i.  The default community property system can be modified by contract.

ii.  Personal gifts exchanged between spouses may be exempt from formal transmutation requirements.

iii.  The rules in this chapter may not apply or may only partially apply to assets in joint form.

#### b. After

After deciding that there is no overriding premarital agreement, transmutation or exempt gift; and that form of title does not give rise to a special title presumption or treatment, continue with the following steps, if applicable:

i.  *Tracing:* The tracing principle holds that property generally takes the character of the property that was used to acquire it. Parties can trace acquisitions to their source to establish character. As discussed in detail below, parties can also trace purchases to or through a bank account either to establish the character of the purchase funds, or to rebut the general community property presumption. If the trace is to or through a *commingled* bank account, contemporaneous, character-specific records of deposits and withdrawals are helpful, if not required, for a successful rebuttal in court. The tracing principle applies regardless of the date of acquisition.

ii. *Commingling:* Admixture, or commingling, occurs when funds or elements of separate and community character are mixed together. The general rule is that commingled funds do not lose their character by the simple fact of being intermixed, as long as the component character elements can be "uncommingled" (that is, conceptually re-separated). At the point when it becomes impossible or impractical to uncommingle funds, the doctrine of confusion, either in judicial or doctrinal form, becomes applicable. It holds that the entire commingled asset becomes community property by operation of law. The doctrine of confusion can apply to property regardless of the date of acquisition.

iii. *Inception of title:* As a general matter, the character of an asset is determined on the date of its acquisition. Disagreements can arise because of a lack of clarifying records. Or they can be fueled by contradicting expectations that can arise when a process of acquisition overlaps both married and unmarried periods in the acquirer's life.

iv. *Borrowed funds:* Credit, creditworthiness, and loan proceeds are characterized as community property if they are obtained during marriage. Depending on the jurisdiction, the separate property proponent can rebut the community property presumption as to borrowed funds either by proving that the lender relied solely on separate property in extending the loan or by proving that the loan was not for a community purpose. Loan proceeds obtained *before* marriage are separate property.

v. *Mortgaged, secured, or deed of trust assets:* Where loan proceeds purchase an asset that secures the loan, jurisdictions differ in how they separate out any community and separate property contributions to purchase. Some jurisdictions apportion interests between the contributing estates. Other jurisdictions characterize the asset as of the inception of the title, but then reimburse any estate of a different character that contributes to the purchase.

vi. *Separate property businesses:* A separate property business is one whose capital is separate property in character. Deciding whether to apportion profits of such a business represents one of the most difficult areas of commingling and confusion. Jurisdictions use different approaches.

vii. *Deferred compensation:* Retirement and other deferred employment benefits are normally apportioned based on a time rule. The rule divides the period of participation in the pension during the marriage by the total time of participation in the pension. The same is done for periods of participation in the pension while single.

viii. *Life insurance:* The trend is to characterize term life insurance policies identically to the last premium paid. Whole life insurance savings components, or savings components of term policies (if any) are apportioned between the contributing estates.

These basic principles and steps are starting considerations only. Additional complications arise in each jurisdiction, and in each case, depending on the equities.

## 2.   COMMINGLING

Commingling occurs when community property is mixed with the separate property of either or both spouses. Bank deposits can be commingled. Purchases can be made with commingled funds. Businesses or business profits can become commingled over time. Deferred compensation plans and pension benefits can be commingled by time in and out of the marriage (pensions) or by deposits (in the case of defined contribution plans like 401(k)s, IRAs and so forth).

When commingling occurs, different outcomes are possible depending on the asset and the jurisdiction.

## a. Complete Ownership

A party buys an asset outright prior to marriage. The asset is separate property from the date of the marriage forward. Or, a party buys an asset with money earned during marriage while domiciled in a community property state. The asset is community property in character.

Complete ownership by the purchasing estate might also obtain despite commingling. This could happen when the commingling is de minimis, as in the following illustration.

*Illustration 6.1:* Prior to marriage H buys a house with a downpayment and a $250,000 purchase money loan that is secured by the house. Title is in H's name alone. On the date of marriage, H owes only $500 on the original purchase money loan. After marriage, H pays the remaining $500 with community property earnings.

In all jurisdictions the house is likely characterized as entirely H's separate property in accordance with the definition of separate property (the house is owned prior to marriage). Although the community makes a $500 contribution to the purchase of the house by its loan principal repayment, that contribution is insubstantial compared to the original purchase money loan of $250,000.

Another option could be to have the separate property estate (H) reimburse the community property estate for its $500 contribution to purchase. In this case, H would reimburse W her one-half of the reimbursement, or $250.

## b. Pro Tanto (Pro Rata) Ownership

Pro tanto ownership indicates that a property interest vests in the contributing estate of a different character with its first contribution to purchase. At dissolution, all contributions to purchase are totaled to determine the quantity of the contribution.

In a community property system, different estates can proportionally own (co-own) property during marriage. Proportional ownership works for some types of assets (for example, securities) but not for other types of assets (for example, property acquired by adverse possession). Louisiana has been the state least willing to recognize proportionate ownership in accordance with a contribution to acquisition.

*Illustration 6.2:* Prior to marriage H buys a house with a downpayment and a $250,000 purchase money loan that is secured by the house. Title is in H's name alone. On the date of marriage H owes a remaining $249,000 on the original $250,000 purchase money loan that was used to buy the house. Assume that during marriage H pays off $200,000 of the loan principal. At dissolution, a pro tanto ownership option would recognize the community as a co-owner of the house as of its first loan principal repayment. Pro rata shares would be determined by adding up the community loan principal repayments and dividing, typically, by the purchase price of the house.

*Illustration 6.3:* The spouses buy a car during marriage for $10,000. They take title in the purchasing spouse's name alone. They use $2,500 of the record owner's provable separate property as a downpayment. They pay the remainder of the purchase price with $7,500 of community property cash. The general presumption initially characterizes the car as community property (because the car was purchased during marriage despite being titled in one name alone). The spouse who contributed separate property to the purchase can seek to rebut the community property presumption by 25%.

An alternate outcome is that the separate property contributor could concede that the car is entirely community property and seek a $2,500 reimbursement to cover the separate property contribution to purchase.

## c. Credit Acquisitions

A credit acquisitions is a purchase made with loan proceeds that are contractually secured by the purchased property.

The minority civil law approach follows the inception of title rule for credit acquisitions. See Section 4 below. The civil law approach holds that the character of a credit acquisition is determined at the

point of purchase. Any contributions to purchase made
of a different character, whether downpayment or loan
principal    repayments,    are    reimbursed.    The
reimbursement would be secured by an equitable lien
on the property.

*Illustration 6.4:* X and Y, a couple domiciled in
Arizona, decide to marry. Soon *before* the date of their
marriage X buys a house in Arizona using a
downpayment and a purchase money loan secured by
the house (Time 1). After the date of marriage the first
loan principal repayment is made with community
earnings (Time 2). The house is separate property by
the inception of title rule; but the community is
entitled to a reimbursement for its loan principal
repayments. At dissolution, community contributions
are added up to determine the amount of the
community reimbursement amount (Time 3).

A majority of states follow the American rule
approach. Here, inception of title determines
character in the initial analysis. But if monies of a
different character are used to contribute to the
purchase of the house (by repaying the purchase loan),
the property can be treated in one of two competing
ways. Either the separate contributor can claim a
proportional ownership share. Or the separate
contributor can ask for a reimbursement. In the latter
case, state law will determine whether the
reimbursement is with or without interest, and
subject, or not, to value limitations in the case of
depreciation.

*Illustration 6.5:* X and Y, a couple domiciled in
California, an American rule state, decide to marry.

Soon *before* the date of the marriage X buys a house for $100,000 using a downpayment of $25,000 and a $75,000 purchase money loan secured by the house. Title is in X's name alone. After the date of the marriage, loan principal repayments are made with community property earnings. The community obtains a vested ownership right on the date of the community's first contribution; each contribution thereafter increases the community's pro rata share of ownership. The community ownership share is based on community property contributions to purchase (here loan principal repayments made with earnings) divided (in most states) by the purchase price of the house.

*Illustration 6.6:* Same facts as Illustration 6.5 above except that *during* marriage the spouses retitle the house so that both names are on title. No other agreements are made at that time as to the character of the house. Later, one spouse petitions for dissolution. In a jurisdiction that has enacted a special community property presumption for assets in joint form title (as California has), the house is characterized as entirely community property for purposes of dissolution. The only way to rebut the special presumption is with a contrary statement in the title or with a contradicting agreement, neither of which the separate property contributor can produce in this case. Nevertheless, the separate property contributor is entitled to a $25,000 reimbursement. That figure is determined by tracing the purchaser's contribution to a separate property source (here, the house was purchased before marriage). State law determines whether interest is calculated on the reimbursement. State law also determines whether there is a value limitation on the reimbursement in a case where the house depreciates in value.

### d. Transmutations by Operation of Law

The judicial option of deeming commingled property to be entirely community property is in full force in a jurisdiction that follows the doctrine of confusion.

The doctrine of confusion holds that when it becomes impossible or impracticable to identify separate and community property contributions, any separate property components are transmuted into community property by operation of law. The argument in support of the transmutation theory is gift-based: allowing property to become commingled to the point of confusion establishes a separate property contributor's donative intent to deliver a gift of his or her separate property percentage of the property to the community. See Chapter 2.

*Illustration 6.7:* Same facts as Illustration 6.6 above, except that during marriage the purchasing spouse refinances and retitles the house several times. Records are inadequate to characterize contributions to purchase. By the time the parties decide to dissolve their marriage, many years down the road, the purchaser's separate property contribution to purchase can no longer be identified. The doctrine of confusion can be invoked as support for characterizing the house as entirely community property. The rationale is that the act of not keeping records is evidence of the separate property contributor's intent to make a gift of that separate property to the community.

## 3.    TRACING RECORDS

Tracing can be relatively basic or specialized. In this context, tracing refers to the process of uncommingling property of mixed characters.

Basic records typically can be used for determining reimbursement amounts.

However, specialized records are sometimes required to successfully assert an ownership interest in a disputed asset purchased from a commingled account.

Specialized records are contemporaneous financial records that keep track of character deposits minus character withdrawals. The family expense presumption applies to subtract family expenses from community property deposits. Net character deposits can then be used to determine character contributions to the purchase of any asset that was bought with commingled sums on deposit in the account.

Except in Wisconsin and an occasional reimbursement code section (as in California), tracing is generally a process originated, authorized, and explicated in all necessary detail by decisional law. This means that tracing can be used despite the literal wording of statutes that define community property.

The following three rationales justify the use of tracing in its myriad forms.

One, some state constitutions protect separate property, thus necessitating tracing to protect constitutional rights.

Two, the inception of title rule characterizes property as of the date of acquisition, but only tracing can account for later-in-time capital or labor contributions to purchase.

Three, an exchange rationale provides either that a community contribution reflects an agreement between the parties that the community will help buy an asset in exchange for an ownership share. Or else it reflects an expectancy interest (helping to pay for something leads to part ownership notwithstanding the title document) that the law should back up as an equitable matter.

The key task of tracing is to account for net character contributions. Net, in this context, means contributions that remain after family expenses are taken into account.

### 4.    INCEPTION OF TITLE VERSUS PRO TANTO OWNERSHIP

The classic civil law approach for credit acquisitions (followed in Arizona, Idaho, Louisiana, Texas, and Washington) is relatively static. Date of inception of title determines character. Reimbursements are determined by proof that a contribution of a different character was made.

The American approach for credit acquisitions (California, Nevada, and New Mexico) is dynamic in the sense that it considers three temporal points. Time

1 is at the inception of title. Time 2 is the date of the first contribution to purchase by an estate of a different character; this contribution gives rise to a concurrent ownership interest in the asset. Where the asset was initially only one character at Time 1, it becomes commingled at Time 2. At Time 3, when partition becomes an issue, pro rata shares are calculated. The American approach allows for a constant process of (re)adjustment in the proportionally owned character of the asset. Some commentators refer to this approach as the community "buy-in" approach.

*Illustration 6.8:* A spouse buys a house *before* marriage, but pays for it during marriage with community property earnings. Title is in the purchasing spouse's name alone. In all jurisdictions, the inception of title rule decides the original character of the house as the purchasing spouse's separate property (Time 1). On the date of the first community property loan repayment, states split on the issue of whether the community acquires a qualified vested ownership interest in the house (Time 2). That difference in state law decides whether, at the end of marriage (Time 3), the community is deemed a co-owner of the house (American approach states) or a creditor of the purchasing spouse that is owed a reimbursement (civil law approach states).

Many but not all credit acquisition cases involve mortgaged real estate. To illustrate some additional time-based acquisition problems in this area, consider the following examples. In each of the examples, if Time 1 is prior to marriage, should the property be characterized as separate or as community at the end of marriage? Different results are reached in different states and sometimes within the same state.

LARGE PURCHASE MADE WITH A REAL ESTATE CONTRACT: H enters into a contract to purchase (in Louisiana, "bond for deed" for) Blackacre at Time 1, pays the consideration from his separate property at Time 2, and receives title at Time 3.

MORTGAGE FORECLOSURE: W sells Blackacre, taking back a mortgage at Time 1; the buyer defaults and W, as creditor, takes a deed in lieu of foreclosure at Time 2.

LAND PATENT: H enters into federal land for land grant purchase at Time 1; a patent is issued at Time 2.

ADVERSE POSSESSION WITHOUT COLOR OF TITLE: W enters into adverse possession (or prescription) without color of title at Time 1; the time for action against the negligent owner, T, is barred by the statute of limitations at Time 2; W perfects her title by legal action resulting in a court judgment at Time 3.

ADVERSE POSSESSION WITH COLOR OF TITLE: H purchases a colorable, but imperfect title at Time 1 and enters into adverse possession (or prescription) with color of title at Time 2; the time for action against the negligent owner, T, is barred by the statute of limitations at Time 3; H perfects his record title by legal action resulting in a court judgment at Time 4.

CONTINGENT FEE: W, an attorney, enters into a contingent fee contract at Time 1, renders service at Time 2, gets a verdict and judgment in her favor at Time 3; the verdict is upheld on appeal at Time 4; the judgment is executed and paid at Time 5.

PERSONAL INJURY CLAIM: W pursues a malpractice claim against a doctor for a duty that was established at Time 1 and breached at Time 2. W does not discover the injury until Time 3.

PENSION: W is employed by Employer at Time 1 through Time 10. Payments are made each year into a pension fund. W's pension rights vest at Time 2. W's pension rights increase in incremental percentages from thereafter. W's pension rights mature at Time 9, subject to conditions which are not completely removed until W actually retires at Time 10.

At what time in the above examples is the inception of right, meaning the time at which H or W establish a legal right to the asset in question?

The inception of title theory usually characterizes property at the point in time when it expands from a mere expectancy to an actionable property right, whether contingent or vested. A term life insurance contract on a living person, the forfeitable pension rights of an employee, the not yet perfected claim of an adverse possessor have each been classified, at times, as a mere expectancy. Expectancies are not subject to the community property system.

The foregoing issues are presented here in connection with a period that starts before and ends after the date of marriage. It is also possible that similar problems will arise over a period that starts during the marriage and ends after a date of separation or a dissolution. Similarly, the period may start while the couple is domiciled in one community (or common law title) property state and end while they are domiciled in another community (or common law title) property state.

Occasionally, a court will use an all-or-nothing approach by declaring that an asset that is the product of both community and separate contributions is entirely community property (or entirely separate property) rather than a proportion of each. The likelihood of this approach varies according to the jurisdiction, the type of asset acquired (realty, life insurance, defined benefit plans, business) and the form of the contributions (cash, loan proceeds, labor). Generally, the all-or-nothing approach varies from strong to weak as the contribution moves through time from labor (sweat equity) to non-cash property items to cash.

## B.   DETAIL

### 1.   TRACING TO AND THROUGH COMMINGLED BANK ACCOUNTS

Tracing often involves bank accounts into which both separate and community property have been deposited. If UMPAA has been adopted in the state with a special community property presumption, then all sums on deposit are presumptively community absent contrary evidence. Tracing in the UMPAA context requires contemporaneous financial records. If

UMPAA has not been adopted, then different tracing
techniques may apply.

## a. Techniques and Options

- Payment of community family expenses could
  be charged to the community property
  deposited, or, conversely, payment of separate
  expenses could be charged to the separate
  property deposited. These methods are
  sometimes successful in eliminating the
  character of property which has the smallest
  amount deposited.

- FIFO ("First In, First Out") is a mechanical
  accounting method by which the chronology of
  deposits and withdrawals determines the
  character of the property acquired by funds
  from the commingled account.

- Equitable application of selected theories is a
  commonly used method for assessing the
  liability of a spouse who commingles. A
  commingling spouse is potentially liable to the
  community estate for damages resulting from
  the conversion of any community property
  funds that were interfered with by the act of
  commingling. Moreover, commingling turns
  the account into a disputed account, as a
  matter of law, by exposing the community
  property to impairment.

- In recognition of the (potential) harms listed in
  the previous bullet point to the community
  property estate, the first spouse to commingle

may have a correlative legal duty to keep adequate records by which funds and purchases can be traced back to their original character, depending on the jurisdiction.

• Absent an agreement, records are generally deemed adequate if they are complete, character specific, and clear enough to allow a claimant spouse to trace the funds *to* the commingled account (thus satisfying his or her claim against the account), and then *through* the account to any assets that are (i) governed by the general community property presumption and (ii) acquired with account money.

• Character-specific records allow the non-commingling spouse to satisfy his or her claim either against the account or against the specific assets.

• When the non-commingling spouse asserts a claim against the commingled account funds (as opposed to the specific asset), the non-commingling spouse may be entitled to the legal fiction that the commingling spouse first withdrew his or her own separate funds. Or, a family expense presumption may apply.

• Community property funds used to pay for family expenses are regarded as an obligation of support. The family expense presumption deducts family expenses (rents, utilities, food, clothing, interest payments, lifestyle expenses, and so on) from community property funds first. If and when the community property funds are exhausted, do family expenses get deducted from available separate property funds.

- Community property sums on deposit minus family expenses identifies *net* community property sums on deposit.

- Separate property sums on deposit minus expenses identifies *net* separate property sums on deposit.

- Separate property funds used to pay family expenses (expenditures for consumable goods), are generally regarded as a gift to the community absent evidence of a reimbursement agreement between the spouses.

- Net separate property funds used to contribute to the purchase of or to make a capital improvement to an asset, are regarded either as the basis for a claim of co-ownership or as the basis for a claim for reimbursement, depending on the jurisdiction.

- Tracing *to* and tracing *through* an account are limited by the lowest intermediate balance of the bank account method. When there are a succession of deposits and withdrawals of separate and community property sums, the claimant is not entitled to more from the account than the lowest intermediate balance in the account between the time of the commingling and the time as of which the rights in the fund are to be determined. Thus for example, if the order of deposits and withdrawals was that at Time 1 the community property sums were exhausted so that at Time 2 separate property sums on deposit were used to pay family expenses, then when community property deposits are added to the account at Time 3 the community property should not be deemed to owe the separate property a reimbursement unless the parties have contracted otherwise.

### b. Common Law Equitable Claims

The Restatement (First) of Restitution (1937) proposes that a claimant who traces assets through a commingled fund into a product of the fund be limited, even as against a conscious wrongdoer, to a share of the product **"in such proportion as his money bore to the whole amount of the fund."** Restatement (First) of Restitution § 210(2). This same provision gives an equitable claim against the property for reimbursement to the owner of money which is wrongfully mingled by another and subsequently used to acquire property. The Restatement section also allows the alternative remedy of a constructive trust if **"the wrongdoer knew that he was acting wrongfully."**

The Restatement (Third) of Restitution and Unjust Enrichment (2011) §§ 58 and 59 is an updated version of the same, and it is consistent with the rules presented in the Restatement (First) of Restitution (1937). The 2011 Restatement suggests **"permitting**

**the claimant (as against a wrongdoer) to claim
the entire advantage of beneficial withdrawals
that can be attributed to the claimant's funds."**
Restatement (Third) of Restitution & Unjust
Enrichment § 59 (2011).

It is still too soon to tell whether the Restatement
(Third) will be accepted by courts as useful in
community property disputes. That said, there is at
least one important difference between the First and
Third Restatements having to do with the difference
between restitution (the claimant is adjudged a co-
owner) and equitable lien (the claimant is adjudged a
creditor), whether the claimant is limited to seeking
one or the other remedy.

If there is a limit on the claim possible, here is the
breakdown:

- *Restitution:* Restitution goes farther than a
  mere lien. Restitution corrects unjust
  enrichment by restoring the claimant to
  property, lost opportunity costs, or to a
  previous state of affairs.

- *Equitable lien only:* In dealing with the
  commingled bank account, the Restatement
  (First) of Restitution (1937) provides in § 211
  for an equitable lien upon the money
  remaining in the account and upon the
  proceeds of the part of the account that was
  withdrawn. § 212 allows a lien only for the
  lowest intermediate balance when all
  subsequent deposits were of the depositor's
  own (i.e., separate) property.

As a practical matter the difference between restitution and an equitable lien lies in what can be recovered. This difference becomes material when an asset appreciates over time. In such a case, an *owner* of an interest in the appreciating item (by constructive trust) will benefit from the increase in value, whereas the *creditor* of a debt secured by an equitable lien upon the item will not.

The Restatement (Third) of Restitution and Unjust Enrichment §§ 54 through 61 describe how tracing establishes the link between the transaction that gives rise to the claim and the property in question. Practically speaking, tracing gives the innocent party the information necessary to make the choice between a constructive trust (i.e., to own a fractional share in the claimed property) or an equitable lien (i.e., to have, as a creditor, a secured position in the asset for the dollar amount owed by the wrongdoer).

The question of whether to prefer an asset or an asset-based remedy versus an equitable lien may arise for any number of reasons, economic and non-economic. The psychological difference may be strong between owning a percentage of an asset (via a constructive trust) versus being a creditor entitled to a reimbursement that is secured by an equitable lien on the asset.

### c. Conversion Damages

The Restatement (Third) of Restitution and Unjust Enrichment (2011) additionally provides that a party who gains a benefit in breach of a fiduciary duty is liable for damages. This is a general principle, but it clearly applies in the marital context.

In the case of commingled funds, the managing spouse (a partnership fiduciary) is liable for conversion, a common law cause of action, at the point of commingling (the point at which the account becomes disputed) or, in states permitting the extension of a statute of limitations by the discovery rule, at the time that the harm is discovered. A cause of action in conversion can also arise from any unjust enrichment that results to the benefitted spouse from the impairment of the other spouse's community property interest.

The Restatement imposes liability for conversion at the point of commingling because, regardless of innocence or blame, the commingling converter obtains advantages that come from sidestepping disclosure, negotiation, contracting, and payment. A breach of fiduciary duty claim addresses these issues. The converter's degree of fault does and should become relevant not in dividing property (as all community property states have adopted no-fault dissolution), but in assessing damages.

California follows these principles in the community property context, as discussed in Section C below. In brief, the first spouse to commingle has the legal duty to keep records, irrespective of blameworthiness. The rationale is that the act of commingling funds results in a disputed account. When commingling is coupled with a breach of fiduciary duty, an adversely affected spouse accrues a claim for the impairment of a community    property    interest.    Cal.Fam.Code

§ 1101(a). If the commingling spouse acts out of ignorance, then the measure of damages is the adversely affected spouse's one-half interest in the impaired community property. Cal.Fam.Code § 1101(g). If the commingling spouse acts out of malice, fraud, or oppression as defined by the penal code, then the measure of damages contemplates disgorgement. Cal.Fam.Code § 1101(h). Attorney fees and court costs are statutorily available no matter the impairing spouse's state of mind.

The trend is against managerial acquittance. Therefore, the need for an approach to managerial fault is obvious. This is so even in a no-fault dissolution era, and especially in light of increasing restrictions and diminishments of postdissolution spousal support. Management and control issues are discussed in Chapter 7.

## 2. COMMUNITY LABOR IN A SEPARATE PROPERTY BUSINESS

In the case of a separate property business the following elements are involved.

*Element 1* is the baseline value of the business at marriage. Marriage does not automatically transmute separate property into community property in the U.S. Absent a transmutation, the premarital business comes to the marriage as separate property. A separate property business also can be started during marriage with provable separate property capital.

*Element 2* is the increase in the value of the business due to the inherent nature of the property or to inflation. The principle here is that a mere change in value does not change the character of the property. To account for this element, the fair market value of the business at the time of dissolution or death is required.

*Element 3* is the net profits from the capital.

In civil law states the rents, issues and profits of separate property are community property during marriage. Thus Element 3 is characterized as community property during the marriage, and returned to the separate property owner at dissolution. However, even in the civil law states, when the value represented by Element 3 is partly or completely left in the business, or partly or completely withdrawn from the business in the form of cash (salary) or stock dividends, Elements 2 and 3 may need to be separated out.

In American rule states, rents, issues and profits of separate property are separate property. Elements 1, 2, and 3, therefore, must be separated out from community property labor that contributed to the profitability of the business.

*Element 4* is the community property labor contribution. Management skills are labor. Other labor contributions may also count so long as they are linked to business profitability. Normally all cash earnings partly or completely withdrawn (or overdrawn) in the form of salary are treated as a business expense. It is only when labor contributes to profits that an accounting becomes necessary.

Ideally, a business will generate enough value to equal the total of capital contributions and returns on capital.

Ideally, the four elements will equal all value that is in the business.

Ideally, useful financial records will be available to identify the relative contributions of labor and capital.

It is only because the ideal situation seldom if ever exists in reality that adjustments of the type described in this chapter are necessary.

In light of the less than ideal situations that abound at dissolution, disputes can arise over the extent of the separate property and community property returns. The separate estate is entitled to a return on investment for its capital contribution. The community estate is entitled to any profits in excess of that return.

## a. The Civil Law Approach versus the American Law Approach

The civil law approach characterizes separate property rents, issues, and profits as community property during the continuance of the marriage. At dissolution, any separate property rents, issues, and profits, are returned to their separate property owner. At dissolution or death, the community may be permitted to seek reimbursement for business growth that traces back to a community property labor component.

The majority American approach, characterizes separate property rents, issues, and profits as separate property during the continuance of the marriage. In the context of a separate property business, the addition of community labor commingles not the business itself, but the business profits. When that happens, the community is permitted to make a claim for excess profits. If community labor was below the legal standard for assigning excess profits to the community, the community still has a right to seek a reimbursement for its net labor contribution.

Both of these elements—apportionment versus reimbursement—are discussed next.

### b. *Pereira* Apportionment versus *Van Camp* Reimbursement

When community property labor helps generate rents, issues and profits, the issue can be handled in two ways. Profits can be apportioned between the separate and community property. Or, profits can be allocated entirely to the separate property, which then reimburses the community for its uncompensated net labor contribution (labor minus family expenses).

### i. *The Apportionment Approach*

The community is entitled to excess profits if community labor helped enhance the profitability of a separate property business. The factual reason (other than transmutation) for allocating excess profits entirely to the community is the active management of the business on the part of one or both spouses.

The scope of covered businesses is broad. Brick-and-mortar businesses (bakeries, retail stores, and so forth, are obviously covered under this rule), but so too are taxable investment accounts, law and other professional firms, consultancy firms, real property, and any other enterprise undertaken for profit.

### ii. The Reimbursement Approach

The reason (other than a transmutation) for allocating profits entirely to the separate property is that profits were due to market forces or inflation, not to community labor.

A reimbursement will not be denied if a de minimis labor contribution was made. So for example, where the owner hires a professional manager to oversee the business, the community can be said to have made little or no contribution to creating business profit. Alternatively, where the owner compensates the community for its labor during the marriage in the form of an industry-standard salary, the community can be said to have been paid for its labor.

Whatever the doctrinal or factual reason for choosing reimbursement over apportionment, one legal tension at play is that an owner of a separate property business has full powers of management and therefore can make decisions and otherwise control the property in a way that can (and probably will) affect the community estate during marriage and the former spouse after dissolution.

All states will admit into evidence the separate property owner's business records. In American rule states, records can assist in determining which approach (apportionment or its rival reimbursement) will achieve substantial justice between the parties.

However, because the amount, timing and nomenclature of the distribution from the business is within the control of the managing spouse, business records as to what was salary and what reinvested dividends may not be objective (or in some cases even kept). Additionally, because the records are kept for other purposes (like tax purposes or liquidity reports), they often are not accurate on the type of data required to apportion the business at dissolution.

In American rule jurisdictions, two rival cases dominate the analysis.

### *iii.* Pereira

In *Pereira v. Pereira*, 156 Cal. 1, 103 P. 488 (1909) the California Supreme Court used total recapitulation accounting to apportion the profits of a separate property saloon business between the separate and the community property. The community's interest was discussed as an equitable ownership right to excess profits as measured by the difference between the fair market value of the business at divorce minus the sum of the original separate property capital plus a fair rate of return on the original capital calculated, at simple interest so as to account for family expenses. The use of simple interest avoids double charging of the community for family expenses.

The original capital was defined as the market value of the business on the date of marriage. The fair rate of return on separate property capital was defined as what the original capital hypothetically would have earned over the length of the marriage had it been invested in securities of reasonable certainty. The *Pereira* court used the legal rate of interest (7%) to calculate the fair rate of return, but allowed for the possibility that the parties could present evidence of an historical rate of interest for the period in question.

By this same logic, if and only if records show that family expenses were paid from a source other than the contested business, then compound interest on the separate property owner's original separate property capital can be argued for. The idea is not to replicate the market or how interest is ordinarily calculated. Rather, as noted above, the idea is to refrain from double charging the community for family expenses.

The *Pereira* formula can be expressed as follows.

*FMV@divorce − (FMV@marriage + FRR) = Excess Profits*

Where:

- "FMV@divorce" is the value of the separate property business at the end of the marriage.

- "FMV@marriage" is the value of the separate property business on the date of marriage.

- "FRR" is the hypothetical fair rate of return on the original separate property capital investment had it been invested in securities of reasonable safety. FRR is calculated on an annualized basis, multiplied by the number of years in question. Simple interest is used by default unless the business did not pay for family expenses.

- "Excess profits" are business gains that remain after the separate property is compensated for the use of its capital. The community award is for excess profits.

- Losses are normally not shared by the community under *Pereira*. Rather, the community takes excess profits as a creditor of the separate property business.

### *iv.* **Van Camp**

*Van Camp v. Van Camp*, 53 Cal.App. 17, 199 P. 885 (1921) held that separate property rents, issues and profits retain their original character where growth of the underlying business is not due to community property labor. Under this formula, the community is entitled to a reimbursement for its net labor. Net labor means that any family expenses paid from the business have been subtracted from any uncompensated labor that was put into the business.

The *Van Camp* formula can be expressed as follows:

*FMV@divorce – (CP labor – Family expenses) = SP*

Where:

- "FMV@divorce" is the fair market value of the separate property business at divorce.

- "CP labor" is the value of community property labor contributions to the business over the time period in question.

- "Family expenses" are family expenses paid from the business over the time period in question.

For purposes of calculating the value of uncompensated community property labor, benchmark salary figures can be used if actual records are not available. Family expenses are subtracted from community property labor only if those expenses were actually paid from the contested business.

### v. Excess Profits or Reimbursement?

In jurisdictions that follow the American rule, the court has discretion to select the formula—*Pereira* or *Van Camp*—that furthers substantial justice between the parties.

An award of excess profits is generally favored as a policy matter, because it compensates the community property independently of any salary or wage that may have been paid to the laboring spouse(s). In California, *Pereira* is also favored as a doctrinal matter by application of the minimum-plus standard of *Beam v. Bank of America,* 6 Cal.3d 12, 98 Cal.Rptr. 137, 490 P.2d 257 (1971), discussed below in Section C, California. In other states (Wisconsin) substantial labor is the standard.

An award of excess profits may be preferable even if the community was compensated during marriage for its labor. The reason is that labor and profits are distinct components of the business. Labor is a business expense. Profits are a return on business capital. Thus, even when the community is compensated by the business for its labor, depending on the amount of labor that went into the business, substantial justice may still require that the community be entitled to an award of excess profits.

A reimbursement is indicated when a low quantum of community labor, as determined by state law, goes into the business. If too little community labor goes into the business, or if that labor is not tied to profitability, then a reimbursement is more appropriate than an award of excess profits. Net, in this instance, indicates that family expenses have been subtracted from community labor.

There is greater variation within each jurisdiction than there is between jurisdictions in the methods used to apportion the rents, issues and profits of a separate property business.

### c. Extent of the Gain

The decided cases have almost always dealt with a successful business. Generally unmentioned in the cases is how to apportioning business losses.

A true separate property business does not get commingled by an infusion of community labor. Rather it remains separate throughout the marriage so long as its operating capital remains separate. Even with *Pereira* accounting the community becomes a creditor of the business, not a co-owner.

## d. Type of Business Organization

The rules of this section apply to unincorporated sole proprietorships and partnerships as well as to corporations. The existence of a close (i.e., entirely or predominately owned by a married person) corporation seems to increase the problems and lead to apportionment questions. This is because in a closely held corporation, the business owner normally has substantial control in deciding whether to reinvest or distribute profits, decide salary, restrict the sale of stock, and so forth.

The separate entity for tax purposes causes greater formality in the arrangement and in the quality of business records. A salary is more likely to be paid if it obtains more income advantages than a dividend; but, on the other hand, corporate earnings may be retained. Accountants may compute the fair market value of the business by including an intangible asset known as "good will" to account for the profitability of the business. If good will is included in a computation at dissolution, it may create a speculative paper profit. Moreover, after the business is apportioned, the owner of the separate property business must pay the community, as creditor; the obligation may subject the business to added debt which may impact or even detract from the business owner's ability to meet other obligations, such as spousal or child support, from the business.

The divorce court occasionally disregards the corporate entity in its discretion, especially if it seems to have been used to conceal assets or to obtain unfair advantage in the dissolution proceedings for the shareholder spouse. Often it makes more sense to distinguish between the close corporation on the one hand and a publicly traded corporation on the other hand (even though both are "corporations") than it does to distinguish between corporations and unincorporated businesses. Idaho has case law making just such a distinction.

Complex problems in all states have arisen when, at divorce, an owner of a closely held family corporation transfers shares of stock to his or her other family members as part of a strategy to block repaying the creditor ex-spouse.

### e.  Contrasts to Community Property Doctrines

There are a number of areas where different rules seem to apply to the separate property businesses. In some cases, the nonapplication of commingling rules (i.e. the all-or-nothing approach) has been discredited and even overruled.

In some states community property law is altered by an express modification of the Uniform Partnership Act to state that a partnership interest is not community property.

Credit acquisitions by a business, especially a corporation, may be subject to the business rules as opposed to the rules concerning the purchase of assets with borrowed funds.

## 3. CREDIT ACQUISITIONS

### a. General Principles

When an asset (like a home) is purchased with borrowed funds, title is taken subject to the mortgage or deed of trust. In cases where contributions to the purchase loan principal payments are of different characters, jurisdictions split on how to handle the purchase. Arizona, Idaho, Washington, Louisiana and Texas follow the civil law inception of the title rule, but reimburse contributions to purchase made of a different character. California, New Mexico, Nevada, and Wisconsin follow the American pro tanto ownership approach.

### b. Character of Loan Proceeds (Borrowed Funds)

In all jurisdictions loan proceeds obtained during marriage are presumed to be community property. So too is credit and creditworthiness. How the separate property proponent rebuts this presumption as to actual borrowed funds that flow into the marriage depends on the jurisdiction. Assessing the character of borrowed funds is useful to either establishing an ownership share or to determining whether a reimbursement is due.

California uses the lender's intent test: loan proceeds obtained during marriage are presumptively community property unless the lender *solely* intended to rely on separate property repayment sources. *Marriage of Grinius*, 166 Cal.App.3d 1179, 212 Cal.Rptr. 803 (1985), clarifying *Gudelj v. Gudelj*, 41

Cal.2d 202, 259 P.2d 656 (1953), which failed to cite precedent. Washington uses the community purpose test: credit obtained during marriage is either community or separate property depending on whether the funds served a community purpose.

Note that the identity of the spouses who actually sign the promissory note is not determinative of the character of the funds obtained. For example, in applying the lender's intent test, courts often disregard the signature of a spouse when the signature was made as an accommodation, for purposes of the lender. Nevertheless, a spouse's signature is important because it represents a contractual obligation incurred by the signing spouse. As such, a signature can subject a spouse's separate property to liability for the loan should the collateral or available community sources prove to be insufficient to satisfy the debt.

### c. Community Property Contributions to the Purchase of Separate Property

The pro tanto approach originated in California law with *Vieux v. Vieux*, 80 Cal.App. 222, 251 P. 640 (1926). The case articulates the principle that the community property gains a pro tanto interest for its contributions to a separate property credit acquisition; and that interest vests on the date that the community contribution to purchase is first made. *Marriage of Moore*, 28 Cal.3d 366, 169 Cal.Rptr. 662, 618 P.2d 208 (1980) sets forth the basic accounting methodology for quantifying the pro tanto interest so as to apportion total appreciation. *Marriage of Marsden* 130

Cal.App.3d 426, 181 Cal.Rptr. 910 (1982) modifies *Moore* so as to apportion (only) marital appreciation. See Section C, California.

The *Moore*, supra, approach uses historic purchase price (contract price) as the denominator. Other states use a different price point. New Mexico, for example, suggests use of the value of the asset on the date of marriage.

### d. A General Approach

The character of a credit acquisition purchased with different character funds is determined in the following seven-step order:

*Valid agreement?* Check for a valid agreement or transmutation. A valid agreement or transmutation between the parties will prevail, regardless of other factors, including the form of title.

*When was the property acquired?* If the property was acquired before marriage, it falls within the definition of separate property, and burden of making a case for a pro tanto ownership falls on the community. Alternatively, if acquired during marriage, the inception of title rule characterizes the property as community, leaving the separate property claimant with the burden of rebuttal.

*If acquired during marriage, does the general community property presumption apply?* Check the form of title. The form of the title does not necessarily control ownership of the asset in a community property jurisdiction. What the form of title determines is which community property presumption applies (general or specific) and, more to the point, what evidence serves to rebut that presumption.

*What character are the loan proceeds?*

If the loan proceeds are obtained during marriage, they are presumptively community property. Some states follow the lender's intent test as a rebuttal method. In those jurisdictions, rebuttal is by proof that the lender relied solely or (in some states primarily) on separate property assets in extending the loan. Loan proceeds obtained prior to marriage are separate property because the lender relies solely on the debtor's premarital (separate) creditworthiness.

During marriage, the loan proceeds are community property in character to the extent that a lender relies on creditworthiness of one or both spouses. In this instance, there is no factual basis upon which to invoke the lender's intent rebuttal.

Other jurisdictions characterize loan proceeds depending upon whether the loan proceeds benefit the community. Loan proceeds that might be recharacterized as separate under the lender's intent test could be characterized as a community under the benefit of the community test. See for example Section C, Washington. The legal question in community benefit states is whether the loan benefitted the community or not. If it did, the loan proceeds are community in character.

*What character are capital contributions, such as the downpayment and loan principal repayments?* Downpayments and loan principal repayments are by definition contributions to purchase. Interest, taxes, insurance, and maintenance expenditures are not; they are normally accounted for as family expenses.

*What are the contributing estates' shares?* Apply the appropriate legal approach for determining pro tanto shares or reimbursement amount.

For property purchased *before* marriage with a separate property loan that is repaid *during* the marriage with community property funds, apportionment theory gives the community a pro tanto share based on its actual contributions to purchase. The community's pro tanto share of ownership determines the community's interest in appreciation or depreciation. Reimbursement theory, by contrast, repays the community for its contributions to purchase.

*What is the state policy?* There are two principle theories that determine the character of property acquired on credit.

The civil law approach protects the separate property owner's title while at the same time (at least in theory) protecting the community's contributions to purchase with a reimbursement. The downside of this approach for the community is that the community does not get to share in asset appreciation over time. The upside is that the community is not exposed to depreciation in a down market.

The American law apportionment theory (developed by California courts) fully protects the separate property owner's title while at the same time recognizing that the community acquires a pro tanto ownership interest for its contributions to purchase. The rationale has rival expressions. One, the parties had an implied contract the terms of which were that community contributions to purchase were in exchange for a percentage of ownership. Or two, the community developed a reasonable expectation of co-ownership, based on its contribution to purchase, that the law should confirm.

Each state handles credit purchases in an increasingly unique way. Keep in mind that, in the context of the community property system, a home purchase involves a dynamic picture of the interplay between personal property (money) and real property (real estate). Moreover, credit and creditworthiness have become property in the traditional sense; therefore, during the marriage, both belong to the community.

## 4.  DEFERRED COMPENSATION

### a.  Types of Deferred Compensation

In accordance with the basic rules discussed in Chapters 3 and 4, deferred compensation earned during marriage is presumptively community property.

Defined *benefit* plans correspond to traditional pension benefits. A defined benefit plan falls into the definition of earnings, even though distribution of the earnings are deferred until a later date. Stock options, profit sharing plans, traditional pension distributions are also examples of defined benefit plans, because all are based on the employment relationship, not on the actual contributions made by the employee or the employer to an identifiable investment fund whose performance is reported to the employee by means of regular statements. The pensioner is an annuitant, not an investor. Moreover, defined benefit plans are generally coordinated with Social Security benefits.

Defined *contribution* plans correspond to retirement savings accounts to which the employee contributes for purposes of investment. The employer may, but need not, match the employee's contribution to an account in the employee's name. The value of a defined contribution plan depends upon the amount of actual employee contributions to the plan made over time, and the rate of return obtained on invested contributions. The term defined contribution plan is very broad. It includes tax deferred and tax protected accounts (as for example a 401(k) or 403(b) account or a Roth IRA).

Some employment benefits, like medical and dental plans, do not create divisible assets, but are in the nature of expense-reducers. Other benefits, like bonuses, thrift plans, and employer-guaranteed loans are routine enough that they do not raise special community property problems. What matters for these assets is timing: only benefits earned during marriage while domiciled in the state are community property.

The remaining benefits raise issues of characterization that must comply with the Internal Revenue Code and, depending on the case, with other complex federal laws like the Employee Retirement, Income Security Act (ERISA), the Retirement Equity Act of 1984 (REACT), or even specific statutes related to civil service employees, military employees, public employees, or health insurance transfers (COBRA). These federal laws are outside the scope of this Nutshell.

## b. Severance, Death, Disability, and Retirement Benefits

As a form of deferred compensation employers often provide one or more benefits designed to alleviate financial problems caused by retirement, disability, or death of an employee. Each can raise problems and issues in community property dissolutions.

Unconditional severance pay is typically regarded as a form of deferred compensation for services previously rendered. As such, severance pay is subject to community property rules by timing, with the question being whether the timing is earned during marriage.

Stock options may or may not be compensation for past, present, or future services. But to the degree they are an alternative to a salary structure offered for tax purposes, they fall within the definition of work compensation and as such are subject to community property rules, if earned during marriage while domiciled in the state. Timing issues related to the granting and exercising of stock options can raise complicated apportionment questions.

Life insurance problems include unresolved contingencies and dramatic value change between contract and the contract proceeds.

Whole life insurance policies are valuable prior to payout and, as such, are subject to community property rules, including apportionment, if acquired during marriage while domiciled in the state.

Term life insurance insures a person at death with renewability roughly based on an assessment of the insured's risk factors for an untimely death. Employers sometimes provide group term life insurance programs. The renewability of group term life insurance policies is not dependent on the insured's actual risk factors; it is dependent on factors like the employee's continued employment and the employer's ongoing economic decision to continue offering its employees the group plan. Term life insurance, group term life insurance and term health insurance contract policies each represent a liability that loses its (potential) pay out value once the contract term expires, at which point the policy become worthless unless it is renewed.

A term life insurance *contract* is characterized by the last premium rule, but the contract itself is typically not an asset subject to division at dissolution. The contract simply goes with the party who is willing to make the next premium payment or, if the contract is part of a group life insurance plan offered by an employer, it goes with the employed party at the end of marriage.

Life insurance proceeds distributed on the death of the insured, take on the character of the life insurance policy by application of the last premium rule. If the last premium was paid by funds of different characters, then the proceeds will be apportioned by character contributions to the payment. Gifts of life insurance proceeds are discussed in Chapter 7.

Veteran's insurance and Federal Employee's Group Life Insurance (FEGLI) are preempted by federal law. *Wissner v. Wissner*, 338 U.S. 655, 70 S.Ct. 398, 94 L.Ed.2d 424 (1950) held that a community property claim contrary to the insured's express designation is precluded by federal statute. The pre-emption ruling was based on language in FEGLI that the insured **"shall have the right to designate"** and change the beneficiary at all times and that payments of proceeds **"shall be exempt from the claims of creditors, and shall not be liable to attachment, levy or seizure by or under any legal or equitable process whatever, either before or after receipt by the beneficiary."**

Disability insurance plans have an evitable contingency (injury), as opposed to the inevitable contingency of life insurance (death). Until the evitable contingency has occurred, the right to disability insurance is a mere expectancy. When the contingency occurs, the inception of title rule looks to the marital status of the recipient to determine the character of the payments. Because disability payments are often designed to replace salary and are further contingent upon the survival of the intended recipient, the question is whether each payment's character should be determined separately. If each payment is not so characterized, the risk is that a spouse may divorce the disabled employee and take one-half of all disability benefits, leaving the injured spouse without a means of support. The difficulty of characterizing recoveries for personal injuries is analyzed in Chapter 4; many of the same principles apply to disability payments.

As to the employee who is entitled to either disability pay or retirement pay but not both, courts have generally held that the employee option cannot defeat the spouse's right to one-half of the community property retirement benefits. Under such a holding, the disability receipts are characterized as community to the extent that retirement pay would have been so characterized.

Chapter 11 of Title 38 U.S.C.A. 301 et seq. covers disability during the line of military duty and pre-existing injuries or diseases aggravated after the separation of military service. The Federal Uniformed Services Former Spouses Protection Act (with its lisping acronym FUSFSPA) does not authorize direct payments of retired disability pay to a former spouse. Disability payments are also protected by the Veterans Benefit Act, 10 U.S.C.A. 1408(a)(4)(B). See below and Chapter 12. Military retirement pay, however, can be covered by community property rules, as discussed in Chapter 12.

Pension rights may be in the form of a pension right in a retirement fund or (for an already retired worker) it may be in the form of a dollar amount payable for the life of the retired employee. Both disability and retirement payments are usually contingent upon the survival of the annuitant, unless the annuitant has contracted with the employer to extend a diminished retirement payment in exchange for extending payments for the life of a surviving spouse or registered domestic partner. Either way, pension rights are deferred compensation subject to community property rules.

With respect to pension benefits, the difficulty arises because retirement income annuities are earned by a prolonged period of employment that may overlap married and unmarried periods, or periods of domicile in both community and non-community property states during the employee's life. When this is the case, it calls for an allocation to or apportionment between the separate and community components.

Difficulties arise in valuing and dividing the pension asset upon divorce. Is a retirement pension one asset or a series of payments?

A minority of states may apportion the pension as a savings account or by contributions. This method apportions by actual money contributions, sometimes augmented by an interest factor for the period that the funds have been held by the retirement fund.

The clear trend, however, is to use the *time rule.*

The time rule holds that the community property share of the pension can be apportioned by a ratio of time earned while married divided by the total time employed.

Here is the formula:

$$\frac{\textit{Time married}}{\textit{Total time employed}} = \textit{CP \% of the pension}$$

$$\frac{\textit{Time unmarried}}{\textit{Total time employed}} = \textit{SP \% of the pension}$$

The time rule makes a rough cut because the task of apportioning a pension benefit can be complex.

California gives a court full authority to **"make whatever orders are necessary or appropriate to ensure that each party receives the party's full community property share in any retirement plan, whether public or private, including all survivor and death benefits."** Cal.Fam.Code § 2610. See below for more on ERISA, QDROs, and state *nunc pro tunc* judgments. Louisiana has held that the court should apportion on the basis of the money contributed by each estate. Wisconsin (and MMPA) describe the marital property element by statute.

## c. Division upon Divorce of Retirement and Disability Benefits

Since both retirement and disability provisions are dependent upon the outcome of so many contingencies, divorce courts have had particular difficulty in dividing the community property while providing for pre-vesting and post-vesting contingencies (further employment, election to retire, not dying etc.), some of which include options within the control of the employee. California has set the theme that normally the wage-earner is given the retirement plan especially where there are balancing assets which can be given to the nonwage-earner as an offset.

Federal law has two attitudes toward retirement plans. As to *private* retirement plans, The Employee Retirement Income Security Act of 1974 (ERISA), 29 U.S.C. §§ 1001 to 1381 demands that they not act like government plans. With private plans the variation in state law turns on vesting of rights in the employee, leaving the issue at dissolution one of apportionment. As to pensions *from* the *government*, discussed next, the employee has no vested right until the prescribed term of service has been rendered; the emphasis is upon the absence of enforceable rights of the employee.

ERISA regulates, at the federal level, retirement funds sponsored by a private employer in which the employee (participant) spouse is eligible for benefits or able to make contributions to the plan over time. The intention of the federal government to preempt the field by ERISA is shown in 29 U.S.C. § 1144, which declares that ERISA's provisions **"shall supersede any and all State laws insofar as they may now or hereafter relate to any employee benefit plan. . . ."** In *Egelhoff v. Egelhoff*, 532 U.S. 141 (2001), the U.S. Supreme Court wrote an extensive explanation of the factors involved in determining whether ERISA preempts state law.

Under 29 U.S.C.A. 1056(d)(3)(A), only a valid **"qualified domestic relations order,"** or QDRO, can provide an exception to the anti-assignment clause of ERISA, and to the express federal pre-emption provision of that statute. Thus, only by a valid QDRO, can a state court address *and create enforceable community property interests* in a federally-regulated pension.

## d. Government Retirement Plans

There is a dividing line between governmental and private retirement plans. The statutory schemes by which public employees are granted retirement benefits have adopted an imperious attitude. The recipient has no right to the retirement or other benefits until the prescribed term of service has been rendered, as defined by federal rules. Benefits are given as a matter of governmental largess.

None of the states follows the old Spanish distinction by which bonus payments to married soldiers who received other compensation were treated as gifts and therefore separate property. The statutory language and approach of governmental employee retirement plans did, however, emphasize the "non-vested" nature of the retirement allowance; this emphasis led the courts in California and Texas to adopt a short-lived doctrine that retirement funds subject to certain contingencies were not "vested" and therefore could not be community property. Both jurisdictions have reversed the holding, but the dichotomy between governmental and private pension plans remains.

Prior to the passage of FUSFSPA, 10 U.S.C.A. § 1408, which removed the federal pre-emption found to exist in *McCarty v. McCarty*, 453 U.S. 210, 101 S.Ct. 2728, 69 L.Ed.2d 589 (1981), federal military retirement benefits could not be characterized as community property—and thus they had to be characterized as the separate property of the military spouse.

The enactment of the FUSFSPA, 10 U.S.C.A. § 1408 reverses the result in *McCarty*, supra. The federal FUSFSPA provision permits the states to apply **"the law of the jurisdiction of such court"** to treat certain **"disposable retired or retainer pay"** as **"property of the member and his spouse."** FUSFSPA § 1408(c). By this language, a state may, by statute or decisional law, treat military veteran's retirement pay as community property divisible at divorce.

Exempt from the above FUSFSPA grant of permission to the states is any amount that the Government deducts **"as a result of a waiver"** that the veteran makes in order to receive **"disability payments."** FUSFSPA § 1408(a)(4)(B). *Mansell v. Mansell*, 490 U.S. 581, 594–595, 109 S.Ct. 2023, 104 L.Ed.2d 675 (1989) interpreted the above language as meaning that a state cannot treat as divisible community property "the waived portion" of the veteran's retirement pay that becomes "nontaxable disability benefits." *Mansell*, supra, involved a waiver that took place before the divorce proceeding.

*Howell v. Howell*, 137 S.Ct. 1400, 197 L.Ed.2d 781, 85 USLW 4245 (2017) raised the same issue, namely whether a state has the authority to divide nontaxable military disability payments. In *Howell*, supra, the veteran spouse was an active member of the Air Force when he divorced. The Arizona divorce court characterized the veteran's military retirement as community property; it then awarded the nonveteran spouse a one-half interest in the veteran's pension whenever the veteran retired. One year later the veteran retired. At that time, both he and his former spouse received a fifty-fifty share of $1500 in monthly retirement pay. Thirteen years later, the husband was adjudged 20% disabled due to a military service injury. At that time, he waived $250 of his retirement pay in order to receive nontaxable disability benefits. The Arizona court ordered the former husband to reimburse the former wife for the amount by which her monthly payments were reduced by the waivers. Appeals were taken to the Arizona Supreme Court, which ultimately affirmed the trial court order. See *In re Marriage of Howell*, 238 Ariz. 407, 408, 361 P.3d 936, 937 (2015). The veteran petitioned for certiorari.

The U.S. Supreme Court held that *Mansell*, supra, applied and, moreover, that it "completely pre-empts the States from treating waived military retirement pay as divisible community property." *Howell*, supra, at 1405, citing *Mansell*, supra, at 109 S.Ct. 2023. The rationale was that because the state court judgment ordering the veteran to reimburse his former spouse for the difference in pre- and postdisability waiver outcomes was without regard to disability, it (impermissibly) vested the former nonveteran spouse in the veteran spouse's nontaxable disability benefits.

*Howell*, supra, recognized that federal pre-emption can work a hardship on divorcing parties.

Nevertheless, it resurrected the rationale given in *McCarty*, supra, as to disability pay:

> "The basic reasons *McCarty* gave for believing that Congress intended to exempt military retirement pay from the state community property laws apply *a fortiori* to disability pay. See 453 U.S. at 232–235, 101 S.Ct. 2728 (describing the federal interests in attracting and retaining military personnel.) And those reasons apply with equal force to a veteran's postdivorce waiver to receive disability benefits to which he or she has become entitled." *Howell*, supra, at 1406.

The outcome in *Howell*, supra, is consistent with the late-twentieth century trend among community property states to assign money and property for bodily injury (an analog to disability pay) to the injured spouse upon dissolution.

FUSFSPA is discussed further Chapter 12.

The application of the federal supremacy clause (U.S. Const. Art. 6, Cl. 2) to community property is discussed in Chapter 12.

Federal statutes by which retirement benefits are awarded may provide that the benefits are for the employee only (non-transferable personal interest) and thus cannot be assigned or reached by process or by attachment (spendthrift provision).

The federal Social Security program has the most widespread retirement coverage of any retirement plan. There is no definitive statement that such benefits are the separate property of the recipient, but it is probable that the Supreme Court of the U.S. would characterize all benefits received under the Social Security program as separate property of the recipient.

Federal law is also inconsistent when it comes to recognizing community property rights in federal governmental benefits and private annuity plans. On one hand, Social Security (retirement) benefits are separate property of the recipient employee despite state community property laws. On the other hand, the REACT amendment to ERISA creates a "super community property" interest for the surviving spouse in death benefits. Under REACT, a QDRO may assign pension rights to a former spouse, even if the participant spouse opts to continue working past the (maturity) date at which he or she is eligible to retire with such rights. The REACT right of a surviving spouse applies in community property states to community property and to non-community property interests.

## C.  INDIVIDUAL STATES

### 1.  ARIZONA

***Bank accounts and sums on deposit.*** Commingled sums on deposit are presumptively community property unless the separate property deposits can be "explicitly traced;" rebuttal rests with the separate property proponent by "clear and satisfactory evidence." *Cooper v. Cooper*, 130 Ariz. 257, 260, 635 P.2d 850, 853 (1981)(in banc). Insubstantial

amounts will not transmute the character of the
account. *Battiste v. Battiste*, 135 Ariz. 470, 662 P.2d
145 (1983). No presumption of a gift arises when
identifiable separate property funds—meaning
deposits that are in fact traceable to a separate
property source—are deposited in the spouses' joint
checking account. *Bowart v. Bowart*, 128 Ariz. 331,
625 P.2d 920 (Ct. App. 1980).

*Separate property businesses.* Separate property
business profits—as distinguished from the
underlying separate property business—fall under the
Ariz.Rev.Stat.Ann. § 25–213(A), which defines the
rents, issues, and profits of separate property as
separate property. All other property obtained during
marriage that is not acquired by gift, devise or descent
is community property under the general statute,
Ariz.Rev.Stat.Ann. § 25–211. And yet, in the separate
property business context, rents, issues, and profits of
the business are "earnings," even though they derive
from separate property.

*Rueschenberg v. Rueschenberg*, 219 Ariz. 249, 196
P.3d 852 (2008) recognized the inconsistency between
Arizona's adherence to the American rule on rents,
issues, and profits and its treatment of the same as
"earnings" in the separate property business context.
The case reconciled the inconsistency in favor of the
general community property statute
Ariz.Rev.Stat.Ann. § 25–211.

A line of cases starting with *Evans v. Evans*, 79 Ariz.
284, 288 P.2d 775 (1955) allows the separate property
proponent to rebut the community property
presumption by showing that earnings obtained

during marriage from rents, issues and profits are derived mainly from the inherent nature of separate property, namely separate property capital and capital investment, and not from community labor. If such proof is made, these "earnings" are redefined as "rents, issues, and profits" under the separate property statutory provision of Ariz.Rev.Stat.Ann. § 25–213(A).

In *Cockrill v. Cockrill*, 124 Ariz. 50, 601 P.2d 1334 (1979) the Arizona Supreme Court reversed its prior all-or-nothing rule in favor of apportioning separate property profits depending on their source (underlying property or community labor). The policy goal is to achieve substantial justice between the parties. There, the issue of apportionment was remanded back to the trial court only to bounce back again to the court of appeal in *Cockrill v. Cockrill*, 139 Ariz. 72, 676 P.2d 1130 (1983).

***Credit acquisitions.*** Arizona is in the minority on credit acquisitions by how it applies the inception of title rule. Property acquired prior to marriage is separate property under Ariz.Rev.Stat.Ann. § 25–213. Separate property retains its character unless the spouses agree otherwise or the asset is transmuted by operation of law. If mortgage principal payments are subsequently made with community property, the community obtains a right of reimbursement, not a pro tanto share. *Potthoff v. Potthoff*, 128 Ariz. 557, 627 P.2d 708 (Ct. App. 1981). Payments made from a commingled account are presumptively credited to the community property.

In *Drahos v. Drahos*, 149 Ariz. 248, 717 P.2d 927 (Ct.App. 1985), the husband purchased a $21,000 residence one day prior to marriage, using a $7,000 downpayment and a $14,000 loan. At dissolution, the house was valued at $80,000. The trial court, applying the inception of title rule, characterized the house as separate property and awarded the wife a one-half equitable lien. On appeal, the court affirmed the separate property characterization of the house, but remanded the case to the trial court for recalculation of the lien. The case was strongly criticized on equitable grounds: even though the house was purchased only the day before the parties married, the outcome under the civil law approach was that the house remained separate property throughout the marriage notwithstanding the community's significant contribution to its purchase, which in the end was (merely) reimbursed.

Ariz.Rev.Stat.Ann. § 25–318, discussed in Chapter 9, allows a court to divide property equitably, and upon request to place a lien on separate property for purposes of reimbursement. Cases have taken a number of divergent paths from that beginning, and courts are not restricted by prior holdings because of the equitable nature of the lien. That said, the general idea seems to be that the lien should be calculated by the "amount spent formula" or by the "value-at-dissolution formula." *Barnett v. Jedynak*, 219 Ariz. 550, 55, 200 P.3d 1047, 1052 (Ct.App. Div. 1 2009). *Valento v. Valento*, 225 Ariz. 477, 482, 240 P.3d 1239, 1244 (Ct.App. Div. 1 2010) applied *Barnett* to articulate a hybrid reimbursement approach, seemingly based on *Marsden* (a California case discussed in Section C, California below), which attempts to capture amount spent, and value-at-purchase, marriage and dissolution factors.

- *When property appreciates during the marriage:* The prescribed value-at-dissolution formula is:

$$C + (\frac{C}{B} \times A) = value\ of\ CP\ lien$$

Where A is the appreciation in value of the property during the marriage, B is the fair market value on the date of marriage, and C is the community contributions to the purchase loan principal.

- *When property depreciates and equity is positive:* The community is reimbursed in the amount equal to the reduction in loan principal indebtedness attributable to the community contribution.

- *When the property depreciates and equity is negative:* The community lien can be valued by this proposed formula:

$$C - (\frac{C}{B} \times D) = value\ of\ CP\ lien$$

Where D is the depreciation in value of the property during the marriage, B is the fair market value on the date of marriage, and C is the community contributions to loan principal or market value. (Note that a depreciation, while a loss in market value, is usually recorded in the form of a tax deduction and therefore it should be a positive number for purposes of the above formula.) According to *Valento* the above formula is "a restatement of *Barnett* in a declining market." *Id.* 482, 1244. Here, community contributions enhance the separate property owner's equity position by decreasing the principal balance of the loan. This is true even if the property owner eventually owes more on the mortgage than the property is worth on the market. *Id.* 483, 1245.

Capital improvements are reimbursed under the value-at-dissolution formula. The community is entitled to share in the enhanced value of the property due to the expenditure of community funds. Not reimbursed are noncapital improvements, taxes, interest, and maintenance.

The intent of the lender test is not used in Arizona. Credit obtained during marriage is community property. Yet some Arizona cases have ignored the credit portion of the acquisition in determining the character of the property by tracing only to the down payment.

***Work related benefits.*** Retirement benefits are apportioned on a time basis.

Disability payments are separate property insofar as they are designed to replace future (postdissolution) income. *Luna v. Luna*, 125 Ariz. 120, 608 P.2d 57 (Ct. App.1979).

Protecting veterans is the plain language of Ariz.Rev.Stat.Ann. § 25–318.01. Added in 2010, the statute mandates that federal disability benefits awarded to a veteran, as in *Luna*, supra, **"shall not"** be considered by the court in making a disposition of property or a determination of spousal support at the end of the marriage.

Inception of title was given support in a dictum in *Rothman v. Rumbeck*, 54 Ariz. 443, 96 P.2d 755 (1939), which indicated that that rule would be applied to life insurance. The inception of title rule was cited with approval more recently in *Everson v. Everson*, 24 Ariz.App. 239, 537 P.2d 624 (Ct.App. 1975) and *Bell-Kilbourn v. Bell-Kilbourn*, 216 Ariz. 521, 169 P.3d 111 (Ct. App. 2007).

## 2. CALIFORNIA

***Bank accounts and sums on deposit.*** As noted above, California has adopted and enhanced uniform laws on multiple parties' accounts. See Chapter 3 for details on the California Multiple Parties Accounts Law.

As a brief review, under CAMPAL account titles determine access to an account. Ownership to sums on deposit in any demand deposit account of a married person, however, are presumptively community in character. The separate property claimant has the burden of rebuttal. That burden can be met by tracing or by producing an agreement specific to the sums on deposit in the contested account.

CAMPAL legislation follows *See v. See*, 64 Cal.2d 778, 51 Cal.Rptr. 888, 415 P.2d 776 (1966) in determining what kind of account records are adequate to trace different character sums held in a single commingled account.

Those rules were developed in relation to purchases made from a commingled account. In *See*, supra, a case that is consistent with CAMPAL, the California Supreme Court ruled that an intentional purchase from a disputed account (meaning an account that is commingled or undisclosed) that is titled in one spouse's name alone is presumptively community property. Rebuttal rests with the separate property proponent to otherwise using specialized account records that, for ease of understanding, can be called *See*-compliant records.

What are *See*-compliant records? Records that (i) are contemporaneous; (ii) show character specific deposits; (iii) apply the family expense presumption and (iv) establish that on the date of the asset's purchase, community property funds were exhausted in whole or part, leaving the separate property sums on deposit to make the purchase. Upon such proof, an inference can be made that the asset was purchased with separate property. Tracing methods set forth in *See*, supra, are also consistent with CAMPAL.

Practitioners occasionally report that they rely on forensic records to prove an ownership interest. But there is a meaningful difference between creating records for purposes of a dissolution proceeding and preparing already existing records for the same purpose. On the eve of dissolution, one might reasonably employ an accountant to review already existing *See*-compliant records; this kind of review does not raise the same specter of perjury as creating records for dissolution does. And, in fact, the latter is contra to the parameters of *See*, supra and of

CAMPAL for at least two reasons. One doctrinal reason is that the duty to keep specialized records arises on the date that the account is first commingled; that date may precede dissolution by years or even decades. Another reason is that the duty to keep *See*-compliant records for a commingled account comes into existence on the date that the account is first commingled. The duty attaches to the first of the spouses to commingle. Thus it is the parameters of this duty that presupposes records are to be kept on or near the date that commingling first occurred.

Forensic records should be (optimally) or may be (more likely) scrutinized as potentially inadmissible for a number of reasons. One, the use of forensic records is contra to the holding in *See*, supra, and particularly the language indicating that it is a significant breach of law and policy for a trial court judge to permit the use of an accounting method that turns a community property interest, which is vested, into an interest that is effectively contingent upon dissolution. Two, *See*, supra, imposed a legal duty on the first spouse to commingle. That duty arises at the time of commingling. Thus it may be reversible error to permit a spouse who has breached the duty keep records in the first place to benefit from his or her negligence. Three, forensic records, unless they start from the date of any initial commingling and move forward to the date of dissolution, may violate the inception of title rule as well as misapply the family expense presumption. Fourth is a policy reason: records created solely for dissolution proceedings increase the risk of perjury.

As tracing is only allowed to rebut the general community property presumption and the presumption for sums on deposit in an account, any asset purchased during marriage, even from a commingled account, and taken in joint title form continues to be governed by Cal.Fam.Code § 2581. See Chapter 5.

If an untitled or sole titled asset is purchased from the commingled account, the asset is subject to the general community property presumption. In that case, only *See*-compliant records showing that community property funds were exhausted on the date the asset was purchased rebuts the presumption. Proportional rebuttal is permissible.

The *Hicks-Mix-Murphy* line of cases allows for the prospective use of *See*-compliant records. This line of cases allows a separate property proponent to plan separate property purchases in advance by using contemporaneous *See*-compliant financial records that show that on or near the date of a purchase (i) both the community property and the separate property sums on deposit were sufficient to make the purchase; (ii) the separate property owner declared in writing an intention to use separate property funds to make the purchase; (iii) the purchase was, in fact, subtracted from separate sums on deposit available on or near the date of purchase; and (iv) the separate property purchaser disclosed the purchase as separate in character to the other spouse optimally before the purchase was made. The declaration of intent must be extrinsic to the account records. In *Marriage of Mix*, 14 Cal.3d 604, 122 Cal.Rptr. 79, 536 P.2d 479 (1975) the court affirmed the non-discretionary rule that *See*-compliant records must be prepared contemporaneously, not in anticipation of litigation; *Estate of Murphy,* 15 Cal.3d 907, 126 Cal.Rptr. 820, 544 P.2d 959 (1976) applies these rules in the probate context.

Cal.Fam.Code § 721(b) fiduciary duties apply to purchases made from a commingled account. A breach of fiduciary duty can occur where a separate property proponent gains **"any unfair advantage"** over the other spouse by the mere fact of making a beneficial purchase for his or her separate property estate at the expense of the community property.

As for *Hicks-Mix,* supra, the reason to require disclosure of a separate property purchase at a time when the community could also make the purchase is that each spouse has a partnership fiduciary duty to inform the other spouse of investment opportunities that the community might undertake.

***Separate property businesses.*** Under *Pereira v. Pereira,* 156 Cal. 1, 103 P. 488 (1909) the community property estate that contributes more than a minimum amount of labor to the separate property business is entitled to any excess profits remaining after the separate property profits and a fair rate of return have been accounted for. *Pereira* accounting is based on several elements: (i) the fair market value of the separate property business at dissolution, (ii) the original separate property capital investment, as measured by the fair market value of the business at marriage, and (iii) a fair rate of return on (the original separate property capital calculated using simple interest, to account for family expenses. The fair rate of return is a hypothetical calculation: what would the original separate property capital have earned had it been invested in securities of reasonable safety?

Here is the *Pereira* formula:

*FMV@ disso – (FMV @ marriage[1] + FROR) = excess profits*

The *Pereira* formula is discussed in Section B above.

*Beam v. Bank of America*, 6 Cal.3d 12, 98 Cal.Rptr. 137, 490 P.2d 257 (1971) held that a non-tax deferred investment account that was brought to the marriage falls within the definition of a covered separate property business. *Beam*, supra, sets the level of labor that gives rise to a community interest as "more than minimal," hence the "minimum-plus standard" mentioned in the previous paragraph.

Under *Van Camp*, if the community contributes only a minimum quantum of labor to the growth of the business during marriage, it is entitled to a reimbursement for its net labor. *Van Camp* accounting is based on several elements: (i) fair market value of the business at dissolution; (ii) uncompensated community property labor over the period of time in question; and (iii) family expenses over the period of time in question.

---

[1]     Assumes a separate property business brought to the marriage.

Here is the *Van Camp* formula:

*FMV@divorce – (CP labor – Family expenses) = SP*

The *Van Camp* formula is discussed in Section B above.

*Marriage of Imperato*, 45 Cal.3d 432, 119 Cal.Rptr. 590 (1975) allows for "reverse *Pereira*" apportionment for a community property business that appreciates in value during a period between a date of separation and a dissolution proceeding, a period of time during which each spouse's labor and accumulations are characterized as separate property.

*Marriage of Koester*, 73 Cal.App.4th 1032, 87 Cal.Rptr.2d 76 (1999), held that the incorporation during marriage of a business that was brought to the marriage is a change in form, not an acquisition during marriage under Cal.Fam.Code § 2581. However, if a court deems that a reimbursement to a separate property owner is due, the approved formula is the *Van Camp* formula.

***Credit acquisitions.*** California recognizes the existence of pro tanto interest for community property contributions to the purchase of separate property.

The following law applies only when the asset (usually a house) is titled in one name alone. Joint titles cannot be rebutted, in a dissolution proceeding, by tracing, as discussed in Chapter 3.

Determining pro tanto shares based on contributions to purchase comes into play when a credit acquisition is made before marriage, then paid down (but not off) during marriage. Refinancing complicates the original picture considerably.

Also, the difference between a pro tanto and an equitable interest is worth noting at this time. A pro tanto interest is one that vests when the community makes its first contribution to purchase. An equitable interest is one that does not vest until it is recognized by judicial action at the end of the marriage. In other words, the pro tanto interest comes into existence independently of judicial action. An equitable interest would not be recognized as having come into existence except through judicial action.

*Vieux v. Vieux*, 80 Cal.App. 222, 251 P. 640 (1926) articulated a twofold rationale in support of the pro tanto approach. One, the implied contract rationale: community property contributions to purchase of a separate property asset are proof that the parties impliedly agreed that the community's contributions would be in exchange for a proportional share of ownership. Two, the expectation rationale: the community develops a reasonable expectation of concurrent ownership based on its dedication of community funds to the purchase of an asset that would otherwise be separate in character.

*Marriage of Aufmuth*, 89 Cal.App.3d 446, 152 Cal.Rptr. 668 (1979), and *Marriage of Moore*, 28 Cal.3d 336, 168 Cal.Rptr. 662, 618 P.2d 208 (1980) affirmed the rationales presented in *Vieux*. Moreover, each went on to become the basis for the formula that establishes a contributing estate's pro tanto ownership share relative to the historic contract price of the disputed credit acquisition. *Aufmuth*, supra, stands for the proposition that loan proceeds constitute a positive contribution to purchase. *Moore* stands for the proposition that each estate's pro tanto share should be based on its actual contribution to purchase, with contribution ordinarily meaning downpayment, loan proceeds, and loan principal repayments. (Interest, taxes, and insurance payments are not contributions to purchase; they are categorized as family expenses.) Under *Moore*, supra, contributions to purchase are ultimately reimbursed, and total appreciation is apportioned by percentage shares. The holding in *Moore* is articulated as a formula below.

*Marriage of Marsden*, 130 Cal.App.3d 426, 181 Cal.Rptr. 910 (1982) expands upon the basic *Moore* formula to allow for the apportionment of marital appreciation. *Marsden*, supra, also confirms that, as a matter of law, the denominator in the *Moore*, supra, formula shall be the contract price (called the "historic purchase price" in *Marsden*, supra), not the fair market value of the house at marriage.

Under *Marsden* each estate's proportional share is multiplied by the appreciation or depreciation that occurs from the date of marriage to the date of dissolution (the "marital appreciation"). The *premarital* appreciation/depreciation, and premarital loan principal repayments are separate property because they are acquired before marriage.

*Marriage of Sherman*, 133 Cal.App.4th 795, 35 Cal.Rptr. 137 (2005) clarified that the fair market value of a residence for purposes of apportioning the property is as of the date of trial, not the date of separation. *Sherman*, supra, also disallowed rental value of the separate property residence to be factored in as a credit for the separate property estate.

Loan proceeds obtained *prior* to marriage are separate property under the general rules set forth in Chapter 4.

Loan proceeds obtained *during* marriage are presumptively community property. As stated above, *Aufmuth*, supra, holds that loan proceeds are a positive contribution to purchase; and if acquired during marriage they constitute a community property asset—in other words, loan proceeds, even though a debt, factor into a pro tanto accounting as a plus, not as a negative. If the separate property claimant wishes to rebut a community property presumption as to loan proceeds, the lender's intent test is the appropriate method for doing so. *Marriage of Grinius*, 166 Cal.App.3d 1179, 212 Cal.Rptr. 803 (1985) controls as a practical, if not a legal, matter. In *Grinius*, supra, the court went to the trouble to "restate the applicable standard: loan proceeds acquired during marriage are presumptively community property; unless the lender intended to rely *solely* on a spouse's separate property and did in fact do so." *Id.* (Italics added.)

The *Moore*, supra, formula applies when there is de minimis asset appreciation prior to marriage. Practically, this occurs when the separate property owner buys the property close to, but still before, the date of the marriage.

*Marsden*, supra, applies when the separate property owner seeks to claim a reimbursement for premarital equity and for premarital appreciation/depreciation. Typically, the house in a *Marsden*, supra, case is purchased well before the date of marriage.

Here are the elements of analysis for *Moore*, supra: (i) the downpayment; (ii) the loan proceeds; (iii) the loan principal repayments; and (iv) the historic purchase price.

Each contributing estate's percentage of ownership is determined by adding up that estate's contribution to purchase and dividing it by the historic purchase price. (Interest, taxes and insurance payments are not included because they are family expenses, as discussed above.)

Here is the *Moore*, supra, apportionment formula:

$$\frac{SP\ dpmt + (SP\ loan - CP\ contribution)}{HPP} = SP\%$$

$$\frac{CP\ contribution}{HPP} = CP\%$$

Multiply the SP and CP percentages by appreciation (or depreciation) to apportion asset appreciation (or depreciation). If premarital appreciation has been established by the separate property claimant, apportion only marital appreciation (or depreciation).

Total appreciation (or depreciation) is found by subtracting from the fair market value at dissolution the fair market value at purchase. Marital appreciation is found by subtracting from the fair market value at dissolution the fair market value at marriage, a value that must be established typically by an appraisal conducted on or near the date of marriage.

*SP% × App (or Dep) = SP share of the App/Dep*

*CP% × App (or Dep) = CP share of the App/Dep*

If a separate property proponent cannot establish an ownership interest (for example where there is an unrebutted joint form title presumption or where the separate property proponent fails to rebut the general presumption), the separate property contributor is nonetheless entitled to a statutory reimbursement, without interest and subject to value limitations. Cal.Fam.Code § 2640, the general reimbursement provision, creates a right of reimbursement that only applies when the asset in question is entirely (100%) community property: **"in the division of the community estate . . . unless a party has made a written waiver of the right of reimbursement or has signed a writing that has the effect of a waiver."** Absent such a waiver, **"the [separate property contributor] shall be reimbursed for the party's contributions to the acquisition of [entirely community] property. . . ."** Tracing determines the amount of the reimbursement, which **"shall be without interest, or adjustment for change in monetary values and shall not exceed**

**the net value of the property at the time of the division."**

Retroactive application of § 2640 was held to be unconstitutional; the addition of a writing requirement being the reason. *Marriage of Heikes*, 10 Cal.4th 1211, 44 Cal.Rptr.2d 155, 899 P.2d 1349 (1995).

*Marriage of Walrath*, 17 Cal.4th 907, 72 Cal.Rptr.2d 856, 952 P.2d 1124 (1998) held that the § 2640 right to reimbursement carries over in the event that the original property is refinanced and the (refinanced) loan proceeds are used to a secure a community asset. If the finance record becomes too complicated to decipher, the doctrine of confusion applies, and the entire asset can be deemed community property.

For purposes of a separate property reimbursement, Cal.Fam.Code § 2640 defines **"[c]ontributions to the acquisition of property"** as including **"downpayments, payments for improvements, and payments that reduce the principal of a loan used to finance the purchase or improvement of the property. . . ."** By the same statute, contributions to purchase **"do not include payments of interest on the loan or payments made for maintenance, insurance, or taxation of the property."**

The legislature modified the rule of *Marriage of Lucas*, 27 Cal.3d 808, 166 Cal.Rptr. 853, 614 P.2d 285 (1980) for purposes of dissolution. Current Cal.Fam.Code § 2640 includes capital improvements within the express meaning of contribution to purchase and provides that they shall be reimbursed. Are contributions to the improvement of property within this definition? Generally, ordinary improvements fall under the rubric of family expenses, as such they are not reimbursable absent a contract providing otherwise. Also not reimbursable are non-capital contributions such as insurance, taxes, interest, and ordinary maintenance, as noted above. This distinction appears in the case law as well.

**Work related benefits.** Business goodwill falls within the community property system. Celebrity identity does too, as it is a property right recognized and protected from commercial use without prior consent by Cal.Civ.Code § 3344. No cases so hold, but presumably a celebrity identity, developed via labor during marriage while domiciled in the state is divisible at dissolution. Elite professional status (talent) has been treated as distinct from celebrity identity, and thus as outside of the community property system; here the courts regard talent, (independently of any income stream it produces) as too personal to its holder to be treated as divisible property. *Marriage of McTiernan & Dubrow*, 133 Cal.App.4th 1090, 35 Cal.Rptr.3d 287 (2005). The rules are just beginning to be articulated.

Cal.Fam.Code § 2641 is a specific reimbursement statute for community contributions to one spouse's education or training. The rule favors threshold marriage dissolutions; meaning cases where the parties are married for a short while, invest in an education for one spouse, but otherwise own no or little divisible property. The reimbursement belongs to the community (not solely to the non-student spouse); and it is (only) for community property contributions to the direct expenses of an income enhancing education or training. *Direct* expenses are tuition, books, fees, supplies, school related travel, and so forth. Payments that reduce the principal portion of an educational loan count as a direct expense. Educational loans are mandatorily assigned to the student spouse at dissolution absent an agreement between the spouses otherwise. Indirect educational expenses (e.g., rent, utilities, cable, etc.) are not reimbursable under this statute, but they form the discretionary basis for a spousal support award to the nonstudent spouse under Cal.Fam.Code § 4320(b).

California uses the apportionment rule to characterize any savings component (cash surrender value) of an ordinary (sometimes referred to as a whole) life insurance policy; both the chose in action and the savings component are divisible on dissolution. See the *Blethen v. Pacific Mutual Life Ins. Co. of Cal.*, 198 Cal. 91, 243 P. 431 (1926) line of cases.

Term life insurance without a savings component has no cash surrender value. It protects against the death of the insured, and as a person gets older or less well the product becomes more difficult to obtain. But rather than risk a loss, the language of insurance puts blame squarely on the individual for becoming "uninsurable." Term life insurance represents a contractual liability that expires at the termination of the specific contract term unless and until the insured dies. Only at the death of the insured, are proceeds paid out.

Disagreement exists at the court of appeal level as to how to characterize a term life insurance policy. In the interests of facilitating dissolution, *Estate of Logan*, 191 Cal.App.3d 319, 236 Cal.Rptr. 368 (1987) follows *Marriage of Lorenz*, 146 Cal.App.3d 464, 194 Cal.Rptr. 237 (1983) and rejects *Marriage of Gonzalez*, 168 Cal.App.3d 1021, 214 Cal.Rptr. 634 (1985). *Logan*, supra, held that a term life insurance policy is not a community asset subject to division on divorce. The rationale is that the term life insurance contract is worthless once the contract term expires.

Even if not divisible, the term life insurance is characterizable by the last premium rule. In the context of spousal managerial rights and duties, naming a beneficiary is an act that disposes of property after death. Thus each spouse can only dispose of one-half of the proceeds of a community life insurance policy.

*Marriage of Spengler,* 5 Cal.App.4th 288, 6 Cal.Rptr.2d 764 (1992) involved renewal rights on a group term life insurance policy offered by an employer. *Spengler* agreed with *Logan* that the term life insurance policy is not itself a divisible asset at divorce, but *Spengler* disagreed with the *Logan* dictum that a renewal right could be community property "if the insured becomes uninsurable during the marriage." *Id.* Thus *Spengler* held that the employment-related policy, despite the husband's terminal illness and uninsurability, was a mere expectancy dependent upon the employer's continuance of the group insurance plan for all of its employees. As a mere expectancy, the life insurance renewal right was not property, and therefore it was not subject to community property laws. By the same rationale, any community property interest in term health insurance ends on dissolution. *Marriage of Havins*, 43 Cal.App.4th 414, 50 Cal.Rptr.2d 763 (1996).

Severance pay is normally understood as deferred compensation. Severance pay was discussed in *Marriage of Horn*, 181 Cal.App.3d 540, 226 Cal.Rptr. 666 (1986), *Marriage of Skadden*, 19 Cal.3d 679, 139 Cal.Rptr. 615, 566 P.2d 249 (1977). A turbulent line of precedent can be found in *Marriage of Gram*, 25 Cal.App.4th 859, 30 Cal.Rptr.2d 792 (1994), which was disapproved of by *Marriage of Lehman*, 18 Cal.4th 169, 74 Cal.Rptr.2d 825, 955 P.2d 451 (1998), which was not extended by *Marriage of Steinberger*, 91 Cal.4th 1449, 111 Cal.Rptr.2d 521 (2001).

Stock options were discussed in *Marriage of Hug*, 154 Cal.App.3d 780, 201 Cal.Rptr. 676 (1984). There the court held that the options were subject to community property rules, and that, given complications raised by issues of timing, their allocation is subject to court discretion.

Disability benefits were discussed in *Marriage of Rossin*, 172 Cal.App.4th 725, 91 Cal.Rptr.3d 427 (2009), a case of first impression. There, the court characterized disability benefits as separate property on a two part showing. One, the disabled spouse had acquired the disability rights (by contract) prior to marriage and thus entirely with separate property funds. Two, the insured's intention was to replace income in the event of injury, not to supplement retirement.

In *Regents of the University of California v. Benford,* 128 Cal.App.4th 867, 27 Cal.Rptr.3d 441 (4th Dist. 2005), a non-employee spouse who predeceased the participant spouse was precluded from devising her community property interest in the university retirement plans. To get around this ruling, the participant spouse would have had to elect a lump sum (rather than an annuity) upon retirement.

*Marriage of Stephenson,* 162 Cal.App.3d 1057, 209 Cal.Rptr. 383 (1984) discusses the method for apportioning a defined benefit plan. *Marriage of Bergman,* 168 Cal.App.3d 742, 214 Cal.Rptr. 661 (1985) discusses the method for apportioning a defined contribution plan.

For the interplay between ERISA and California law, see *Kennedy v. Plan Adm'r for Dupont Sav. & Inv. Plan,* 555 U.S. 285, 129 S.Ct. 865, 172 L.Ed.2d 662 (2009). For a discussion and explication of ERISA and the necessity of creating a valid QDRO for purposes of Cal.Fam.Code § 2346, which authorizes a court to enter a judgment *nunc pro tunc* in any dissolution proceeding that seeks to reserve jurisdiction over decedent's ERISA pension, see *Marriage of Padgett,* 172 Cal.App.4th 830, 91 Cal.Rptr.3d 475 (2009).

Generally, California continues to apportion retirement benefits most often by use of the time rule. The ultimate decision of what denominator to use, however, (time, points, contributions) is left to the discretion of the court, but the denominator should make sense in the context of the pension plan. If the employer uses points, the court also should probably use points. See for example *Marriage of Poppe*, 97 Cal.App.3d 1, 158 Cal.Rptr. 500 (1979). Calculations can be laborious, expensive, and subject to intense scrutiny, as illustrated by *Marriage of Green*, 56 Cal.4th 1130, 158 Cal.Rptr.3d 247, 302 P.3d 562 (2013).

## 3.   IDAHO

***Accounts and sums on deposit in an account.*** *Gapsch v. Gapsch*, 76 Idaho 44, 277 P.2d 278 (1954) is an often cited case on commingling of separate and community property. For a purchase from commingled funds, Idaho does not require specialized records to rebut the general presumption, suggesting that a total recapitulation method of accounting (rather than the contemporaneous accounting method used in California, for example) is permitted.

***Separate property businesses.*** Idaho follows in civil law on separate property rents, issues, and profits. Thus, in Idaho, separate property rents, issues and profits are community property during the continuance of the marriage. Additionally, *Gapsch*, supra, is often cited for the principle that the natural enhancement of separate property remains part of the underlying separate property. (Natural enhancement presumably refers to asset appreciation, not asset income streams.) Despite this legal scaffolding, it may still be necessary to seek an accounting at dissolution or death. What gets accounted for are profits that can be traced back to separate property elements versus profits that can be traced back to community property elements.

Idaho Code § 32–906 was amended to read **"[t]he income, including rents, issues and profits, of all property, separate or community is community property. . . ."**

In *Speer v. Quinlan*, 96 Idaho 119, 525 P.2d 314 (1974) and in *Simplot v. Simplot*, 96 Idaho 239, 526 P.2d 844 (1974) the Idaho Supreme Court held that retained corporate stock dividends are not income or rents or profits as that term is used in Idaho Code § 32–906. The rationale is that until corporate stock dividends are distributed, they remain the property of the corporation. *Swope v. Swope*, 112 Idaho 974, 739 P.2d 273 (1987) declined to extend *Simplot*, insofar as it held that the earnings of a partnership, whether retained or distributed, are income under Idaho Code § 32–906. The rationale relied on in *Swope*, supra, is that a partner has a vested interest in partnership earnings, whether retained or distributed.

*Speer*, supra, also held that retained corporate earnings do not constitute commingling, even when the separate property business owner has substantial influence in the decision to reinvest the corporate stock dividends in the company. The *Speer* court was unwilling to allocate the closely-held corporation, even though the separate property proponent was the majority shareholder who made the decision to reinvest the stock dividends. The divorce court had discretionary power to divide the community property in a just manner, and to protect the community's rights with an equitable lien, but it could not stop the business owner from transferring shares to his family. Thus the wife was granted an equitable lien on a percentage of the withheld corporate stock retained by her former spouse's separate property business, but that ruling led to substantial post-divorce litigation over who, among the separate property business owner's family members, actually owned the disputed shares of stock.

Idaho uses a benchmark salary test to determine the amount of the business attributable to the community estate as compensation for its labor. *Speer*, supra, stated that the trial court should adequately compensate the community for its labor at the standard rate it would take to "secure a non-owner employee to perform the same services which were rendered by the community." *Id*. 135, 330. Once the compensation rate is determined, any rents, issues and profits obtained during marriage are apportioned between labor (the community's reimbursement) and natural increase (the underlying business).

*Credit acquisitions.* The purchase of property with a loan secured by the property has received disparate treatment in Idaho, but generally Idaho follows the inception of the title rule. An early bankruptcy case, *Wilkerson v. Aven*, 26 Idaho 559, 144 P. 1105 (1914), seemed to allow the separate property character of the down payment to determine the character of the property overall. The actual source of payments was used on a condition subsequent basis in *Cargill v. Hancock*, 92 Idaho 460, 444 P.2d 421 (1968). The civil law inception of title approach was followed in *Estate of Freeburn*, 97 Idaho 845, 555 P.2d 385

(1976), a case recently cited by *Credit Bureau of Eastern Idaho, Inc. v. Lecheminant*, 149 Idaho 467, 235 P.3d 1188 (2010).

***Work related benefits.*** Idaho has moved toward the last premium rule for community property term life insurance proceeds. *The Travelers Insurance Company v. Johnson*, 97 Idaho 336, 544 P.2d 294 (1975). This case was followed in *Thompson and Thompson*, 2011 WL 2694245 (U.S. Bankruptcy Court, D. Idaho (2011). Whole life insurance policies with a savings component continue to be governed under the inception of title rule.

In *The Traveler's Insurance Co.* the insured named a third party (his former wife not his current wife) as the sole beneficiary on his group term life insurance policy. At the death of the insured, the surviving spouse claimed a one-half interest in the life insurance proceeds. The trial court apportioned the proceeds between the former wife and the surviving wife. The Idaho Supreme Court eventually reversed. The court held that an insurance policy issued on the life of a married person without the knowledge or consent of the other spouse gives rise to a one-half community interest to the proceeds in favor of the surviving spouse. The rationale for this outcome relies on the commonly accepted distinction between testamentary and nontestamentary acts In the context of spousal managerial rights and duties the naming of a gratuitous life insurance POD is a testamentary act; even so, each spouse has the authority to dispose of (only) his or her one-half of the proceeds of a the policy.

In *Banner Life Insurance v. The Mark Wallace Dixson Irrevocable Trust*, 147 Idaho 117, 206 P.3d 481 (2009), the court announced a move toward Washington's "risk payment theory" for characterizing proceeds. The court articulated the risk payment rule as follows: A life insurance policy acquired during marriage is presumed community property unless the last premium was paid for with separate property.

Pensions are apportioned on a time basis between periods when the employee was or was not married and domiciled in Idaho. *Ramsey v. Ramsey*, 96 Idaho 672, 535 P.2d 53 (1975). *Ramsey* was overruled by *Rice v. Rice*, 103 Idaho 85, 645 P.2d 319 (1982) insofar as it conflicted with *McCarty*, supra, (discussed above and in Chapter 12).

Congress effectively overruled *McCarty*, supra, in 1982 with the USFSPA, 10 U.S.C.A. § 1408 (1982), which permits the states to apply **"the law of the jurisdiction of such court"** to treat certain **"disposable retired or retainer pay"** as **"property of the member and his spouse."**

*Rice*, supra, in turn, was subsequently overruled by *Griggs v. Griggs*, 107 Idaho 123, 686 P.2d 68 (1884), a case in which the Idaho Supreme Court exercised its plenary justification power under Art. § 5 and § 9 of the Idaho Constitution to reinstate the holding in *Ramsey*, supra, as to military retirement pay.

In the case of divorce, Idaho Code § 32–712 provides that the existence and extent of retirement benefits, including **"social security, civil service, military**

**and railroad benefits"** is a factor which bears upon a **"just"** assignment of community property. **"Just"** division need not be an equal division under the discussion in *Griggs*, supra. Thus, consideration of such benefits under Idaho Code § 32–712(7) need not run counter to the reasoning of *Hisquierdo v. Hisquierdo*, 439 U.S. 572, 586, 99 S.Ct. 802, 810, 811, 59 L.Ed.2d 1 (1979), which held that to allow an offsetting award to the non-employee spouse would defeat the purpose of barring the anticipation of covered government pensions and benefits. While Idaho Code § 32–712 provides that **"the community property must be assigned by the court . . . ,"** it also gives the court discretion to give **"due consideration"** to federally protected retirement benefits in making a **"just"** assignment.

## 4.    LOUISIANA

*Accounts and sums on deposit.* Louisiana historically required greater clarity of intent in order to preserve the separate character of property acquired by exchange during marriage. LSA–C.C. Art. 2342 carries on this tradition by requiring a declaration of separate property on an asset-by-asset basis, at the time of acquisition. The use of a declaration presumably applies to accounts and sums on deposit. A separate property declaration can be controverted by a community property proponent who traces the asset back to a community source. LSA–C.C. Art. 2342, as discussed in Chapters 3 and 4.

LSA–C.C. Art. 2343 and Art. 2343.1 cover commingling issues. Under the first provision, a spouse may **"transform a community property interest into separate property;"** when this occurs by an act of donation, **"an equal interest of the donee is also transformed into separate property ... [to] form part of the donee's separate property."** Under the second provision, separate property can be transferred to the community, and it retains its character if there is no **"stipulation that it shall be part of the community."** Note however that in *Graffeo v. Graffeo*, 576 So.2d 596 (La.App. 1991), a change in the title of a bank account was sufficient stipulation of an intent to transmute the account from separate to community.

*Separate property businesses.* LSA–C.C. Art. 2368 allows a statutory scheme by which a separate property business retains its separate character even during marriage. If the business increases in value as a result of **"uncompensated common labor or industry of the spouses,"** then **"the other spouse is entitled to be reimbursed from the spouse whose property has increased in value one-half of the increase attributed to the common labor."** The business owner can rebut the reimbursement with evidence that some or all of the growth was the result of non-labor factors. *Bordelon v. Bordelon*, 942 So.2d 708 (La.App. 2006).

*Credit acquisitions.* The inception of the title rule had a variation in Louisiana that looked to the time of vesting, rather than purchase. In a bond for deed for the purchase of an immovable (called a contract for deed or a real estate contract in other jurisdictions), the inception of title arises when the contract for the sale of realty is made, but the time of vesting in the purchaser does not occur until the deed is delivered, often years many years after execution, when all contract obligations have been fulfilled by the purchaser.

The use of community property funds to pay a separate property obligation is covered by LSA–C.C. Art. 2364. The use of separate property funds to pay a community property obligation is covered by LSA–C.C. Art. 2365. Purchase money mortgage cases are reported under both provisions.

Contributions to purchase (mortgage principal payments), use, improvement or other benefits are covered by LSA–C.C. Art. 2366 (community to separate) and LSA–C.C. Art. 2367 (separate to community).

Generally, if property of one character has been used to satisfy a purchase money mortgage obligation of another character, under the inception of title rule, the character of the property does not change, but, a reimbursement is due to the contributing estate. The same is true for contributions to acquisitions more generally, as this is the civil law approach. See also *Betz v. Riviere*, 29 So.2d 465 (La. 1947). However, an incipient line of cases takes the American rule approach, starting with, *Curtis v. Curtis*, 388 So.2d 816 (La.App. 1980), an equal management era case that recognizes proportional ownership on the theory that reimbursement is not adequate to keep up with inflation.

***Work related benefits.*** LSA–C.C. Art. 2369 provides that **"a spouse owes an accounting to the other spouse for community property under his control at the termination of the community property regime."** This obligation is not predicated upon a showing of fraud, as it is under LSA–C.C. Art. 2354, discussed in Chapter 7. The accounting is due as matter of course, but it applies going forward only to property under one former spouse's control at the termination of the community. Retirement benefits, insurance contracts, corporate stock, former community enterprises, usufruct, and the like would be covered under the provision.

Louisiana has applied the inception of the title rule to life insurance policies and proceeds. *Succession of Verneuille,* 45 So. 520 (La. 1908). At the termination of the community, a reimbursement is due for a community life insurance policy with a cash surrender value that gets allocated to one spouse. Reimbursement is not the amount of one-half of the premiums paid, but rather one-half of the cash surrender value of the policy at the time of partition and award, if any. *Westcott v. Westcott,* 11 So.3d 45 (La.App. 4 Cir. 2009). There is no right of reimbursement for term life insurance without a cash surrender value. *Connell v. Connell,* 331 So.2d 4 (La. 1976).

In *Sims v. Sims,* 358 So.2d 919 (La. 1978), the Louisiana Supreme Court apportioned retirement benefits between the contributing estates on the basis of contribution, not time. See LSA–C.C. Art. 2336. The effect of the ruling was to except private retirement plans and benefits from the inception of title rule. At the termination of the community, each spouse is entitled to a pro rata share of the retirement assets based on a ratio of character contribution divided by total value of plan.

In the public retirement fund area, Louisiana tracks the federal approach of deciding that some retirement funds do not belong to the community of acquets and gains. *Kennedy v. Kennedy*, 391 So.2d 1193 (La.App. 1980) involved the Firefighter's Pension and Relief Fund, *Scott v. Scott*, 179 So.2d 656 (La.App. 1965) involved the State Teacher's Retirement System, and *Brouillette v. Brouillette*, 51 So.3d 898 (La.App. 2010) involved Combat Related Special Compensation Benefits. Relief from the harshness of this rule for the nonemployee spouse is given in the form of a right of reimbursement to the community for any contributions that were made to the separate property retirement system.

## 5.   NEVADA

***Accounts and sums on deposit.*** Purchases made during marriage from a commingled account are presumptively community property absent clear and convincing evidence otherwise. *Malmquist v. Malmquist*, 106 Nev. 231, 238, 792 P.2d 372, 376 (1990) recites the California approach on this topic.

***Separate property businesses.*** The rents, issues and profits of separate property obtained during marriage are also separate property, following the American rule approach. Historically, Nevada followed the all-or-nothing approach to rents, issues and profits of a separate property business. But *Johnson v. Johnson*, 89 Nev. 244, 510 P.2d 625 (1973) disallowed the all-or-nothing approach and instead adopted the California approach as stated in *Beam v. Bank of America*, supra, which confirms that *Pereira*, supra, and *Van Camp*, supra, provide rival accounting methods. Today, the preferred accounting method in Nevada is *Pereira*, supra. But the court has discretion to use the method that will achieve substantial justice between the parties.

A relatively recent Nevada application of *Van Camp*, supra, is *Devries v. Gallio*, 128 Nev.Adv.Op. 63, 290 P.3d 260, 263 (2012). There, the wife owned a separate property cattle ranch during the 12-year marriage. The husband introduced evidence of the growth in the value of the wife's business, but "minimal evidence of what labor, if any" the community had contributed. *Id.* After extensive tracing of the cattle company growth, the trial court applied *Van Camp*, supra, because the increase in value of the wife's business "appeared to come solely from the sale and acquisition of cattle and equipment . . . purchased with [the wife's] separate property or the rents thereof." *Id.*

***Credit acquisitions.*** Nevada courts have recognized that the community is entitled to a pro rata ownership share for contributions to the purchase of separate property. *Robison v. Robison*, 100 Nev. 668, 670, 691 P.2d 451, 454 (1984).

As to apportionment, *Malmquist v. Malmquist*, 106 Nev. 231, 238, 792 P.2d 372, 376 (1990) announced that Nevada would follow a slightly modified version of California law, and specifically of *Aufmuth/Moore* apportionment, as discussed in Section C, California above. The Nevada approach is fully developed and discussed in Peter M. Moldave, *The Division of the Family Residence Acquired With a Mixture of Separate and Community Funds*, 70 CAL.L.REV.1263 (1982). The stated rationale is simplicity and fairness.

***Work related benefits.*** Deferred compensation in the form of pension benefits is apportioned by time.

Term life insurance is not divisible upon divorce. Term life insurance proceeds are characterized by the last premium rule.

The savings component of a whole life insurance, if any, is apportioned based on character contributions.

## 6.   NEW MEXICO

***Accounts and sums on deposit.*** Purchases from commingled bank accounts are community property, unless the separate property proponent can trace the asset back to separate property funds. New Mexico does not appear to have tracing rules specific to commingled bank accounts, thus suggesting that courts allow the total recapitulation method of accounting. Copies of checks, records of deposits, bank account statements, and purchase receipts may be used to rebut the community property presumption.

***Separate property businesses.*** *Laughlin v. Laughlin*, 49 N.M. 20 (1944) involved a separate property agricultural enterprise made profitable by community property labor. New Mexico's Supreme

Court rejected the approach in *Estate of Pepper*, 158 Cal. 619, 112 P. 62 (1910), the start of yet a different line of California cases that involve separate property agricultural enterprises. Instead, the court opted for *Pereira*, supra, accounting. The New Mexico Supreme Court specifically cited the *Pereira*, supra excess profits versus *Van Camp*, supra reimbursement approach with approval since in New Mexico (as in California) rents, issues, and profits of separate property are also separate property. *Laughlin*, held that even in the case of a separate property agricultural enterprise, the separate property is entitled to the rental value of the land (either in cash or in the proceeds of crops sold from it), while the community property is entitled to the balance of income produced from the land by the labor, skill, or management of the parties.

***Credit acquisitions.*** For credit acquisitions, *Dorbin v. Dorbin*, 105 N.M. 263, 731 P.2d 959 (1986) holds that New Mexico has long apportioned interests where property is purchased with separate *and* community property; pro rata shares are based on capital contributions to purchase. Where an asset is acquired with a separate property downpayment and a separate property loan *and* where community property principal payments are made to the separate property loan, the estates' shares are the ratio of their respective contributions to purchase divided by the value of the asset upon marriage.

*Dorbin*, supra, cited *Chance v. Kitchell*, 99 N.M. 443, 659 P.2d 895 (N.M. 1983) to affirm the use of a modified California *Moore/Marsden* formula. In New

Mexico percentages are determined by dividing contributions by the value of the property on the date of marriage, not by the historic purchase price (i.e. the contract price) as in California. The policy in apportioning interests is to seek substantial justice between the parties.

Neither New Mexico case law nor statutes authorize a reimbursement for payment of interest, taxes and insurance.

***Work related benefits.*** New Mexico applied the inception of title rule for determining the character of "war risk" life insurance proceeds, *White's Estate*, 43 N.M. 202, 89 P.2d 36 (1939). *Phillips v. Wellborn*, 89 N.M. 340, 552 P.2d 471 (1976) **moved toward the last premium rule.** But otherwise, pension benefits are characterized by marital status when earned, and thus can be adjudged commingled. *LeClert v. LeClert*, 80 N.M. 235, 453 P.2d 755 (1969).

## 7.   TEXAS

***Accounts and sums on deposit.*** Texas cases recognize a community property presumption when separate and community property are commingled so that they cannot be separately traced. In addition, V.T.C.A.Fam.Code § 3.102(b) provides a presumption concerning management, control and disposition of commingled community property, as discussed in Chapter 7.

For funds in a bank account to be characterized as separate property, the burden is on the separate property proponent to prove by clear and convincing evidence. *Vardilos v. Vardilos*, 219 S.W.3d 920 (2007), *Pearson v. Fillingim*, 332 S.W.3d 361 (2011). The separate property claimant's testimony, without corroborating evidence, is not sufficient. *Sprague v. Sprague*, 2012 WL 456936.

***Separate property businesses.*** Texas follows the civil law rule on separate property rents issues and profits. This means that income earned by separate property funds is community property during the marriage, as discussed in Chapters 3 and 4. See also Section C, Idaho above.

***Credit acquisitions.*** Loan proceeds (borrowed money) obtained during marriage are presumed to be community property unless the creditor agreed to look only to the separate property of the contracting party for satisfaction of the credit extended. *Goodloe v. Williams*, 302 S.W.2d 235 (Civ.App.1957). Unpublished opinions continue this rule. V.T.C.A.Fam.Code § 3.402(a)(4)(C) codifies this lender's intent test in its definition of an "economic contribution," as discussed in the next paragraph.

V.T.C.A.Fam.Code § 3.401 et. seq. allows for claims for economic contribution and reimbursement as effective September 1, 1999. Amendments were made in 2001. V.T.C.A.Fam.Code § 3.402 defines an **"economic contribution"** as the **"reduction of the principal amount of the debt."** The provision covers the following: separate property loans secured by the property; home equity loans secured by the property; debts secured by other property; refinancing loans; and capital improvement loans. **"Expenditures for ordinary maintenance and**

**repair or for taxes, interest, or insurance"** or
sweat equity in the form of spousal labor do not fall
under the definition of economic contributions.

V.T.C.A.Fam.Code § 3.403 allows for **"a claim for
economic contribution"** in a case where one marital
estate makes an economic contribution to property
owned by another marital estate.

Consistent with the civil law inception of title rule,
an economic contribution claim does not affect the
character of the asset. V.T.C.A.Fam.Code § 3.404(a),
which explicitly states, in subsection (b), that **"the
claim for economic contribution ... does not
create an ownership interest in property, but
does create a claim against the property of the
benefited estate by the contributing estate. The
claim matures on dissolution of the marriage or
the death of either spouse."** In *Langston v.
Langston*, 82 S.W.3d 686, on subsequent appeal 183
S.W.3d 479 (Ct.App. 2002), a trial court was held to
have abused its discretion when it awarded an
ownership interest to a contributing estate. Abuse of
discretion, because the mandated statutory outcome is
to secure the contributing estate's claim with an
equitable lien on the benefitted property.
V.T.C.A.Fam.Code § 3.406.

Offsets are allowed.

A statutory right to waive, release, assign or
partition an economic contribution by a marital
property agreement is found at V.T.C.A.Fam.Code
§ 3.410.

***Work related benefits.*** Generally, the definitions of community and separate property, along with the conceptual guide of the inception of title rule help characterize assets like non-ERISA governed insurance policies. *Marriage of Skarda*, 345 S.W.3d 665 (2011). Whether property is separate or community is determined by its character at inception, and this general rule seems to apply to life insurance policies.

If an insurance contract is community property at the time of the insured spouse's death, then the surviving spouse is entitled to one-half the proceeds as his or her share of the community estate; this is so even if the deceased spouse's designates a nonspousal POD beneficiary. *Amason v. Franklin Life Ins. Co.*, 428 F.2d 1144, 1146–47 (5th Cir. 1970).

At dissolution, when the life insurance policy has a cash value—as when community property paid for the policy in a lump sum or where there is a cash surrender value—the inception of the right rule holds that the ownership of the community property life insurance policy remains co-owned by the (now) ex-spouses. However, title defaults to tenants in common absent a valid property settlement concerning the term life insurance policy or a divorce court division of the policy. In the case of the change from community property to tenants in common the now ex-spouses own the policy as if they had never been married, with each tenant in common getting a one half share of the insurance proceeds in the event of the death of the insured. Alternatively, where the policy itself does not have a cash value after divorce—

as with a term life insurance policy—then the unmatured policy—because it has no property value—is not subject to division, as was explained in *Grost v. Grost*, 561 S.W.2d 223 (1977).

A term life insurance policy that is separate in character that gets reissued during the marriage becomes community property by the last premium rule. *Newberry v. Newberry*, 351 S.W.3d 552 (2011); and *Person v. Fillingim*, 332 S.W.3d 361 (2011).

## 8.  WASHINGTON

### *Accounts and sums on deposit.*

All property acquired after marriage is presumptively community property, even property in TIC or JTWROS title form. Wash.Rev.Code § 64.28.020 states that an interest in favor of two (or more) persons is an interest in common, and that a joint tenancy can be created in the state. But that code section also provides that interests in common in the names of persons who are married to each other (or RDPs) are **"presumed to be community property."** Thus a bank account in the name of two married persons is presumptively community in character, as are sums on deposit acquired during marriage. The spouses can opt, by community property agreement, for a right of survivorship; but a community property agreement does not change the character of the account from community to separate. What the community property agreement does is, one, impress upon the parties that they are agreeing to dispose of community property by survivorship and, two, provide clear and convincing written evidence of each spouse's intent. See Chapter 5.

In 1885 Washington abrogated the doctrine of survivorship as an incident of joint tenancies. Later, exceptions were made for demand deposit accounts of various sorts. Commentary explained that what Washington abolished was the technical appending of the right of survivorship to the joint tenancy once the four unities had been met (as in the common law). Washington did not bar the use of a JTWROS, so long as there was written evidence of the parties' intent to dispose of the property by survivorship.

For married persons, the right to agree to a right of survivorship is secured by Wash.Rev.Code § 64.28.030, again as long as there is written evidence of intent. See Chapters 2 and 5. Moreover, the above statute expressly states that, as to bank deposits and community property agreements, the law **"shall not restrict the creation of a joint tenancy in a bank deposit ..., nor restrict the power of both spouses or both domestic partners to make [community property] agreements ...."**

Moreover, if the spouses use a community property agreement to dispose of sums on deposit by right of survivorship, the account and the sums remain community in character. The account is community property because it is included in a community property agreement; the sums on deposit are community property because they are acquired during marriage absent proof to the contrary and held within a community property account.

***Separate property businesses.*** In allocating the profits of a separate property business to which community labor has been added, the courts in Washington have looked at the respective importance of labor or capital in the particular business, and have considered the sufficiency of amounts withdrawn from the business as salary. The Washington approach—called the segregation approach—is intended to give the separate property owner the authority to self-apportion the business. The rationale is that the court should not second-guess the separate property business owner on management issues and on the more particular issue of how business records are or should be kept during the marriage.

***Credit acquisitions.*** In determining the character of property acquired on credit, Washington follows the general community property presumption. A number of local peculiarities and inconsistencies have developed and appear to be in play.

For example, consistent with other community property states, Washington's general approach is to treat borrowed funds and promissory notes obtained during marriage as community property. But rebuttal is not by the lender's intent test. Rather rebuttal is by proof of one of the following: (i) the spouses had an agreement to treat the funds as separate property, (ii) the loan was secured by separate property, or, (iii) most generally, the funds were not intended to be or in fact used for a community purpose.

The character of an asset purchased with acquired borrowed funds depends on the character of the downpayment *and* on the character of the purchase loan. In *Merkel v. Merkel*, 39 Wash.2d 102, 234 P.2d 857 (1951), one spouse acquired two parcels of land, one before marriage and one during marriage by inheritance; each parcel was subject to a mortgage secured by its respective parcel. The court ruled that both parcels were separate property, both mortgages were separate property obligations, and that the use of community property funds to repay the separate property obligation gave rise to a right of reimbursement in the community. See also, *Marriage of Johnson*, 28 Wash.App. 574, 576, 625 P.2d 720 (1981).

*Barlow v. Barlow*, 107 Wn. 1050, 182 P. 588 (2001) adds to *Merkel* and *Johnson*. In *Barlow*, supra, the wife took out an equity line of credit on her separate property during marriage for the purpose of constructing a community property house on a different parcel. The trial court characterized the loan as a community obligation (not a separate one) because it was for a community purpose ("the couple's dream house"). On appeal, this characterization was held to be within the trial court's discretionary power. If the money was borrowed for community purpose, the court ruled, the borrowed funds were community in character. For more on characterizing contract obligations, see Chapter 10.

Washington has granted an equitable lien for the amount of improvements when separate and community property are commingled by an improvement made by one character of property to the other. Likewise when the separate property of one spouse is used to improve the separate property of the other spouse, as in *Estate of Trierweiler*, 5 Wash.App. 17, 486 P.2d 314 (1971). Washington also indicates that the measure of the lien is the amount expended rather than the amount by which the value of the improved property is enhanced.

***Work related benefits.*** A life insurance policy is analyzed as property, not as a mere expectancy. Therefore, historically, whole and term life insurance policies (and their proceeds) were apportioned using a ratio of character contributions to premiums, *Coffey's Estate*, 195 Wash. 379, 81 P.2d 283 (1938). Of note, however, is that the last premium rule emerged in Washington for term life insurance policies in a dissent in *Small v. Bartyzel*, 27 Wash.2d 176, 185, 177 P.2d 291, 397 (1947).

The risk-payment theory was adopted in *Aetna Life Ins. Co. v. Wadsworth*, 102 Wash.2d 652, 689 P.2d 46 (1984). There, the court held that a married insured has the testamentary right to dispose of one-half of the proceeds of a community property life insurance policy. *Aetna Life Ins. Co.* overruled *Small*.

The time rule was applied to a pension in *Marriage of Jacobs*, 20 Wash.App. 272, 579 P.2d 1023 (1978). See also *Farver v. Department of Retirement Systems of State of Washington*, 97 Wash.2d 344, 644 P.2d 1149 (1982). The percentage of benefits earned during the marriage is subject to division under Wash.Rev.Code § 26.16.030, which is the general community property statute. Percentages earned outside of marriage are separate property under Wash.Rev.Code § 26.10.10 or 26.10.20. See also *Arnold v. Department of Retirement Systems*, 128 Wash.2d 765, 912 P.2d 463 (1996).

## 9. WISCONSIN

*Commingled property generally.* Wis.Stat. § 766.63 states the general rules for commingled property in subsection (1) and for improvements and businesses in subsection (2):

1. **[Except for life insurance policies and proceeds and deferred employment benefits] mixing marital property with property having any other classification reclassifies the other property to marital property unless the component of the mixed property which is not marital property can be traced.**

2. **Application by one spouse of substantial labor, effort, inventiveness, physical or intellectual skill, creativity or managerial activity to either spouse's property other than marital property creates marital property attributable to that application if both of the following apply:**

   a. **Reasonable compensation is not received for the application.**

   b. **Substantial appreciation of the property results from the application.**

Notice that subsection (1) above raises more than a presumption in favor of the marital community. It actually reclassifies the entirety of the commingled property unless the individual (separate property) component can be traced.

Subsection (2) above uses a substantial labor standard to determine which of any covered property is transmuted by default into marital property. Transmutation by law occurs if the marital partnership is not reasonably compensated for its labor contribution *and* if the property in question has substantially appreciated as a result of the marital labor contribution. This standard appears to meld the excess profits (*Pereira*, supra) and reimbursement (*Van Camp*, supra) approaches in recognition that the marital partnership's substantial investment in an appreciated enterprise is a reasonable basis upon which the marital partnership can claim a superior property interest in the enterprise relative to the individual owner.

***Work related benefits.*** Life insurance policies and proceeds are extensively treated in Wis.Stat. § 766.61. The general idea is that the ownership interest and proceeds of a life insurance issued after a determination date are marital property regardless of the classification of property used to pay the premiums.

Deferred employment benefits are extensively covered in Wis.Stat. § 766.62. Generally, **"a deferred employment benefit attributable to employment of a spouse occurring after the determination date is marital property."** Various mixed property scenarios and multipliers are detailed in the statute.

# PART 3
# MANAGEMENT AND CONTROL

# PART 9

# MANAGEMENT AND CONTROL

# CHAPTER 7
# MANAGEMENT AND CONTROL

## A. OVERVIEW

Management and control is the collective name for a number of important rights and liabilities that attach to property ownership. They include the right to use, consume, destroy, abandon, sell, convey, donate, encumber, mortgage, lease, expend, assign, create a security interest in, dispose of, place into trust, institute or defend a legal action over, and otherwise exercise control or decision making power over an asset and its component parts.

The clear trend is to extend equal management and control rights to both spouses. Whether equally, jointly, or dually depends on the asset and on the jurisdiction.

Management rights and liabilities extend to community property, including any commingled with separate property.

Liabilities for mismanagement of property can and increasingly do arise at the end of a marriage.

## B. DETAIL

### 1. MANAGEMENT AND CONTROL

Most U.S. community property states have adopted equal management legislation that "either" spouse has identical (equal) legal rights to manage and control community personal property.

Even so, in every state there are gradations of control permitted, depending on the asset, the enterprise, and the degree of commingling.

Gradation categories for management and control can include the following.

- Sole control, meaning exclusive control by default, for uncommingled separate property.

- Equal control for community personal property.

- Joint control for community real property.

- Dual control, as in the Texas system.

- Primary control, typically used for community property businesses.

- Exclusive control, meaning sole control obtained by court order over a specific community property asset for a limited time.

Some of the equal management states require that the spouses act jointly when dealing with certain categories of community property, such as real estate.

Texas is unique for its dual management system. In Texas spouses have sole management, by statutory default, over community property that each would have owned individually had the marriage not existed. If one spouse's solely managed property becomes commingled with the other spouse's solely managed community property, dual management becomes the default rule for the commingled *community* property. As a practical matter, the adoption of the "dual management" system retains a de facto earner's (male) management bias in families where only one spouse works outside the home.

Arizona is unique by how it allows one spouse to make a gift of identified community property earnings to the other spouse. Upon delivery the earnings become the separate property of the donee spouse.

In Louisiana, significant amounts of management and control are given to the spouse who registers movables (personal property) in his or her name alone.

With respect to a community property business, California, Louisiana, Nevada, Washington and Wisconsin recognize the right of one spouse to exercise "primary control" over that business. Primary control is not the same as exclusive control. The main limitation on primary control is that if the managing spouse decides to transfer substantially all of the business assets to a third party, he or she is statutorily required to obtain the consent of the non-managing spouse.

Finally, in a majority of states, one spouse can move for a protective order to obtain exclusive control over one or more community property assets.

The particular task of management and control rules is to balance the rights of spouses, third parties who transact with married persons, and the public.

## a. Community Property in General

The general rule for equal management and control of community property allows either spouse to act alone. Each of the statutory schemes contains exceptions. Thus in equal control states, certain actions or types of property may require either the action of both spouses, or the consent of the nonacting spouse.

Specific statutory provisions allow the spouses to agree to a different scheme of management and control in Idaho, Texas, and Wisconsin. In Louisiana a spouse may expressly renounce the right to concur in actions which would otherwise require both spouses to join in the transaction.

The consent of a spouse may be obtained in advance by a power of attorney in accordance with statutory provisions in California, Idaho, Nevada, and Texas. Generally, an action requiring consent can be ratified after the fact, expressly or by acquiescence, and during life or after death (by means of an estate plan that validates the acting spouse's transaction).

In California, one spouse may bring a motion to dispense with the consent requirement, on a transaction-by-transaction basis. This can happen when the other spouse arbitrarily refuses to give consent, or is physically or mentally incapacitated, or has been absent from the family for a prolonged period of time. Cal.Fam.Code § 1101(e). Wisconsin has a similar provision that permits a court to appoint a conservator or guardian to exercise a disabled spouse's right to manage and control marital property. Wis.Stat. § 766.52.

Statutes and cases normally distinguish between real and personal community property.

## b. Community Personal Property

Personal property is defined as all property not real property. A wide range of assets fall into the category of personal property. Money, stock, bonds, pension rights, employment contracts, sums on deposit, furniture, clothing, cars, and companion animals are examples of personal property.

For community personal property transactions, either spouse has authority to act alone subject to statutory limitations.

In most U.S. community property states one spouse has a positive right to manage community personal property; and the nonacting spouse has a corollary statutory to avoid certain nonmutual transfers. Litigated nonmutual transfers typically involve gifts and sales of furniture or family clothing to third parties.

When both spouses do not act, the statutory remedy is to give the nonacting spouse a cause of action either in conversion (against the spouse who initiated the transaction) or in replevin (against the transferee).

## c. Community Real Property

Real property is broadly defined as land and structures affixed. Items of personal property become part of the realty if they are affixed.

Community real property transactions, if they are consequential, require the joint action ("joinder") of both spouses. Practically speaking, joinder means that both spouses must sign any document that affects community property rights in the asset.

Arizona and Washington require joinder for the purchase of community property real estate. The absence of joinder exposes the transaction to avoidance.

### d. Separate Property

The rule is exclusive management and control when it comes to uncommingled separate property.

### e. Commingled Property

Once separate property is commingled with community property, the equal management and control principle may and likely will attach to the entirety of the commingled property. See e.g. *Marriage of Walker*, 138 Cal.App.4th 1408, 42 Cal.Rptr.3d 325 (2006). Therefore, as managers of community property, spouses owe each other, at minimum, a duty of good faith with respect to the management of community property and of commingled property.

### f. Partnership Fiduciary Duties

Increasingly spouses are recognized as having management duties as to community property. Many states permit a court to create a constructive trust to hold impaired or undisclosed assets for the benefit of the adversely affected spouse. Wisconsin does so by statute, as does California

California, by statute, explicitly specifies that spouses are in a fiduciary duty akin to that of nonmarital business partners. Cal.Fam.Code § 721. The duty requires good faith and loyalty at the very least. Good faith is often defined in case law as honesty in fact. Loyalty is linked to financial disclosure.

If a breach of the fiduciary duty impairs the non-managing spouse's past, present or future community property interest in the (mis)managed property, Cal.Fam.Code § 1101 provides a series of (apparently) independent claims by which the impaired spouse can sue the impairing spouse for breach of fiduciary duty. Remedies include court ordered accountings, title changes, consent waivers, and damages (with court costs and attorney's fees).

Protection of third parties is furnished by a number of provisions without much uniformity among the states. California, Idaho, Washington, and Wisconsin include express provisions that validate certain pre-existing documents. Washington protects mechanics' and materialmens' liens. New Mexico has express provisions for management based upon the form of documentary title to personal property. Nevada and Wisconsin have a specific provision concerning payments from employee benefit plans.

## 2.   THE PARTNERSHIP FIDUCIARY STANDARD

Under the obsolete male management model, a fiduciary standard of varying stringency was generally imposed upon the husband in his role as the legal manager of the community property estate. Real property transactions more typically required joint action between the spouses, but personal property transactions did not. This meant that the husband acting alone, as a managing agent of the community, had exclusive control over all personal property transactions involving money, encumbrances, securities, bonds, businesses, tort causes of action, tort settlements, bank accounts, retirement accounts, monetized home equity, and so forth. Depending on the jurisdiction, the husband was held to competing fiduciary standards ranging from good faith on the lax end to (far less commonly) the fiduciary duties of a professional trustee on the strict end. The range of models continues today. But it is applied in gender neutral form to the legal manager (either spouse) who transacts with community personal property (the de facto managing spouse for the transaction).

On the lax end, because either spouse has the legal power of absolute disposition over the community personal property, a de facto managing spouse has the right to use community personal property as if it were his or her own separate property. Some hints of this language remain in the California and Nevada provisions, which describe the power of the manager to deal with community personal property as absolute.

The apparent freedom of the absolute power of disposition standard should not be taken literally. The standard is modified by recognition (often statutory) that the spouses are in a confidential relationship that gives rise to a fiduciary duty that comes into existence, as a matter of law, on the date of marriage.

Generally, upon proof of any unfair dealing by a spouse, a presumption of undue influence arises. Unless the presumption is rebutted (with evidence of voluntariness, usually), taking unfair advantage of a confidant's trust exposes the de facto managing spouse to legal liability on a number of grounds. Those grounds may be: breach of good faith; failure to keep records; failure to make records accessible; failure to disclose financial information; obtaining any unfair advantage in a transaction between the spouses; impairing a nonacting spouse's past, present or future community property interest; obtaining an advantage over the other spouse by fraud, duress, undue influence, oppression; or any other sharp practice that is a cause for judicial concern. All of these are example grounds for challenging a de facto manager's actions.

On the other extreme of the fiduciary standard, some cases have gone so far as to suggest that a spouse is a "trustee" in relation to the community. But what kind of trustee?

A professional trustee has multiple statutory duties—like the duty to make the trust property productive (or suffer surcharge against one's own property); the duty to follow certain investing strategies (like modern portfolio theory); the duty to account on a periodic basis (or suffer removal from the trustee position). During the marriage a spouse may not (and likely will not) meet this exacting and formal standard as a general matter, and definitely will not meet the standard as to each and every potentially challengeable transaction.

A business partner, by contrast, owes partnership fiduciary duties to the other partners, but the business partner's duties are measured by a far less exacting standard than are the professional trustee's duties.

Plus, the business partner's liability is limited by the business judgment rule in a way that the professional trustee's liability is not. The business judgment rule tends to recognize only claims that arise from acts of gross negligence.

Between the doctrinal extremes of what constitutes a "fiduciary" duty are a number of possible alternatives. Most have had or still have adherents in some community property states.

The duty not to commit fraud is clearly a part of the de facto managing spouse's obligation in every state. But loss due to the actions of a negligent or incompetent spouse are (still) considered risks of marriage in most jurisdictions.

Success of an employed spouse in his or her career is not required by the law. Although the breach of an employment contract by non- or substandard performance may be actionable as an impairment of a present or future community property contract right.

A manager is permitted to be inept, inefficient, or clumsy, so long as he or she is honestly so; but here again, the inept de facto manager may be liable if ineptness is adjudged the cause of impairment to the other spouse's past, present or future community property interest. Cal.Fam.Code § 1101.

Over a century of case law in each of the community property jurisdictions teaches that at the end of a marriage, given the nature of the dissolution process, each spouse may, should, and probably will be called upon to account for his or her stewardship of the community property.

## 3.   TIME FRAMES

Statutes that govern management and control of community property are most likely to come into play at the termination of the marriage by dissolution. Perhaps this is because spouses manage their finances, as a practical matter, without the aid of the law. It is only when marital discord or dissolution arises that the law is consulted to determine how management should have proceeded.

As a case-management matter, time frames for analysis can include periods during the marriage, a period of separation, the period during the dissolution proceeding, and (depending on the court order) any time postdissolution in which the parties continue to hold property together.

As a doctrinal matter, explanatory materials that collect cases of a certain historical era (pre-mid-1970s) are normally decided on the now-obsolete male-management principle (the idea that the husband was the legal manager of the community property by virtue of his gender alone). If these mid-1970s explanatory sources may not reevaluate the cases in light of the sea change that equal management and control has brought to community property law, they must be scanned for implicit gender bias on management and control issues.

Liability for debts is often linked to management and control. See Chapter 8.

## 4.   GIFTS

Gifts and low value transfers have historically been contentious areas because they often involve a spouse who is wrongfully attempting to dissipate the community property in anticipation of a dissolution.

Spanish law gave the husband the right to make gifts of community property to third persons as part of management and control of community personal property. The legal limit to this power was that the husband could not defraud his wife. Most community property states followed the Spanish lead.

Today, U.S. community property states give spouses equal management and control rights over community personal property. (Real property requires joint action of the spouses for each discrete transaction.) Equal rights means that either spouse can make legal decisions about the use of community property without consulting the other.

The statutes typically also recognize a corollary right in the nonacting spouse to challenge an acting spouse's decisions on a transaction-by-transaction basis. Historically, the nonacting spouse's challenge was framed around the issue of consent. Transactions to which the nonacting spouse did not consent were invalidated as to the third party (replevin) or else charged against the separate property of the donor spouse (conversion).

Additionally, the trend has been and still is to offer some default protection to third parties in transactions with a married person. Transactions that involve gifts or even market value transfers of family

furniture and clothing can be negotiated and even
conducted by one spouse. Yet, the other spouse has the
right to challenge the transaction by suing either the
third party or the other spouse. California is a leader
in extending the consent requirement from gifts
(gratuitous transfers made by one spouse acting alone)
to low-value transactions and even to market value
transactions. A low value transaction would be
exemplified by a situation where one spouse sells the
$20,000 family piano for $10. A market transfer might
involve the sale of family furniture and clothing for
fair market value.

## a. Gifts of Community Property Made by One Spouse to the Other Spouse

Gifts of community property, real or personal, from
one spouse to the other spouse pose few problems so
long as transmutation formalities are met.
Transmutations are discussed in Chapter 2.

Even so, the law presumes the existence of a
confidential relationship between spouses. This
confidential relationship, in theory, precludes spouses
from manipulating the marriage in order to procure
any unfair advantage over each other.

A gift that transmutes property, because it changes
the character of property, is a transaction between the
spouses. Thus upon evidence that the benefitted
spouse took advantage of the adversely affected
spouse, a presumption of undue influence is raised.
Rebuttal requires proof that the gift was made
voluntarily with adequate disclosure.

Evidence that the parties were married when the gift was made is not in and of itself enough evidence upon which to properly raise a presumption of fraud or undue influence. Nor is evidence that one spouse exited the marriage with less property than the other.

### b. Gifts or Low Value Transfers of Community Personal Property Made by One Spouse to a Third Party

A nonmutual gift made by one spouse to a third person passes title upon delivery, subject to an avoidance claim by the non-consenting spouse.

Two other general ideas are useful to bear in mind at this point. The law does not bother with trifles. But neither should it tolerate fraud. The area the between trifle and fraud is gray.

Small customary gratuities remain fully within the general management power of a spouse and, as such, they do not require the other spouse's consent. Louisiana has codified and extended this rule. In Louisiana **"concurrence of the spouses"** is required by statute, except that **"a spouse acting alone may make a usual or customary gift of a value commensurate with the economic position of the spouses at the time of the donation."** LSA–C.C. Art. 2349.

In California, either spouse has full management powers to make a nonmutual gift of community personal property. But because written consent is required, if a spouse makes a nonmutual gift of community personal property to a third party, the absence of consent exposes both donor spouse and donee to an avoidance claim by the non-consenting spouse.

Nevada and Washington require only the "express or implied consent" of the non-acting spouse.

Wisconsin requires that both spouses act together to create gifts that exceed a specific dollar amount per donee in a calendar year. If the gift exceeds that annual dollar amount, it may still be valid if it is reasonable in relation to the economic position of the spouses.

A gift to a third party otherwise requiring the consent of both spouses is valid and free from the claims of the non-consenting spouse if the non-consenting spouse authorizes the gift in advance, by a power of attorney, or posthumously, by a trust or estate plan that is consistent with the making of the gift. See for example *Spreckels v. Spreckels*, 172 Cal. 775, 158 P. 537 (1916). Other types of ratification, including acquiescence, might be used to validate a gift that would otherwise be subject to an avoidance claim by a non-consenting spouse.

Despite statutory consent requirements, fraud persists. A gift made to a third party with the fraudulent purpose of injuring the other spouse, or of impairing his or her interest in community personal property, can and should be set aside. Likewise, a gift made by undue influence, mistake, or misrepresentation should be avoidable by the non-consenting spouse.

Relevant to the analysis of whether a gift is more trifle than fraud are the following factors. What is the relationship of the donee to the donor? What is the value of the gift as compared to the community estate? What motivated the particular gift? These are all potential factors that courts have considered in determining whether one spouse's gift to a third party is in fraud of the other spouse's community property rights.

*Illustration 7.1:* Without the other spouse's knowledge, a spouse gives a sibling $3,000 of community property cash to care for an ailing parent. The net worth of the community estate is $500,000.

In most states, the argument for avoiding the gift is that it was nonmutual. The non-consenting spouse's cause of action for avoidance acts as a cloud on the donor spouse's transfer, notwithstanding that the value of the gift is small compared to the total value of the community estate. California uses this approach.

A counterargument for validating the gift is that $3,000 is a small sum compared to the total community property net worth of $500,000. Louisiana and Wisconsin use this approach.

*Illustration 7.2:* Same facts as 7.1 above except that the net worth of the community estate is only $5,000.

The argument in favor of avoiding the gift is now twofold. One, it was nonmutual. Two, $3,000 is a large sum relative to the $5,000 net worth of the community.

The fact that the gift is made for a greater family purpose could, in some states, make a difference material enough to support a ruling in favor of validity. But, given that the gift is a large part of the total community estate, equity-based arguments in favor of avoiding the gift likely outweigh technical arguments in favor of confirming it.

*Illustration 7.3:* Same facts as 7.2 above except that the $3,000 gift is made to a nonspousal sexual partner.

The argument for avoiding the gift is now threefold. One, the gift of community property was nonmutual. Two, the gift of $3,000 is not a small sum relative to the $5,000 net worth of the community. Three, the intimate nature of the donor's relationship to the third party donee could increase the likelihood that the donor may be involved not just in a single nonmutual gift, but in a series of nonmutual secretive gifts that could impair the other spouse's present and future community property interest. The third party or the donor spouse—depending on whom the non-consenting spouse sues—can defend the validity of the gift by presenting evidence of the non-consenting spouse's knowledge, ratification or acquiescence. If the non-consenting spouse sues the donor spouse, the gift likely will be deemed valid as to the third party recipient.

## c. Portion of the Gift That Is Set Aside

If the donor spouse makes a gift to a third person without the consent as in California, Nevada, Washington, or in excess of the permissible standard as in Wisconsin, or in fraud of the non-consenting spouse's rights (as in other states), what remedies are available if the non-consenting spouse sues the third party? Is the purported gift void ab initio or voidable? How much of the gift should be set aside? One half? All in excess of the standard? All or a fraction based on the value of the gift at the time of its delivery?

In an equal management jurisdiction, because either spouse has the power to manage and control community personal property, any gift made by one spouse, acting alone, to a third party is voidable, not void. In other words, delivery of the gift transfers title, but that title is subject to the claims of the non-consenting spouse who has a period of time to avoid the gift or recover its value as of the time of transfer.

A claim for avoidance can be initiated by the non-consenting spouse against the third party donee or against donor spouse (or his or her estate). In some states, the non-consenting spouse can also sue the donor spouse to recover damages for any impairment of the claimant's community property interest. A court might place the property into constructive trust for the benefit of the non-consenting spouse. See for example Chapter 9, Section C, Wisconsin.

In short, the law balances three issues. One, it defines the equal management rule to include gifts that are made by one spouse, acting alone, to a third party. Two, it protects the third party donee by making the gift voidable upon delivery rather than void. Three, it protects the non-consenting spouse by providing a basis, often statutory, upon which he or she can challenge the validity of the gift. What the law does not allow for is the donor spouse to avoid the gift.

As between the donor spouse and the third party donee, therefore, the gift is valid upon delivery.

If the non-consenting spouse insists on retrieving *the property itself*, he or she must sue the third party donee or (if the property was subsequently transferred) the current possessor of the property.

If the non-consenting spouse sues for the *value* of the gift, the amount that can be declared void and brought back into the community estate might vary. The trend is to base those variances on whether the marriage is intact or not.

- The non-consenting spouse can seek to recapture the entire value of the gift (100%) on behalf of the community estate, assuming the community is still in existence.

- If the community has been terminated (whether by agreement, physical separation (in some states), court action, or death), the non-consenting spouse has the right to recapture only one-half of the value (50%) of the gift.

- Another remedy which is possible at the termination of the community is to award to the non-consenting spouse, from the community property remaining on hand, one-half the value of the gift. With this technique, if enough community wealth remains on hand, the non-consenting spouse need not sue the gift recipient to recover value.

A one hundred percent (100%) recovery, when the marriage is intact, prevents a de facto managing spouse (the donor in this context) from giving progressive halves of the community estate away by successive unconsented to gifts of community property. In Wisconsin the non-consenting spouse may recover the property or a compensatory judgment equal to the amount by which the gift exceeded the permissible standard. Recovered property is characterized as community property.

A fifty percent (50%) recovery, when a marriage is ending, allows the other one-half of the property to remain with the third party donee on one of two standard theories. One, from the perspective of the end of the marriage, the transfer is tantamount to dissolution. Hence, the donor has the right to make a gift of one-half of the property now being dissolved. Two, under the common law of gifts the donor's title (one-half of the gifted community property) irrevocably transferred to the donee upon delivery; here, the law is understood to protect the community during the marriage. The donor is not protected as an individual and indeed should be estopped from challenging the validity of a gift intentionally made and delivered

### d. Gifts Made by One Spouse to a Nonspousal POD Beneficiary in a Term Life Insurance Policy

One of the most frequently litigated issues, especially at the end of a marriage by death, concerns gifts of community property in the form of a term life insurance policy.

Disputes arise because of this particular clash: On one hand, purchasing a term life insurance contract is a *nontestamentary* act involving community personal property; as such, it is an act governed by equal management and control rules. On the other hand, designating a pay-on-death (POD) beneficiary is a *testamentary* act; as such, it is outside the scope of equal management and control rules.

So, with respect to term life insurance, what exactly is the gift and when exactly is it made? Is it made at the time that each premium is paid? Is it made when the proceeds are paid?

If the policy has not yet matured (i.e. the insured policy owner is alive) a "gift" might be construed as having been made to a third party with each premium payment that was made while the third party POD was named a beneficiary on the life insurance contract. In such a case the "gift" is really a series of multiple gifts that, together, are properly defined as the sum total of cash that was used to pay the policy premium(s). If the premiums constitute a significant value of the total community property estate, the question of consent on the part of the spouse who was adversely affected by the payments can be raised.

If the insured is deceased the "gift" occurs when the beneficiary receives the life insurance proceeds, meaning the contract pay out. Where relevant, the proceeds (usually a much larger gift than the gift of premiums) are measured against the net community estate remaining after the payment of debts. In jurisdictions that distinguish between testamentary and nontestamentary acts in the management and control of community property, the character of the policy is important. If the policy is a separate property asset, then the decedent had the right to name a nonspousal POD beneficiary for the entirety (100%) of the proceeds. But if the policy is community property, how much the named POD beneficiary takes depends on state law. In a state where the naming of a POD beneficiary is a testamentary act not subject to consent requirements, the decedent has the right to make (only) a gift of his or her one-half (50%) of the proceeds.

In this context, testamentary act does not mean that the proceeds will or do fall into the deceased's probate estate. Rather, it means more generally that the insured, prior to death, made a decision to dispose of assets after death.

Additionally, the revocability or irrevocability of the POD beneficiary designation is a key touchstone for determining what the gift is and when it was made.

Normally the beneficiary designation is revocable, and a gift of the proceeds is not made until the death of the insured. An irrevocable beneficiary designation, by contrast, effects an immediate gift, with all subsequent premium payments being additional cash gifts. Some uncertainty exists concerning the retention of other rights which can indirectly change the beneficiary, such as the right to surrender the insurance policy, the right to borrow against the policy or the right to allow coverage to expire by the nonpayment of premiums. Generally such rights are disregarded, or considered to be in the nature of conditions subsequent upon an otherwise-completed gift of the life insurance premiums.

Insurance company practices and protective statutes reduce the probability the insurer will be called upon to pay the proceeds twice. Many companies request or even require that the spouse of the insured policy owner indicate, in writing, his or her consent to any nonspousal POD. By consenting to the other spouse's POD, the consenting spouse relinquishes any community property interest he or she might have to the proceeds upon the insured's death.

Additionally, most states have enacted statutes that permit insurance companies to pay out policy proceeds in accordance with the POD beneficiary designation unless the surviving spouse asserts his or her claim in a timely manner. This practice permits insurance companies to make fast pay outs. If the spouse does assert a claim contrary to the beneficiary designation, the company usually pays the money into court and interpleads the claimants. Interpleader protects the insurance company from paying twice, but it does not determine legal right to the proceeds. Absent interpleader, the spouse asserts his or her claim first against the insurance company; but if the insurer has already paid the proceeds, the spouse is left to assert a claim against the POD beneficiary.

The source of the above rules is the management and control limitation upon gifts made by a managing spouse to third parties. It is possible that a reciprocal arrangement between nonspousal business partners to name each other as life insurance beneficiaries was supported by consideration. If so may be treated as a contract, not an avoidable gift.

## C.  INDIVIDUAL STATES

### 1.  ARIZONA

Arizona follows a managerial system based on an equal management and control statute that covers both community personal and community real property.

The management and control statute is found at Ariz.Rev.Stat.Ann. § 25–214:

**"A. Each spouse has the sole management, control and disposition rights of each spouse's separate property.**

**B. The spouses have equal management, control and disposition rights over their community property and have equal power to bind the community.**

**C. Either spouse separately may acquire, manage, control or dispose of community property, or bind the community, except that joinder of both spouses is required in any of the following cases:**

**1.  Any transaction for the acquisition, disposition or encumbrance of an interest in real property other than an unpatented mining claim or a lease of less than one year.**

**2. Any transaction of guaranty, indemnity or suretyship."**

Since 1913, one spouse (a wife) was recognized as having a right of action against the other spouse (a husband) for conversion of separate property. *Eshom v. Eshom*, 18 Ariz. 170 (1916).

Additionally, in the equitable division of marital property, Ariz.Rev.Stat.Ann. § 25–318 **"does not prevent the court from considering all actual damages and judgments from conduct that results in criminal conviction of either spouse in which the other spouse or child was the victim, excessive or abnormal expenditures, destruction, concealment or fraudulent disposition of community, joint tenancy and other property held in common."** The divorce implications of this topic are discussed further in Chapter 9.

## 2.    CALIFORNIA

California adopts a managerial system based on equal management and control. The system is straightforward, yet it turns on four distinctions. One, community personal property is governed by the equal management and control rule. Two, community property businesses are governed by a special primary management and control rule. Three, community real property is governed by a joint management rule. Four, by court order, specific community property assets can be brought under the exclusive control of one spouse for a limited period of time.

*Equal management and control for community personal property.* As to community personal property, **"[e]ither spouse has the management and control of the community personal property ... with like absolute power of disposition, other than testamentary, as the spouse has of the separate estate of the spouse."** Cal.Fam.Code § 1100. The clear limitation on this rule is that gifts, low value transfers, and transfers of furniture, and clothing may not be made **"without the written consent"** (or ratification) of the non-acting spouse. Cal.Fam.Code § 1100(b) and (c).

*Primary management and control for a community property business.* A community property business, which is community personal property, is exempt from the equal management and control rule. Instead, a community property business is governed by a superseding **"primary"** (not sole) management and control provision. See Cal.Fam.Code § 1100(d). The manager of a community property business **"may act alone in all transactions,"** except that the managing spouse must give **"prior written notice to the other spouse of any sale, lease, exchange, encumbrance, or other disposition of all or substantially all of the personal property used in the operation of the business ... , whether or not title to that property is held in the name of only one spouse."** *Id.*

*Joint management and control for community real property.* As to community real property, Cal.Fam.Code § 1102 provides that **"either spouse has the management and control of the**

**community property,"** . . . but both spouses must execute **"any instrument by which that community real property or any interest therein is leased for a longer period than one year, or is sold, conveyed, or encumbered."** A spouse can petition a court to avoid an instrument that he or she did not join in. However, a grant of such a petition does not include with it cancellation of the underlying debt that was created by the instrument. *Lezine v. Security Pacific Financial Services, Inc.*, 14 Cal.4th 56, 58 Cal.Rptr.2d 76, 925 P.2d 1002 (1996). Subject to the limitations of the lender's intent test, borrowed funds obtained during marriage are presumed to be community personal property, as discussed in Chapters 3, and 6. This is so even if the loan proceeds are monetized home equity fraudulently obtained by one spouse acting without the knowledge or consent of the other spouse.

*Exclusive control by court order.* During a dissolution and during a marriage, it is possible for a spouse to petition for exclusive control of a specific asset so as to prevent its impairment or dissipation.

Additionally, the California Family Code has specific provisions that can (by an injured spouse's option) or do (automatically) provide a legal basis for divesting an abusive spouse of community property or for otherwise affecting his or her rights of management and control. Some statutes apply in a dissolution proceeding. See for example Cal.Fam.Code § 2045. Other remedies are trigged by the wrongdoer spouse's conviction of an enumerated crime against the other spouse See for example

Cal.Fam.Code § 4324 and § 4324.5. Other statutes apply categorically to assets. See for example Cal.Fam.Code § 1101.

California has adopted the Domestic Violence Prevention Act (the DVPA for short) within its Family Code. See Cal.Fam.Code §§ 6200 et seq. DVPA provisions are broad enough to reach acts of financial violence.

*Preventing undue influence.* As to all community personal property, Cal.Fam.Code § 1100(e), a self-updating provision, incorporates the most recently amended version of Cal.Fam.Code § 721(b), which provides that **"in transactions between themselves, spouses are subject to the general rules governing fiduciary relationships which control the actions of persons occupying confidential relations with each other."**

The fiduciary relationship is a partnership duty. As such it is compared to that of a **"nonmarital business partner,"** not to that of a professional trustee. There is no general duty to keep records. But if records are kept the recordkeeping spouse is required to provide access to records and disclosure of financial information to the other as set forth in Revised Uniform Partnership Act provisions that are expressly incorporated into Cal.Fam.Code § 721(b), as self-updating provisions.

Cal.Fam.Code § 1101 sets forth the bases and remedies for community property impairment claims. Generally, Cal.Fam.Code § 1101(a) gives a spouse **"a claim against the other spouse for any breach of** the fiduciary duty that results in impairment to the claimant spouse's present undivided one-half interest in the community estate, including, but not limited to a single transaction or a pattern or series of transactions, which transaction or transactions have caused or will cause a detrimental impact to the claimant spouse's undivided one-half interest in the community estate."

Recovery percentages, court costs, and attorney fees are set out in Cal.Fam.Code § 1101(g)—50% plus attorney fees and court costs for impairments due to ordinary negligence—and (h)—100% and court costs for impairments resulting from fraud, oppression, or malice as defined in the state Penal Code.

More generally under Cal.Fam.Code § 1101, a claimant spouse can sue: for an accounting; to add a name to **"community property held in the name of the other spouse alone"** with some business exceptions; and to **"dispense with the requirement of the other spouse's consent"** if the "proposed transaction is in the best interest of the community" and **"consent has been arbitrarily refused or cannot be obtained due to physical incapacity, mental incapacity, or prolonged absence of the nonconsenting spouse."** Limitation periods are set forth in the statute.

For term life insurance policies, the character of the last premium paid determines the character of insurance proceeds, as discussed in Chapter 6. Relevant to management and control principles, however, is that naming a POD beneficiary is deemed a testamentary act, and as such it is exempt from the ordinary lifetime management and control powers that either spouse otherwise enjoys.

As discussed above, a testamentary act determines the disposition of property upon death. Either spouse, acting alone, has the equal management and control right to make a gift of his or her one-half of a community property life insurance proceeds by naming a nonspousal POD beneficiary. But neither spouse has the management and control power to give away the other spouse's one half of the proceeds by that same act. Thus, a community property policy that names a nonspousal (third party) POD beneficiary is subject to the claims of the surviving spouse for one-half of the proceeds. This is similar to the risk-payment theory outcome developed by Washington. See Chapter 6 for more on life insurance.

### 3.   IDAHO

Idaho Code § 32–912 adopts a managerial system based on equal management and control.

**"Either the husband or the wife shall have the right to manage and control the community property, and either may bind the community property by contract, except that neither the husband nor wife may sell, convey or encumber the community real estate unless the other joins in executing the sale agreement, deed or other instrument of conveyance, by which the real estate is sold, conveyed or encumbered, and any community obligation incurred by either the husband or the wife without the consent in**

**writing of the other shall not obligate the
separate property of the spouse who did not so
consent; provided, however, that the husband or
wife may by express power of attorney give to
the other the complete power to sell, convey or
encumber community property, either real or
personal. All deeds, conveyances, bills of sale, or
evidences of debt heretofore made in
conformity herewith are hereby validated."**

Idaho Code § 32–906 characterizes the income of all
property, separate or community, as community. This
brings the separate property rents, issues, and profits
under the state equal management and control rule.
However, if separate property rents, issues, and
profits obtained during marriage are transmuted into
separate property, the property becomes subject to the
management of **"the spouse owning the property."**

Under Idaho Code § 32–916: **"The property
rights of husband and wife are governed by this
chapter, unless there is a marriage settlement
agreement entered into during marriage
containing stipulations contrary thereto."**

## 4. LOUISIANA

Louisiana follows a managerial model that is based
on equal management and control and is consistent
with the state's civil law tradition.

Ownership in Louisiana is allodial (freehold); it
confers present, direct, and exclusive ownership over
the thing owned, without bifurcation into legal and

equitable interests. Instead, usufruct rights are recognized, as discussed in previous chapters.

State statutes distinguish between "immovables" (land) and "movables" (not land), and between property rights and contract rights.

LSA–C.C. Art. 2346 provides: **"Each spouse acting alone may manage, control, or dispose of community property unless otherwise provided by law."** Concurrence—which sounds much like joinder—of the spouses is required for specified transactions, listed below.

When **"concurrence is required by law,"** LSA–C.C. Art. 2353 provides that **"the alienation, encumbrance, or lease of community property by a spouse is relatively null unless the other spouse has renounced the right to concur."** This rule applies to community property businesses (and other enterprises) as well.

The concurrence of both spouses is statutorily required for **" . . . the alienation, encumbrance, or lease of community immovables, standing, cut, or fallen timber, furniture or furnishings while located in the family home, all or substantially all of the assets of a community enterprise, and movables issued or registered as provided by law in the names of the spouses jointly."** Also, by this provision, concurrence is required for **"the harvest of community timber."** LSA–C.C. Art. 2347(a).

LSA–C.C. Art. 2348 provides: **"A spouse may expressly renounce the right to concur in the**

**alienation, encumbrance, or lease of a community immovable or all or substantially all of a community enterprise. He also may renounce the right to participate in the management of a community enterprise. The renunciation may be irrevocable for a stated term."**

With respect to gifts made by one spouse to a third party LSA–C.C. Art. 2349 controls. This statute provides that a spouse acting alone **"may make a usual or customary gift of a value commensurate with the economic position of the spouses at the time of the donation."** The provision, in effect, gives spouses the right to exercise exclusive control over the donated property.

LSA–C.C. Art. 2350 covers a community property business generally by how it provides that **"[t]he spouse who is the sole manager of a community enterprise has the exclusive right to alienate, encumber, or lease its movables unless the movables are issued in the name of the other spouse or the concurrence of the other spouse is required by law."** This general provision, as legislative comments make clear, governs when the specific rule on concurrence, found at LSA–C.C. Art. 2353, is deemed inapplicable. The general rule can be invoked "in favor of commerce" when deemed necessary.

Louisiana includes exclusive control provisions for the following:

- LSA–C.C. Art. 2351: **"A spouse has the exclusive right to manage, alienate, encumber, or lease movables issued or registered in his name as provided by law."**

- LSA–C.C. Art. 2352: **"A spouse who is a partner has the exclusive right to manage, alienate, encumber, or lease the partnership interest."**

When community property is impaired by fraud or bad faith, a cause of action arises in the adversely affected spouse. LSA–C.C. Art. 2354 creates liability **"for any loss or damage caused by fraud or bad faith in the management of the community property."** Case law recognizes within this provision a duty to disclose. For example, One spouse's pattern of failure to disclose financial information was found by a jury to be fraud in *Theriot v. Theriot*, 622 So.2d 257 (La.App. 1993), writ denied.

## 5.   NEVADA

Nevada follows a managerial system based on equal management and control.

Equal management of community property is governed by Nev.Rev.Stat. § 123.230, which is based on California law. Notice that the statute requires joinder (joint management and control) for consequential real estate transactions; and allows primary control for community property businesses.

"A spouse may, by written power of attorney, give to the other the complete power to sell, convey or encumber any property held as community property or either spouse, acting alone, may manage and control community property, whether the community property was acquired before, on or after July 1, 1975, with the same power of disposition as the acting spouse has over his or her separate property, except that:

1. Neither spouse may devise or bequeath more than one-half of the community property.

2. Neither spouse may make a gift of community property without the express or implied consent of the other.

3. Neither spouse may sell, convey or encumber the community real property unless both join in the execution of the deed or other instrument by which the real property is sold, conveyed or encumbered, and the deed or other instrument must be acknowledged by both.

4. Neither spouse may purchase or contract to purchase community real property unless both join in the transaction of purchase or in the execution of the contract to purchase.

5. Neither spouse may create a security interest, other than a purchase money security interest as defined in NRS 104.9103, in, or sell, community household goods, furnishings or appliances unless both join in executing the security agreement or contract of sale, if any.

**6. Neither spouse may acquire, purchase, sell, convey or encumber the assets, including real property and goodwill, of a business where both spouses participate in its management without the consent of the other. If only one spouse participates in management, he may, in the ordinary course of business, acquire, purchase, sell, convey or encumber the assets, including real property and goodwill, of the business without the consent of the nonparticipating spouse."**

Notwithstanding the basic management and control provisions, it appears that an employed spouse has exclusive control, relative to that spouse's employer, over employee benefits. Practically this is the case across the board, at least during the continuance of the marriage. But Nev.Rev.Stat. § 123.240 elevates the concept to a statutory rule which provides that " . . . **whenever payment or refund is made to an employee, former employee, or his or her beneficiary or estate pursuant to a written retirement, death or other employee benefit plan or savings plan, such payment or refund shall fully discharge the employer and any trustee or insurance company making such payment or refund from all adverse claims thereto . . . "** unless notice is given of the surviving spouse's claim.

Nev.Rev.Stat. § 123.250 gives each spouse the power of testamentary disposition over his or her interest in the community property, with or without the other spouse's consent. The numerical limit on this power appears to be one-half.

## 6. NEW MEXICO

New Mexico follows a managerial system based on equal management and control.

N.M.Stat.Ann. § 40–3–14 (1978) provides that **"either spouse alone has full power to manage, control, dispose of and encumber the entire community personal property."**

Subsections (B) and (C) of that same code section create title and agreement based exceptions where sole or joint management become the rule:

**"Where only one spouse is:**

**(1) named in a document evidencing ownership of community personal property; or**

**(2) named or designated in a written agreement between that spouse and a third party as having sole authority to manage, control, dispose of or encumber the community personal property which is described in or which is the subject of the agreement, whether the agreement was executed prior to or after July 1, 1973; only the spouse so named may manage, control, dispose of or encumber the community personal property described in such a document**

evidencing ownership or in such a written agreement.

Where both spouses are:

(1) named in a document evidencing ownership of community personal property; or

(2) named or designated in a written agreement with a third party as having joint authority to dispose of or encumber the community personal property which is described in or the subject of the agreement, whether the agreement was executed prior to or after July 1, 1973; both spouses must join to dispose of or encumber such community personal property where the names of the spouses are joined by the word "and." Where the names of the spouses are joined by the word "or," or by the words "and/or," either spouse alone may dispose of or encumber such community personal property."

As for community real property, joinder is required.

Except for purchase-money mortgages, "the spouses must join in all transfers, conveyances or mortgages or contracts to transfer, convey or mortgage any interest in community real property and separate real property owned by the spouses as cotenants in joint tenancy or tenancy in common." Additionally, the spouses must join in "all leases of community real

**property or separate real property owned by
the spouses as cotenants in joint tenancy or
tenancy in common if the initial term of the
lease, together with any option or extension
contained in the lease or provided for
contemporaneously, exceeds five years or if the
lease is for an indefinite term."** N.M.Stat.Ann.
§ 40–3–13 (1978).

## 7. TEXAS

Texas uses a dual management system that gives
each spouse sole management and control over
separate property and over community property
(including personal income) that would have been
separate had the person not been married. Once one
spouse's community property is commingled with the
other spouse's community property, however, the rule
becomes one of joint management and control for the
commingled property.

The statutory provisions for management, control
and disposition of separate and community property
and the protection of third parties are as follows:

V.T.C.A.Fam.Code § 3.101 gives each spouse **"the
sole management, control, and disposition of
that spouse's separate property."**

V.T.C.A.Fam.Code § 3.102 provides that **"during
marriage each spouse has the sole
management, control, and disposition of the
community property that the spouse would
have owned if single."** This power extends to
**"personal earnings; revenue from separate**

property; recoveries for personal injuries; and the increase and mutations of, and the revenue from, all property subject to his or her sole management, control, and disposition."

Under    V.T.C.A.Fam.Code    § 3.102(b)    "If community property subject to the sole management, control, and disposition of one spouse is mixed or combined with community property subject to the sole management, control, and disposition of the other spouse, then the mixed or combined community property is subject to the joint management, control, and disposition of the spouses, unless the spouses provide otherwise by power of attorney in writing or other agreement.

Except as provided in Subsection (a), community property is subject to the joint management, control, and disposition of the spouses, unless the spouses provide otherwise by power of attorney in writing or other agreement."

V.T.C.A.Fam.Code § 3.104: "(a) During marriage, property is presumed to be subject to the sole management, control, and disposition of a spouse if it is held in that spouse's name, as shown by muniment, contract, deposit of funds, or other evidence of ownership, or if it is in his or her possession and is not subject to such evidence of ownership.

(a) A third person dealing with a spouse is entitled to rely (as against the other

**spouse or anyone claiming from that spouse) on that spouse's authority to deal with the property if:**

**(1) The property is presumed to be subject to the sole management, control, and disposition of the spouse; and**

**(2) the person dealing with the spouse:**

> **(A) is not a party to a fraud on the other spouse or another person; and**

> **(B) does not have actual or constructive notice of the spouse's lack of authority."**

When joint management and control applies, gifts made by one spouse to a third party can be avoided. Texas retains the civil law fraud test for setting aside a gift by the manager of the community. It also extends the test's coverage by reliance on the concept of constructive fraud. Additionally, the person who attempts to uphold the gift has the burden to prove that the gift was reasonable under the circumstances in which it was made.

Texas upholds many community property life insurance beneficiary designations when the beneficiary is a relative or former relative to whom a duty to support exists. The existence of the duty negates fraud upon the spouse so long as the community funds expended for the insurance are not unreasonably out of proportion to the community assets remaining.

## 8.   WASHINGTON

The statutory provisions for management and control in Washington are found at Wash.Rev.Code § 26.16.030, reproduced below. Joint management and control is required for consequential real estate transactions. Primary management and control is the rule where one spouse alone manages a community property business. Otherwise Washington is a managerial system based on equal management and control.

**"Property not acquired or owned, as prescribed in RCW 26.16.010 and 26.16.020, acquired after marriage or after registration of a state registered domestic partnership by either domestic partner or either husband or wife or both, is community property. Either spouse or either domestic partner, acting alone, may manage and control community property, with a like power of disposition as the acting spouse or domestic partner has over his or her separate property, except:**

**(1) Neither person shall devise or bequeath by will more than one-half of the community property.**

**(2) Neither person shall give community property without the express or implied consent of the other.**

(3) Neither person shall sell, convey, or encumber the community real property without the other spouse or other domestic partner joining in the execution of the deed or other instrument by which the real estate is sold, conveyed, or encumbered, and such deed or other instrument must be acknowledged by both spouses or both domestic partners.

(4) Neither person shall purchase or contract to purchase community real property without the other spouse or other domestic partner joining in the transaction of purchase or in the execution of the contract to purchase.

(5) Neither person shall create a security interest other than a purchase money security interest as defined in RCW 62A.9–107 in, or sell, community household goods, furnishings, or appliances, or a community mobile home unless the other spouse or other domestic partner joins in executing the security agreement or bill of sale, if any.

(6) Neither person shall acquire, purchase, sell, convey, or encumber the assets, including real estate, or the good will of a business where both spouses or both domestic partners participate in its management without the consent of the

> other: PROVIDED, That where only one spouse or one domestic partner participates in such management the participating spouse or participating domestic partner may, in the ordinary course of such business, acquire, purchase, sell, convey or encumber the assets, including real estate, or the good will of the business without the consent of the nonparticipating spouse or nonparticipating domestic partner."

A spouse or domestic partner may protect his or her marital rights to property that is titled in the other spouse's name alone. The spouse does this by filing and recording a written instrument that identifies his or her interest in the property. The instrument provides record notice to third parties. When a spouse fails or decides not to protect marital rights in the above manner, the result is that **"full legal and equitable title"** passes to **"any actual bona fide purchaser"** who had no knowledge of the marriage and could not have obtained knowledge of the marriage. Wash.Rev.Code § 26.16.100.

## 9. WISCONSIN

Spouses are held to the standard of good faith with respect to marital property. Wis.Stat. § 766.15 provides:

> (1) "Each spouse shall act in good faith with respect to the other spouse in matters involving marital property or other property of the other spouse. This

> obligation may not be varied by a
> marital property agreement.
>
> (2) Management and control by a spouse of
> that spouse's property that is not
> marital property in a manner that
> limits, diminishes or fails to produce
> income from that property does not
> violate sub. (1)."

A spouse has a claim against the other spouse for
breach of the duty of good faith resulting in damage
to the claimant spouse's property. There is a six year
statute of limitations from the time the claimant
spouse gains actual knowledge of the breach.
Wis.Stat. § 766.70(1) sets out this and other
remedies.

The management and control statute, Wis.Stat.
§ 766.51, reads as follows:

> (1) "A spouse acting alone may manage and
> control:
>
> (a) That spouse's property that is not
> marital property.
>
> (am) Except as provided in subs. (2) and
> (3), marital property held in that
> spouse's name or not held in the name of
> either spouse.
>
> (b) Marital property held in the names
> of both spouses in the alternative,
> including marital property held in a
> form designating the holder by the

       words "(name of one spouse) or (name of other spouse)."

  (c) **A policy of insurance if that spouse is designated as the owner on the records of the policy issuer.**

  (d) **Any right of an employee under a deferred employment benefit plan that accrues as a result of that spouse's employment."**

By the same statute, **"for the purpose of obtaining an extension of credit for an obligation [incurred by a spouse in the interest of the marriage or the family], a spouse acting alone may manage and control all of the marital property."**

Also under Wis.Stat. § 766.51(b), note that:

- Joinder is required for marital property held in the names of both spouses; and

- Either spouse's right to act alone in managing and controlling marital property does not extend to enumerated business interests.

Wis.Stat. § 766.51(1m)(b)(4) provides that: **"the right to manage and control marital property permits gifts of that property."**

Related to this provision, Wis.Stat. § 766.53 sets out relevant value limitations, as follows.

**"A spouse acting alone may give to a 3rd person marital property that the spouse has the right to manage and control only if the value of**

the marital property given to the 3rd person does not aggregate more than either $1,000 in a calendar year, or a larger amount if, when made, the gift is reasonable in amount considering the economic position of the spouses. Any other gift of marital property to a 3rd person is subject to [§ 766.70(6)'s recovery remedy during the marriage] unless both spouses act together in making the gift. Under this section and for the purposes of [§ 766.70(6)'s recovery remedy during the marriage], in the case of a gift of marital property by a spouse to a 3rd person in which the donor spouse has retained an interest, the gift shall be valued at the full value of the entire transfer of marital property, regardless of any retained interest or interest donated to the other spouse. For purposes of this section only, a gift of a life insurance policy by a spouse to a 3rd person shall be valued at the amount payable under the policy if the insured died at the time the gift was made."

The remedies available to a non-consenting spouse for gifts of marital property made by the other spouse to a third person are set out in Wis.Stat. § 766.70(6) to (8).

# CHAPTER 8
# LIABILITIES

## A. OVERVIEW

The traditional civil law followed the entity approach, according to which the marital community is a formal legal entity with authority to incur its own liability, independent of the marital partners. At dissolution, assets are characterized. So are liabilities. Of the U.S. community property states, only Louisiana continues to follow this model.

The other community property states follow some version of a managerial approach. Under the managerial approach community property is a method of holding assets. Community property assets can be seized by creditors depending on whether and to what degree the spouse who incurred the debt had the legal right to manage and control the property. Each spouse acts an agent for the community with actual, implicit, and apparent power to bind the community property.

One key difference between the entity and the managerial approach is that the former deducts community liabilities from gross community assets in a sort of partnership liquidation process, while the latter looks to gross assets when determining creditors' rights, but then marshals those assets by character.

Another key difference is that a managerial model does not characterize liabilities. It marshals liabilities by the character of property.

The difference in the two models can be illustrated by the following equation:

**Gross and Net Liabilities:
Community Entity Versus Managerial Models**

**Both managerial and community entity models characterize assets to identify gross CP assets.**

**A managerial model *only* characterizes assets. Liabilities are not characterized; instead they are paid from gross assets, which are then marshaled by character.**                                    GROSS CP ASSETS

**A community entity model goes a step further to characterize liabilities for repayment. CP liabilities are repaid from gross CP assets. SP liabilities are repaid from gross SP assets**                    (CP LIABILITIES)

**After repayment, remaining CP assets, if any, are distributed to the spouses:**                                      NET CP ASSETS

The word liabilities is a generic label. It is used without regard to the time incurred; the way in which the obligation was created; or the time schedule for which payment on the obligation is due. In Louisiana, the term "obligations" is used in lieu of the term "liabilities."

Liabilities breaks down into three broad categories: contract liabilities, tort liabilities, and other liabilities.

*Contract liabilities*, are obligations that one spouse or both spouses incur by exchange and agreement with a third party. Typically a contract liability is memorialized by signing a written document that can be enforced as a contract.

*Tort liabilities* arise when the tort occurs.

*Other liabilities* arise from court judgments. Other liabilities are not based in contract or in tort. A judgment confirming a support payment owed by one spouse to a former spouse or minor child is an example of a debt that falls into the category of "other liabilities." A tax debt is another.

If and when a community property asset is levied on, both spouses lose the asset, whether it be real estate, personal property, deposits, or earnings.

Some states limit a judgment creditor to reaching the debtor-spouse's one-half of any levied community property. But even in these states, the lien creditor's repayment can and often does result in an unfortunate outcome whereby the non-debtor spouse comes to own the property with the creditor. This outcome can lead to a next round of litigation or negotiation, now between the creditor and the non-debtor spouse, over partition of the community property asset that was ultimately used to satisfy the debt.

Property is exempt if it is not subject to levy by the sheriff. In a managerial state, marshaling is the process whereby the creditor determines which character of property is reachable first, and which is temporarily exempt.

In a case where the creditor is initially limited to reaching separate property, community property falls into the category of exempt property, meaning property beyond the creditor's reach during the levy process. If there are no available separate property assets or if separate property assets become insufficient to repay the debt, then the creditor may benefit from going back to court to marshal the next-in-line community property asset(s).

If the creditor is entitled to reach both community and separate property, the question of marshaling also arises. The answer to which character of property is reachable first (community or separate?) and which second (community or separate?) determines what, if any, assets remain (temporarily) exempt from the reach of the creditor in the first round of the levy process, at the creditor's option.

State law varies widely in terms of how much protection it extends to debtors and, if married, to their spouses.

## B.   DETAIL

Among the areas of divergence in various states are the following, in order of importance.

*When was the liability incurred?* A liability can be incurred before, during or after marriage.

*Which character estate is reachable by a creditor?* As noted above, there are three possible estates that a creditor can or may seek to reach: one spouse's separate property, the other spouse's separate property, or community property.

*How was the liability incurred?* A liability can be incurred by contract, tort, or by statutory process (as discussed above support obligations and tax debts are examples of general obligations).

*If contractual, who incurred the debt and for what reason?* A contract liability can be incurred by one spouse, by the other spouse, or by both spouses. If one spouse incurs the debt, he or she may do so by signature, or, if not, as a manager of the community estate, or, if not, because the debt is incurred for a necessary (standard of) living expense during marriage or a (basic) common necessary expense during a period of separation.

For a contract debt incurred by one spouse acting alone, the judgment creditor can typically reach the community property before reaching the separate property of the married person who incurred individual (separate) liability by signature.

*If tort, who is the tortfeasor spouse and what conduct gave rise to the tort?* A tort liability arises when the tort occurs. One spouse alone may be the tortfeasor. Or both spouses may be tortfeasors.

In relation to a tort obligation, the community is generally liable if the tort arose from conduct that benefitted the community. The tortfeasor's intent is not dispositive. What tends to matter today is whether the community actually benefitted from the wrongful conduct. If it did, then the community property is reachable by the tort judgment creditor.

A tort can arise out of conduct that initially benefits the community but then veers off into conduct that has no community purpose whatsoever. See e.g., *deElche v. Jacobsen*, 95 Wash.2d 237, 622 P.2d 835 (1980) (*en banc*) (Horowitz J., dissenting), discussed below in Section C, Washington. In such a case, the community property may be exempt from the reach of the tort creditor. Or, as in most states, community assets are marshaled into second place, after the judgment debtor's separate property.

State law determines what property the sheriff can and cannot levy against. *Non-exempt* property is reachable by the creditor. *Exempt* property is shielded from the creditor's reach, if not temporarily (due to marshaling), then absolutely, depending on state law.

In a minority of U.S. community property states, one-half of the community assets may be deemed exempt for purposes of satisfying a separate tort judgment. If so, the judgment creditor can reach the tortfeasor spouse's separate property first, and the tortfeasor's one-half interest in the community property second, but the tortfeasor cannot reach the non-tortfeasor spouse's one-half of the community property. New Mexico achieves this result by statute. Washington achieves it by case law in certain circumstances.

The (majority) managerial system does not assign debt repayment to the community as an entity. Even so, assets and liabilities are divided for analytic purposes into three major categories: one spouse's separate, the other spouse's separate, and their community.

Chapters 2 through 6 indicate the methods used to characterize and apportion assets.

The community property rules for dealing with liabilities do not enjoy the same degree of consensus that the rules for characterizing assets do. Practically speaking, one target asset or another may be more or less desirable or accessible to certain creditors. On the statutory side of things, while there are many similarities among the states, there are also material differences.

## 1. LIABILITY OF COMMUNITY PROPERTY

### a. For Contract Obligations Incurred During Marriage

The safest ground in this area of quicksand is the sure liability of the community property for contractual debts incurred during marriage for a community purpose.

Community debts are satisfied against community property by signature, type of claim, time, managerial authority, and purpose. Contract debts for a community purpose or for family living expenses incurred during marriage (called *necessaries of life*) normally qualify contract creditors to execute a judgment against non-exempt community property assets as well as against the separate property assets of the spouse who is otherwise not liable by a signature.

While debtors may obtain some protection against unsecured creditors, no state protects debtors from their voluntary liens. For that reason, most community property states require that both spouses sign an encumbrance or a voluntary lien (a security interest or deed of trust) on community real property. These laws, known as joinder laws, give the nonjoining spouse a remedy—even if a very limited and time sensitive one—against the creditor who does not secure both spouses' signature on the real property security interest or deed of trust. See Chapter 7.

The tort creditor is in an entirely different position than the contract creditor. For negligent torts, the issue might be phrased in terms of the reasonableness of insuring against the risk. For intentional torts, a different set of issues asks whether the tortfeasor was acting as an agent of the community when the tort occurred. Such issues implicate the community purpose doctrine, which holds that if the conduct from which the tort arose benefitted the community, then the judgment debtor should be permitted to reach non-exempt community property, even if it is marshaled behind the tortfeasor's separate property.

The community purpose doctrine can come up in relation to tort creditors. But its key meaning is also made clear in the context of contract law. Here, the idea is that the spouses have a duty to support each other and their children by the present marriage. Obligations undertaken to that end are in keeping with community purpose. At the center of the duty of support during marriage is the duty to provide standard of living expenses. Because such obligations benefit the community, they are theoretically collectable first from community property assets and then, if the community assets are inadequate, from the separate property of both spouses.

Obligations incurred during the marriage are presumed to be community obligations unless it is clearly shown that they were not for the benefit of the community. Basic living expenses clearly benefit the community. Standard of living expenses do too. Expenses that exceed the community's ordinary standard of living, however, can lead to sound arguments that the community should be shielded from the reach of the creditor. Likewise expenses that are contrary to the community purpose.

If a liability incurred during the marriage is adjudged to not benefit of the community, some states allow the judgment creditor to levy on the debtor's separate property first and his or her one-half of the community property second, as mentioned above. Others marshal the assets so that the judgment creditor must levy on the debtor's separate property first, before seeking permission to levy on the entirety of the community property.

The community purpose doctrine is not necessarily an explicit part of the statutory creditors' rights scheme in managerial states like California, Idaho, New Mexico, Texas and Wisconsin; plus, it is out of favor with courts in Washington. Nevertheless, if a judgment creditor's rationale for being able to seize property is that either spouse acting alone can serve as an agent for the community, then questions of express, implied, and apparent authority are sometimes litigated, just as they would be in a nonmarital partnership.

Obligations incurred after a date of separation can fall within the general duty of support. These obligations may be contractual or general. If the spouses move into separate residences, both have the right to manage and control accumulated community property, if any. If one spouse is more productively employed than the other, the spouse in need of support may incur contractual debt for common necessaries, meaning basic living expenses. The contracting spouse is liable in first position; but if necessary, the creditor can satisfy a default against the other spouse's separate property.

A spousal support order from a prior marriage, or a child support obligation to children of a prior marriage or relationship are satisfiable first from the judgment debtor's separate property. The state has a compelling interest in seeing that support judgments are enforced. For that reason in some states—California is an example—if the debtor's separate property is nonexistent or insufficient to satisfy the support obligation, the community property of the debtor's subsequent marriage is liable. The rules are intended to protect parties who rely on the execution of support judgments, but even so, support judgments are reputed to be among the most difficult to collect.

If it turns out that a judgment debtor's subsequent community property must be used to satisfy a support obligation from a prior marriage or relationship, some states provide the subsequent community with a right of reimbursement against the judgment debtor. The reimbursement may or may not be with interest. It is payable (either voluntarily or as a lien) from the judgment debtor's existing or after-acquired separate property.

## b. For Obligations Incurred Before Marriage

Historically, civil law concepts exempted community property (or at least one-half of it) from liability for premarital obligations; the rationale was that the debts, if they pre-exist the marriage, are not contracted on behalf of the community. The exemption proved extremely inconvenient for creditors since all income (whether earned or, under the traditional civil law rule, generated by an existing separate property asset) is characterized as community property during marriage. If the married couple had only income from work, the rules of the community property system effectively barred the creditor from satisfying the premarital obligation.

Today, there is a tendency to subject community property to premarital liabilities. One reason is practical: revolving debt, for example, is recontracted during the marriage. Another reason is analytic: the obligations that a spouse brings to the marriage certainly will impact the community if the spouse intends to use earnings obtained during marriage to satisfy the debt. The third is conceptual: for the price of a marriage license, a person could frustrate the claims of premarital creditors with a so-called "two dollar bankruptcy" (the pre-inflation price of a marriage license).

Subjecting the entire community to liability for a premarital obligation was not favored in the civil law, as discussed in the previous paragraph, but it nevertheless could be done. Historically, a distinction was based upon whether the debtor was the manager of the community. At other times, the decision to hold the community liable for premarital (separate) debts turned on whether the debtor was the producer of the community income. Both distinctions tended to subject the community to liability, but only when the earning spouse was also the debtor.

Today, under the managerial model with its equal management rule, either spouse, even acting alone has, the legal authority to manage and control community personal property. By virtue of the legal right to manage and control, spouses can expect that the premarital creditors of either spouse may, and probably will be able to reach all community property to satisfy a default. Marshaling rules may apply to subordinate the community property to the debtor's separate property, depending on the type of debt (revolving or nonrevolving).

That said, there are statutes that may exempt a portion of the community property from the reach of certain premarital creditors of a person's spouse.

The range of rules below illustrates the extent to which U.S. community property states can and have diverged from their civil law origin as well as from each other.

- Arizona holds community property liable for the premarital separate debts or other liabilities of a spouse, but only to the extent of the value of that spouse's *contribution to* (not interest ın) the community property. Ariz.Rev.Stat.Ann. § 25–215.

- California allows a spouse to fully exempt (shield) his or her (actual) community property earnings from **"a debt incurred by the person's spouse before marriage."** Cal.Fam.Code § 911. The shield does not apply to revolving debt. The earnings must be fully removed from the debtor spouse's legal management and control in order to be fully exempt from the reach of the other spouse's premarital creditors.

- Early Idaho precedent permitted a premarital creditor of the husband, but not a premarital creditor of the wife, to reach community assets. The gender specificity of the precedent is an obsolete holdover from the male management era discussed above.

- Louisiana permits a premarital creditor to reach the community property, but provides for reimbursement between the spouses upon termination of the marital regime.

- Nevada provides that one spouse's share of the community property is not liable for the debts of the other spouse if contracted before marriage. The statute, by its own terms, should not include revolving debt, since what makes debt revolve is that it is recontracted each month with the delivery and acceptance of a monthly statement.

- New Mexico lists separate debts by statute. It then allows separate debts (including premarital obligations of either spouse) to be collected from the debtor spouse's one-half *interest in* (not contribution to, as described in Arizona above) the community property. Marshaling rules require that a separate debt creditor reach the debtor spouse's separate property before attempting to seize that spouse's one-half interest in any listed community property. This reverses the prior rule that sought to exempt the entirety of community property from the reach of separate debt creditors.

- Texas, a dual management state, allows the satisfaction of all premarital debts from commingled community property that is under dual control. It subjects property under the sole management and control of one of the spouses only to the premarital debts of that spouse, and not to the premarital debts of the other spouse.

- Washington shields the non-debtor spouse's separate property from the reach of premarital creditors, but then creates a non-community status of the debtor spouse's community property earnings and accumulations. The earmarked earnings can be used to satisfy a premarital liability of the debtor spouse.

- Wisconsin provides that an obligation incurred by a spouse before or during marriage that is attributable to an obligation arising before marriage (contract), or to an act or omission occurring before marriage (tort), may be satisfied only from property of that spouse that is not marital property (including the unique Wisconsin "unclassified" or "all other" property). Such debts can also be satisfied from that part of marital property which would have been the property of that spouse but for the marriage. The category of property that would have been individual property but for the marriage most obviously refers to separate property income streams. See Chapter 3, Section 3, Wisconsin.

## c. For Other Obligations

Most jurisdictions assume that spousal support for a previous spouse and support payments to the children of a prior or different relationship are premarital debts.

Louisiana has arrived at the opposite conclusion, however. In Louisiana, the obligation arises not because of the termination of the first marriage, but because of the passage of time during the second marriage. By this rationale, the obligation is categorized as a community obligation of the second marriage. The logic of the Louisiana approach, it seems, may be difficult to explain to the second spouse.

## d. For Tort Liability Adjudged Against One Spouse

In the civil law system the separate property of one spouse was not liable for the "delict" (roughly defined as the tort or crime) of the other. Similarly, only the community property managed and controlled by the wrongdoing spouse was subject to liability and then only if the delict was committed while the manager was engaged in an activity that benefitted the community.

Today, some trends for one spouse's tort liability are as follows:

- The community is liable in Arizona and Louisiana for a tort committed by the person who is a manager of the property if the activity that gave rise to the tort was being performed for or resulted in a benefit to the community or the other spouse.

- California, New Mexico, and Washington follow a marshaling approach by which the community property can be reached even for a tort that is a result of one spouse's activity that did not benefit the community. By statute, the separate property estate of the tortfeasor is primarily liable, but all or at least one-half of the community estate, depending on the jurisdiction, remains secondarily liable. If all the community property is reached by the creditor, the community obtains a right of reimbursement against the tortfeasor spouse.

- Texas subjects the community to liability by statute.

- Wisconsin provides that an obligation incurred by a spouse for a tort during marriage may be satisfied from property of that spouse which is not marital property ("all other property" in the words of the statute) and from that spouse's interest in marital property.

## e. Liability of One-Half of the Community

If a separate debt cannot be collected from *both* halves of the community property, may the creditor collect against one-half of the community?

The problem is theoretical because on one hand, if analytic stress is placed on the concept of *ownership*, the community is owned concurrently by the two spouses. This means that one-half of the community is as much the property of the debtor spouse as is his or her separate property. By this rationale, because a creditor can reach property that the debtor has legal rights to manage and control, a sound argument can be made that all, or at the very least one-half, of the community property should be reachable by the separate creditors of one spouse. On the other hand, if the analytic focus is on the *concurrent* feature of community property ownership, an equally sound argument can be made that the community should be shielded, if not deemed exempt altogether, from the reach of certain separate creditors of one spouse.

If the civil law "net community" approach is used, the exact amount of the community share cannot be accurately ascertained until the payment of all community debts and the division of the property is made at the termination of the marital regime. To allow collection of a separate debt against one-half of the community would be to allow a preference to this separate obligation over later community obligations (including support needs of the family). It would also raise unanswered accounting questions relevant to the types of problems discussed in Chapter 6. For example: if a creditor reached one-half of community earnings, would the earnings of the remaining one-half of the community belong entirely to the other spouse? Such issues could possibly be contracted around, but there are no clarifying default rules when they are not.

There have been some breaks in the traditional reluctance of community property jurisdictions to allow collection of a separate debt from one-half (but not the whole) of the community property.

- Arizona implies, by how it allows a spouse's premarital creditors to reach the debtor spouse's contribution to the community estate, that the community estate can be conceptualized as nonconcurrent halves for certain purposes.

- California (by statute) and Washington (by case law) adopts a marshaling approach for separate tort judgments. This suggests a policy choice to stress the concurrent aspect of half ownership.

- Louisiana allows a separate property debt to be satisfied from all community property. This places the stress on the ownership aspect of concurrent ownership. Nevertheless, the law permits a right of reimbursement for the community against the debtor spouse. That right accrues upon the termination of the marital regime, not before.

- Nevada implies that one-half of the community is liable for the premarital debts by stating, in Nev.Rev.Stat. § 123.050, that the community *share* of a married person is not liable for the premarital debts of that person's spouse.

- New Mexico and Wisconsin marshal one-half of the community property only after the separate (and in Wisconsin unclassified "all other") property of a debtor spouse is reached.

- Texas statutory law leaves the order of marshaling to the discretion of the court.

- Washington case law adopts a marshaling approach for the payment of separate tort judgments. The judgment creditor can reach the tortfeasor's separate property and one-half of the community property, as determined on a case-by-case basis. This approach may be modified depending on whether the tortious conduct was intentional or negligent.

For a sociological discussion of the relationship between debt collection, marriage and bankruptcy, see ELIZABETH WARREN, ET. AL. THE FRAGILE MIDDLE CLASS (2000).

## 2. LIABILITY OF SEPARATE PROPERTY

Previously, Spanish civil law authorities proclaimed that any liability incurred during the marriage for the benefit of the community was a community liability.

Rebuttal followed for debts incurred by the manager (then the husband) for his separate benefit. The wife, not being the manager, did not have a full right to bind the community by her contracts.

The civil law marshaled the couples' assets but then subjected both community and separate property to liability for community contractual debts. The right of reimbursement diminished the distinction between debts and expenses in the sense that payment of a liability from the inappropriate character property gave rise to a right of reimbursement from the property that would otherwise have been legally liable for repaying the debt.

Louisiana, with its matrimonial regime approach, remains the most faithful to the traditional civil law model. Among the U.S. community property states, Louisiana has the most detailed statutes to govern the characterization of obligations (debts) as community or separate. See Section C, Louisiana below.

Washington formerly used an entity approach that characterized the liability itself as separate or community. Separate property was liable for separate debts and community property was liable for community debts (a term that excluded both premarital debts and separate tort judgments). Today, in Washington, any rigid distinction between these points has been erased by statutes and cases. As applied to separate tort judgment creditors, the entity approach no longer shields all of the community property from seizure, as it once did. Instead, a separate tort judgment creditor can reach both the tortfeasor spouse's separate property and one-half of

his or her community property, especially in the case
of an intentional tort, as discussed below in Section C,
Washington below.

Otherwise, most of the U.S. community property
states have developed a managerial approach that
treats community property as a form of holding gross
assets without regard to liabilities, as the chart in
Section A indicates.

The basic idea behind a managerial model is that a
creditor should be able to satisfy a debt in default from
whatever property a spouse has the *legal right* to
manage and control. In most U.S. community property
states, under equal management rules, either spouse
acting alone can manage and control the entirety of
the community personal property, as well as their own
separate property. Agency principles make separate
property liable for contractual debts even if the spouse
did not bind his or her separate property with a
signature.

To better protect their interests, contract creditors
often ask both spouses to voluntarily assume personal
liability for a loan by a signature.

But absent a signature, there are default methods
to hold a spouse's separate property liable. The
doctrine of *necessaries of life*, meaning standard of
living expenses, applies during marriage. The doctrine
of *common necessaries*, meaning basic living expenses,
applies in a period of separation. Both are discussed
below.

Additionally, doctrines like the lender's intent test
allow a lender to proactively place a spouse's separate

property in priority position in case of default. The lender's intent test is discussed in Chapter 6.

### a. For One Spouse's Individual Debts During Marriage

There is no controversy about the rule that the separate (and in Wisconsin the unclassified "all other") property of each spouse is liable for his or her individual debts.

A separate liability may arise as a matter of civil, contract or tort law; and it may be individual or joint with the other spouse:

Civil liability may occur by reason of the duty of support, although most other provisions imposing liability by virtue of the marital relationship (other than spousal support and community property rules) have been abolished.

Contract liability may arise as a result of one's own promise (alone, jointly or as guarantor of the other spouse's promise), by consent or other agreement (including transmutation), or by giving authority to the other spouse, such as by a power of attorney or other specific agency arrangement.

This is understandable enough, but absent a signature how does one spouse become personally liable for a contract debt incurred by the other spouse?

To start with, spouses owe each other a duty of support during marriage. During marriage, the community is liable for necessaries of life (standard of living expenses while married), regardless of which spouse incurs the debt. During a period of separation the community is usually liable for common necessaries (basic living expense, during a period of separation), again regardless of which spouse incurs the debt. If there is no accumulated community property, then statutes invoke the duty of support to impose default separate liability on the spouse who is most gainfully employed for common necessaries (debts for basic living needs) that the less gainfully spouse incurs during a period of separation. This is true regardless of the fact that the more financially able spouse did not personally sign the contract, did not act as an agent, and will not personally benefit from the contract services or products.

Tort liability, in addition to being for one's own torts, may be vicarious or derivative. The other spouse may commit a tort which is attributed to the first spouse by virtue of the agency doctrine of respondeat superior or because of ownership, such as with vehicle registration liability. There can also be owner liability derived from community property ownership.

## b. For Debts Incurred During Marriage as a Community Manager

There is still some authority for subjecting the separate property of the manager of the community to liability for acts done as manager of the community.

One part of the obsolete male management rule which is definitely eliminated is the liability of the separate property of the husband only (and no liability of the separate property of the wife) for community debts because the husband had legal and actual management and control of the community. Today, under equal management rules, when one spouse obligates the community personal property either the separate property of both spouses is bound, as when both spouses sign a loan contract, or the separate property of neither is bound (as in Arizona).

Two variations reflect how the higher earning spouse, who obtains a statutory benefit as a matter of economics, might also be exposed to greater liability than the other lower earning spouse. The first variation is the ability of a higher earning spouse to bind the property over which he or she would have had control if not married. Typically this category of property is the spouse's earnings, as in Texas, or separate property rents, issues, and profits. The second variation is illustrated by the following Louisiana provision. Under a **"separation of property regime"** spouses are made liable for family expenses not on an equal basis, but **"in proportion to his or her means"** in the language of LSA–C.C. Art. 2373. By rules like these, a higher earning spouse's economic exposure to personal liability, practically speaking, is greater than a lower earning spouse's is both during marriage and during any period of separation.

Generally, if both spouses signed or agreed to the contract for a community debt, the separate property of both can be used to satisfy the debt. If only one spouse contracted the community debt, the separate property of that spouse is also liable for that same community debt. The spouse who didn't incur the

debt may be liable under duty of support or benefit to
the community principles.

Some states specify by statute that when the
community property is marshaled in first position,
the separate property of the manager shall be
reached only after the community property has been
exhausted.

## C.   INDIVIDUAL STATES

### 1.   ARIZONA

Arizona follows a two-part hybrid approach. Part
one incorporates a managerial approach for contracts
and acts and omissions taken in furtherance of the
community purpose. Part two follows an entity
approach for intentional torts.

Ariz.Rev.Stat.Ann. § 25–215(D) permits **"either
spouse"** to **"contract debts and otherwise act for
the benefit of the community"** except as provided
by Ariz.Rev.Stat.Ann. § 25–214, which requires
joinder for **"any transaction for the acquisition,
disposition or encumbrance of an interest in
real property."** In the case of joinder, when liability
results, the spouses are sued jointly. Satisfaction
comes **"first, from the community property, and
second, from the separate property of the
spouse contracting the debt or obligation."** *Id*.

Otherwise, during the marriage, the separate
property of each spouse is liable for his or her own
separate debts, but **"shall not be liable for the
[separate debts or obligations of the other**

**spouse,] absent an agreement to the contrary."**
Ariz.Rev.Stat.Ann.        § 25–215(A).        This        statutory
language may block third party creditors from directly
reaching a non-debtor spouse's separate property.
However, in a property settlement agreement or
decree of dissolution, **"[o]n request, a court can
impose a lien against the separate property of a
spouse to secure payment of debts that the court
orders that spouse to pay."** Ariz.Rev.Stat.Ann.
§ 25–318(F). See Chapter 4.

Arizona does not follow the necessaries doctrine.

A property settlement agreement between the
spouses or a dissolution decree cannot cancel a debt;
for that reason, a spouse can expect to remain liable
for whatever contractual obligation may exist between
that spouse and a creditor. In a legal separation or
dissolution proceeding, each spouse has a statutory
right to obtain a copy of the other spouse's credit report
so as to assess what, if any, liability the requesting
spouse has to the creditor. Ariz.Rev.Stat.Ann. § 25–
318(F).

Prior to the passage of the controlling statute
Ariz.Rev.Stat.Ann. § 25–215, in 1973, the entirety of
the community property was also exempt from
liability for the premarital separate obligations of
either spouse. As discussed above, that rule changed
with Ariz.Rev.Stat.Ann. § 25–215(B), which was
enacted to create a disincentive for avoiding existing
obligations to creditors through the voluntary act of
marriage. Ariz.Rev.Stat.Ann. § 25–215(B) now
provides that **"[t]he community property is liable
for premarital separate debts or other liabilities**

of a spouse, incurred after September 1, 1973 but
only to the extent of the value of that spouse's
contribution to the community property which
would have been such spouse's separate
property if single."

*Schilling v. Embree*, 118 Ariz. 236, 575 P.2d 1262
(1977), held that the application of Ariz.Rev.Stat.Ann.
§ 25–215(B) is limited to debts and liabilities incurred
prior to marriage; the rationale being that the phrase
**"premarital separate"** modifies both **"debts"** and
**"other liabilities."** By this interpretation the
community is not liable for payment of separate
liabilities during the marriage, but is liable for
premarital debts to the extent of the debtor spouse's
**"*contribution* to the community property,"** not
*share* or *interest* in the community property. (Italics
added.) Modification by agreement is covered by
Ariz.Rev.Stat.Ann. § 25–215(A)).

Ariz.Rev.Stat.Ann.       § 25–215(D)     does     not
distinguish between contract and tort liabilities"
**"either   spouse   may   contract   debts   and
otherwise act for the benefit of the community."**

The two types of obligations appear to be treated the
same under Arizona case law. *Elia v. Pifer*, 194 Ariz.
74, 977 P.2d 796 (1998), *rev. denied*, for example,
affirms that the community is liable for contracts
made during marriage, just as it is liable for
intentional torts committed by one spouse while
performing an activity in furtherance of the
community's interest. Nevertheless, the statutory
language reflects that Arizona historically has
followed Washington law on the question of whether

to make the community property liable for the intentional torts of one spouse acting alone without benefit to the community.

The community purpose doctrine, introduced above, holds that if a tort is committed with the intent to benefit the community, the community property can be reached to satisfy the judgment, even if the community does not receive an actual benefit from the wrongful conduct. *Shaw v. Greer*, 67 Ariz. 223, 194 P.2d 430 (1948).

But where the tort is also (i) "a malicious tort" committed by one of the spouses "without knowledge, consent, or ratification of the other" and (ii) does not result in a "benefit to the community" the community property cannot be reached. *Id.* at 34. In such a case, the tortfeasor's debt becomes the separate obligation of the tortfeasor and the community is entirely shielded from liability. *Howe v. Haught,* 11 Ariz.App. 98, 462 P.2d 395, 397 (1969). So too is the separate property of the innocent spouse. Ariz.Rev.Stat.Ann. § 25–215(A).

With intentional torts there is a presumption in favor of shielding the community from liability for the delicts of one spouse. A married tortfeasor is presumed to cause malicious or intentional harm while acting outside the community purpose, and thus outside the scope of any managerial authority. The presumption is rebuttable, either with proof that the community benefitted from the tort or that the non-tortfeasor spouse knew about, consented to, or ratified the other spouse's act or omission. Nonintervention while present at the scene of the tort does not per se constitute knowledge, consent or ratification of the innocent spouse in the tortfeasor's wrongdoing. *Howe* supra at 398. Neither does ignorance. *Selby v. Savard*, 134 Ariz. 222, 655 P.2d 342, 349 (1982), citing *Howe*, supra.

## 2. CALIFORNIA

The California approach to liability is managerial.

For purposes of the family code, a **"debt"** is **"an obligation incurred by a married person before or during marriage."** A debt can arise from contract, tort, or otherwise. Cal.Fam.Code § 902. Debts are incurred at specific times. For a contract, the debt is incurred when the contract is made; for a tort, at the time the tort occurs; and in other cases, at the time the obligation arises. Cal.Fam.Code § 903.

Statutes and decisional law distinguish between necessaries of life and common necessaries.

The necessaries of life doctrine makes the community liable for **"a debt incurred by either spouse before or during marriage,"** up until a date of separation. Cal.Fam.Code § 910. By this rule, the creditors of one spouse can reach community property for obligations whose purpose is to meet the spouses' basic needs, the family's standard of living expenses, and the educational expenses of minor children. A court has discretion, within the definition of necessaries of life, to include business debts incurred for the purpose of creating income for the family (for example, computers for a community property business).

After a date of separation, the common necessaries doctrine, discussed below, applies.

By statute, a spouse can exempt his or her community property earnings during marriage from the reach of the other spouse's premarital creditors **"so long as** [the shielding spouse's community property earnings] **are held in a deposit account in which the person's spouse has no right of withdrawal and are uncommingled with other property in the** *community estate,* **except property insignificant in amount."** Cal.Fam.Code § 911 (italics added). The shield automatically drops if and when the exempt community property earnings are commingled with any other community property funds, or if and when the account becomes accessible by both spouses. The rationale is one of legal control: once the debtor spouse obtains access to the shielding spouse's account, the debtor spouse gains legal control of the sums on deposit in that account, which in turn exposes sums on deposit in the account to the reach of both spouses' creditors.

A spouse's separate property is liable for debts incurred by that spouse before or during marriage. By the same rationale, the general rule is that a spouse's separate property is not liable for a debt incurred by the other spouse before or during marriage. Cal.Fam.Code § 913. *Note carefully that this general rule is dwarfed by exceptions.*

Cal.Fam.Code § 914 states those exceptions by reference to the common necessaries doctrine, mentioned above. The common necessaries doctrine provides that a married person's separate property is liable for debts " . . . for "**necessaries of life of the person's spouse while the spouses are living together**" and for "**common necessaries of life of the person's spouse while the spouses are living separately.**" Cal.Fam.Code § 914(a)(1) and (2).

Necessaries of life are defined as expenses related to each spouse's statutory obligation to support the other during marriage. Again, such expenses are broadly measured by a standard of living metric that includes basics, amenities, and, depending on the family finances, even luxuries like vacations, club fees, private school tuition, and other lifestyle expenditures.

In a period of separation, the duty of support continues, but in a pared down fashion. The common necessaries doctrine permits each spouse's creditors to reach (i) accumulated community property and (ii) absent a signature, the other spouse's post-separation earnings and accumulations (which, after separation, are characterized by statute as the earner's separate property). The spouse who incurs the debt is the supported spouse. The spouse whose income and accumulations are liable to satisfy the debt is the supporting spouse. Absent an agreement, creditors are permitted to reach the supporting spouse's post-separation earnings and accumulations, by default, for debts that go toward common necessaries, meaning basic living expenses: rent, food, utilities, transportation, and possibly basic medical care. Standard of living expenses are not covered by the common necessaries doctrine.

Conditions governing any right of reimbursement appear in Cal.Fam.Code § 920.

With respect to tort liability, California modifies the managerial approach with satisfaction of order rules. The community property is liable for a tort judgment, and marshaled either in first or second position depending on whether the tort was committed **"while the married person was performing an activity for the benefit of the community."** Unlike in Arizona or Washington, the community is not entirely shielded from one spouse's tort debts; indeed, the community may be find itself all or partially liable to the injured plaintiff depending on the tortfeasor's separate property resources.

Cal.Fam.Code § 1000 provides in part:

**(a) "A married person is not liable for any injury or damage caused by the other spouse except in cases where he or she would be liable therefor if the marriage did not exist.**

**(b) The liability of a married person for death or injury to person or property shall be satisfied as follows:**

**(1) If the liability of the married person is based upon an act or omission which occurred while the married person was performing an activity for the benefit of the community, the liability shall first be satisfied from the community property and second**

> from the separate property of the
> married person.
>
> (2) If the liability of the married person
> is not based upon an act or omission
> which occurred while the married
> person was performing an activity
> for the benefit of the community, the
> liability shall first be satisfied from
> the separate property of the married
> person and second from the
> community property."

Additionally, the debt allocation provisions of
Cal.Fam.Code § 2625 include in the definition of
**"separate debts"** contract obligations **"that were
not incurred for the benefit of the community."**
So, for example, under this provision, the purchase of
an airplane during marriage using a joint savings
account as collateral was defined as a separate debt
when the spouse who incurred the debt did so in
anticipation of separation. *Marriage of Mahone*, 123
Cal.App.3d 17, 176 Cal.Rptr. 274 (1981). A contract for
attorney fees related to one spouse's criminal defense
was assigned to the criminal defendant spouse as a
separate debt because the criminal charge
"culminated in financial consequences at the time the
marriage was coming to an end." *Marriage of Stitt*, 147
Cal.App.3d 579, 195 Cal.Rptr. 172 (1983), cf. *Marriage
of Hirsch*, 211 Cal.App.3d 104, 259 Cal.Rptr. 39
(1989). And a contract made after separation by one
spouse for the services of a private investigator hired
to locate the other spouse was confirmed without offset
to the spouse who made the contract *Marriage of*

*Munguia,* 146 Cal.App.3d 853, 195 Cal.Rptr. 199 (1983).

## 3.  IDAHO

The major statutory provision is Idaho Code § 32–912, which is also excerpted in Chapter 7, Section C, Idaho. That provision states a managerial approach: **"Either the husband or wife shall have the right to manage and control the community property, and either may bind the community property by contract, except that neither the husband nor wife may sell, convey or encumber the community real estate unless the other joins in executing the sale agreement, deed or other instrument of conveyance by which the real estate is sold, conveyed or encumbered, . . ."** This language suggests either spouse acting alone can bind the community personal property for secured and unsecured promissory notes or obligations. The Idaho Attorney General issued an advisory statement in 2005 indicating it is unlikely that one spouse acting alone can bind the community property to an unsecured promissory note or loan obligation. OAG 05–1.

The Attorney General's advisory reflects the current rule among the U.S. community property states for community real property, however. The rule is that both spouses shall join in encumbering the community real property. Joinder is required in Idaho, but unlike in California, in Idaho joinder rule is not applied on a document-by-document basis so much as on a transactional basis. Therefore, in a transaction, absent collusion between the creditor and the spouse who incurs the contract debt, if only one spouse signs a promissory note or loan contract but later both spouses sign a deed of trust, then the creditor, opines the Attorney General, should be able to reach the community real property despite the absence of joinder on the loan contract. OAG 05–1, supra. The Attorney General refers to Idaho case law in general but does not cite actual cases.

On the issue of community property real estate, case law often seems inconsistent with the premise that joinder refers to transactions rather than to documents. One possibly inconsistent case involving community property real estate, is *New Phase Invs., LLC v. Jarvis*, 153 Idaho 207, 280 P.3d 710 (2012). There the court held that it is only the nonsigning spouse, not a creditor, who can bring an action to declare a real estate transfer void under Idaho Code § 32–912. The purpose of the provision, the court went on to say, is to benefit the non-signing spouse by providing that spouse with a shield for protecting his, her or their interest in community real property. A default rule that focuses on the transaction rather than on the documents upon which the transaction is built weakens the shield, an issue the Attorney General did not address. Also contradicting the Attorney General's statement is the holding in *Credit Bureau of Eastern Idaho, Inc. v. Lecheminant*, 149 Idaho 467, 235 P.3d 1188 (2010). There the court ruled that a debt need not be for a community purpose in order to bind the community. Idaho law is in need of clarification. Should the default serve as a shield for the creditor or for the non-joining spouse?

In light of the Attorney General's statement, that same statute—Idaho Code § 32–912—may also provide the non-signing spouse with a shield for protecting an interest in community personal property.

Additional clarification would be useful on separate property exemptions as well. Idaho exempts some separate property from liability for certain community obligations. Idaho Code § 32–912, for example, provides that: **"any community obligation incurred by either the husband or the wife without the consent in writing of the other shall not obligate the separate property of the spouse who did not consent."**

The statutory scheme requires the written consent of a person to any community contract which binds his or her separate property. For example, Idaho Code § 32–904 gives **"the wife ... absolute powers of disposition of her separate property."** Idaho Code 32–903, 23–904, and 32–905 are all gender specific, and this seems a remnant of the male management era. Therefore, one would expect a court to follow precedent and apply the rules in gender-neutral form, especially after *Suter*, supra. But even so, the Idaho Code remains in dire need of the legislature's attention.

Idaho follows the civil law rule that rents, issues, and profits of separate property are characterized as community for the duration of marriage. But Idaho Code § 32–906 speaks to the case where the separate property owner has transmuted the rents, issues, and profits back to separate property. In such a case, the transmuted property is not exempt from liability. Prepare yourself for three negatives: the rule stated is that neither the separate property nor its income streams **"shall not be liable for the debts of the other member of the community."** *Baruch v. Clark*, 154 Idaho 732, 302 P.3d 357 (2013) and *Credit Bureau of Eastern Idaho*, supra, are Idaho Supreme Court cases on point.

In *Williams v. Paxton*, 98 Idaho 155, 559 P.2d 1123 (1977), applied well accepted principles to allow a creditor to reach a wife's separate property where the creditor had obtained a judgment on a joint promissory note that the spouses contracted during marriage. The creditor was permitted to levy against the wife's separate property regardless of what the purpose of the contract was deemed to be. The court's rationale was that if the act of signing a loan contract during marriage obligates the community, it also personally obligates the signing spouse; therefore, a judgment creditor can execute against the signing spouse's separate property. *Credit Bureau of Eastern Idaho*, supra, makes a similar point.

Community funds that are used to pay off premarital debts are not necessarily reimbursed upon an Idaho divorce, depending on how the court applies Idaho Code § 32–712. The statute allows a court discretion to assign community debts to a higher earning spouse.

If community funds satisfy separate debt and, by doing so, enhance the separate property, a reimbursement may be due the community. See e.g., *Vanwassenhove v. Vanwassenhove*, 134 Idaho 198, 998

P.2d 505 (Ct. App. 2000), ruling that the magistrate erred in denying the community a reimbursement for its principal payments on the husband's separate property farm. But if community funds satisfy separate debt without a corresponding enhancement to the separate property, then a reimbursement is likely not due. See e.g. *Bliss v. Bliss*, 127 Idaho 170, 898 P.2d 1081 (1995) where the court denied a reimbursement to the community for its contributions to paying off the husband's premarital judgment debt. The rationale of the *Bliss*, supra, could be fairly characterized in this way: a debt that does not result in an enhancement of the community estate is not a family expense.

The law is unclear about whether the separate property of one spouse should be exempt from liability for the torts or delicts of the other spouse.

## 4.  LOUISIANA

Louisiana is the most faithful adherent to the community regime concept by how it classifies obligations as separate or community. See LSA–C.C. Art. 2359. **"Community obligation"** is defined in LSA–C.C. Art. 2360 as **"[a]n obligation incurred by a spouse during the existence of a community property regime for the common interest of the spouses or for the interest of the other spouse. . . ."** Attorney fees and costs in an action for divorce are community obligations prior to the **"the date of the judgment of divorce,"** but not after. LSA–C.C. Art. 2362.1.

Separate obligations are enumerated in LSA–C.C. Art. 2363 and further described as debts incurred **"prior to the establishment of a community property regime, or . . . during the existence of a community property regime though not for the common interest of the spouses or for the interest of the other spouse,"** and after the community terminates. **"An obligation resulting from an intentional wrong not perpetrated for the benefit of the community, or an obligation incurred for the separate property of a spouse to the extent that it does not benefit the community, the family, or the other spouse, is likewise a separate obligation."**

Under the above statute, a premarital obligation is characterized as separate because it negatively impacts marital net worth as, for example, when it is repaid with community funds. By comparison, an obligation assumed during marriage—contract or tort—is characterized by whether (and to what extent) its effect is to benefit the family. Benefit is dispositive, here; not the intent of the spouse who incurred the obligation (as in Arizona). Debts incurred after the community regime terminates are separate on the theory that they can have no impact on the community.

During the existence of the marital regime a separate obligation may be satisfied from the separate property of the spouse who incurred the obligation and from the community property. LSA–C.C. Art. 2345.

Upon termination of a community property regime, when community property has repaid a separate obligation, the spouse who did not incur the obligation (or heirs) may have a reimbursement claim against the spouse who did incur the obligation. The amount of the reimbursement due is one-half of the amount (if money was used), or one-half the value at the time of use (if things other than money were used). LSA–C.C. Art. 2364.

A spouse who uses separate property to satisfy a community obligation is likewise entitled to a reimbursement at the end of the community regime. The reimbursement is from the other spouse to the community. It is limited to the amount or value of one-half the payment made. It is taken from the reimbursing spouse's net share of the community. In the language of the statute it is " . . . **limited to the value of [the reimbursing spouse's] share in the community after deduction of all community obligations.**" LSA–C.C. Art. 2365. If there are no community assets, then no reimbursement is due.

A major exception is made " . . . **[i]f the community obligation was incurred for the ordinary and customary expenses of the marriage, or for the support, maintenance, and education of children of either spouse in keeping with the economic condition of the community, the spouse is entitled to reimbursement from the other spouse regardless of the value of that spouse's share of the community.**" For this enumeration of the major exception, the spouse who pays the expense is entitled to a reimbursement. If there are insufficient community assets to satisfy the debt, then a reimbursement is due from the reimbursing spouse's separate property.

Similarly, a reimbursement is due when a spouse uses separate property to improve the other spouse's separate property. LSA–C.C. Art. 2367.1. Reimbursement is due from the benefitted spouse to the contributing spouse, and measured by the amount or value the contributing **"assets had at the time they were used."**

The right of reimbursement is heritable.

The provisions quoted above are concerned with the allocation of the burden between the spouses. They do not deal with the rights of creditors. Even so, creditors may intervene and object in the proceeding by which the spouses resolve their rights.

## 5.    NEVADA

Among the few provisions which give guidance in this area is Nev.Rev.Stat § 123.050: **"Neither the separate property of a spouse nor his share of the community property is liable for the debts of the other spouse contracted before the marriage."**

There appears to be an exception for **"articles necessary"** in a case where **"the husband neglects to make adequate provision for the support of his wife."** The gender specific language complicates rather than clarifies. But, as written, the "husband's" creditors can reach his separate property if the community property is insufficient to satisfy a debt for "articles necessary," meaning one presumes necessaries of life. Nev.Rev.Stat. § 123.090. The language of the provision is obviously a remnant from the male-management era. One can expect that Nevada courts would apply the rule on a gender-neutral basis. Here, again, the state code is in need of update.

## 6.   NEW MEXICO

New Mexico has a relatively complete set of statutory provisions that divide debts into separate and community, and that direct an order of marshaling for satisfying each category of debt.

Generally, a debt incurred during marriage is presumptively a community debt absent proof that the debt falls into one of the categories of separate debts listed in N.M.Stat.Ann. § 40–3–9(A)(1) through (6) (1978).

The statutory provisions for the definition of separate and community debts are set forth as N.M.Stat.Ann. § 40–3–9(A) (1978):

**A. "Separate debt" means:**

   **(1) a debt contracted or incurred by a spouse before marriage or after entry of a decree of dissolution of marriage;**

   **(2) [or legal separation]. . . .**

   **(3) a debt designated as a separate debt of a spouse by a judgment or decree of any court having jurisdiction;**

(4) a debt contracted by a spouse during marriage which is identified by a spouse to the creditor in writing at the time of its creation as the separate debt of the contracting spouse; or

(5) a debt which arises from a tort committed by a spouse before marriage or after entry of a decree of dissolution of marriage or a separate tort committed during marriage. . . .

**B. "Community debt" means a debt contracted or incurred by either or both spouses during marriage which is not a separate debt.**

As for community contract debts, the either or both spouse language means that either spouse acting alone can contractually bind the community unless he or she identifies the contract debt **"to the creditor in writing at the time of its creation as the separate debt of the contracting spouse."** N.M.Stat.Ann. § 40–3–9(A)(4) (1978).

In other words, New Mexico is a managerial approach state for community debts. But is it one for separate debts as well? How much of the community property can a creditor of an enumerated separate debt reach? Case law answers that (even) a spouse who incurs separate debts is a manager of the community. As a manager that spouse can incur debts that ultimately expose the community property to the reach of creditors. When that happens, however, only one-half of the community property is made available.

By distinguishing between the debtor spouse's and non-debtor spouse's one-half of the community property, New Mexico shields (exempts) one-half of the community property from the reach a spouse's separate creditors.

In 1997, New Mexico enacted N.M.Stat.Ann. § 40–3–9.1 (1978), a statute specific to gambling debts. It provides that **"[a] gambling debt incurred by a married person as a result of legal gambling is a separate debt of the spouse incurring the debt."**

The New Mexico order of marshaling separate debt is unique among the states in other ways. The next paragraph is the marshaling order.

Separate debts are covered under N.M.Stat.Ann. § 40–3–10 (1978).

**A. The separate debt of a spouse shall be satisfied first from the debtor spouse's separate property, excluding that spouse's interest in property in which each of the spouses owns an undivided equal interest as a joint tenant or tenant in common. Should such property be insufficient, then the debt shall be satisfied from the debtor spouse's one-half interest in the community property or in property in which each spouse owns an undivided equal interest as a joint tenant or tenant in common, excluding the residence of the spouses. Should such property be insufficient, then the debt shall be satisfied from the debtor spouse's interest in the residence of the spouses. . . . Neither spouse's interest in community property or separate**

property shall be liable for the separate debt of the other spouse.

B. The priorities or exemptions established in this section for the satisfaction of a separate debt must be claimed by either spouse under the procedure set forth in Section 42–10–13 NMSA 1978, or the right to claim such priorities or exemptions is waived as between a spouse and the creditor.

C. This section shall apply only while both spouses are living, and shall not apply to the satisfaction of debts after the death of one or both spouses.

During a period of separation, a party may petition that a debt be declared an **"unreasonable debt."** An unreasonable debt becomes a separate debt, payable by the party who incurs the debt. A debt is unreasonable **"if it was incurred by a spouse while the spouse was living separate and apart and the debt did not contribute to the benefit of both spouses or their dependents."** This standard seems to further narrow the already narrow common necessaries doctrine. It narrows by requiring a benefit to both spouses, not just to the needy spouse, or to their dependents.

Community debts fall under N.M.Stat.Ann. § 40–3–11 (1978).

**"A. Community debts shall be satisfied first from all community property and all property in which each spouse owns an undivided equal interest as a joint tenant or tenant in common,**

excluding the residence of the spouses. Should such property be insufficient, community debts shall then be satisfied from the residence of the spouses, except as provided in Section 42–10–9 NMSA 1978. Should such property be insufficient, only the separate property of the spouse who contracted or incurred the debt shall be liable for its satisfaction. If both spouses contracted or incurred the debt, the separate property of both spouses is jointly and severally liable for its satisfaction.

B. The priorities or exemptions established in this section for the satisfaction of community debts must be claimed by either spouse under the procedure set forth in Section 42–10–13 NMSA 1978 or the right to claim such priorities or exemptions is waived as between a spouse and the creditor.

C. This section shall apply only while both spouses are living, and shall not apply to the satisfaction of debts after the death of one or both spouses."

The residence of the spouses (in excess of the homestead exemption) is not exempt and thus reachable to satisfy a community debt.

The above statute leaves open the question of how to characterize a tort committed by one spouse during the marriage. The doctrine that decides the character of a tort is the family purpose doctrine that turns on whether the tortfeasor's conduct benefitted the community. If not, the tort creates a liability separate in character. *Dell v. Heard*, 532 F.2d 1330 (10th Cir. 1976). For separate torts, the statutes and cases make clear that a spouse who commits a separate tort (intentional or negligent) is individually liable for damages that arise therefrom. The community or separate property assets of the innocent spouse are not liable and therefore cannot be reached by the tort judgment creditor.

If the tortfeasor's conduct benefitted the community, then the tort is community in character. As such, the wrongful conduct creates a community liability. The judgment is collectible under the community property provisions set forth above. Those provisions provide that the judgment creditor can seek a judgment lien against the tortfeasor's one-half of the community property. This includes permission for the judgment creditor to reach one-half the income of the non-debtor spouse. *Cent. Adjustment Bureau, Inc. v. Thevenet*, 101 N.M. 612, 686 P.2d 954 (1984).

Additionally, depending on the reach of the state family purpose doctrine, even if a plaintiff only has a cause of action against one spouse, once a judgment is obtained, if and when the judgment creditor goes to satisfy the judgment, the separate property of both spouses, if any, may be jointly and severally liable and hence reachable. *Dell*, supra.

## 7.   TEXAS

V.T.C.A.Fam.Code § 5.61 provides the basic theme of liability of community property: Property subject to the sole management and control of one spouse is liable for that spouse's marital contract debts.

All the dually managed community property is subject to liability for torts committed during the marriage. So too is property under the sole management of the spouse who incurs the liability.

Here is the text of V.T.C.A.Fam.Code § 5.61:

(a) **A spouse's separate property is not subject to liabilities of the other spouse unless both spouses are liable by other rules of law.**

(b) **Unless both spouses are liable by other rules of law, the community property subject to a spouse's sole management, control, and disposition is not subject to:**

  (1) **any liabilities that the other spouse incurred before marriage; or**

  (2) **any nontortious liabilities that the other spouse incurs during marriage.**

(c) **The community property subject to a spouse's sole or joint management, control, and disposition is subject to the liabilities incurred by him or her before or during marriage.**

(d) **All the community property is subject to tortious liability of either spouse incurred during marriage.**

Texas couples the managerial approach with marshaling. But order of priority (marshaling) is expressly left to the discretion of the judge by V.T.C.A.Fam.Code § 5.62:

   (a) A judge may determine, as he deems just and equitable, the order in which particular separate or community property will be subject to execution and sale to satisfy a judgment, if the property subject to liability for a judgment includes any combination of:

      (1) a spouse's separate property;

      (2) community property subject to a spouse's sole management, control, and disposition;

      (3) community property subject to the other spouse's sole management, control, and disposition; and

      (4) community property subject to the spouses' joint management, control, and disposition.

   (b) In determining the order in which particular property will be subject to execution and sale, the judge shall consider the facts surrounding the transaction or occurrence upon which the suit is based.

## 8. WASHINGTON

Wash.Rev.Code § 26.16.200 protects each spouses separate property from the other's premarital creditors. The statutory basis for that interpretation is a reference in the statute to **"the rent or income of the** *separate property* **of either . . . ."** (Italics added.) *Haley v. Highland*, 142 Wash.2d 135, 12 P.3d 119, 123–125 (2000).

The same statute does not protect community personal property from the reach of creditors, premarital or marital. Practically, this means that the separate property of the nonliable spouse is not subject to writ or levy for the liable spouse's premarital debt, but any property they acquire during marriage as community property is. See also Wash.Rev.Code § 26.16.010 and 26.16.20.

Despite the above rule, during marriage community property remains more insulated from a creditor's reach if the separate debt is in contract, less insulated if the debt arises from a liquidated tort claim. The relevant part of the statute provides **"[t]he earnings and accumulations of the spouse or domestic partner shall be available to the legal process of creditors for the satisfaction of** *debts* **incurred by such spouse or domestic partner prior to the marriage."** (Italics added.) *Id.* Debts, as noted above, is a general term that includes contractual liability, liquidated tort liability, and support obligations to a former spouse or to children from a prior union.

Under state statutory and decisional law, community property is generally not available to satisfy the separate debts of either spouse. The following general rule appears at Wash.Rev.Code § 26.16.200: **"Neither husband or wife is liable for the debts or liabilities of the other incurred**

**before marriage, nor for the separate debts of each other ..."** See also *Nichols Hills Bank v. McCool*, 104 Wash.2d 78, 701 P.2d 1114 (1985). This rule was enacted in 1881 and modified in 1969 with the addition of two provisos (including the quoted statutory language above).

Three exceptions potentially expose the community property to liability for separate debt.

One, the exception for premarital liabilities that have been are reduced to judgment within three years of the marriage of the parties. Wash.Rev.Code § 26.16.200. Note however that *Caplan v. Sullivan*, 37 Wash.App. 289, 679 P.2d 949 (1984) held that an unliquidated tort claim does not fall into the category of "debts" for purposes of Wash.Rev.Code § 26.16.200, an interpretation affirmed in *Haley*, supra, at 127.

Two, the exception for support obligations to former spouses or children from a prior marriage. *Fisch v. Marler*, 1 Wash.2d 698, 97 P.2d 147 (1939).

Three, the exception for tax liabilities.

Separate debts that are incurred by one spouse during marriage cannot generally be satisfied with the non-debtor spouse's separate property.

But Wash.Rev.Code § 26.16.205, the "necessaries" statute, carves out a huge exception for family expenses: **"The expenses of the family and the education of the children, including stepchildren, are chargeable upon the property of both husband and wife, or either of them, and they may be sued jointly or separately."** Scope and timing determine whether an expense is a family expenditure (and thus a community debt) or not (and thus a separate debt). See e.g. *Smith v. Dalton*, 58 Wash.App. 876, 795 P.2d 706 (1990)(ski boat purchased one month before separation was held not to be a family expense, leaving husband's separate property and his one-half of the community property reachable by the seller).

As for torts, Wash.Rev.Code § 26.16.190 exempts the nontortfeasor spouse's separate property from the execution of a separate tort judgment unless there would be joint liability even if the marriage did not exist.

Are separate tort judgment creditors limited to reaching the tortfeasor's separate property? Can they also reach the tortfeasor spouse's one-half of the community property? Is there a marshaling rule? Or, as was historically the rule in Washington, is a separate tort creditor barred from executing against community property?

The answer is that creditors are not limited to reaching the tortfeasor's separate property, but they must first execute the judgment against any existing separate property. Only if there is insufficient separate property to satisfy the judgment, can a creditor petition to execute against the tortfeasor spouse's one-half of the community property. *deElche v. Jacobsen*, 95 Wash.2d 237, 622 P.2d 835 (1980) (*en banc*) (Horowitz J., dissenting) lowered the bar for execution of community *personal* property. *Keene v. Edie*, 131 Wash.2d 822, 935 P.2d 588 (1997) lowered it for the execution of community real property Notice the marshaling rule embedded in the decisional law. The rule is that the separate tort judgment creditor must execute against and exhaust the tortfeasor's separate property (if any) before executing against the tortfeasor's one-half of the community property.

What is a separate tort? Here again, when it comes to tort liability the community purpose doctrine applies. A separate tort is one that does not benefit the community. A community tort is one that does benefit the community. Prior law exempted all community property from liability for liquidated separate tort claims by defining "community purpose" broadly. But *DeElche*, supra, a split decision, canceled the community property exemption. (New Mexico achieves the same outcome by statute.)

*DeElche*, supra, involved a married couple that hosted a party on their community property sail boat (a community activity, a community purpose, hosted on a community asset, and paid for with community funds). After the party, one spouse trespassed onto a third person's boat and committed a violent act. The tort was deemed a separate tort. The tortfeasor had no separate property with which to satisfy the tort judgment. The creditor sought to reach the tortfeasor's one-half of the community personal property. The previous rule would have shielded all community property from the reach of a separate tort judgment creditor. *deElche* reversed. The rationale was threefold. One, the community is not a legal entity (like a corporation), therefore the spouses, not the entity, incur liability. Two, the spouses have a present and vested interest in community property, as such, the tortfeasor's one-half community property interest should be subject to execution for a judgment debt. Three, it is unfair to immunize tortfeasors or deny remedy to their victims simply because the tortfeasor happens to be married.

*Keene*, supra, the separate judgment creditor attempted to execute the judgment against the tortfeasor spouse's separate property. When that was insufficient, the creditor attempted to execute against the tortfeasor's community real property. *De Elche*, supra, had canceled the exemption for community personal property. *Keene*, supra, raised the next obvious issue of whether the ruling in *De Elche* extended to community real property. The court ruled it did, citing public policy concerns and the absence of any statutory exemption for community real property from involuntary encumbrances, the Washington Supreme court overruled prior law and expended the rule in *deElche*, supra. *Keene*, supra, at 594–595. *deElche*, supra, is widely cited. There was a dissent in the case; it argued that the legislature, not the courts, should have changed the prior rule.

If community property is reached to satisfy a separate tort judgment, a right to reimbursement in the community typically arises by equitable lien. The purpose of the community lien is to ensure that the innocent spouse receives the same amount of community property he or she would have received had the tortfeasor's one-half of the community property not been used to satisfy the separate tort judgment.

The distinction between community and separate liabilities was historically more important (and more frequently litigated) in Washington than in other community property states. This is because—again historically—most separate debts could not be collected from community property and most community debts could not be collected from separate property. The source of the relative immunity of community property was the judicial interpretation of a statute that subjects community real property to mechanics' liens and materialmen's liens obtained for community debts.

Washington courts have authority to draw the line between community and separate debts. But what serves as a guidepost for where they tend to draw it?

One answer is evidence. There is a rebuttable presumption that a liability incurred by a married person during the continuance of the marriage is a community liability. That presumption can be properly raised on evidence that the debt was incurred during the marriage, either to acquire something, to manage community property, or to benefit the community. Rebuttal is by proof that the expense was directly related to the separate property of the married person who incurred the debt. Alternatively, rebuttal can be made with proof that the liability was incurred by one spouse in the act of making of a nonmutual gift to a third party.

Another answer is the original purpose of the debt. If a debt is incurred for a community purpose, it is a community debt. The courts have been liberal in finding community purpose and consequently community liability. Recreational activities, expectation of employment, benefit to a corporation of which the spouse is an officer or director, and even a debt for funds borrowed on the security of separate property have been classified as community debts. Each was shown to have benefitted the community, either directly or indirectly. Therefore, each met the community purpose test.

Intent to benefit the community may of course factor into an analysis of actual benefit, but intent alone is not dispositive. In *Northern Bank & Trust Co. v. Graves*, 79 Wash. 411, 140 P. 328 (1914), a separate obligation was not transformed into a community obligation merely because both spouses signed the promissory note with the intent to benefit the community. The case arose in the male-management era, a time in which the husband was the legal manager of the community property and the wife had no obligation to sign the promissory note in order to bind the community. It was decided that by signing the promissory note, husband and (additionally) wife did not create a community debt. Rather they incurred two separate debts, one that obligated husband's separate property and one that obligated wife's separate property.

## 9. WISCONSIN

Wisconsin adds to the already detailed UMPA provisions to specify which classifications of property are liable for enumerated types of spousal obligations incurred prior to and during marriage.

Family purpose is determined by timing. Wisconsin presumes that an obligation incurred by one spouse during marriage is undertaken for a family purpose, or in the language of Wis. Stat. § 766.55, reproduced below, **"in the interest of the marriage or the family."**

Relevant Wisconsin cases are federal bankruptcy cases. Still, it is useful to bear in mind that a debtor's property interests affected by his or her bankruptcy filing are determined by state law.

In Wisconsin, when an obligation is satisfiable from all "marital property," it is satisfiable from both spouses' community property wages, regardless of which spouse incurred the debt. *In re Passmore*, 156 B.R. 595 (Bkrtcy. E.D. Wis. 1993) raised the issue of whether a prepetition order to garnish the wages of the non-debtor spouse (Mary) was voided by the automatic stay that arose after the debtor spouse (Mary's husband) filed a bankruptcy petition. The court answered in the affirmative and ordered Mary's creditor to return to those of her wages that had been garnished from her after the stay in her husband's case. The reason for including Mary's wages in the automatic stay occasioned by her husband's bankruptcy is that the married bankruptcy debtor, as a Wisconsin domiciliary, owns an undivided interest in all marital property. That undivided interest cannot be partitioned by the creditor. Nor can it be unilaterally severed by the spouse in order to avoid a creditor. Thus when the Mary's husband filed a bankruptcy petition, the automatic stay of collection claims against him also barred Mary's creditors from continuing to garnish her (community property) wages.

If a spouse is not also personally liable for the debt, then the property that is not marital property (i.e. all other property) is not reachable. *Smith v. Capital One Bank (USA) N.A.*, 545 B.R. 249 (Bkrtcy. E.D. Wis. 2016) (credit card debt).

Generally these principles govern contract debt incurred during marriage, but here again there is variation among the states on whether and (if so) how the spouse who does not incur the debt can shield his or her earnings from the reach of certain creditors. Lack of knowledge about the debt has been held insufficient to overcome the Wis. Stat. § 766.55 (1) presumption that the debt is in the interest of the marriage or family, at least in the context of a bankruptcy proceeding. *In re Dahle-Fenske*, 525 B.R. 912 (Bkrtcy. E.D. Wis. 2015).

Wis. Stat. § 766.55 (2) and (2)(cm), both reproduced below creates an exception from the Wis. Stat. § 766.55 (1) presumption that debt incurred during marriage is in the interest of the marriage or the family. That same kind of presumption applies to a tort claim brought during marriage against (only) one spouse.

Wis.Stat. § 766.55 provides in part:

(1) **An obligation incurred by a spouse during marriage, including one attributable to an act or omission during marriage, is presumed to be incurred in the interest of the marriage or the**

family. A statement separately signed by the obligated or incurring spouse at or before the time the obligation is incurred stating that the obligation is or will be incurred in the interest of the marriage or the family is conclusive evidence that the obligation to which the statement refers is an obligation in the interest of the marriage or family, except that the existence of that statement does not affect any interspousal right or remedy.

(2) After the determination date all of the following apply:

    (a) A spouse's obligation to satisfy a duty of support owed to the other spouse or to a child of the marriage may be satisfied only from all marital property and all other property of the obligated spouse.

    (b) An obligation incurred by a spouse in the interest of the marriage or the family may be satisfied only from all marital property and all other property of the incurring spouse.

    (c) 1. An obligation incurred by a spouse before or during marriage that is attributable to an obligation arising before marriage or to an act or omission occurring before marriage may be satisfied only from property of that spouse that is not marital property and from that part of marital property which would have been the property of that spouse but for the marriage.

(c) 2. An obligation incurred by a spouse before, on or after January 1, 1986, that is attributable to an obligation arising before January 1, 1986, or to an act or omission occurring before January 1, 1986, may be satisfied only from property of that spouse that is not marital property and from that part of marital property which would have been the property of that spouse but for the enactment of this chapter.

(cm) An obligation incurred by a spouse during marriage, resulting from a tort committed by the spouse during marriage, may be satisfied from the property of that spouse that is not marital property and from that spouse's interest in marital property.

(d) Any other obligation incurred by a spouse during marriage, including one attributable to an act or omission during marriage, may be satisfied only from property of that spouse that is not marital property and from that spouse's interest in marital property, in that order.

(2m) Unless the dissolution decree or any amendment to the decree so provides, no income of a nonincurring spouse is available for satisfaction of an obligation under sub. (2)(b) after entry of the decree. Marital property assigned to each spouse under that decree is available for satisfaction of such an obligation to the extent of the value of the marital property at the date of the decree. If a dissolution decree provides that the nonincurring spouse is responsible for satisfaction of the obligation, the obligation may be satisfied as if both spouses had incurred the obligation.

Wis.Stat. § 766.56(1) provides that a creditor "shall consider all marital property under s. 766.55(2)(b) [reproduced above] to satisfy the obligation in the same manner that the creditor, in evaluating the creditworthiness of an unmarried credit applicant, considers the property of an unmarried credit applicant available to satisfy the obligation."

The general rule is that a marital agreement does not adversely affect the interest of a creditor who transacts with a married person, even if that agreement is recorded. Wis.Stat. § 766.56(2)(a) explicitly states that recordation of a martial agreement does not provide actual or constructive notice to third party creditors.

Wis.Stat. § 766.56(2)(b) provides for an adequate notice provision. The statutory section is in the form of a general rule (a marital agreement does not adversely affect the interest of a creditor) and an exception: " . . . **unless the creditor, prior to the time the credit is granted, is furnished a copy of the agreement, statement or decree or has actual knowledge of the adverse provision when the obligation to the creditor is incurred. The notice requirement does not apply to renewals, extensions or modification or the use of an open-end credit plan."**

# PART 4
# END OF MARRIAGE

# CHAPTER 9
# DIVORCE

## A. OVERVIEW

The community regime may be terminated by separation, dissolution, a change of domicile, or the death of a spouse.

Legal separation terminates the community regime in all states. Physical separation terminates it in some states. A final dissolution judgment divides property. Only a court judgment terminates a marriage by changing the parties' status from married to single. Among the community property states, Texas is alone in permitting informal marriage. No community property state recognizes informal (sometimes mislabeled common law) divorce.

Void marriages never come into existence but, in many states, still must be formally annulled. Voidable marriages come into existence but are subject to annulment or dissolution, at the option of one or both parties. The equitable putative spouse doctrine addresses property issues that can come up in a void or voidable marriage.

As to the division of community property, a majority of states follow the equal division principle. A minority follow the equitable division principle.

## B. DETAIL

### 1. ENDING THE COMMUNITY

The community property system admits to it, by default, a married person who is domiciled within the jurisdiction. However, certain events, enumerated next, end or significantly alter the way in which the community property rules apply to that person.

Changing domicile to a separate property state removes a married person or persons (if both spouses change their domicile) from the system of their former domicile and includes them in the system of their new domicile. This is so even if the change is from one community property state to another.

*Illustration 9.1:* H and W are domiciled in California. They move to New Hampshire and establish a domicile there. H and W leave the California community property system and enter the New Hampshire common law marital property system as of the date of the domicile change.

*Illustration 9.2:* H and W are domiciled in California. They move to Texas and establish a domicile there. H and W leave the California community property system and enter the Texas community property system as of the date of the domicile change.

The transition from one domicile to the next may effect a consequential change in marital and property rights and duties since the laws of each U.S. state vary.

Assuming that there is no change in domicile, the following events will end the community's ability to acquire property.

a.  Informal (physical) separation;

b.  A separation agreement;

c.  Separation of property regime by court procedure;

d.  Legal separation of the spouses;

e.  A property settlement agreement;

f.  A final judgment of dissolution; or

g.  The death of a spouse.

Separation, whether informal or by court process, ends the community's ability to acquire (although not to hold) property. In most states, post-separation earnings and accumulations belong to the earning spouse as his or her separate property. For that reason alone date of separation can be and often is vigorously disputed in the context of dissolution.

An informal separation occurs when one or both parties decide that the marriage is over. States have different rules about when an informal period of separation commences as a matter of law. Some states require proof that one of the spouses moved out of the family residence. Other states admit any evidence that goes toward proving that a separation has occurred.

A separation agreement that terminates the community estate is governed by the contract modification principles, as set forth in Chapter 2. A separation agreement is an agreement between the parties pinpointing the date of separation and the community's ability to acquire and accumulate property after that date. Where allowed, a separation agreement may or may not include other important issues relating to property rights, property dissolution, or support awards. Parties who negotiate an enforceable separation agreement must still petition for a final judgment of dissolution in order to legally terminate the marriage.

A regime of separation of property can be created by court order in Louisiana.

Legal separation of the spouses generally involves all of the elements of a divorce, including the division of property, and the award of spousal support (where necessary). A judgment of legal separation does not restore the parties' legal status to single. When parties are legally separated, they continue to retain their status as married individuals, which means that each individual is precluded from contracting a valid subsequent marriage.

A judgment of dissolution finalizes property issues and restores the parties to single status.

The end of marriage by the death of a spouse is discussed in Chapter 10.

## 2. ANNULMENT, LEGAL SEPARATION, DISSOLUTION

There are three general categories of proceedings by which a community (as opposed to a community estate or regime) is terminated: annulment, legal separation and dissolution.

## a. Annulment

Because of a major defect such as bigamy or too close a degree of kinship (incest), certain marriages never come into existence and are therefore adjudged void from the beginning. A void marriage does not acquire community property

Other marriages are voidable because of correctable defects that exist at the time of the marriage. A voidable marriage is presumed valid and so can acquire community property, but it is subject to annulment at the option of one or both parties. In the context of a voidable marriage, annulment voids the marriage whereas dissolution ratifies it.

Community property (or an analog to it) may come into existence during a void or voidable marriage. This happens by application of the equitable putative spouse doctrine, which holds that if one or both parties believed in good faith that their otherwise void or voidable marriage was valid, they may seek a court order for putative spouse status. For purposes of community property law, a putative spouse has most if not all of the rights of a spouse; and a putative marriage acquires assets until a decree of nullity or dissolution is issued by a court. See Chapter 11.

## b. Legal Separation

By separation agreement (in some states) or by legal procedure, the community's ability to acquire earnings and accumulations is suspended, as discussed above.

During a period of separation, the parties are in the process of moving toward a final dissolution, but they are not yet divorced. Therefore, the parties' obligations to each other to manage and control existing community property continue to exist until the issuance of a final judgment of dissolution. A separated person is still married, and as such not eligible to legally contract a subsequent marriage.

### c. (Absolute) Divorce

No U.S. state recognizes informal divorce. All divorce is by court order.

Historically, absolute divorce has proceeded from a status of non-existence (meaning it was not permitted) to separate maintenance, to absolute divorce for fault (adultery, cruelty, desertion, imprisonment, insanity etc.) and eventually to no-fault divorce.

Today, the concept of fault is largely avoidable, if not practically eliminated, as a ground for divorce. In a no-fault divorce system, a court is mandated to disregard fault when dividing (partitioning) community property.

A majority of states follow a default equal division rule; a minority call for equitable division. In both regimes the analytical starting point is that each spouse owns a one-half vested interest in each community property asset, by legal right. Parties are free to negotiate a different split. If they reach an ımpasse, a court shall step in. Courts in equal division states step in to make a fifty-fifty split. Courts in equitable division states can effect an arithmetically unequal split so long as it is equitable or fair under the circumstances. In either case, whether division is equal or equitable, dissolution of community property is not by fault, but by right.

Likewise, in setting spousal support. Typically courts are directed—by statute or case law—"to ignore marital fault and ... to base any determination solely on the circumstances of the parties, including the duration of their marriage and the ability of the supported spouse to engage in gainful employment." *In re Marriage of Rosan*, 24 Cal.App.3d 885, 892, 101 Cal.Rptr. 295 (1972). Some states have mandatory statutory checklists for determining a spousal support award based on need. Others do not.

## 3.  DISSOLUTION OF PROPERTY

### a.  The Theoretical Ideal

As a purely theoretical matter, the dissolution of property interests upon divorce would call for each spouse to acknowledge ownership of separate property and of his or her one-half of the community property as to each asset, by inventory. The need to inventory property at the end of a marriage is seasoned by reality as well as, in some states, by judicial mandate. In California, the Judicial Council has prepared a form that parties can use to inventory community and separate assets (Form FL-160).

After dissolution, co-ownership of each asset is often impractical especially if the family has one or two major assets (the home and a car) and much of their remaining wealth is in non-liquid form, like for example life insurance or retirement plans.

Ideally, in a divorce action, the parties and the court would be fully informed about and agree to the disposition of all community assets and liabilities. Liabilities would be assigned fairly, with community liabilities assigned in line with ability to pay. After the liabilities were addressed, net community assets would be divided equally or equitably, by the parties themselves, in a way that best supports each party's aspirations for exiting the marriage.

During the negotiation process, no community property interest or asset would be omitted from the final inventory. No community property interest, asset or even potential interest would be left undisclosed. Cooperative and full disclosure would be the cultural norm. If there were a lapse in disclosure, a legal mechanism would quickly address it. Overall, the law would ensure that the parties understand exactly what it is that they are agreeing to with the partition.

Fairness would be a dissolution norm. There would be no fraud, duress, perjury, pressure or mistake of law or fact. Each party would be represented by his or her own attorney. Negotiations would be in a language understood by the parties. If not, adequate translation would be available. Negotiations would be memorialized in a language in which the parties are proficient.

Where necessary, a comprehensive and fair support award would be negotiated. The support award would honored (paid) on a timely basis.

These would be the bare parameters of an ideal situation, defined as an outcome meant to enhance veracity, fairness, and voluntariness.

Unfortunately, the ideal situation rarely if ever arises.

Among the factors that compromise the ideal are the following:

- Misunderstanding about whether oral agreements are enforceable (they typically are not);

- Concealing or omitting assets from the initial asset inventory;

- Failing to disclose or insufficiently disclosing information about the possible or actual existence of a community property interest;

- Mistake and misconduct—misinformation, coercion, fraud, duress, undue influence, misrepresentations, and domestic violence—in the negotiation process;

- Conduct (management and control issues) during marriage that may have dissipated or impaired the community property;

- Misconduct in the management and control of property during marriage, such as unauthorized gifts or transfers, or the absence of joinder for consequential transactions involving real estate or statutorily designated community property business operations;

- Accounting failures;

- Taking unfair advantage of the other spouse in a transaction between them;

- Reaching an impasse in the negotiation process;

- Power differentials in bargaining position;

- Misusing or abusing private dispute resolution processes;

- Valuation issues;

- Assignment issues;

- Property outside the court's jurisdiction, especially realty located in a non-community property state.

A process that diverges from the ideal, increases the risk of litigation during the dissolution and even after a final judgment is issued. Impasse, time delays, discovery misconduct, and the like have the potential to lead to formal discovery motions, sanctions, postdissolution judgment motions to adjudicate omitted assets, post-judgment motions to set aside a final dissolution judgment, appeals, and even (in some cases) criminal indictments. What could be a process for efficiently winding up the affairs of an intimate partnership instead becomes a rocky legal road whose many tolls exact a high personal and economic cost from the parties.

## b. Separate Property

Some states by statute do not grant a court jurisdiction over the separate property of either spouse unless the spouses otherwise consent.

Even in these states, however, courts have discretion to impose an equitable lien on the separate property of either spouse so as to effect a division of the community property. The lien on separate property is a device to protect and satisfy the community property interest of the spouse who does not own the separate property asset. A majority of states employ the device liberally by how they permit a court to impose an equitable lien upon either spouse's separate property or marital property award.

There are many reasons to use a lien on one spouse's existing separate property to protect and secure the other spouse's community property interest. Two specific reasons stand out. A lien on one spouse's separate property may be a fair way to secure a community property interest in a separate property asset that the community helped acquire. Or a lien may be necessary to enforce payment of support obligations.

## c. Community Property

U.S. community property states differ in their approach, even if they remain close in result, when the issue is the division of the community property.

The majority of the statutes give little guidance to the family court (and little basis for appeal from its decision). They state that the division of the community property shall be "equitable" or "substantially equal" or "just." As discussed above, equitable (or just) is not necessarily arithmetically equal, as the theoretical model would seem to require. Arizona, Idaho, Washington and Wisconsin are states that describe relevant factors that a court may consider in dividing the community property. The Wisconsin factors are similar to the mandatory factures used in California to calculate postdissolution spousal support.

The rationale for an equal division mandate is that each spouse holds a present and vested one-half interest in each community property asset as of the date of its acquisition. Even when it appears that the court is using offsets and trades to partition the community estate, the equal division principle mandates that the court account for each and every community property interest. Accurate accounting protects each party's due process rights.

## 4.  COMPLICATIONS

### a. Concealed Assets

Today, with equal management and control, either spouse has the right to manage community property. Consequently, both spouses are legally obligated to the duties that apply to persons in relationships that are adjudged confidential. In the case of marriage, a majority of states follow the rule that a confidential relationship arises on the date of marriage as a matter of law. A minority hold that the confidential relationship starts as early as the engagement.

States allow an exception to the equal division principle when the concealment of assets is suspected.

If an asset is omitted from the division of the community, whether because of concealment, honest error, or difference of opinion as to its character, the asset is converted from community property to tenancy in common by the divorce of the parties. A party may also typically file a motion for a postdissolution adjudication of the parties' rights in the omitted asset. Statutory limitations apply.

A postdissolution set-aside statute serves three goals. One, it erases the line between extrinsic and intrinsic fraud, a historically problematic distinction that has frustrated attempts to correct judgments procured through deception. Two, it expands the definition of fraud to include perjury, duress, undue influence, and even mistakes of law or fact that the innocent party makes as a consequence of the other party's deception or misrepresentation. Three, it extends the statute of limitations for claims by adopting the discovery rule. The claimant's cause of action accrues not when the coercion occurred or when the judgment was issued, but when the misconduct was discovered, a point that can be occur long after the final dissolution of judgment.

If the time period for a postdissolution judgment adjudication has passed, and the time for all appeals has also passed, it may still be possible for a party to move to set aside the dissolution judgment. Such a motion would be granted for fraud related reasons.

A nonmutual gift to or the sale of an asset to a third person may give rise to an allegation of concealment by one spouse against the other.

### b. Omitted Assets

Parties can negotiate a settlement agreement to dispose of the community. Absent such an agreement, the court shall divide the community between them either along equal or equitable lines, depending on state law. The latter equitable division standard allows the court greater discretion and reduces the ground for appeal that the division was not equal.

If the parties do reach a negotiated settlement agreement, the interaction of the court varies from state to state and from action to action. It is desirable to allow parties to settle their own differences, whether through lawyers, mediators, or collaborative law specialists. Yet even when parties are represented by counsel, and especially when one or both are not, courts are understandably wary of the specter of collusive or coerced agreements. Judicial wariness has its source in the balancing of competing policies. For example, the policy against fraud is a strong counterweight to the policy in favor of final dissolution judgments.

Assuming the permissibility and fairness of a marriage settlement agreement, a further question arises as to the effect of the court decree upon such an agreement. Is the agreement merged in the decree so that it can be enforced by contempt proceedings? Or is it a contract enforceable by a breach of contract action? Who can change the terms of the executed agreement, the court or the parties? Tax and other consequences have flowed from the answers to these questions.

Finally because a negotiated settlement agreement assigns to the parties net community property, which is to say assets minus liabilities, creditors have a stake in the proceedings. Every community property state has a long history of protecting the rights of creditors. In part, protection comes in the technicalities of debt assignment and securitization; and the smooth functioning of the economy, at the very least, requires that third parties have confidence in dealing with married persons. Consequently, it is imperative that the policy in favor of finality be furthered absent compelling reasons to re-open or set aside a final judgment of dissolution that is tainted by perjury, fraud, or coercion

## c. Difficult to Divide Assets

Generally, for purposes of division, assets are to be valued at the time of dissolution.

The equal (or equitable) division principle applies to all assets, even those that are difficult to divide, value or liquidate. Some assets are difficult to divide because they are commingled. Others are difficult to divide because of valuation or liquidation issues; sometimes, for example, with a business, a formal appraisal can be prohibitively expensive, leaving the parties to cite their personal opinions on the value of the business. Others assets are difficult to divide because of severe fluctuations in market value.

When the problem with division is traced to a breach of fiduciary duty, an impairment of one spouse's community property interest may occur. In California, statutory provisions connect the dots between misconduct (such as for example a failure to disclose) and valuation problems. Remedies for the impairment of community property due to a breach of fiduciary duty by one spouse **"shall be determined to be [the asset's] highest value at the date of the breach of fiduciary duty, the date of the sale or disposition of the asset, or the date of the award by the court."** Cal.Fam.Code § 1101.

Life insurance has special valuation considerations. Either a life insurance policy is transient in value or even worthless if the premium payments lapses, as with term life insurance. Or a policy is difficult to liquidate during the life of the insured, as with whole life insurance. And yet, the nearly valueless or difficult to liquidate asset can be irreplaceable (due to uninsurability) or subject to a great increase in value upon the insured's death (in the form of the policy proceeds).

If for some reason, a court awards the spouse one-half of the value of the premiums or contributions paid to maintain the policy, this award combines with the recipient spouse's existing one-half interest to give the recipient full rights in the policy. The same is true if one spouse is awarded the life insurance policy in exchange for a transfer to the other spouse of off-setting property.

Either outcome gives that spouse the right to name a contractual POD designee.

Additionally, the act of extinguishing one spouse's community property interest in the life insurance policy (meaning the contract), insures that, in the event of the insured's death, the life insurance proceeds will belong entirely to the policy owner's POD beneficiary (or beneficiaries), should they pay out during the contract term.

Retirement plans may be difficult to disperse for several reasons. They may not be vested. Or, if vested, they may not be matured. They may also pose problems of management. Sometimes they are difficult to value because of other contingencies. If the retirement benefit is community property and both spouses are entitled to participate in its management and control, then it follows that options given to the employee under the retirement plan belong to both spouses.

If an annuity is viewed as property, it is an asset for division upon divorce. This is the common approach. On the other hand, the stream of income produced by the annuity can be viewed as the postdissolution income of one party. Support for the other spouse (or the parties' children) may be ordered, based upon that income right. Care must be taken so that the non-employee spouse is not given two bites of the apple. This could happen if the retirement fund is divided in half and the non-employee is given both the non-employee's half and a share of what is viewed of as postdissolution income from the employee's half.

Federal law requires that a state court issue a "qualified domestic relations order" (a QDRO for short) in order to direct payments from a pension, annuity, profit-sharing, or stock bonus plan, 26 U.S.C.A. § 414(p), ERISA § 206(d)(3). See Chapter 6 and 12.

Some states exempt federal retirement or disability benefits from the reach of community property laws: Arizona and Louisiana are examples.

Among the options which are likely to be found in retirement plans are the following:

- Disability retirement income in lieu of ordinary retirement income. If the employee is entitled, at his or her election, to receive either *community* property *retirement* benefits or *separate* property *disability* benefits, the court may require the employee to apply the higher disability benefits as if they were retirement income to the extent that retirement benefits would have been received.

- Lump sum payment or an annuity. Should the spouses be required to select the same plan or could one spouse (typically the non-employee) cash out (take the lump sum payment option as to his or her community property share) and leave the remainder to the employee spouse as an annuity?

- Self or self-and-survivor (or joint) annuity.

- Whether to retire or to stay employed. Occasionally, a court will order a spouse who elects not to retire to pay benefits to his or her ex-spouse as if retirement had occurred. Such an order gives the non-employee spouse an option as to when to receive otherwise deferred income.

## d. Conflict of Laws

The marital or separate property may be outside the jurisdiction of the divorce court.

A court may not enter in rem orders affecting the title to realty outside the forum, but it may enter an in personam order which purports to direct a person over whom the court has personal jurisdiction to convey, transfer or take other action with reference to property, especially realty, located outside the forum.

At the other end of the scale is property acquired outside, and then brought to the community property forum state. Several states use the concept of quasi-community property to address the issue.

Paradoxes exist.

State and federal constitutions can be invoked. Arizona, California and Texas, for example, have had litigation in connection with community property divisions that resulted in the arithmetically unequal division of one or more assets. The legal issue is whether an unequal division deprives one party of state and federal constitutionally protected rights. One such right is the state constitutional right to own separate property during marriage. Other implicated rights are state and federal due process and equal protection. Competing state fiscal protections and mandates also may be implicated, especially in the case where one spouse exits marriage needing public support for self and children while the other spouse exits with (separate property) assets sufficient to comfortably commence life as a single person.

From an economic perspective, characterizing property determines the partnership's profits over time. From a legal perspective, characterizing property imposes jurisdictional limits on a court's power to divide community assets; a court that has jurisdiction over community property may not necessarily have it over separate property. From a social perspective, characterizing property gives the parties a manageable proxy for discussing the basis upon which the state can regulate private (family) matters.

### e. Separation

In addition to property rights, another theoretical basis for the equal sharing of the income and property acquired during marriage derives from the support obligation that spouses owe each other during marriage.

Often there is a period of psychological and physical separation of spouses prior to the divorce. If the period before a dissolution judgment is short, the termination point for the community is the date of the judgment. But if the physical separation is long, then readjustment of the community property regime is necessary. In a clear majority of states, earnings and accumulations of a spouse who lives separate and apart from the other spouse is characterized as separate property, as discussed in Chapter 4. Absent an agreement, management and control rights and duties might change, depending on the context.

The theoretical basis for voluntarily sharing income and gains weakens considerably when married persons separate. Even so, the earnings of the higher earning spouse may be liable for common necessaries (basic living expenses) of the other spouse, as discussed in Chapter 8.

## 5. SPOUSAL SUPPORT

Historically, maintenance derived from two concepts: alimony and spousal support. Alimony was analogous to an annuity or a pension awarded to a spouse at the end of a marriage. Spousal support was more in the nature of a temporary award intended to enable the supported spouse to find gainful employment. Today, spousal support is the more commonly used process of the two.

A spousal support award obligates the postdissolution (or post-separation) net income of the supporting spouse for the benefit of the supported spouse. The supporting spouse becomes debtor, the supported spouse a creditor with a priority claim to the supporting spouses postdissolution (or post-separation) net income. The creditor spouse's priority claim is typically limited to a certain time period; but within that time it survives a subsequent marriage or the death of the supporting spouse.

The concept of alimony has a complex and gendered history that developed in tandem with the concept of fault. Alimony is distinct from community property. In Louisiana, for example, prior to 1855, a wife who obtained a divorce was not entitled to alimony. When LSA–C.C. Art. 160 passed in 1855, a court could grant alimony to the wife out of the husband's property (not including his earnings). But an award of alimony was predicated on proof of the husband's fault. Those husbands who were deemed without fault and had earnings but no property were relieved from any alimony obligation. In 1916, the same statute was amended to make alimony payable out of the husband's property and earnings. In 1926, alimony was conceptualized as a "pension" to the wife that lasted unless and until the wife contracted a subsequent marriage; here again, alimony had to be predicated on proof of the husband's fault.

As alimony got culturally and legally delinked from fault, it began to be understood not as a pension, but as an extension of the spousal support obligation. At first, the obligation was conceived of as lifelong. Today, alimony, now more accurately called postdissolution spousal support, is understood as a temporary award. Its purpose is to assist the supported spouse with finding a job, with education, or with (re)training.

A spousal support award is satisfied with the debtor ex-spouse's individual (postdissolution) property, income, earnings, accumulations, and so forth. Spousal support obligates individual property rather than community property because it is, by definition, paid after the final judgment of dissolution is issued.

In the language of business statements, at dissolution, each soon-to-be-ex-spouse in a community property partnership is given his or her equal (or equitable, depending on the jurisdiction) ownership share in the *assets* that are inventoried on the balance sheet of the partnership, as of the end of the marriage. These assets represent the amount of income received during the marriage that was not consumed for community expenses. But while *assets* are distributed to the spouses by halves, subject to the rights of secured creditors, a spousal support award consists of the future *net income* of the supporting spouse.

Spouses do not necessarily exit marriage on an equal financial footing. Therefore, whatever the arguments for or against, spousal support exists and continues to be necessary even in a community property system.

Statutory changes have made the spousal support obligation gender neutral. Community property systems recognize the housekeeper's contribution as a conclusive contribution to the acquisition of community assets, as discussed in Chapter 1. Even so, leaving a marriage with assets must ultimately be distinguished from leaving a marriage with a secure earning capacity.

When a housekeeper spouse contributes to the marital partnership, the possibility of a support award recognizes her or his contribution as one that, depending on the circumstances, enhanced the human capital of the earning spouse. Human capital necessarily belongs to its holder; it cannot be practicably divided at dissolution. Nevertheless, a

spousal support award permits a court to order an
earning ex-spouse to financially assist the other ex-
spouse to train for gainful employment.

## C.  INDIVIDUAL STATES

### 1.  ARIZONA

Arizona is an equitable division state.
Ariz.Rev.Stat.Ann. § 25–318 authorizes, upon
dissolution of the marriage or legal separation, an
equitable (and therefore not necessarily equal)
division the community property. The authorization
extends also to property owned by the spouses as joint
tenants or as tenants in common with each other.

Fault is not relevant for the division, unless the
spouses have entered into a covenant marriage, in
which case the fault-based grounds for divorce can be
found at Ariz.Rev.Stat.Ann. § 25–903.

Arizona does not permit the divorce court to award
the separate property of one spouse to the other.
However, upon request, liens may be imposed on
separate property for reimbursement or to secure
payment of support obligations.

Ariz.Rev.Stat.Ann. § 25–318(C) authorizes liens on
separate property or the marital property awarded to
either party for:

(1) **Any interest or equity the other party
has in or to such property.**

(2) **Community debts that the court has
ordered to be paid by the parties.**

(3) **An allowance for child support spousal maintenance or both.**

(4) **All actual damages and judgments from conduct that results in criminal conviction of either spouses in which the other spouse or child was the victim.**

Provision is specifically made in Ariz.Rev.Stat.Ann. § 25–318(A) for quasi-community property, which is defined as **"property acquired by either spouse outside of this state . . . if the property would have been community property if acquired in this state."**

The key portion of Ariz.Rev.Stat.Ann. § 25–318 provides that **"[i]n a proceeding for dissolution of the marriage, or for legal separation, . . . the court shall assign each spouse's sole and separate property to such spouse. It shall also divide the community, joint tenancy and other property held in common equitably, though not necessarily in kind, without regard to marital misconduct. . . ."**

## 2.   CALIFORNIA

California is an equal division state. However, the Family Law court is a court of law and equity with considerable discretion.

Dissolution or legal separation may be based on one of two grounds. **"Irreconcilable differences,"** meaning **"the irremediable breakdown of the marriage"** is one ground. Another is **"[p]ermanent legal incapacity,"** meaning medical or psychiatric proof that **"the spouse was at the time the petition was filed, and remains, permanently lacking the legal capacity to make decisions."** Cal.Fam.Code § 2310 and § 2311. A judgment of nullity is an option for any void or voidable marriage. One important reason to require a judgment of nullity for a void marriage is to provide third parties with notice of its nonexistence.

California led the way in no-fault divorce. **"except as otherwise provided by statute, in a pleading or proceeding for dissolution of marriage or legal separation of parties, including depositions and discovery proceedings, evidence of specific acts of misconduct is improper and inadmissible."** Cal.Fam.Code § 2335.

Identifying and implementing alternatives to adversarial litigation is and has been a strong legislative policy. Parties are encouraged to use private mediation, arbitration, and collaborative law methods to negotiate marriage settlement agreements. Cal.Fam.Code § 2013 states the goal of such a preference as being **"to resolve disputes . . . on an agreed basis without resorting to adversary judicial intervention."**

In a private negotiated settlement process, the parties are entitled to use different disclosure standards than those that appear in the Family Code. Typically, parties agree to (summary) disclosure standards that are lower than the standards found in the Family Code. Lower disclosure standards may cause continuing problems in the division of property,

especially if the parties have also agreed (as is often
the case with arbitration) to waive the right to appeal.
Support agreements are modifiable and severable
unless the parties specifically agree otherwise.
Property agreements, by comparison, are final, absent
an expanded definition of fraud found at
Cal.Fam.Code § 2122.

A negotiated marriage settlement agreement is the
preferred method for dissolving a community estate.
But if the parties reach an impasse, adversarial
intervention to obtain judicial help is available.
Parties who own a modest community estate, defined
as not exceeding $50,000, can be submitted by a court
for arbitration. Cal.Fam.Code § 2554.

The court has jurisdiction over community property
and quasi-community property; the parties may also
request that the court divide any separate property
interests held by the parties, in another jurisdiction in
joint tenancy or tenancy in common. Cal.Fam.Code
§ 2660. (California has a special community property
presumption that applies to jointly titled assets in a
dissolution proceeding, as discussed in Chapter 3.)
Valuation is as of the time of trial. Cal.Fam.Code
§ 2552. When dissolution involves the rights of a third
party who is not a creditor, the concern is with the
third party's due process rights (notice and the
opportunity to be heard) relative to the dissolution
proceeding, an issue discussed in *Muckle v. Superior
Court*, 102 Cal.App.4th 218, 125 Cal.Rptr.2d 303
(2002).

**"During the continuance of the marriage,"** the
spouses' interests in community property are

**"present, existing, and equal."** Cal.Fam.Code § 751. At dissolution, Cal.Fam.Code § 2550 restates the equal division principle. It provides: **"Except upon the written agreement of the parties, or on oral stipulation of the parties in open court, or as otherwise provided in this division, in a proceeding for dissolution of marriage or for legal separation of the parties, the court shall, either in its judgment of dissolution of the marriage, in its judgment decreeing the legal separation of the parties, or at a later time if it expressly reserves jurisdiction to make such a property division, divide the community estate of the parties equally."**

Among the numerous statutory exceptions to the general concept of equal division of community property at dissolution are the following:

- *Economic circumstances.* The court may award an asset entirely to one party **"[w]here economic circumstances warrant ... on such conditions as the court deems proper to effect a substantially equal division of the community estate."** Cal.Fam.Code § 2601.

- *Deliberate misappropriation.* An additional award or offset is possible if the court determines that one party has **"deliberately misappropriated"** a part of the community estate **"to the exclusion of the interest of the other party in the community estate."** Cal.Fam.Code § 2602.

- *Community estate personal injury damages.*
  Money and property received in settlement of a
  personal injury claim that arose during the
  marriage, defined in Cal.Fam.Code § 2603(a)
  are subject to a mandatory assignment rule at
  dissolution. Such money and property **"shall
  be assigned to the party who suffered the
  injuries unless the court, after taking into
  account the economic condition and
  needs of each party, the time that has
  elapsed since the recovery of the damages
  or the accrual of the cause of action, and
  all other facts of the case, determines that
  the interest of justice require another
  disposition."** If a court deviates from the
  mandatory assignment rule, **"at least one-
  half of the damages shall be assigned to
  the party who suffered the injuries."**
  Cal.Fam.Code § 2603(b).

- *A default judgment involving a small estate.* A
  net community estate of less than five
  thousand dollars ($5,000) may be awarded
  entirely to one spouse if the other spouse
  cannot be located **"through the exercise of
  reasonable diligence."** Cal.Fam.Code
  § 2604.

- *A deferred sale of the family home.* A family
  home sale may be deferred by a court order
  that awards, to the custodial parent,
  temporary exclusive use and possession of the
  family home. The order can defer sale during
  the child's minority or, in the case of an adult

dependent with disabilities, as long as the
dependent requires continuing support.
Cal.Fam.Code § 3800 through § 3808 set forth
the basis for a deferred sale of a family home
order. A court has authority to consider
economic and noneconomic criteria in
reaching its decision. Cal.Fam.Code § 3801
codifies the decision in *Marriage of
Stallworth*, 192 Cal.App.3d 742, 237 Cal.Rptr.
829 (1987).

Detailed provisions for the allocation of debts are
contained in Cal.Fam.Code § 2620, et seq. The
provisions generally correspond to what parties might
expect. However, pursuant to Cal.Fam.Code § 2622
**"[t]o the extent that the community debts
exceed community and quasi-community assets,
the excess debt shall be assigned as the court
deems just and equitable, taking into account
factors such as the parties' relative ability to
pay."** In essence, this provision means two things.
One, each party's separate property or future
(postdissolution) income may be liable for obligations
incurred during marriage. And two, a party who has a
greater relative ability to repay creditors can expect to
be assigned a greater share of the debt.

A special reimbursement statute found at
Cal.Fam.Code § 2641 returns to the community
eligible contributions to the direct costs of an income
enhancing education or training of a spouse. The same
provision mandatorily assigns educational debt to the
student spouse. The spouses can modify the
assignment by agreement. Community contributions

CH. 9             *DIVORCE*            527

to indirect expenses are calculated into a postdissolution spousal support award under Cal.Fam.Code § 4320.

California does not permit the divorce court to award the separate property of one spouse to the other. Nevertheless, liens may be imposed against separate property for reimbursement, or to secure payment of a support obligation. *Fox v. Fox*, 18 Cal.2d 645, 117 P.2d 325 (1941).

California has two quasi-community property statutes: one in the Family Code and another in the Probate Code. The basic theme of each is that quasi-community property is property that the parties would have held as California community property had they been domiciled in state when the property was acquired. The definition of quasi-community property given for the purposes of dissolution is found at Cal.Fam.Code § 125; the definition for probate purposes is found at Cal.Prob.Code § 66. See Chapter 3.

For dissolution purposes, quasi-community property is treated as if it were California community property. Cal.Fam.Code § 125 provides: **"As used in this part, "quasi-community property" means all real or personal property, wherever situated, heretofore or hereafter acquired in any of the following ways:**

    **(a) By either spouse while domiciled elsewhere which would have been community property if the spouse who acquired the property had been**

**domiciled in this state at the time of its acquisition.**

**(b) In exchange for real or personal property, wherever situated, which would have been community property if the spouse who acquired the property so exchanged had been domiciled in this state at the time of its acquisition."**

Additionally, California at times uses the concept of the community estate, which is a broader concept than that of community property. **" 'Community estate' includes both the community and quasi-community assets and liabilities of the parties."** Cal.Fam.Code § 63.

In the case of a putative spouse, the quasi-marital estate is comprised of **"property acquired during the union "that would have been community or quasi-community property had the union not been void or voidable."** Cal.Fam.Code § 2251(a)(2).

If, after all efforts to reach an equal division of the community estate, an asset is omitted, a party can bring a motion for postdissolution adjudication. Personal jurisdiction is required over the defendant because any such judicial action would be wholly independent from the original dissolution proceeding. The defenses of laches and res judicata apply, as do statutory limitations. Spousal support is calculated by a mandatory fourteen point statutory list found at Cal.Fam.Code § 4320.

The putative spouse doctrine is discussed in Chapter 11.

The link between property characterization and separation is discussed in Chapter 4.

### 3.   IDAHO

Absent compelling reasons, equal division is the rule in Idaho. In dividing the property, the court weighs factors set out in Idaho Code § 32–712:

"**In case of divorce by the decree of a court of competent jurisdiction, the community property and the homestead must be assigned as follows:**

**1. The community property must be assigned by the court in such proportions as the court, from all the facts of the case and the conditions of the parties, deems just, with due consideration of the following factors:**

**(a) Unless there are compelling reasons otherwise, there shall be a substantially equal division in value, considering debts, between the spouses.**

**(b) Factors which may bear upon whether a division shall be equal, or the manner of division, include, but are not limited to:**

**(1) Duration of the marriage;**

**(2) Any antenuptial agreement of the parties; provided, however, that the court shall have no authority to amend or rescind any such agreement;**

(3) **The age, health, occupation, amount and source of income, vocational skills, employability, and liabilities of each spouse;**

(4) **The needs of each spouse;**

(5) **Whether the apportionment is in lieu of or in addition to maintenance;**

(6) **The present and potential earning capability of each party; and**

(7) **Retirement benefits, including, but not limited to, social security, civil service, military and railroad retirement benefits."**

Idaho does not permit the divorce court to award the separate property of one spouse to the other, but liens may be imposed against separate property for reimbursement or to secure payment of support obligations. *Radermacher v. Radermacher*, 61 Idaho 261, 100 P.2d 955 (1940).

Among the community property states, reciprocal duties of (extended) family support were recognized in Idaho Code § 32–1002 up until 2011, when those code sections were repealed. A similar statutory responsibility existed at Idaho Code § 32–1008A for nursing home costs, but that section was also (only recently) repealed.

In *Jones v. State*, 85 Idaho 135, 376 P.2d 361 (1962), where both parents were found unfit for the custody of their children and financially irresponsible, the trial court exercised its discretion and authority in the parents' divorce action to establish a trust of community property to support and educate the children. The trust was subject to continuing supervision of the divorce court.

Idaho allows a homestead to be assigned either from community property or from one spouse's separate property. If assigned from community property, the homestead can be assigned absolutely or for a limited period of time. Absolute assignments will be factored into the ultimate distribution of the community property. If the homestead is assigned from separate property, the homestead **"must be assigned to the former owner ... subject to the power of the court to assign it for a limited period to the other spouse."** Idaho Code § 32–712.

## 4. LOUISIANA

Louisiana is an equal division of community property state with procedures for a regime of separation of property by which the parties (or one member for cause) agree (or obtain a judgment) that the community regime shall not arise or shall cease to exist. See LSA–C.C. Art. 2370 through Art. 2376. The protective nature of this procedure (the non-voluntary form) can be inferred from the causes for which a judgment of separate property regime can be obtained: LSA–C.C. Art. 2374 permits a judgment decreeing separation of property when **"a community property regime is threatened to be diminished by the fraud, fault, neglect, or incompetence of the other spouse, or by the disorder of the affairs of the other spouse ..."** The judgment

**"terminates the regime of community property retroactive to the date of the filing of the petition or motion . . ."**

In Louisiana, divorce is by petition of either spouse.

A divorce shall be granted if the spouses have been living apart for a statutory time period of either 180 days or 365 days (LSA–C.C. Art. 103.1), or because of adultery or conviction of a felony and sentence to death or imprisonment at hard labor. LSA–C.C. Art. 103. Obviously, proof that the statutory period was met requires establishing a clear date of separation. A separation from bed and board must first be obtained before an absolute divorce can be obtained. The separation from bed and board immediately terminates the community regime and entitles the parties to move for division of the community property.

In a covenant marriage, LSA–R.S. Art. 9:307 lists the grounds for separation from bed and board as: adultery; conviction of a felony and sentence to death or imprisonment at hard labor; abandonment; physical or sexual abuse of the spouse seeking the divorce or of a child of one of the spouses; living apart for extended period of times without reconciliation. In a covenant marriage, a prerequisite to a divorce or to a separation from bed and board is that the parties must seek counseling.

## 5.   NEVADA

Nevada is an equal division of community property state.

Nevada once had a national reputation for a relaxed attitude toward divorce, primarily because of its six week residency requirement for establishing domicile. Nev.Rev.Stat. § 125.020. The state grants divorces upon grounds of insanity, living apart for one year, or incompatibility. Nev.Rev.Stat. § 125.010.

In awarding alimony and adjudicating property rights, the divorce court **"shall, to the extent practicable, make an equal disposition of community property,"** but the court is also given discretion to make a **"just"** disposition **"if the court finds a compelling reason to do so and sets forth in writing the reasons for making the unequal disposition."** Nev.Rev.Stat. § 125.150(b). Cases point to financial misconduct as a compelling reason for an unequal division.

The court has jurisdiction over and power to divide property placed in joint tenancy. Nev.Rev.Stat. § 125.150(2). This statute was amended in 2013.

A limited power over separate property as a source for alimony is given in Nev.Rev.Stat. § 125.150, the relevant portion of which reads:

**"In granting a divorce, the court may also set apart such portion of the husband's separate property for the wife's support, the wife's separate property for the husband's support or the separate property of either spouse for the support of their children as is deemed just and equitable."**

## 6.   NEW MEXICO

The division of property is governed by
N.M.Stat.Ann. § 40–4–7.B (1978), which also gives the
divorce court power to order alimony in a single sum
or in installments out of a spouse's separate property.
An additional provision permits the divorce court to
**"set apart out of the property of the respective
parties, such portion thereof, for the
maintenance and education of their minor
children, as may seem just and proper."** The
statute does not specifically permit an unequal
division of the community property upon divorce, and
precedent appears to require equal division of the
community property, *Michelson v. Michelson*, 86 N.M.
107, 520 P.2d 263 (1974).

New Mexico has two statutory procedures for
ending the community. The first is dissolution of
marriage on the grounds of **"incompatibility; cruel
and inhuman treatment; adultery; or
abandonment"** (N.M.Stat.Ann. § 40–4–1). The
second is division of property without a dissolution of
marriage     (N.M.Stat.Ann.     § 40–4–3     (1978).
Incompatibility is defined in N.M.Stat.Ann. § 40–4–2
(1978) as existing when **"because of discord or
conflict of personalities, the legitimate ends of
the marriage relationship are destroyed
preventing any reasonable expectation of
reconciliation."** This standard can be used to
establish date of separation.

## 7.  TEXAS

V.T.C.A.Fam.Code § 6.001 permits a grant of divorce without regard to fault.

Cruelty, adultery, conviction of a felony, abandonment, living apart without cohabitation for at least three years, and confinement in a mental hospital are all grounds for divorce, even if seldom used. Fraud, duress, or force in inducing a person to marry, concealed divorce, and conducting a marriage ceremony within the 72 hour waiting period following the issuance of the marriage license are all grounds for an annulment. V.T.C.A.Fam.Code §§ 6.002 through 6.110.

Additionally, to facilitate the legal process, a court, on the parties' or on its own motion, may refer a suit for dissolution to mediation; or the parties may agree to a collaborative law process. V.T.C.A.Fam.Code §§ 6.602 and 6.603.

Once eligibility for spousal support is established, the preferable duration of maintenance orders is the **"shortest reasonable period"** that allows a spouse to develop work skills that will provide for his or her **"minimum reasonable needs through employment."** A court may not order spousal support that remains in effect **"three years after the date of the order."** V.T.C.A.Fam.Code § 8.054. There are exceptions for a disabled spouse, and for a spouse who will care for infant or disabled children, but even they are limited in duration. The flexibility lost by the three-year limitation on spousal support is partly recaptured (when there are assets, as opposed to earning power) by allowing the divorce court to divide the quasi-community property and community property **"as the court deems just and right, having due regard for the rights of each party and any children of the marriage."** V.T.C.A.Fam.Code § 7.001. The duration of spousal support appears to be one of the most litigated sections in the Texas Family Code.

It would seem that Texas has further reduced the chance of spousal support because it does not permit the divorce court to divest either spouse of the title to separate real estate. The code section for this proposition (V.T.C.A.Fam.Code § 3.63) was repealed, but precedent may continue to hold. *Cameron v. Cameron*, 641 S.W.2d 210 (Tex. 1992) extends the rule to separate personalty, though the case has some negative treatment.

Liens may be imposed against separate property for reimbursement or to secure payment of support obligations. Moreover, the statutory protection of separate property from divorce obligations has been weakened by cases permitting a divorce court to award one spouse a homestead for life in the separate property of the other spouse, and authorizing subjection of the income, rents, or revenues of the separate real estate to the support of the other spouse or to the education and support of the children. *Hedtke v. Hedtke*, 112 Tex. 404, 248 S.W. 21 (1923). *Burney v. Burney*, 225 S.W.3d 208 (Tex.App. 2006) and *Motley v. Motley*, 390 S.W.3d 689 (2012) are related cases.

The community property system is modifiable by contract. Therefore, parties have the right to enter into a property settlement agreement that provides for extended or conditional spousal support payments that replicate something akin to long term alimony.

## 8.    WASHINGTON

Equitable division is the default rule.

Washington grants a no fault dissolution of marriage or legal separation upon a finding that the marriage is irretrievably broken. Wash.Rev.Code § 26.09.030. A petitioner must be a Washington resident, a member of the armed forces stationed in Washington, or married to someone who fits one of the above two categories. The parties to a marriage may enter into a separation contract to dispose of any property owned by both or either of them under Wash.Rev.Code § 26.09.070. This same provision authorizes the recording and publishing of notice of such a contract.

Wash.Rev.Code § 26.09.080 mandates a **"just and equitable"** division. Factors for the court's consideration are set forth as follows:

**"In a proceeding for dissolution of the marriage [or] legal separation ... the court shall, without regard to marital misconduct, make such disposition of the property and the liabilities of the parties, either community or separate, as shall appear just and equitable after considering all relevant factors including, but not limited to:**

**(1) The nature and extent of the community property;**

(2) The nature and extent of the separate property;

(3) The duration of the marriage; and

(4) The economic circumstances of each spouse at the time the division of property is to become effective, including the desirability of awarding the family home or the right to live therein for reasonable periods to a spouse having custody of any children."

## 9.    WISCONSIN

In Wisconsin, a court may grant a judgment of divorce or legal separation only upon finding that a marriage is **"irretrievably broken."** Wis.Stat. § 767.07(2) and § 767.12(2).

The default rule for marital property is equal division, but a court has discretion to effect an equitable division upon consideration of circumstances enumerated at Wis.Stat. § 767.255, excerpted here.

**"Upon every judgment of annulment, divorce or legal separation, or in rendering a judgment in an action [for property division], the court shall divide the property of the parties and divest and transfer the title of any such property accordingly . . . .**

**Any property shown to have been acquired by either party prior to or during the course of the marriage as a gift, bequest, devise or**

inheritance or to have been paid for by either party with funds so acquired shall remain the property of such party and may not be subjected to a property division under this section except upon a finding that refusal to divide such property will create a hardship on the other party or on the children of the marriage, and in that event the court may divest the party of such property in a fair and equitable manner. The court shall presume that all other property is to be divided equally between the parties, but may alter this distribution without regard to marital misconduct after considering:

(1)  The length of the marriage.

(2)  The property brought to the marriage by each party.

(2r) Whether one of the parties has substantial assets not subject to division by the court.

(3)  The contribution of each party to the marriage, giving appropriate economic value to each party's contribution in homemaking and child care services.

(4)  The age and physical and emotional health of the parties.

(5)  The contribution by one party to the education, training or increased earning power of the other.

(6)  The earning capacity of each party, including educational background, training, employment skills, work experience, length of absence from the job market, custodial responsibilities for children and the time and expense necessary to acquire sufficient education or training to enable the party to become self-supporting at a standard of living reasonably comparable to that enjoyed during the marriage.

(7)  The desirability of awarding the family home or the right to live therein for a reasonable period to the party having custody of any children.

(8)  The amount and duration of an order ... granting maintenance payments to either party, any order for periodic family support payments ... and whether the property division is in lieu of such payments.

(9)  Other economic circumstances of each party, including pension benefits, vested or unvested, and future interests.

(10) The tax consequences to each party.

(11) Any written agreement made by the parties before or during the marriage concerning any arrangement for property distribution; such agreements

shall be binding upon the court except that no such agreement shall be binding where the terms of the agreement are inequitable as to either party. The court shall presume any such agreement to be equitable as to both parties.

(12) Such other factors as the court may in each individual case determine to be relevant."

The discovery of concealed property after entry of a judgment dividing the spouses' property is dealt with by Wis.Stat. § 767.27(5):

"If any party deliberately or negligently fails to disclose information required ... and in consequence thereof any asset or assets with a fair market value of $500 or more is omitted from the final distribution of property, the party aggrieved by such nondisclosure may at any time petition the court granting the annulment, divorce or legal separation to declare the creation of a constructive trust as to all undisclosed assets, for the benefit of the parties and their minor or dependent children, if any, with the party in whose name the assets are held declared the constructive trustee, said trust to include such terms and conditions as the court may determine. The court shall grant the petition upon a finding of a failure to disclose such assets as required. ..."

# CHAPTER 10
# DEATH

## A.  OVERVIEW

When a marriage ends by the death of a spouse, the community's ability to acquire property ends. At that point, the decedent spouse's probate estate comes into existence. The term probate estate is used here to indicate the assets of a decedent that are subject to the scheme of distribution under the state's probate administration laws.

### 1.  THE DECEDENT'S ESTATE

The probate estate includes the property owned by the decedent at death. Excluded from the probate estate are assets that do not belong to the decedent and assets which are disposed of by other means, such as by right of survivorship or by inter vivos gift. Alternatives to probate administration include joint tenancy (which passes to the surviving joint tenant), trusts, and life insurance (each of which would pass to the designated beneficiary or beneficiaries). These alternatives are discussed in previous chapters.

State probate law determines how a decedent's estate is distributed.

The assets of the decedent's probate estate are consumed to pay debts or distributed.

The order of payment is as follows.

- Taxes are paid first.

- Expenses and debts of administration are paid second.

- The set aside of homestead property, exempt property, the elective share of the spouse (in a common law state), and any family allowance to the surviving spouse or dependent children or both are paid.

- Beneficiaries designated by a valid will (which includes codicils) or those indicated as substitute beneficiaries in cases involving lapse, renunciation, or other circumstances affecting the distribution of testate estates receive their gifts.

- Heirs (intestate takers) or those indicated as substitutes for heirs (in cases involving renunciation or other circumstances affecting the devolution of intestate estates) take their statutory share of any property that is disposed through the state intestacy statute.

If there are no beneficiaries or heirs the decedent's property escheats to the state.

In some states, family protections are or may be paid before the debts of creditors are paid. See for example Texas, discussed below.

Only those assets that are left over after the exhaustion of the preceding categories pass to subsequent categories. Thus, a decedent's spouse or children or both may exhaust a small probate estate by taking exempt property or a family allowance. A person could die with assets insufficient to pay all creditors and nothing would pass to his or her will beneficiaries. A valid will that effectively disposes of the entire estate to will beneficiaries who are not also intestate heirs could deprive the intestate heirs of any inheritance.

Uniform Probate Code 1969 (the UPC for short) or the amended UPC (1989 and 1990) has been adopted by eighteen states. Some of these states have adopted the UPC in its entirety. Others have adopted the UPC with significant modifications.

Of the U.S. community property states, Arizona, Idaho, and New Mexico have adopted versions of the revised UPC (1989 or 1990). California imports individual sections of the UPC for certain issues. Details about the UPC are outside the scope of this Nutshell.

## 2. COMMUNITY PROPERTY VARIATIONS

In a community property state, the death of a married person terminates the community character of property.

A note on terminology: A decedent spouse's community property share is "former community property" rather than community property. Nevertheless, for efficiency of expression, here, former community property is called community property.

For a person who is married at their death, it would seem that only the separate property of the decedent and his or her one-half of the community property should fall in the probate estate.

If property in joint tenancy form was determined to be community property, then probate administration (and liability for taxes, expenses of administration, and debts) necessarily follows upon the death of one of the owners. If the property is truly joint tenancy property, community property with the right of survivorship, or (as in Wisconsin) survivorship marital property, that titled asset passes by right of survivorship. Survivorship property is nonprobate and, therefore, neither subject to the decedent's debts nor included in his or her probate estate.

Liability for debts in a probate estate usually follows the same rules as the liability of the community for debts during the marriage. However some states impose a greater liability upon the community half of a decedent for his or her separate debts.

The right of the surviving spouse to family allowance is a family protection. It is a continuation of the obligation of support owed by one spouse to the other. The family allowance also alleviates economic difficulties caused by the termination of the marriage by death. The concept of exempt property and homestead, a family protection, was initiated in Texas, as discussed in Chapter 5. The homestead idea has been adopted in one form or another by almost all of the states.

In addition to third party creditors, a married person may die leaving the surviving spouse as a creditor. The basis for a surviving spouse's claim can a tort judgment, a community property impairment claim, a claim for reimbursement for community funds used to make capital improvements to the separate property of the decedent, or any other reimbursement allowed by state law.

The net probate estate is what remains after payment of taxes, administration expenses, debts and family support priority items are satisfied. The net probate estate is distributed in accordance with the effective provisions of the decedent's last will (including any codicils). Assuming that the character of the property has been determined to be community, there are two areas where litigation tends to occur:

a. Provisions made by the decedent's will are less generous to the surviving spouse than are the intestacy statutes.

b. The decedent attempts to dispose of more than he or she is entitled to dispose of by will, or attempts to impose conditions or restrictions upon the share that the surviving spouse is entitled to receive outright and in kind.

## B. DETAIL

### 1. PROBATE ADMINISTRATION OF COMMUNITY PROPERTY

Administration of the estate of a decedent (loosely called "probate" after the proof of a will) is the process by which a personal representative (executor or administrator) is appointed by the local court to gather the assets of the decedent, to pay taxes, administration expenses and debts, and to distribute the estate to the decedent's will beneficiaries or heirs. The probate process is also used to prove or clear title to assets. Probate administration provides a legal forum in which the community or separate character of property can be determined. Probate administration has not been popular with the ultimate takers of the probate estate because of the length of processing time and the possibility of estate shrinkage, the latter being caused largely by administration expenses, including attorney fees.

Some states, including California, attempt to alleviate the problem of overly long processing times. Those states either allow summary probate estate proceedings or else hold that probate is not necessary under certain circumstances. Cal.Prob.Code § 13000 et seq. Texas and Washington were leaders in this movement with the concept of the independent executor who qualified with, and reported a list of assets to, the probate court, but then operated informally, meaning independent of probate court supervision. The UPC allows both formal and informal probate administration.

Each combination has advantages. If the community property is entirely included in the probate administration, proof of title and collection of debts are simplified. If only the decedent's half of the community is included, the equal ownership of each spouse is recognized. If probate administration is completely avoided, there are savings in time and cost for the surviving spouse, but less protection to the creditors and will beneficiaries.

## a. Administration of Community Property

The functions of the personal representative duplicate some, but not all, of the functions of the manager of community property.

Many of the community property states have not, and some still do not, require probate administration of the community property, especially when the decedent's half of the community property passes by intestacy to the surviving spouse.

## b. Present Rules for the Administration of Community Property

The UPC permits less formal probate procedures when simplicity, rather than protection, appears appropriate.

The trend is to define small probate estates by statute so as to allow for informal probate in those cases.

High net worth estates will almost always require probate, even if only to wrap-up stray assets not covered by trusts and non-probate transfers.

## 2.    FORCED ELECTIONS AND FAMILY PROTECTIONS

In the U.S. community property states, a decedent spouse cannot disinherit the surviving spouse of community property. Nevertheless, the decedent can put posthumous financial pressure on the surviving spouse to decide whether to take under or against the decedent's will.

## a. Taking Under the Decedent's Will

A forced election scenario happens when the decedent spouse purports to use a will to devise the surviving spouse's share of the community property in exchange for substitute provisions. If the surviving spouse acquiesces to the substitution(s), then he or she takes in accordance with the deceased spouse's will. If not, the surviving spouse must formally renounce the will and take the decedent's property under the state intestacy laws.

Most community property states declare that the surviving spouse is entitled to one-half of each asset, outright and in kind. Therefore, the testator forces the surviving spouse to an election when the testator manifests the clear intent to devise either the entire interest in a community asset (or, in some states, more than one-half of the aggregate community wealth) to a nonspousal beneficiary in exchange for other devises made in the will to the surviving spouse. Arizona would look to the total aggregate amount received by the surviving spouse before declaring that the survivor is forced to elect.

Another way to force an election is for the testator to put limitations on property that belongs to the surviving spouse. This happens, for example, if surviving spouse's community one-half is placed into an irrevocable trust (usually paired with the testator's half of the community for more efficient management of the whole). Indeed, the forced election has been used consensually in estate tax planning. Some of the tax importance has been reduced by the federal estate tax unlimited marital deduction and upward changing values of the unified credit.

If forced to an election, the surviving spouse may either take the property that would transfer by the will to him or her (thus electing to allow his or her share of the community property to pass in accordance with the deceased spouse's will), or retain his or her share of the property and relinquish all inconsistent gifts under the decedent spouse's will.

What is an inconsistent gift?

Courts often indulge in the presumption that the testator intended to dispose only a portion of the property which he or she owned, i.e., his or her one-half of the community, if the asset is community property. A bequest of "my automobile" is often construed as "my community property interest in our automobile." A bequest of "one-half of my estate to my brother, the other half to my wife" may be construed to give the brother one fourth of the community property since the decedent had the right to dispose of only the decedent's one-half of the community estate.

If this presumption is not raised or if the language of the will is too clearly indicative of an unmistakable intention to dispose of property which was not entirely his or her own, then the decedent spouse's will may be deemed to force the surviving spouse to an election.

## b. Taking Against the Decedent's Will

Theoretically, the vested nature of the community property interest protects the surviving spouse from disinheritance. Even so, family protections are an important part of any community property system.

If the decedent's will does not make adequate provision for the surviving spouse, he or she also may assert the right to take a specified fraction of the estate, or additional assets up to that fraction of the estate. When this protection is invoked, the surviving spouse is said to take *against* the provisions of the will. (The UPC permits the surviving spouse to take a share of an "augmented estate," meaning an estate defined by the UPC for the purpose of supporting the surviving spouse.)

### 3.    INTESTACY STATUTES

Succession statutes apply when a decedent dies intestate. A person dies intestate in any one of the following situations.

- The person dies without a will;

- The person dies without a valid will;

- The person dies with a valid will that disposes of only part of the decedent's property; or

- The person dies with a will that disposes of all of the decedent's property, but the will is (only) partly valid.

State intestacy statutes mandate how an intestate estate will be distributed.

In community property states, when a married decedent dies intestate, (only) one-half of the community property but all of the separate property descends through the state intestacy statute. In all community property states except Arizona, different disposition schemes exist for community as opposed to separate property.

In a community property state, the surviving spouse owns one-half of the community property. The decedent has the right to dispose of his or her one-half by will, as discussed above. If the decedent dies intestate, only one-half of the community property (the decedent's one-half) descends by intestate succession. Some of the variations are as follows:

- In California, Idaho, Nevada, New Mexico and Washington, the decedent's community property passes to the surviving spouse regardless of the number of issue of the decedent.

- In Wisconsin, the surviving spouse shares community property with the issue of the decedent who are not also the issue of the surviving spouse.

- Louisiana retains *legitime*, a modified forced heirship system originating in Roman law. Legitime in Louisiana prevents a decedent from disinheriting children who are younger than 23 years of age or disabled. The legitime cannot be reduced by the surviving spouse's claim to an intestate share.

Separate property of the decedent is subjected to a different and usually more complicated distribution scheme, except in Arizona and Wisconsin. The disposition scheme for separate property normally requires that the surviving spouse share with the deceased spouse's descendants, collaterals, or ancestors, as mandated by statute. The rationale behind the intestacy statute governing separate property distribution is to provide for the surviving spouse while also recognizing those of the decedent's intestate heirs who are not also the heirs-apparent of the surviving spouse.

*Illustration 10.1:* B and C are married. B dies intestate survived by children who are not also C's children. B and C own community property valued at $100,000. B owns no separate property. After accounting for taxes, debts, family allowances, and support obligations, the most likely distribution would be that C takes B's one-half of the community property by intestate succession. Thus C, who already owns $50,000 of the community property, succeeds to B's $50,000 of community property. B's children take $0.

*Illustration 10.2:* B and C are married. B dies intestate survived by children who are not also C's children. B and C own community property valued at $100,000, and B owns separate property valued at $100,000. After accounting for taxes, debts, family allowances, and support obligations, the most likely distribution is as follows. C takes B's one-half of the former community property by intestate succession, as in Illustration 10.1 above; and B's children are entitled to B's separate property in proportional shares, as mandated by the state intestacy statute.

## 4. INDIVIDUAL RETIREMENT ACCOUNT ASSETS

Individual retirement account assets (IRA assets for short) are tax deferred or protected accounts, as discussed in Chapter 6. IRA assets are disposed of by a pay on death (POD) designation in a beneficiary form on file with the IRA institution. Because IRA assets do not pass by will, they are categorized as nonprobate assets.

The IRS has many different rules for a married IRA asset owner depending on whether the IRA owner names a spousal beneficiary or a nonspousal beneficiary. The rules are complex and outside the scope of the Nutshell. Even so, one major distinction concerning minimum distribution calculations bears noting here.

If the married IRA asset owner dies on or after the required minimum distribution date (after the age of 70½), and names a spouse as the sole beneficiary of an IRA asset, the IRS allows the spousal beneficiary to use his or her own life expectancy (recalculated every year) for determining the minimum distribution required. Life expectancy numbers are found in the Uniform Lifetime Table, IRS Publication 590.

If, on the other hand, the married IRA asset owner dies on or after the required minimum distribution date, and names a nonspousal beneficiary, IRS rules lock in an initial time-certain period for calculating minimum distributions. This time period is reduced by one for each year following.

For taxpayers who have accumulated significant balances in IRA assets in the form of tax deferred and protected accounts, federal estate tax and state tax liabilities may become an issue in any number of situations.

- If the taxpayer dies without a surviving spouse, no marital deduction is available on the taxpayer's death.

- If the taxpayer dies with a surviving spouse, but the marriage was subject to a premarital agreement that affected or eliminated the marital deduction in whole or part, then federal and state estate tax may be due.

- If the federal estate tax exemption is too low to cancel out federal estate tax liability on an estate, then federal and state estate tax may be due.

- If the IRS audits the deceased spouse's estate and concludes that more federal estate taxes are owed, then federal and state tax estate may be due.

States can eliminate a state tax by repealing the tax altogether, as Arizona does. Or impose a stand-alone tax, as Washington does.

States can lower the estate tax by raising exemptions. In these states, a state estate tax is imposed only if the decedent's estate is taxable under federal estate tax law. The policy aim is to impose estate taxes on decedent's who leave substantial estates upon death.

## C.  INDIVIDUAL STATES

### 1.  ARIZONA

Arizona has adopted and revised the UPC.

Ariz.Rev.Stat.Ann.  § 14–2101  provides  that **"[a]ny part of a decedent's estate not effectively disposed of by will passes by intestate succession to the decedent's heirs. . . ."**

The decedent's estate is made up of his or her separate property *and* his or her one-half vested interest in the community property.

Ariz.Rev.Stat.Ann. § 14–2102 clarifies that only the decedent's one-half of the community property passes by will or intestate succession. The surviving spouse retains his or her one-half vested share.

Ariz.Rev.Stat.Ann. § 14–2102 provides for the following intestate distribution:

**"The following part of the intestate estate, as to both separate property and the one-half of community property that belongs to the decedent, passes to the surviving spouse:**

1. **If there is no surviving issue or if there are surviving issue all of whom are issue of the surviving spouse also, the entire intestate estate.**

2. **If there are surviving issue one or more of whom are not issue of the surviving spouse, one-half of the intestate separate property and no interest in**

**the one-half of the community property that belonged to the decedent."**

Formerly, Arizona law gave a surviving spouse rights to the decedent spouse's entire *intestate* estate only if the decedent died without issue. Today, Ariz.Rev.Stat.Ann. § 14–2102 gives the surviving spouse the entire **"intestate estate"** if the decedent dies without issue, or if the decedent dies survived by issue who are also issue of the surviving spouse. The idea here is that children of the decedent and the surviving spouse remain the natural bounty of the surviving spouse, and therefore retain rights as the intestate heirs of the surviving spouse. The **"intestate estate"** only breaks down into its **"separate property and community property"** components when the surviving issue of the decedent are not also the issue of the surviving spouse (i.e. when the issue of the decedent are not also the birth or adopted children of the surviving spouse). But even then, all of the decedent's community property descends to the surviving spouse; only the decedent's separate property is subject to division between the surviving spouse and those of the decedent's issue who are not also issue of the surviving spouse.

Arizona repealed the estate tax in 2006. Ariz.Rev.Stat.Ann. §§ 42–4001 through 42–4008 were repealed by Laws 2006, Ch. 262, § 3.

## 2. CALIFORNIA

Cal.Prob.Code § 28 expressly converts into California community property, for purposes of the California Probate Code, **"property *acquired*** during marriage while domiciled in the state, . . . **all personal property wherever situated and all real property situated in this state ... *acquired* during marriage by a married person while domiciled elsewhere, that is community property, or a substantially equivalent type of marital property under the laws of the place where the acquiring spouse was domiciled at the time of the acquisition, ... "** and all property acquired **"in exchange"** for the above property. So, for example, if a decedent owns, for example, Texas or Louisiana community property, for purposes of the probate proceeding that property is characterized as California community property upon the domiciled spouse's death.

The need for a probate-specific quasi-community property concept arose from the situation in which persons retired, after working in a common law state, then moved to California. In the common law state, the surviving spouse would have had a statutory elective share right against a will that did not provide for her or him. A similar right does not exist in California because of the community property system.

Thus, for the retired couple who did not engage in the labor force while domiciled in California (they were no longer working, their assets had been acquired in another state, and any capital gains of separate property were themselves separate property under California law), the surviving spouse of a retiree could lose the alternative legal protections against disinheritance that he or she would have enjoyed in a common law state. He or she also would be unable to claim the existence of community property. To rectify the situation, the California legislature created a new character of property called "quasi-community property," and deemed that it would descend, upon intestacy, in the same manner as community property.

Cal.Prob.Code § 66 defines quasi-community very broadly for purposes of probate:

**As used in this code, "quasi-community property" means the following property, other than community property as defined in Section 28:**

> **(a) All personal property wherever situated, and all [California] real property ... acquired by the decedent while domiciled elsewhere which would have been the community property of the decedent and the surviving spouse if the decedent had been domiciled in [California] at the time of its acquisition.**

> **(b) All personal property wherever situated, and all [California] real property ... acquired in exchange for real or personal property, wherever situated, which would have been the community property of the decedent and the surviving spouse if the decedent had been domiciled in this state at the time the property so exchanged was acquired.**

Cal.Prob.Code § 6402.5 provides special intestacy rules for ancestral property, defined as former property (separate, community, and quasi-community) of a predeceased spouse if the surviving spouse (the present decedent) dies intestate after 1984 without (a subsequent) spouse or issue surviving. The provision deals only with property governed by the intestacy statute. The historical source of the property covered by this statute is unique in the sense that it is (i) the ancestral property of the present decedent's predeceased spouse (ii) that passed to the present decedent when his or her former spouse died within a certain period (15 years for realty, 5 years for personalty). If the present decedent dies without a surviving spouse or issue of his or her own, then the statute provides that the ancestral property shall descend to certain of the decedent's predeceased spouse's relatives (issue, parents, or issue of parents) rather than to relatives of the present decedent. Ancestral property provisions do not often come into play, since they apply only to property that falls into the present decedent's intestate estate. For that reason, estate planning that brings the property into the decedent's probate estate or passes the property by a nonprobate method will nullify the application of the statute in all cases.

Cal.Prob.Code § 6401 provides that the intestate share of a surviving spouse consists of the decedent's one-half of community property, as defined in Cal.Prob.Code § 28; the decedent's one-half of quasi-community property, as defined in Cal.Prob.Code § 66; and a portion of the decedent's separate property which varies depending upon the relationship of other surviving kindred of the decedent (who are the takers of the balance of the decedent's estate under Cal.Prob.Code § 6401(c)).

Cal.Prob.Code § 6401(c), provides that:

- The surviving spouse inherits **"the entire intestate [separate property] estate"** if the decedent left no surviving issue, parent, sibling, or issue of a deceased sibling. Cal.Prob.Code § 6401(c)(1).

- The surviving spouse inherits **"one-half of the intestate [separate property] estate"** if the decedent is survived by only one child, or the issue of a deceased child; or if the decedent is not survived by issue but is survived by a parent or parents, or their issue (siblings), or the issue of either of them (step-siblings of the decedent). Cal.Prob.Code 6401(c)(2).

- The surviving spouse inherits **"one-third of the intestate [separate property] estate"** if the decedent is survived by more than one child living; or one child living and the issue of one or more deceased children; or the issue of two or more deceased children. Cal.Prob.Code 6401(c)(3).

- § 6402.5 ancestral property is exempt from the reach of this statute.

California has provisions for small estate set asides, homestead exemptions, family protections, support provisions, and many other provisions designed to protect the surviving spouse.

California prohibits the imposition of tax on transfers made by reason of death (see Cal.Rev. & T. 13301) unless the taxpayer is also liable for federal estate tax. If so, then the California estate tax is **"equal to the portion, if any, of the maximum allowable amount of the credit for state death taxes, allowable under the applicable federal estate tax law, which is attributable to property located in the State of California."** Cal.Rev. & T. § 13302. State tax liability cannot exceed federal estate tax liability.

### 3. IDAHO

Idaho has adopted and revised the UPC.

**"As to community property,"** Idaho Code § 15–2–102(b) provides that **"the one-half of community property which belongs to the decedent passes to the surviving spouse."**

The surviving spouse takes all of the community property, and all of the separate property of the decedent if it has a value of less than $50,000 after the homestead exemption.

As to separate property, Idaho Code § 15–2–102(a) provides that if the decedent leaves neither surviving issue nor parents, the surviving spouse is entitled to all of the separate property intestate estate of the decedent. If the decedent leaves surviving issue (children, grandchildren, or more remote lineal descendants), the surviving spouse is entitled to one-half of the separate property intestate estate; the surviving issue share the other one-half. If the decedent leaves no surviving issue but is survived by parents, then the surviving spouse takes one-half of the separate property intestate estate; the decedent's parent or parents share the other one-half.

Idaho grants a surviving spouse the right to take a forced share of the estate augmented by any quasi-community property. See Idaho Code § 15–2–202 and § 15–2–203. Quasi-community property is described and distributed in language almost identical to the California definition. All quasi-community property is subject to the debts of decedent.

Idaho Code 14–403(1), the Estate and Transfer Reform Act of 1988, provides that **"[a] tax in the amount equal to the federal credit is imposed on the transfer of the taxable estate of every resident."**

### 4. LOUISIANA

Louisiana's civil law heritage shows strongly in the provisions for administration and distribution of a decedent's estate. To give just one example, Louisiana permits the legitime, a Roman law action meant to protect heirs against lifetime donations (gifts) that were made by the decedent with the intent to deprive his descendants of their (forced) heirship.

Louisiana recognizes two types of succession, by valid will and by intestacy statute.

In the case of intestate succession, Louisiana divides intestate heirs into classes, called "orders." While the surviving spouse has a primary status in other community property states, in Louisiana the class of descendants has primacy over the class of parents and siblings, which in turn has primacy over the surviving spouse.

The surviving spouse—defined as a spouse who is not juridically separated from the decedent—succeeds to the decedent's share of community property only if there are no descendants, parents, siblings, or descendants from siblings. Otherwise, the surviving spouse takes by a right of usufruct. LSA–C.C. Arts. 888, 889 and 890. Usufruct gives the surviving spouse, as usufructuary, the right to use the property for a certain period of time. A usufructuary is not an outright owner of the property, as discussed in Chapter 3.

Separate property succession devolves in accordance with LSA–C.C. Art. 894. That article reads: **"if the deceased leaves neither descendants, nor parents, nor brothers, sisters, or descendants from them, his spouse not juridically separate from him shall succeed to his separate property to the exclusion of other."**

As noted above, Louisiana recognizes the concept of forced heirship and therefore allows for legitime. The institution of forced heirship has undergone changes in Louisiana, but still today the state prohibits a property owner from disinheriting certain descendants, as discussed below. The traditional common law gave a decedent full legal rein to intentionally disinherit descendants, collaterals, ancestors, and even the surviving spouse. Therefore, there is no equivalent to the legitime in the common law.

As incorporated into the 1974 Louisiana Constitution, Art. XII, § 5 on October 21, 1995, legitime currently only applies to certain descendants. By this amendment, the legislature has a duty to provide a law for forced heirship as it applies to descendants who are **"23 years of age or younger ... or ... any age who, because of mental incapacity or physical infirmity are incapable of taking care of their person or administering their estates."**

A testator can affect the legitime by a subsequent marriage or remarriage. *Succession of Becker*, 660 So.2d 61 (La.App. 1995).

Louisiana recognizes the marital portion, a concept that was incorporated into Louisiana law in 1808. The marital portion appears to be a benefit that the law obligates the decedent's estate to provide to a surviving spouse under certain conditions. The time for a surviving spouse to make a claim for the marital portion is upon the death of the other spouse. The surviving spouse's marital portion is "irrespective of the rights of heirs, forced or otherwise, and of the legatees ... [and it] is demandable in a testate, as well as in an intestate succession." *Malone v. Cannon*, 41 So.2d 837, 839 (La. 1949).

LSA–C.C. Art. 2432 articulates the need for and scope of the marital portion: **"When a spouse dies rich in comparison with the surviving spouse, the surviving spouse is entitled to claim the marital portion from the succession of the deceased spouse."** A long line of cases make the point that, as between individual spouses "rich" is a relative term. And LSA–C.C. Art. 2433 provides that a **"marital portion is an incident of any matrimonial regime."** The marital portion **"may be claimed by the surviving spouse, even if separate from the deceased. . . ."** The marital portion also may be claimed if the deceased spouse disinherited the surviving spouse by will.

LSA–C.C. Art. 2434 sets forth the quantum of the marital portion, often referred to in case after case as the "marital fourth." (Why the marital portion equals one-fourth relates to the legitime action, which would set aside three-fourths of a succession for the forced heir(s).) This statute provides that **"the marital portion is one-fourth of the succession in ownership if the deceased died without children, the same fraction in usufruct for life if he is survived by three or fewer children. In no event, however, shall the amount of the marital portion exceed one million dollars."** Recall, as noted above, that children are in the primary class of descendants, but they take subject to the surviving spouse's marital portion. Revision Comments 1979.

The surviving spouse is receiving the marital portion (or marital fourth) in usufruct, rather than in outright ownership. For that reason, she (or he) is subject to the rights and duties of a usufructuary. Even so, the spouse is not otherwise required to post a security.

Whether usufruct is terminated by the surviving spouse's remarriage seems an often-litigated issue. Generally, a surviving spouse's remarriage

terminates the right to a marital portion by usufruct
unless the decedent has provided otherwise in a valid
will provision. Nonmarital cohabitation ("living in
open concubinage" as some of the cases put it) long
has been held not to terminate the surviving spouse's
right to a marital portion by usufruct. See e.g. *Benoit
v. Benoit*, 379 So.2d 270 (La.App. 1979), *Kelley v.
Kelley*, 198 La. 338, 3 So. 641 (1941), *Moore v. Moore*,
1868 WL 4316 (La. 1868), *Succession of Vaiaud*, 1856
WL 4534 (La. 1856), footnoted and discussed in
KATHRYN VENTURATOS LORIO, SUCCESSIONS AND
DONATIONS (2009) at § 2.16. Nonmarital cohabitation
is discussed in Chapter 11.

**"A legacy left by the deceased spouse to the
surviving spouse and payments due to him as a
result of death are deducted from the marital
portion."** LSA–C.C. Art. 2435.

A periodic allowance for the maintenance of the
surviving spouse is also allowable, but it is dependent
upon the right to, and subtracted from, the marital
portion (or marital fourth) as finally fixed. LSA–C.C.
Art. 2437.

Louisiana imposes an estate tax, but for taxpayers
whose death occurs after 1992, the Louisiana
inheritance tax statute exempts from the calculation
**"the total amount or value of the inheritance,
legacy, donation or gift made in contemplation
of death to a surviving spouse of a decedent . . . "**
LRS 47:2402, as amended by 1987 La. Acts, No. 236.
The legal usufruct of a surviving spouse also may be
exempt from taxation. *Succession of Marsal*, 42 So.
778 (La. 1907).

## 5.   NEVADA

Nevada's intestacy statutes (similar to California) pass the decedent's one-half of the community property to the surviving spouse (Nev.Rev.Stat. § 135.060.

Nev.Rev.Stat. § 134.040 divides the decedent's separate property between the surviving spouse and the decedent's issue. If the decedent dies survived by a spouse and one child (or **"the lawful issue"** of one child), the division of separate property is one-half to the surviving spouse and one-half to the child. If the decedent dies survived by a spouse and more than one child living, or a child and **"the lawful issue"** of one or more deceased children, then the separate property estate goes one-third to the surviving spouse and two-thirds to the decedent's children or their issue.

Nev.Rev.Stat. § 132.055 excludes (one presumes unadopted) stepchildren and foster children from the definition of child; thus stepchildren, foster children, step-grandchildren, foster grandchildren, and so on are not **"lawful issue"** for purposes of Nev.Rev.Stat. § 134.040.

If the decedent dies leaving no issue, Nev.Rev.Stat. § 134.050 divides the decedent's separate property between the surviving spouse and the decedent's parents equally, or to the survivor of them. If neither parent survives the decedent, the property goes to the decedent's parent's descendants (i.e. to the decedent's siblings or their issue) by right of representation. If no member of the immediate family (i.e., no parent, sibling, nephew, or niece) survives the decedent, then the surviving spouse takes all of the separate property over more distantly related heirs.

Nevada imposes a tax on the transfer of a taxable estate of resident and nonresident decedents. Nev.Rev.Stat. § 375A.100. For residents and nonresidents, tax is calculated **"in the amount of the maximum credit allowable against the federal estate tax for the payment of state death taxes on all."** Nev.Rev.Stat. § 375A.100.1 and § 100.2.

For resident decedents, property included in the calculation is real estate, tangible personal property located in the state, and intangible personal property in or outside the state but otherwise subject to the jurisdiction of the state at the time of the owner's death. Nev.Rev.Stat. § 375A.100.1(a) and (b).

For nonresident decedents, property included in the calculation is real estate, tangible personal property located in the state, and intangible personal property. Intangible personal property includes any stock of a Nevada corporation and any interest in a Nevada business, a federal corporation, or national bank that has its place of business or does the major part of its business in Nevada. Personal bank deposits are excepted unless they are used in connection with a Nevada business. Nev.Rev.Stat. § 375A.100.2(a) and (b).

### 6. NEW MEXICO

New Mexico adopted and revised the UPC.

N.M.Stat.Ann. § 45–2–102 (1978) transfers to the surviving spouse the decedent's **"one-half of the**

**community property as to which the decedent could have exercised the power of testamentary disposition."**

The separate property intestate estate is divided one-fourth to the surviving spouse and three fourths to the surviving issue of the decedent. If there are no surviving issue, N.M.Stat.Ann. § 45–2–102 (1978) transfers the entire separate property intestate estate of the decedent to his or her surviving spouse.

All of the community property is subject to the payment of community debts. N.M.Stat.Ann. § 45–2–804 (1978) also provides: **"The deceased spouse's separate debts and funeral expenses and the charge and expenses of administration are to be satisfied first from his separate property excluding property held in joint tenancy. Should such property be insufficient, then the deceased spouse's undivided one-half interest in the community property shall be liable."**

N.M.Stat.Ann. § 45–2–804 (1978), revised in 2012, automatically revokes probate and nonprobate transfers in the event of a divorce. If applicable, property otherwise title in joint tenancy could properly find its way into the decedent's probate estate. This is part of the UPC.

New Mexico imposes an estate tax in an amount equal to the federal credit on **"the transfer of the net estate of every resident."** See N.M.Stat.Ann. § 7–7–3.A (1978). The net estate is the taxable estate as defined by I.R.C. § 2051.

## 7.  TEXAS

On January 1, 2014, the Texas Probate Code, which had been in effect since 1956, was repealed by the Texas Estates Code (2013 Tex. Sess.Law Serv.Ch. 1136 (H.B. 2912) (VERNON'S), effective January 1, 2014.

The Texas Probate Code had distinguished between personalty and realty. Its replacement, the Texas Estates Code, makes substantive changes in Texas law that may alter where the distinction had previously been drawn.

Texas originated two concepts that affect the passage of property at death (in addition to lifetime implications). The first is the concept of the independent executor. The second is the concept of the homestead right.

The independent executor concept emphasized the non-intervention of the Probate Court after the qualification of the personal representative. V.T.C.S.Prob.Code § 155 exempted the community property estate from administration; it was repealed, effective January 1, 2014, but no change was made to the language: **"[w]hen a husband or wife dies intestate and the community property passes to the survivor, no administration thereon shall be necessary. . . ."** The idea is that the community intestate estate of a decedent passes entirely to the surviving spouse if the decedent leaves no living descendants, or if the decedent's surviving issue are also issue of the surviving spouse. V.T.C.S. Probate Code § 45. The disposition is subject to payment of the debts, but the use of **"shall"** suggests that a creditor cannot force an administration.

The concepts of the homestead right, discussed in Chapter 5, and of exempt personal property originated in Texas. Although designed primarily to protect a family farm or home, and certain minimum amounts of clothing, furnishings and work equipment from execution of creditors, the protection has been extended after the death of a spouse or parent. The extension is logical because otherwise death would terminate legal protection given to family members when they may most need it. The exemption from creditors has also been applied to work as an exemption when a decedent dies with a valid will. Thus in Texas, as in many jurisdictions, the spouse or the children of the decedent claim their homestead and other family protections before creditors can reach the decedent's property. A family allowance may also be ordered paid, as a preferred item from the decedent's estate, again prior to creditors.

Texas labels the estate tax an inheritance tax. V.C.T.A. § 211.051(a) imposes **"[a] tax equal to the amount of the federal credit imposed on the transfer at death of the property of every resident."** This includes property that passes by devise. Real property, tangible personal property, and intangible personal property wherever located including notes, bonds, stock certificates and interests proved by other evidence all fall within the category of property that is subject to the state inheritance tax. *Id.* Property that vests before the decedent's estate is subject to inheritance taxes is not included in the category of assets upon which state inheritance tax is imposed. Homestead property in particular is not subject to state inheritance tax.

## 8. WASHINGTON

Washington subjects both halves of the community property to probate administration when either spouse dies. This allows a continuing control of community debts and payment from the probate estate.

Wash.Rev.Code § 11.02.070 provides that upon the death of a decedent, **"a one-half share of the community property shall be confirmed to the surviving spouse or the surviving domestic partner."** The balance of the section makes clear, however, that it is a net one-half of the community *after* the **"payment of obligations and debts of the community, the award in lieu of homestead, the allowance for family support, and any other matter for which the community property would be responsible or liable if the decedent were living."**

If the decedent dies wholly or partially intestate, the surviving spouse or domestic partner, in addition to having his or her one-half of the community property confirmed in him or her, receives the decedent's one-half of the community property by succession.

As to the net separate property estate, Wash.Rev.Code § 11.04.015 gives the surviving spouse one-half if the decedent was survived by issue

Those issue take the other half of the separate property. If the decedent is not survived by issue, the spouse takes three fourths of the net separate property estate and the immediate family (parents if both are alive, surviving parent if one is alive, or issue of the parents by right of representation if neither parent survives the decedent) take the other fourth. If the decedent is not survived by issue or parent or sibling, the surviving spouse takes all of the net separate property estate.

Wash.Rev.Code § 11.04.095 provides a special rule for certain types of ancestral property. It comes into play when a surviving spouse or surviving domestic partner who received all or substantially all of the property of his or her previously deceased spouse or domestic partner (during the joint lifetime or at the death of the first spouse or domestic partner to die) dies without a will or an heir. In that case, if the covered property would otherwise escheat, the property of the second to die passes by intestacy to the surviving issue of the first to die. See California.

As in California, the Washington ancestral property provision applies only to the intestate estate, and thus is easily avoided by use of a will, trust, or nonprobate transfer.

Although during the continuation of the community Washington separate property is not liable for community debts and Washington community property is not liable for separate debts, different rules apply to timely filed creditors' claims in the probate estate. The community debts are paid from the total community, producing a net community estate; then, the separate claims against the decedent are asserted against his or her half of that net community estate.

Wash.Rev.Code § 26.16.120 authorizes spouses or domestic partners to make a contract which disposes of the community property upon the death of the first of them. This survivorship contract does not have to be executed with the formalities of a will. It is a contract, meaning (absent a specific provision to the contrary) that one spouse, acting alone, ordinarily cannot terminate or revoke the parties' agreement (as one could with a joint tenancy or a will, respectively). See Chapter 2.

Washington imposes an estate tax by Wash.Rev.Code § 83.100.040(1), which was revised in 2013, effective Jan. 1, 2014. The statute reads: **"A tax in an amount computed as provided in this section is imposed on every transfer of property located in Washington."** The estate tax due is computed by reference to a table found in Wash.Rev.Code § 83.100.040(2)(a). The estate tax is calculated on estate valuations that proceed in increments of $1,000,000. So for example, estates under $1,000,000 pay a $0 **"initial tax amount"** plus a **"tax rate %"** of 10%. *Id.* Estates between $1,000,000 and $2,000,000 pay a $100,000 initial tax amount plus a tax rate percentage of 14%. *Id.* (In other words, in 2014 the state exemption was reduced from $2,000,000 to $1,000,000.) The statutory table provides initial tax amounts and tax rate percentages for estates up to $9,000,000 and over, which pay a $1,490,000 initial tax amount plus a tax rate percentage of 20%. *Id.*

Unlike the estate taxes of the other community property states, the Washington estate tax is a stand-alone estate tax. As such the Washington estate tax is **"independent of any federal tax obligation and is not affected by termination of the federal estate tax."** Wash.Rev.Code § 83.100.040(3).

## 9. WISCONSIN

Wisconsin revised its probate administration and intestate and testate succession laws, effective January 1, 1986, the same time that it became a community property state.

The intestate share of a surviving spouse of a Wisconsin domiciliary who dies after 1985 consists of the following:

1. The deceased spouse's entire intestate estate if no issue survive or if the surviving issue are all issue of the decedent and the surviving spouse; or

2. One-half of the deceased spouse's property other than marital property and other than deferred marital property (defined below) if there are any surviving issue who are not also issue of the surviving spouse.

Wisconsin law permits each spouse to will his or her portion of each item of marital property and his or her nonmarital (i.e., individual and unclassified) property, subject to the surviving spouse's elective rights.

Only the decedent's one-half of marital property is subject to probate administration. Survivorship marital property, like joint tenancy, belongs by operation of law to the survivor; therefore, survivorship marital property is not subject to administration, nor does it pass by will.

Wis.Stat. § 766.58(3)(f) permits spouses to enter a marital property agreement containing provisions that act as a will substitute to transfer property without probate administration:

**"Providing that upon the death of either spouse any of either or both spouses' property, including after-acquired property, passes without probate to a designated person, trust or other entity by nontestamentary disposition. If a marital property agreement provides for the nontestamentary disposition of property, without probate, at the death of the 2nd spouse, at any time after the death of the first spouse the surviving spouse may amend the marital property agreement with regard to property to be disposed of at his or her death unless the marital property agreement expressly provides otherwise and except to the extent property is held in a trust expressly established under the marital property agreement."**

To afford surviving spouses some additional economic protection (to cover Wisconsin's legal transition from a separate property title state to a community property state), an elective right (rather than the automatic property interest envisioned by the UMPA) is provided to a surviving spouse. By this right the surviving spouse may elect to receive up to one-half of certain nonmarital property called "deferred marital property" in the deceased spouse's probate estate. Deferred marital property is property acquired during marriage that would have been marital (community) property had the marital property law applied when the property was acquired. This provision is designed to sunset.

A surviving spouse may also elect to receive up to one-half of the value of the "augmented marital (community) property estate." The augmented marital property estate (a concept borrowed from the UPC) consists of certain nonprobate transfers effected on or after April 4, 1984 (the date on which the Governor signed the law). Those nonprobate transfers must be of deferred marital property to third parties, and they can include certain trusts, joint tenancies and life insurance. The amount elected by the surviving spouse is reduced by amounts transferred by the decedent to the surviving spouse. The surviving spouse is eligible to collect the amount remaining after deferred marital property is transferred. See Wis.Stat. § 861.03 to § 861.17.

Unlike the other community property states, Wisconsin makes clear at the outset that its purpose in imposing an estate tax is to obtain a benefit for the state, and thus laws governing the estate tax are **"to be liberally construed to effect this purpose."** Wis.Stat. § 72.005. The amount of the state estate tax is **"the maximum credit allowable upon the United States estate tax . . . ."** Moreover, **"[a]n estate tax is imposed upon the transfer of all**

**property that is subject to a federal estate tax
and that has a taxable situs in [the] state."**
Wis.Stat. § 72.02.

# PART 5
# SPECIAL PROBLEMS

# CHAPTER 11
# NONMARITAL RELATIONSHIPS

## A.  OVERVIEW

A valid, or lawful marriage, is a solemnized marriage that is licensed in accordance with the state's internal law. States generally recognize as valid a marriage validly contracted in another state.

A licensed marriage, though seemingly valid, could be subject to a legal defect. The purported marriage might be void because of bigamy or because the spouses are too closely related as a matter of biology. Or, the marriage may be voidable because of an adjudged lack of consent or a defect in legal formalities.

The judicial procedure by which a void or voidable marriage is declared invalid is called an annulment. An annulled marriage is one that never came into legal existence. A dissolved marriage, by contrast, is one that did come into legal existence between the dates of the executed marriage license and the final divorce decree. In principle, spouses must be lawfully married in order to be within the community property system.

With the important exception of domestic violence provisions, the legal concerns of nonmarried cohabitants fall outside of the community property system.

## B.   DETAIL

### 1.   THE PUTATIVE SPOUSE AND THE DIVISION OF PROPERTY

The common law rule was that an invalid marriage is invalid for all purposes. The rule was adopted in community property states, but then made considerably less harsh by application of the equitable putative spouse doctrine.

A putative spouse is an innocent member of a void or voidable marriage who maintains a good faith belief in the validity of the marriage. One or both members of a defective marriage may be a putative spouse in fact. But only a court judgment awards putative spouse status as a matter of law. That status is important to dissolving a putative marriage because it gives the petitioner access to the state family code and it shields the parties from criminal liability related to the technical invalidity of the marriage.

A common law spouse and a putative spouse do not share the same legal status. A common law spouse who marries in a state that permits informal marriage contracts *is* lawfully married. A putative spouse is not lawfully married but—upon proof of his or her good faith belief in the validity of the marriage—is nevertheless *treated as if* he or she had been lawfully married.

Not all states accept the putative spouse doctrine. Certainly not all states have codified the doctrine. But of those that have, courts vacillate between understanding the putative spouse as an actor who must demonstrate a good faith belief that his or her marriage was *valid* versus one who must demonstrate a good faith belief that his or her marriage was *lawful*.

This is a fine distinction that can nevertheless determine property rights. So for example, a person who is domiciled in a community property state that does not recognize informal marriage might, in good faith, albeit mistakenly, believe that his or her informal marriage is valid, but that same person could not in good faith believe that the marriage is lawful since the marriage was not solemnized and licensed in accordance with jurisdictional requirements. By the same token, a person might act in accordance with the jurisdictional requirements, thus believing that the marriage is lawful, but because of a defect in formalities the marriage might still be invalid.

Of the states that have adopted the putative spouse doctrine by statute or by decisional law, not all of them accept it for all purposes (such as spousal support). California, for example, uses the doctrine to resolve property and support issues in line with the family code, which recognizes putative spouses as being in a confidential relationship. The state civil code, by comparison, would presume arm's length transactions absent actual proof of a confidential relationship.

In the event of death, there may be multiple survivors, one of whom is a lawful spouse and the other a putative spouse. Where there is only one survivor, the putative spouse doctrine offers that survivor the protections that a lawful spouse would otherwise enjoy under the family law. Where there are two or more survivors, courts have divided on how the property of the various unions should be divided. When there are two claimants in the form of a lawful spouse and a putative spouse, Louisiana and California have solomonically divided the property, awarding one-half to the lawful spouse as community property and the other one-half to the putative spouse either as quasi-marital property, some other community property analog, or perhaps even community property.

Illustration 11.1 below has historically been more likely to occur in the case of a probate proceeding than a dissolution proceeding. Still, there is no bar to the application of the putative spouse doctrine in a dissolution proceeding, and in fact it is often invoked in that context.

*Illustration 11.1:* H lawfully marries W1, ineffectively divorces her, and later ceremonially "marries" W2. Having no knowledge of the H-W1 marriage, W2 believes in good faith that the H-W2 marriage is valid. In this scenario, W1 is H's lawful spouse; W2 has a factual basis for claiming putative spouse status.

Complications arise in the break-up context if all three of the parties are employed or have earnings related assets: Is W2 entitled to a share of W1's income? Is W1 entitled to H's share of W2's income? Is H entitled to a part of each of their earnings? If H earns less than either W1 or W2, and he is deemed a putative spouse, does that status entitle him to a share of both W1 and W2's earnings? Few cases have dealt with these problems.

*Illustration 11.2:* H lawfully marries W1, ineffectively divorces her, and later ceremonially "marries" W2. Having no knowledge of the H-W1 marriage, W2 believes in good faith that the H-W2 marriage is valid. H subsequently dies intestate. How should H's estate be distributed?

Complications arise in the probate context as well. W1 is H's surviving spouse. But W2 is H's surviving putative spouse. What is community property of the H-W1 marriage? What is the property of the H-W2 relationship? Are the claims of W1 superior to those of W2; or are W2's claims superior to W1's? More cases have dealt with these problems, with courts trying, in the end, to do what is fair for all involved.

## 2. NONMARRIED COHABITANTS

Nonmarried cohabitants are defined as persons who live together in a sexual relationship without intending to formalize their relationship by marriage or RDP status. The general rule is that a nonmarried cohabitant does not, by cohabitation alone, acquire rights in the accumulations of the other cohabitant.

States take different approaches to the rights of nonmarried cohabitants in the context of a break-up or death.

On one side of the spectrum is Washington, which equitably grants nonmarried cohabitants access to the community property system on a case-by-case basis.

On the opposite side of the spectrum is Louisiana, which neither grants the parties access to the marital regime nor recognizes agreements made in the context of a nonmarital relationship that is sexual in nature.

California takes the middle ground of enforcing pooling contracts—including implied and tacit contracts—between nonmarried cohabitants. But this is in lieu of granting nonmarried cohabitants access to the community property system and the parties must in fact be living together. The expressed policy concern for the exclusion is to prevent the creation of a back-door marriage option. Another reason has to do with a societal concern about nonconsensual marriage.

Contracts can provide for property earned during the cohabitancy, whether through labor, talent, or gift. Additionally, some states permit quantum meruit claims to be brought by nonmarital partners whose relationship has ended.

These are allowances, but they bring home the fact that nonmarried cohabitants are not entitled, by default, to use the family law to resolve their disputes. Contract law, property law (title documents), unjust enrichment, the law of trusts, partnership, quasi-partnership and joint venture law must be used instead as theories upon which to govern the division of property between nonmarried cohabitants. In the event of wrongdoing, resulting and constructive trusts can be sought by the wronged party.

Creditors of nonmarried cohabitants must likewise look to general law rather than to family law (community property) for protection of their rights.

There are a number of theories of general law available to a person who seeks to obtain or recover property from or as a nonmarried cohabitant at the termination of the cohabitancy.

## a. Contract

Nonmarried parties may contract between themselves over property and support rights. Consideration is required. A contract between nonmarried partners can relate to a period of time or to a specific asset or assets acquired during their relationship. It can also relate to post-breakup support.

When the consideration involves support solely in exchanges for sex, it falls into the category of meretricious consideration. Meretricious consideration is illegal and therefore insufficient to support a contract.

## b. Implied Contract

Often nonmarried cohabitants have implied or tacit understandings about property and support issues. These understandings sound in contract and thus create reasonable expectations. If one cohabitant keeps house, cares for children, assists in the developing the other cohabitant's career, lost opportunity costs as well as a change in position point to the existence of a bargained for exchange (no matter how implicit the bargain might have been). The exchange is that one cohabitant will provide financial support (including possibly property ownership of assets titled in the employed cohabitant's name alone) in exchange for the other cohabitant's labor contributions. Claims for long periods of service may be cut short by statutes of limitation, so that only the final two, three, four or six years of service can serve as the basis for a claim.

An alternative to an implied or tacit contract theory (either of which can create a post-breakup support obligation) is the quasi-contract theory. A quasi-contract claim is limited to the value of the labor actually expended (past tense) in support of the family or the other cohabitant's wellbeing or career.

Contract is a remedy that seeks to execute the parties' exchange. A contract claim is based on the idea that the cohabitants negotiated for a certain outcome in the event of a future breakup. For a plaintiff to prevail, proof is required of offer, acceptance, and consideration.

A quasi-contract (quantum meruit) claim is based on the idea that a cohabitant who expends labor during the relationship without financial compensation is entitled to a reimbursement so as to avoid unjustly enriching the benefitted party. For the plaintiff to prevail, proof is required of the parties' intent to compensate the laboring party for specific, identifiable services.

Equitable ownership claims may be included in any suit by one former cohabitant against the other. A recovery that sounds in property is based on the idea that contributions to purchase, including labor contributions, create a reasonable expectation of shared ownership as to a specific asset.

For the equitable ownership theory, the claimant must identify his or her contributions to the purchase of the asset(s) that were untitled or titled in the other's name alone.

### c. Partnership

Partnership theory allows a nonmarried person to seek compensation in the context of a breakup. A formal partnership agreement is useful to this end but not necessary for an adjudication of rights and duties. The partnership can be equal or unequal. It can duplicate many of the features of community property. Generally, courts uphold partnership agreements if a business (or real property) is involved, and there is adequate proof of the partnership agreement. Occasionally, a court embraces approximately the same principles, but calls the combination a joint venture rather than a partnership.

A pooling of earnings of both parties during the relationship tends to demonstrate the existence and possibly the terms of a partnership or joint venture as to property obtained throughout the cohabitancy period. Pooling implies a one-half split between the parties, which means that a claim that the parties intended to pool their resources is most plausible when there are not large discrepancies in the parties' actual respective cash contributions to their shared household.

### d. Form of Title

As to title forms, the general rule is that form of title controls ownership. A title in one nonmarried cohabitant's name alone is that person's individual property. A concurrent title is owned by both cohabitating persons.

The form of holding title is less important in civil law countries; and it can be shown to fail to reflect the parties' understanding about ownership of the titled asset. Nevertheless, the general rule holds. Therefore, form of title remains good protection for the person in a nonmarried relationship whose name alone is on title. And yet, the form of title principle is reputed to encourage craft and selfishness in the intimate relationship when honesty, openness and selflessness are presumed to be the practice.

If the parties have contributed equally in money or goods to the purchase of property, either joint tenancy or an equal tenancy in common will accurately reflect the cohabitants' intentions as to ownership.

If, however, the contributions by the cohabitants are unequal, only a tenancy in common in the same proportions as the parties' respective contributions will prevent an unintended gift or unjust enrichment.

Labor (sweat equity) is typically not considered a contribution to purchase for purposes of credit acquisitions, but it may be the basis for a quasi-contract claim.

Labor will be the factored into the apportionment of a separate property business.

## e. Unjust Enrichment

Generally, nonmarried cohabitants are not in a confidential relationship as a matter of law. With parties who deal at arm's length, even if they are in an intimate relationship and live together, courts are reluctant to compensate for goods or services contributed to the household in whatever voluntary arrangement the parties adhere to. Overbearing by one person in a relationship toward the other, however, is a legitimate legal basis upon which a court can order protection for the adversely affected party, especially if a confidential relationship can be established between the two as a matter of fact for a particular transaction.

The contribution of money or goods is more likely to invoke judicial protection than one of labor (sweat equity). Normally, there must also be a discrepancy between the position of the cohabitants, either because of the strength of the position of the person in possession of (or having title to) the property or because of the relative fragility (mental, emotional, educational or psychological) of the other party.

If the title to property was acquired (either directly or by use of funds belonging to the wronged party) by fraud or mistake, an unjust enrichment claim likely accrues. The remedy is a constructive trust.

## f. Constructive Trust

A constructive trust is a remedy whereby the court orders the record title owner or possessor (as "trustee") to carry out his or her sole duty. That one duty is to transfer title to the wronged party whose funds were used to make the purchase without attribution. The wronged party is an equitable owner and thus the beneficiary of the constructive trust.

## g. Resulting Trust

A resulting trust arises when one party, without intending a gift, supplies the purchase price of a property for which title is taken in the name of a second party. The person whose name is on title holds the property for the benefit of the equitable owner, which is to say the party who supplied the purchase price.

## h. General Equitable Principles

The courts of equity have long exercised powers to correct legal imbalances. The increasing number of non-marital relationships produces greater demands on systems of law and equity for correction of inequalities between the parties.

## C.　INDIVIDUAL STATES

### 1.　ARIZONA

Arizona does not permit informal marriages, but it does recognize such marriages as valid if they are validly contracted in a jurisdiction that allows them. Ariz.Rev.Stat.Ann. § 25–111 and § 25–112. Arizona does not recognize informal divorce. Therefore, informally married spouses who move to the state must still obtain a formal divorce.

Bigamous marriages are void and illegal upon proof that a person knowingly married another person in a manner that would be valid but for the defendant's ongoing marriage. *State v. Guadagni*, 218 Ariz. 1, 178 P.3d 473 (2008). Only marriages that are void or voidable may be annulled. Valid marriages are dissolved. Nevertheless, the granting of a dissolution does not preclude the granting of a valid decree of annulment under *Hodges v. Hodges*, 118 Ariz. 572, 578 P.2d 1001 (Ct.App. 1978) and *Medlin v. Medlin*, 194 Ariz. 306, 981 P.2d 1087 (Ct.App. 1999).

Arizona acknowledged the putative spouse doctrine in *Stevens v. Anderson*, 75 Ariz. 331, 256 P.2d 712 (1953), but does not appear to have scrutinized it with great frequency at the appellate level. The general rule is that if parties are not lawfully married, they cannot predicate property rights on marital status. *Cross v. Cross*, 94 Ariz. 28, 381 P.2d 573 (1963). They can, however, seek recovery on theories of partnership or contract.

## 2. CALIFORNIA

Consent, license, and solemnization make for a valid marriage. Consent refers to mental competence. Solemnization means that the ceremony is witnessed. A license, once recorded, becomes the marriage certificate. Not recording a license will not invalidate an otherwise valid marriage; but neither will recording a marriage license turn an otherwise void or voidable marriage into a valid one.

A void marriage is one that is bigamous, polygamous, or between relatives of a certain degree of kinship. One type of bigamy is potentially excusable under Cal.Fam.Code § 2210(b); it is where a spouse (spouse 1) who has been **"absent and not known to the other spouse ... for a period of five successive years . . ."** shows up after the abandoned spouse (spouse 2) has married a different person (spouse 3). The mere absence of a spouse does not raise a presumption of death, but there is case law that suspends the first marriage (between spouse 1 and 2) once the second marriage (between spouse 2 and 3) is contracted. After suspension, either spouse 1 or spouse 2 can seek a judgment of nullity or a judgment of dissolution as to the Spouse 1–2 marriage.

A voidable marriage is one with a defect that vitiates consent. A voidable marriage is presumed valid unless and until one party (or both), during life, seek an annulment. Upon the death of one party to the union, a voidable marriage becomes valid.

California codified the putative spouse doctrine Cal.Fam.Code § 2251 such that **"if a determination is made that a marriage is void or voidable and the court finds that either party or both parties believed in good faith that the marriage was valid, the court shall declare the party or parties to have the status of a putative spouse."** A putative spouse can opt to claim his or her share of **"quasi-marital property,"** which is defined as **"that property acquired during the union which would have been community property or quasi-community property if the union had not been void or voidable."** Putative spouses can also claim spousal support rights (unlike in Nevada, as discussed below).

A recent line of cases holds that being adjudged a putative spouse requires a subjective good faith belief in the validity of an otherwise void or voidable marriage. That line starts with *Ceja v. Rudolph &*

*Sletten, Inc.*, 56 Cal.4th 1113, 158 Cal.Rptr.3d 21, 302 P.3d 211 (2013).

Cal.Fam.Code § 297 et seq. brings registered domestic partners (RDPs) completely into the community property system. Cal.Fam.Code § 297.5 specifically provides that RDPs **"shall have the same rights, protections, and benefits, and shall be subject to the same responsibilities, obligations, and duties under law, whether they derive from statutes, administrative regulations, court rules, government policies, common law, or any other provisions or sources of law, as granted to and imposed upon spouses."** Under this same provision, former RDPs have the same rights and obligations as former spouses. Formal termination of a RDP is required before a subsequent RDP or marriage can be entered into.

Nonmarried cohabitants are generally outside the reach of the Family Code. Their property and support issues (if any) are governed by the general laws discussed in Sections A and B above. However, the state Domestic Violence Prevention Act (DVPA) does apply to nonmarried cohabitants. So does most of CAMPAL, with the exception of the special community property presumption for sums on deposit in an account.

California is the place that made contracts between nonmarried cohabitants, known as *Marvin* contracts, famous. *Marvin v. Marvin*, 18 Cal.3d 660, 134 Cal.Rptr. 815, 557 P.2d 106 (1976) continues to be a leading case on the issue of a nonmarital cohabitant's breakup remedies. There, the California Supreme Court considered the appropriateness of two breakup remedies. One was the enforcement of an implied pooling (sharing) contract for which the consideration was alleged as housekeeping. The other was the appropriateness of rehabilitation, meaning post-breakup financial support.

The trial court dismissed the plaintiff's contract claims as to certain assets (like a Los Angeles mansion) for lack of consideration, but it awarded her $104,000 of rehabilitation on general equitable principles. Appeals were ultimately taken to the California Supreme Court. As to contract enforceability issue, the state supreme court held that implied or tacit pooling contracts between nonmarital cohabitants are enforceable upon proof of (i) the terms of the contract (ii) valid consideration for the contract, and (iii) breach. There is an extensive case law on what constitutes sufficient consideration to support a *Marvin* contract. The trial court's grant of post-breakup support was ultimately reversed, however, on the rationale that the nonmarried cohabitants, not having been married to each other, are not eligible to access the community property system for purposes of seeking spousal support. The policy consideration that loomed large was the state's concern about opening a back door to the recognition of informal (unlicensed) marriage.

A later case, *Byrne v. Laura*, 52 Cal.App.4th 1054, 1063, 60 Cal.Rptr.2d 908 (Cal.App.Ct. 1st Dist. 1997) extended *Marvin*, supra, to oral agreement for lifetime post-breakup support from a decedent nonmarital partner's estate.

A *Marvin* claim can be consolidated with an existing family law case, as for example when nonmarital cohabitants marry and then eventually dissolve their marriage. But in the end, a *Marvin* claim is a civil action, not a family court action.

The doctrine of estoppel (because of the cohabitancy itself) precludes application of the statute of frauds as a defense. See *Marvin*, supra, and *Byrene*, supra. Different statutes of limitation apply depending on the claims, as indicated in the state Civil Code. Finally, the *Marvin* contract does not implicate the state Labor Code. *Whorton v. Dillingham*, 202 Cal.App.3d 447, 248 Cal.Rptr. 405 (Cal.App.Ct. 4th Dist. 1988).

Just as nonmarried cohabitants are outside of the Family Code, lovers who do not cohabitate are outside of the *Marvin*, supra, rule. See e.g., *Bergen v. Wood*, 14 Cal.App.4th 854, 18 Cal.Rptr.2d 75 (2nd Dist. 1988), holding that lovers who do not cohabitate are barred from bringing *Marvin* contract claims.

California does not permit informal marriage, but the state will recognize as valid such a marriage lawfully contracted in another jurisdiction. California does not recognize informal divorce.

### 3.   IDAHO

Idaho recognizes marriage as a civil contract, but no longer permits informal marriages after January 1, 1996. The change is non-retroactive. Prior to January

1, 1996, cohabitation alone could give rise to presumption of an informal marriage. Such a marriage was defined as one that arose by the parties' mutual and non-licensed assumption of marital rights, duties, or obligations. After January 1, 1996, the operative statute is Idaho Code § 32–201, which currently reads: **"Consent alone will not constitute marriage; it must be followed by the issuance of a license and a solemnization as authorized and provide by law."**

Idaho recognizes as valid a common law marriage lawfully contracted outside of Idaho.

Idaho never did and does not now recognize informal divorce.

Idaho Code § 32–208 is a unique code provision among the U.S. community property states. It releases a party from a marriage contract **"made in ignorance of the other's want of personal chastity."** Additionally, **"either is released"** from a contract to marry **"by unchaste conduct on the party of the other, unless both parties participate therein."** There is no case law on this code provision.

Idaho has not adopted the putative spouse doctrine, except to permit putative spouses to sue for wrongful death under Idaho Code § 5–311. See also, *Reichert v. Sunshine Mining Co.*, 95 Idaho 647, 516 P.2d 704 (1973).

## 4.   LOUISIANA

The Louisiana Constitution had been amended accordingly to block same-sex marriage and other "marriage-like" relationships. The *pre-Obergefell,* supra, era statute, now defunct, reads: **"Marriage is a legal relationship between a man and a woman that is created by civil contract. The relationship and the contract are subject to special rules prescribed by law."** LSA–C.C. Art. 86.

LSA–R.S. Art. 9:272 permits covenant marriage (after premarital counseling and the execution of a declaration of intent). A covenant marriage is defined as **"a marriage entered into by one male and one female who understand and agree that the marriage between them is a lifelong relationship."** Grounds for covenant marriage are found at LSA–R.S. Art. 9:307.

LSA–C.C. Art. 40.62 **"Any person born in Louisiana who has sustained sex reassignment or corrective surgery which has changed the anatomical structure of the sex of the individual to that of a sex other than that which appears on the original birth certificate of the individual, may petition a court of competent jurisdiction as provided in this Section to obtain a new certificate of birth."** Equal protection issues may arise as a result of an absence of language on how to deal with a pre-operative marriage documents that would reveal a person's pre-operative sex. Until the statutory gap is addressed, transgender petitioners who were or are currently married, as compared to petitioners who have never been married, may receive disparate treatment under Louisiana law. Additionally, LSA–C.C. Art. 40.62 contains no direction for how it reconciles with LSA–C.C. Art. 86.

Louisiana codified the putative spouse doctrine which it adopted from the civil law. LSA–C.C. Art. 96 provides: **"An absolutely null marriage nevertheless produces civil effects in favor of a party who contracted it in good faith for as long as that party remains in good faith."** "Civil effects," as to the marriage, allow the putative spouse access to the matrimonial regime (LSA–C.C. Art. 2336), and extend protections to the children of the union.

A recent modification appears in the second sentence of the same provision: **"When the cause of the nullity is one party's prior undissolved marriage, the civil effects continue in favor of the other party, regardless of whether the latter remains in good faith, until the marriage is pronounced null or the latter party contracts a valid marriage."** The rationale for this modification, according to the Revision Comments, is that in such a situation:

> "The party whose prior undissolved marriage is the cause of nullity is the one who has the dispositive power to rectify the nullity (by divorcing his former spouse and remarrying his present one). The other party cannot do so. Accordingly, the second sentence of this Article permits the spouse who has acted in good faith

and whose prior marriage was not the cause of the nullity to enjoy the civil effects of marriage even after he ceases to be in good faith. This additional period ends when the party benefitted by it contracts a valid marriage (whether with the other party to the null union or with a third party), or when the nullity of the bigamous marriage is judicially recognized, whichever occurs first." Revision Comments 1984.

Contracts between nonmarried cohabitants— Louisiana cases use the obsolete terms "concubinage," "concubine," and "paramour"—have been held unenforceable as against public policy. LSA–C.C. Art. 2030 provides: **"A contract is absolutely null when it violates a rule of public order, as when the object of a contract is illicit or immoral. A contract that is absolutely null may not be confirmed."** Equitable lien and quantum meruit claims have also been denied on similar policy grounds.

In *Schwegmann v. Schwegmann*, 441 So.2d 316, 324 (La.App. 1983) writ denied sub nom. *Blackledge v. Schwegmann*, 443 So.2d 1122 (La. 1984), after her nonmarried cohabitant's stroke, the plaintiff sued her cohabitant, his children, and his multiple corporate business entities to enforce an oral agreement, an implied agreement, equitable liens, quantum meruit for uncompensated domestic services (cooking, cleaning, chauffeuring, child care, assisting the defendant after his stroke), and quantum meruit for uncompensated services as a business advisor, a political assistant, and a business confidant. The court called the 12-year relationship a "concubinage." The plaintiff became a "concubine," which the court defined as "a woman who occupies position, performs duties, and assumes responsibilities of the wife, without title and privileges flowing from legal marriage." The man was cast as a "paramour," which the court defined as "a man with whom [a] concubine lives." The court then dismissed the plaintiff's claims related to the "concubinage," but allowed the uncompensated business services claim on the ground that it might not be related to the "concubinage." (Eventually, that claim was denied as well.)

The rationale on the dismissal of the contract claims was that they were void for public policy. The rationale on the dismissal of the equitable lien and quantum meruit claims was that "nonmarried cohabitation does not give rise to property rights analogous to or similar to those of married couples," and that "concubines have no implied contract or equitable liens that afford them any rights in the property of their paramours." The court said, of its policy, that "although Victorian, the values sought to be protected by the formulation of those legal concepts are imperative if we are to maintain our civilized society."

## 5. NEVADA

Couples over a certain age can solemnize their relationship under the Nevada Domestic Partnership Act. Nev.Rev.Stat. § 122A.010 appears to parallel the

California legislation in extending the rights and liabilities of marriage to RDPs. Formal termination of the domestic partnership is required.

*Hay v. Hay,* 100 Nev. 196, 199, 678 P.2d 672, 674 (1984) quoted *Marvin v. Marvin,* 18 Cal.3d 660, 134 Cal.Rptr. 815, 557 P.2d 106 (1976), to expressly hold that *Marvin* contracts are enforceable in Nevada.

The Nevada Supreme Court, in *Williams v. Williams* 120 Nev. 559, 97 P.3d 1124 (2004), adopted the putative spouse doctrine in annulment proceedings for purposes of property division, but rejected the doctrine as a basis of awarding equitable spousal support. The rationale was that Nevada's annulment statutes do not provide for an award of support upon annulment. The court also stated in dicta that although a bigamous marriage is void under the plain meaning of Nev.Rev.Stat. § 125.290, an annulment proceeding is nonetheless necessary to legally sever the relationship. *Id.* at 564. *Marriage of Seaton,* 200 Cal.App.4th 800, 807–08, 133 Cal.Rptr.3d 50, 56 (2011) discussed *Williams* in a case involving a spouse who entered into a void marriage in Nevada and subsequently married a different person in California.

## 6.   NEW MEXICO

New Mexico has not formally recognized the putative spouse doctrine. However, the rights of spouses in an invalid marriage have been protected by judicial decision. See e.g., *Estate of Lamb,* 88 N.M. 157, 655 P.2d 1001 (1982), and *Prince v. Freeman,* 45 N.M. 143, 112 P.2d 821 (N.M. 1941).

## 7. TEXAS

Texas had, on its books, a now defunct constitutional amendment banning same-sex marriage and other marriage-like relationships. It also had a license prohibition for persons of the same gender who sought to marry. V.T.C.A.Tex.Fam.Code § 2.001.

Post-*Obergefell*, supra, Texas case law continues to cause obstacles for transgender persons. By case law, gender assignment at birth, not the person's gender at the time of the marriage determines a person's gender for purposes of determining the validity of a formal marriage. *Littleton v. Prange*, 9 S.W.3d 223 (1999), *rev. denied, rehearing of petition for review overruled, cert. denied* 531 U.S. 872, 121 S.Ct. 174, 148 L.Ed.2d 119. *Obergefell*, supra, nullifies the part of the above holding that goes toward marriage validity. But other problems remain. For example, a charge of false swearing may be brought against a person who swears a gender different than one assigned at birth. V.T.C.A.Tex.Fam.Code § 2.004(c) and Op.Att'y Gen. No. M–1277 (1972).

Texas recognizes informal, or common-law, marriage for different-sex partners upon proof offered in a **"judicial, administrative, or other proceeding"** by the party claiming the validity of the marriage. V.T.C.A.Fam.Code § 2.401. It is unclear how and in what way *Obergefell*, supra, implicates the Texas rules on informal marriage, which clearly contemplates a gender-binary union.

To establish an informal marriage, three elements must be proved. One, the partners agreed to be married. Two, the partners lived together in Texas as spouses. And three, the partners held themselves out as married.

Each case of claimed common-law marriage is determined on its own facts. *Joplin v. Borusheski*, 244 S.W.3d 607 (2008). The burden of proof is by a preponderance of the evidence. *Small v. McMaster*, 352 S.W.3d 280 (2011), petition for review filed.

A conditional agreement made by the parties to live together for a trial period does not constitute a valid informal marriage. The precedent here is a line of cases interpreting element one (the agreement element) to require a present, unconditional, and unqualified, bilateral agreement between the parties *to be married*. See e.g., *Schwingle v. Keifer*, 105 Tex. 609, 153 S.W. 1132 (1913), *Texas Employers' Ins. Ass'n v. Borum*, 834 S.W.2d 395 (1992), *Nguyen v. Nguyen*, 355 S.W.3d 82 (2011).

Additionally, an agreement to be spouses must be followed by cohabitation *as spouses*. The idea being that the parties' conduct must give them a public reputation of being married, not just one of being engaged, cohabitating, or in a trial period of cohabitation. *Smith v. Deneve*, 285 S.W.3d 904 (2009). *Grigsby v. Reib*, 105 Tex. 597, 153 S.W. 1124 (1913)— a rather interesting case—ruled that cohabitation as spouses need not be continuous, once the three elements for establishing the informal marriage are met.

An informal marriage may be declared and registered under V.T.C.A.Fam.Code § 2.401. Bigamy is a criminal offense in Texas, and an unterminated common-law marriage can form the basis for a bigamy prosecution. *Melton v. State*, 71 Tex.Crim. 130, 158 S.W. 550 (1913). Common-law divorce is unknown to Texas law; therefore, once an informal marriage is established, it must be dissolved in the same way as a ceremonial marriage. In *Claveria v. Claveria's Estate*, 597 S.W.2d 434 (1980), the court recognized common-law divorce, but this decision and the rationale of common-law divorce were reversed on appeal in *Claveria's Estate v. Claveria*, 615 S.W.2d 164 (1981).

Where two marriages are alleged, the most recent marriage is presumptively valid against each marriage that precedes it, unless the party who asserts the validity of an earlier marriage proves otherwise. *Nguyen v. Nguyen*, 355 S.W.3d 82 (2011). In the event that an earlier marriage is proved valid as against a later in time marriage, Texas protects the good faith later-in-time putative spouse through an equitable doctrine that entitles the putative spouse to one half of the product of the joint efforts acquired while believing in good faith that a marriage existed. The courts have not been consistent with terminology. Some cases have declared the share to be community; others have stated the shares to be the separate property of each party. The lesson here is that putative spouse status will not necessarily support a community of property in Texas—no matter what it is ultimately called—as it does in California.

Nonmarried cohabitants, even if they live together, are not spouses, and thus they lack the right to avail themselves of the benefits of the community property system. Their remedies against each other rest in legal theories applicable to nonmarried persons such as agreements for contract, quantum meruit, and partnership or joint venture claims when there have been contributions of labor or capital to the life shared together.

## 8.   WASHINGTON

Washington recognizes marriage as a **"civil contract between two persons . . . ."** Additionally, Washington passed broad registered domestic partnership legislation in the pre-*Obergefell*, supra, era so as to protect the right of same-sex couples to formalize the relationship. Wash.Rev.Code § 26.16.030. Formal termination of a registered domestic partnership is required to terminate a domestic partnership.

An mid-twentieth century case, *Creasman v. Boyle,* 31 Wash.2d 345, 196 P.2d 835 (1948), denied nonmarried cohabitants access to the community property system, thus leaving them to resolve their property rights by contract, business partnership, trust, or constructive trust (in cases of fraud).

*Creasman* was overruled in *Matter of Marriage of Lindsey,* 101 Wash.2d 299, 678 P.2d 328 (1984), which held that courts must " 'examine the [parties'] relationship and the property accumulations and make a just and equitable disposition of the property.' " *Id.* at 307. Proof is required of what was once called a meretricious relationship but today is called an equitable relationship. Proof of an underlying contract, business relationship, or wrongdoing necessitating a constructive or resulting trust is not required.

An equitable relationship is defined as one that is stable, marital-like, and built on the intention to pool and share resources (and apparently) acquisitions. See e.g. *Marriage of Pennington*, 142 Wash.2d 592, 14 P.3d 764 (2000). By this rationale (but not the outcome) any one of two parties domiciled in the state who can (but nevertheless choose not to) marry can invoke the protections of *Lindsey*, supra. *Vasquez v. Hawthorne*, 141 Wash.2d 1025, 11 P.3d 825 (2000).

By tradition and by precedent, as in *Brenchley's Estate*, 164 P. 913 (Wash. 1917), as well as by the logic applied to equitable relationships, Washington protects the rights of the putative spouse, at least as to property obtained during the putative marriage. It also allows for spousal support.

## 9.  WISCONSIN

Limited domestic partnership legislation exists in Wisconsin, as Wisconsin was one of the states that banned same sex marriage by state constitutional amendment. Wis.Stat. § 770.01. RDPs in Wisconsin do not have access to Wisconsin marital property statutes.

In 1922—long before Wisconsin's adoption of UMPA—Wisconsin allowed recovery on an implied contract theory in a case involving a putative spouse.

The putative widow believed in good faith that she had been validly married to the decedent, who knew the marriage was invalid. See *Estate of Fox*, 178 Wis. 369, 190 N.W. 90 (1922). Today, under Wis.Stat. § 765.24, if there is an impediment to a lawful marriage, once the impediment is removed, the parties can have their marriage recognized as lawful.

The Wisconsin Supreme Court has held that nonmarried cohabitants may raise claims based on unjust enrichment following the termination of their relationship. The claim accrues when one party attempts to retain an unreasonable amount of the property acquired through the efforts of both. See *Watts v. Watts*, 137 Wis.2d 506, 405 N.W.2d 303 (1987) and *Lawlis v. Thompson*, 137 Wis.2d 490, 405 N.W.2d 317 (1987).

Wis.Stat. § 766.01 does not subject the spouses to marital property rules unless both are domiciled in the state.

# CHAPTER 12
# FEDERAL PROBLEMS

## A. FEDERAL SUPREMACY

### 1. OVERVIEW OF THE FEDERAL SYSTEM

The U.S. federal system contemplates a full body of state laws in each state and a superimposed network of federal laws.

The federal laws are generally not all encompassing. Instead, federal laws envision fuller interpretation by use of the various state laws. For example, bankruptcy is federal law, but state law determines which property is not subject to execution.

Most of the fields with which this Nutshell is concerned—property interests, creditors' rights, marriage, divorce, and probate administration—are almost entirely a matter of state law with very little federal intrusion. Whenever federal law and state law conflict, however, the federal law (if constitutional) is given priority under the supremacy clause, Constitution of the United States, article VI, clause 2.

If a state law is considered destructive of the spirit and purpose of federal legislation, the federal legislature or courts can reject it. For example, *Free v. Bland*, 369 U.S. 663, 82 S.Ct. 1089, 8 L.Ed.2d 180 (1962) asserted federal supremacy in the form of ownership of U.S. Series E and F Savings Bonds. As a matter of federal law, the "or" form of ownership established a survivorship between the parties (similar to joint tenancy); but Texas provisions (the local law) purported to declare the "or" form of bond ownership to be community property (without a survivorship feature). In this instance, the state (local) law was required to yield to the federal law.

An analytic approach to constitutional interaction of federal and state laws is as follows.

*Constitutionality.* Is the federal law constitutional? What power granted to the federal government authorizes the statute? Is the federal statute prohibited by any constitutional provision?

Few federal statutes are deemed to be in excess of the constitutional power to enact laws which are necessary and proper to carry out the enumerated federal powers. There is a remote possibility that a statute might be deemed to attempt to take property without due process. If so, the statute would violate the 5th Amendment to the U.S. Constitution.

*Pre-emption.* Does the federal statute purport to preempt the field or does it defer to state law? Federal laws may preempt a field, but not all federal laws necessarily do so.

*Federal interests.* Does the state law do major damage to clear and substantial federal interests? Some state laws are inconvenient to the federal law without being damaging to federal interests. See for example *Poe v. Seaborn*, 282 U.S. 101, 51 S.Ct. 58, 75 L.Ed. 239 (1930), the U.S. Supreme Court required the modification of the federal tax laws in order to eliminate the advantage otherwise available only in community property states. A more recent example is the legalization of same-sex marriage in *Obergefell*, supra, discussed in Chapters 1 and 11.

## 2.   FEDERAL PRE-EMPTION

*Wissner v. Wissner*, 338 U.S. 655, 70 S.Ct. 398, 94 L.Ed. 424 (1950) is the doctrinal ancestor of current cases dealing with the interaction of state and federal law. In that case, National Service Life Insurance on the life of a deceased California serviceman who was domiciled in California was held exempt from the state community property laws. Evidence for pre-emption was found in Federal Employee's Group Life Insurance (FEGLI) Act statements that the insured "shall have the right to designate" and change the beneficiary at all times and that payments of proceeds "shall be exempt from the claims of creditors, and shall not be liable to attachment, levy or seizure by or under any legal or equitable process whatever, either before or after receipt by the beneficiary." *Wissner*, supra, is discussed in Chapter 6.

*Hisquierdo v. Hisquierdo*, 439 U.S. 572, 99 S.Ct. 802, 59 L.Ed.2d 1 (1979); and *McCarty v. McCarty*, 453 U.S. 210, 101 S.Ct. 2728, 69 L.Ed.2d 589 (1981) are decisions of the U.S. Supreme Court that concern the application of state community property laws to federal retirement plans, and specifically to military retirement plans. *Hisquierdo*, supra, has consistently been relied upon, but *McCarty*, supra, is red flagged because it was reversed by statute on the military retirement issue; recently, however, the case, was resurrected as stating the rationale for pre-emption of nontaxable disability pay. See *Howell,* supra, discussed below and in Chapter 6.

*Hisquierdo,* supra, dealt with the federal Railroad Retirement Act (the RRA for short), a federal law that the U.S. Supreme Court wrote "resembles both a private pension program and a social welfare plan". The case involved a married worker's railroad retirement benefits, earned during marriage while domiciled in California, and covered by the RRA. The legal question was whether the covered benefits were divisible at dissolution, and if so, whether an offsetting award to the non-employee spouse would defeat the purpose of the RRA. The U.S. Supreme Court held that RRA covered benefits are not community property subject to division upon divorce. Consequently, an offsetting award to the non-employee spouse would defeat (damage rather than merely inconvenience) the purpose of the RRA.

In its rationale, *Hisquierdo,* supra, summarized the federal pre-emption doctrine, as enforced by the Supremacy Clause, as follows. The subjects of domestic relations and probate administration belong to the laws of the individual states rather than to the laws of the federal government. State laws must do major damage to clear and substantial federal interests before the supremacy clause of the federal constitution will override the state law. The tests applied are whether the asserted right conflicts with the express terms of federal law and whether its consequences sufficiently injure the objectives of the federal program to require nonrecognition. *Hisquierdo,* supra, classified as preempting language a provision in the RRA against attachment or anticipation of a specified beneficiary's interest. *Hisquierdo*, supra, is discussed in Chapter 6.

*McCarty*, supra, held that federal military retirement benefits could not be characterized as community property because the valid federal retirement plan objectives would be injured. The court in that case quoted *Hisquierdo*, supra, for tests which appear to be stretched by the application made of them. Ultimately *McCarty*, supra, was reversed by FUSFSPA), 10 U.S.C.A. § 1408. The FUSFSPA provision removed, as to military retirement pay, the federal pre-emption found to exist in *McCarty*. The result is that states are now permitted to apply their own (local) laws to determine whether military retirement pay is divisible as a marital asset. FUSFSPA § 1408(c).

Exempt from the FUSFSPA grant of permission to the states is any amount that the Government deducts **"as a result of a waiver"** that the veteran makes in order to receive **"disability payments."** FUFSPA § 1408(a)(4)(B).

*Mansell*, supra held that a state cannot treat "the waived portion" of the veteran's retirement pay that becomes "nontaxable disability benefits" as divisible community property. *Id.*

*Howell*, supra, applied *Mansell*, supra, to decide the outcome in a case where the veteran's disability waiver took place several years after the final divorce judgment had been issued. The Arizona court had ordered the veteran to reimburse his former spouse for the waived disability portion of his monthly military retirement pay. The Arizona Supreme Court ultimately affirmed the state trial court order. See *In re Marriage of Howell*, 238 Ariz. 407, 408, 361 P.3d 936, 937 (2015). The veteran petitioned for certiorari.

The U.S. Supreme Court took the case and held that *Mansell*, supra, "completely pre-empts the States from treating waived military retirement pay as divisible community property." *Howell*, supra, at 1405, citing *Mansell*, supra, at 109 S.Ct. 2023. Recognizing that federal pre-emption can work a hardship on divorcing parties, *Howell*, supra, relied on the federal purposes and objectives rationale, and specifically on the federal government's interests in attracting and retaining military personnel.

FUSFSPA is discussed further Chapter 6.

The possibility of federal pre-emption remains in other areas. For example, one legal question in need of clarification is how federal and state laws on educational loan liabilities might interact.

## B.  STATE CONSTITUTIONAL PROVISIONS

### 1.  OVERVIEW: FEDERAL AND STATE CONSTITUTIONS

Areas in which community property problems tend to arise under the U.S. Constitution include:

- Supremacy clause problems.

- Fourteenth Amendment problems involving either the due process or the equal protection provisions of the Constitution of the U.S. as applied to the state.

- Privileges and immunities problems which arise primarily between domiciliaries and non-domiciliaries of the state.

Each of the community property states also has its own constitution. The contested areas under state constitutions tend to be:

- Clauses that are identical to the U.S. Constitution.

- Separate property clauses.

- Equal rights provisions. In the absence of such a provision, states can still protect equal rights by application of the equal protection provision of the federal constitution, New Mexico has added such a provision to its constitution.

- Retroactive applications of substantive rule changes.

*Suter v. Suter,* 97 Idaho 461, 546 P.2d 1169 (1976), for example, declared unconstitutional a sex-based distinction that appeared in a provision for the character of property acquired while a couple is separated. A prior Idaho case, *Reed v. Reed,* 404 U.S. 71, 92 S.Ct. 251, 30 L.Ed.2d 225 (1971), had invalidated on the same grounds an Idaho statute that preferred males in the appointment of administrators of decedents' estates; other courts have declined to extend the case. Bans on same-sex marriage provisions, which remain on the books in several U.S. community property states, have been nullified by the U.S. Supreme Court in *Obergefell*, supra. Same-sex marriage is licensable in every U.S. state as the Fourteenth Amendment of the U.S. Constitution protects fundamental liberties, such as the right to marry. *Obergefell*, supra. *U.S. v. Windsor*, 133 S.Ct. 2675, 186 L.Ed.2d 808 (2013) held a same-sex spouse is included within the definition of "spouse" as that term is used in federal statutes. In *Windsor*, supra, when Edith Windsor succeeded to her deceased spouse Thea Spyer's estate, she sought a tax exemption as a surviving spouse under the U.S. Internal Revenue Code. Windsor was initially barred from claiming the exemption; ultimately the U.S. Supreme Court ruled in Windsor's favor.

Pre-*Obergefell*, supra, the U.S. community property states took different approaches to same-sex marriage. Washington and California permitted same-sex marriage; New Mexico was neutral; and Idaho, Louisiana, Nevada, Texas, and Wisconsin passed state constitutional amendments banning same-sex marriage. The state patchwork created significant human rights problems with respect to marriage and divorce. States with constitutional provisions that banned same-sex marriage did not recognize such marriages even if they were validly established in another state—a practice *Obergefell*, supra, now bars. Nevertheless, under the pre-*Obergefell* patchwork, validly married same-sex couples who subsequently changed their domicile to a community property state that banned same-sex marriage could not divorce in their new domicile state. Today, the previous legal patchwork uniformly resolves in favor of equal protection rights for same-sex marriage and its corollary, same-sex divorce.

Against the backdrop of *Obergefell*, supra, marriage remains a state law procedure, as does divorce. Different U.S. community property states allow for different relationship options. All permit licensed marriage. Only Texas permits informal marriage. Likewise, as to divorce, all states require a final judgment of dissolution to terminate a *valid* marriage, whether licensed or unlicensed. No state permits informal divorce.

At the time this Nutshell goes to press, California, Nevada, and Washington have registered domestic partnership (RDP for short) legislation that gives RDPs the same rights and obligations as married persons. Wisconsin has limited domestic partnership legislation—the limitation was due to the state's constitutional amendment banning same-sex marriage. Arizona, Idaho, Louisiana, New Mexico, and Texas have no domestic partnership legislation. In the states that permit them, RDPs must be formally entered into (hence they become "registered"); and, as a consequence, they must be formally terminated in accordance with the parameters of the statute that authorizes them.

## 2.   STATE CONSTITUTIONAL DEFINITIONS OF SEPARATE PROPERTY

California, Nevada and Texas have state constitutional provisions that define separate property. The constitutional provisions have served as a limitation upon actions by the legislature in making and amending community property laws.

*The character of rents, issues, and profits obtained during marriage.* As discussed in Chapters 2, 3, and 6, the separate property rents, issues, and profits receive different treatment, during marriage, depending on state law.

At one time, the text of the three state constitutional provisions concerning rents, issues, and profits was identical. Subsequent amendments have changed the wording of all three constitutions. But even when the wording was identical, however, different interpretations arose.

The major difference in interpretation was whether the income from separate property should be characterized, during marriage, as community or as separate property California held in *George v. Ransom*, 15 Cal. 322 (1860) that separate property income remains separate property. Nevada indicated by dictum in *Lake v. Lake*, 18 Nev. 361, 382–84, 4 P. 711, 722–23 (1884) as modified by *Johnson*, supra that it would follow the California (American rule) approach. But Texas held in *Arnold v. Leonard*, 114 Tex. 535, 273 S.W. 799 (1925) that such income is community. Additionally, both Texas and California held unconstitutional statutes that attempted to transmute, by operation of law, rents, issues, and profits received during marriage.

In *George*, supra, the California court based its decision upon what it called the fixed meaning in the common law of the term separate property. In *Arnold*, supra, the Texas court viewed the omission of the term "rents, issues and profits" from its constitutional definition of separate property as an indication that separate property rents, issues, and profits were not included within that definition. The Texas court went on to say that the legislature could neither enlarge nor diminish a spouse's separate property because of the state constitutional definition.

Commentators generally agree that the California court used a common law analysis in reaching its result and that Texas was truer, by comparison, to civil law tradition. Some commentators have called the California rule a mistake. But even if it is, it is not likely that the California rule will be reversed in furtherance of theoretical civil law purity. As we have seen, a majority of states follow the California approach. Moreover, the direction of change among those states that do not follow the American rule is nevertheless in the California direction. In 2013, Texas voters rejected a proposal to amend the Texas Constitution in favor of adopting the American approach.

## 3.   RETROACTIVE CHANGES IN COMMUNITY PROPERTY LAWS

### a.  Retroactivity

There can be an initial ambiguity in how to define the concept of retroactivity when applying changes in community property laws.

A statute may have an effective date that is determined as a general rule applying to all statutes.

Or, it might include a date for that particular statute. This happens, for example, with emergency legislation. If not, a discrete statute may specifically address the retroactivity issue for purposes of its application.

The effective date of a statute can be prospective as to some operative event, but retroactive as to some other operative event. This type of legislative change—presumption as to character, ability to donate, rights to devise or manage, changes in the rights of third parties relative to the spouses—may dictate what operative event should serve as the line between retroactive and prospective operation.

Sometimes a question arises as to whether the legislature intended the statute to operate prospectively or retroactively. The intention may be express, implied, or inferred. As a general matter, if, after considering all pertinent factors, the court is unable to determine the legislative intent, the statute will be presumed to operate prospectively and not retroactively.

Even more generally, a guiding principle is that constitutional questions are avoided by rules of statutory construction or of general property law, absent statutory language to the contrary. The presumption here is that retroactive application is not intended unless it is specifically stated in the language of the statute itself.

In California, *Spreckels v. Spreckels*, 116 Cal. 339, 48 P. 228 (1897), imposed a constitutional prohibition upon retroactive changes. The case questioned an

1891 legislative amendment that required a wife's consent to gifts of community personal property made by the husband to a third party. The amendment was held constitutionally inapplicable to property acquired before the effective date, the rationale being that each spouse had vested rights in community property, and, therefore, it was beyond the power of the legislature to deprive a spouse of his or her vested right without due process of law. California passed a comprehensive Family Code in 1992, effective 1994. The Family Code abrogates much of the prior law as a general matter. Nevertheless there remains a considerable body of case law on whether amendments to the community property laws can be applied retroactively.

## b. Vested Rights

Often, the inquiry over the quality of a right revolves around a determination of whether the right is vested. Cases tend to start the analysis with the proposition that the interest being changed was (or was not) a property right; from there the analysis moves to whether the right is vested, contingent, or a mere expectancy.

Amendments that seek to change in any manner the vested rights of the spouses between themselves cause an enlargement of the interest of one spouse at the expense of the other spouse. Therefore, as to property already acquired during marriage, one spouse may be deprived of a potentially vested property right by the retroactive application of a newly enacted statute. If the deprivation is without due process or without compensation, or if it denies one party the equal protection of law, there is a basis for holding that the legislation has been applied in an unconstitutional manner. It is also remotely possible that the legislation could be treated as impairing the obligation of the marriage contract.

Constitutional objections are sometimes avoided by deciding that the interest is not a vested right, or that the legal approach does not affect a vested right. Thus the attribute of the community property law that is being changed (such as the ability to make gifts of community property without the consent of the other spouse or the need for a written contract) can be declared to be merely an incident to a right rather than a right itself. Or, the legal approach in question— as, for instance, a special community property presumption that goes into effect as of a certain date— can be deemed merely to start the conciliation proceeding, not to affect vested property rights.

Historically, the constitutional analysis focused on asking whether there was any impairment of a vested right. Modernly, a more nuanced analysis prevails. Even if there is an impairment, the analysis goes a step further to ask (i) how much of an impairment (ii) of how important a right (iii) and for how important a reason. The emphasis, for constitutional purposes, therefore, is on the due of due process. Is the change under consideration sufficiently necessary to the public welfare to justify the impairment?

In determining the value of the change, the factors to be considered include "the significance of the state interest served by the law, the importance of the retroactive application of the law to the effectuation of that interest, the extent of reliance upon the former law, the legitimacy of that reliance, the extent of actions taken on the basis of that reliance, and the extent to which the retroactive application of the new law would disrupt those actions," *Marriage of Bouquet*, 16 Cal.3d 583, 592, 128 Cal.Rptr. 427, 432, 546 P.2d 1371, 1376 (1976).

Finally, there can be reasons to make a statute retroactive.

If the basis of a change in a default law is in furtherance of a compelling social policy, then only retroactive application will bring about the change for all spouses.

Prospective-only application, by contrast, delays the implementation and uniformity of the changes, leaving some spouses protected and some not.

Another complexity with prospective-only legislation is that a new class of community property is created with each legislative change. As a result, administrative difficulties tend to increase, and the default system of community property laws tends to become more complex.

## c. Texas Due Course

Texas has interpreted its constitution as imposing limits upon the extent to which a divorce court can assign the separate real property of one spouse to the nonowning spouse upon divorce.

In *Eggemeyer v. Eggemeyer*, 554 S.W.2d 137 (Tex.1977), the Texas Supreme Court prohibited such a transfer on the basis that it was contrary to two constitutional provisions—the definition of separate property in Tex. Const. Art. XVI, § 15 and the due course provision of Tex. Const. Art. I, § 19. The Texas due course provision, it turns out, is almost identical to the due process provisions of the federal and other state constitutions. Moreover, the Texas due course provision was deemed to require not only procedural, but also substantive, due course. *Id.*

Finally, *Eggemeyer*, supra, applies as much to personal property as it does to real property. And it applies to each spouse's one-half share of the community property as well as to separate property. Thus it is not inconceivable that *Eggemeyer*, supra, could be applied so as to declare unconstitutional most provisions for the division of property upon divorce if those provisions tend to divide property "equitably" between the parties to the marriage without rigid conformity to previous ownership or character.

*Eggemeyer*, supra, also could be viewed as an attempt to create consistency between divorce and other areas where community property law is applied. The probate court is required to divide community property equally and is not authorized (except in homesteads and family allowances) to assign the property of one spouse to the other spouse. Creditors generally cannot reach more than the debtor's interest, in the absence of fraud.

Nevertheless, divorce courts have traditionally divided property or assigned property nominally owned by one party to the other party.

## C.   CONFLICT OF LAWS

### 1.   CHOICE OF LAW

The federal system permits diversity so that each state can decide whether it will have a community property system and what attributes that community property system will have. A price of the federal system is that the laws of various states can conflict, meaning they can reach opposing conclusions depending upon which system of law is chosen.

To resolve conflicts of laws, courts seek to use one or more contacts. The method of choice of law is often to seek the jurisdiction with the most significant contacts with the subject matter of the litigation. Among the significant contacts are the forum, domicile, location of realty, and place where a tort occurred.

### a.   Forum

The forum is the jurisdiction which contains the court in which a lawsuit is filed.

A state could declare that it intends to apply its own law to all situations regardless of the domicile and location of the parties and persons who come before it. In addition to constitutional and jurisdictional problems, this would make the applicable law almost entirely the choice of the plaintiff, since the choice of forum is made by the plaintiff.

The easiest law for the forum court to apply is its own law. In many instances, a choice of law problem is ignored because the existence of a contradictory system is not called by the parties to the attention of the court. For example, if a couple who own community property are divorced in a non-community property state; the divorce court might ignore community property problems because one or both parties and their attorneys have failed to point out the conflict. When this happens, one spouse may be adversely affected, relative to the other spouse, in terms of property division.

Similarly, the presumption that the law of another jurisdiction is the same as the law of the forum puts the burden of proving the different law upon the person who asserts that there is a difference.

Finally, the total law of the forum includes both its internal law and its choice of law provisions. Therefore it is imprecise to say that the forum court is applying its own law *or* the law of another state. The internal law of another state may be applied through the choice of laws law of the forum.

## b. Domicile

Domicile is the legal status of citizenship and residency in a state.

Generally, domicile results from a combination of physical presence in the state, and the intention to remain (or at least not to leave) the state. Generally, a person's legal domicile is the state in which the person resides. But residence and domicile are not identical terms. A residence can be a permanent or a temporary address, but a domicile is the individual's permanent, legal address.

In the male-management era, which ended for all community property states in the mid-1970s, the (now rejected) rule was that the husband's domicile determined the wife's domicile unless the wife was justified in establishing a separate domicile for herself.

The rule, from the mid-1970s forward is that each person in a marriage establishes a domicile. Any person, married or not, has (only) one domicile at a time. Spouses typically share the same domicile as a practical matter. But today it is also possible for persons who are married to each other to establish different domiciles, and a person's domicile can change during marriage. Objective facts determine a person's domicile: personal residence, family residence, place of employment, voter registration, vehicle registration, and any other fact tending to show that the party has a present intent to permanently reside in the state. Once domicile is established, it remains the same until it is reestablished elsewhere.

Sometimes a person is present in the state but not domiciled there. Some examples follow. A military person who is stationed in a community property state may be physically present in the state but not domiciled there. A college student can be a physical resident of a state without being domiciled there. Likewise, a person housed in a federal prison may have a permanent legal residence in another state.

If spouses are domiciled in different states, the marriage will be governed by the state with the most significant relationship to the spouses and the property at issue.

Domicile is the most important criterion in determining the application of community property law.

The validity of the marriage itself is tested by the law of the place where it is executed, but the domicile of the parties may nevertheless declare the marriage invalid if the marriage is contrary to a strong policy of the domicile.

Definitions of community property laws are based upon the domicile of the parties at the time that property is acquired. Generally, all property acquired during marriage while domiciled in the state is community property under the laws of that state. Thus, if a married couple change their domicile from one community property state to another, they may acquire different categories of community property. When this happens, the married persons may own State A community property—governed by State A's community property rules—and State B community property—governed by State B's community property rules.

If the community is terminated by dissolution, the domicile of one or both parties is the proper jurisdiction for the dissolution action.

If the community is terminated by death, the domicile of the decedent is the proper jurisdiction as to personal property to administer the probate estate, to judge the validity and effect of any will, and to apply its intestacy rules.

Jurisdiction over a defendant is usually most easily obtained at the defendant's domicile. Thus, the defendant's domicile is frequently also the forum.

## c. Situs

Realty, the classic immovable, is generally governed by the law of its situs, or location.

Further, the concept of quasi-community property is a labeling device. It does not give the court of one state jurisdiction over property in another state.

For the above reason, ancillary probate administrations are necessary in the estate of a decedent who dies owning property in states other than the domiciliary state. The choice of laws law of the situs state, like that of the forum, may look to the domiciliary state law in order to determine the character of property.

## d. Place Where Tort Committed

The choice of law rule for torts generally looks to the law at the place where the tort was committed, the lex loci delicti.

For the above reason, if community property state domiciliaries are tortiously injured in a non-community property state, the law of the place of the tort appears to be the proper law to apply.

A number of conflicts of laws could arise. For example, if the community property domiciliary rules make the non-injured spouse a necessary party to the tort action and the non-community property site of the accident requires only the injured spouse be named as a party, a question may arise as to whether the non-injured spouse is a necessary party to the action.

## 2. MOVING TO A COMMUNITY PROPERTY STATE

### a. Multistate Problems

There are a number of ways in which the laws of more than one state may be involved in deciding which law to apply to determine the character of property. Married couples may move to, from, or between community property states, own property or become involved in a tort in a state other than the state of domicile.

There is seldom community property unless and until a married couple has both married and establish domicile in a community property state. Just as there is no community prior to marriage, there is no community without domicile. Minor exceptions do exist. A wedding gift to a couple about to be married can be community property in a minority of jurisdictions; or, a couple can marry with the plan to soon after establish a new domicile in a community property state.

### b. Retiring in a Community Property State

The Sun Belt of the U.S. historically has drawn retirees from colder parts of the country. Several of the Sun Belt states (Arizona, California, Nevada, New Mexico and Texas) are community property states. The flow of married couples into community property states is therefore not an isolated phenomenon.

Upon the death of a primary wage earning spouse, the different approaches of community and non-community property states can leave a gap in coverage for the immigrant surviving spouse. The spousal protection statutes of a separate property state (forced share dower substitutes, for example) will not be part of the law of a community property state.

In this case, the surviving spouse's protection, if any, must come from the decedent's estate plan.

## c.  Privileges and Immunities Problems

The first attempt by California to define quasi-community used entry into the state as the trigger for changing the character of an immigrant couple's out-of-state property. That attempt was held unconstitutional in *Estate of Thornton*, 1 Cal.2d 1, 33 P.2d 1 (1934), where the court ruled that the use of entry into the state as a trigger for characterizing property within the community property system was a deprivation of property without due process and a denial of the privileges and immunities of those who moved to California. The result is that establishing a domicile in a community property state is not enough, without more, to bring the party or parties' property into the community property system of the person's new domicile.

*Thornton*, supra, is now superseded by a quasi-community property statute. That statute names the filing of a petition in a California court (not mere entry into the state) as the event that gives a California court authority to characterize out-of-state property within the California community property system.

*Addison v. Addison*, 62 Cal.2d 558, 43 Cal.Rptr. 97, 399 P.2d 897 (1965) upheld the application of California's quasi-community property statute to the dissolution situation.

*Addison*, supra, distinguished *Thornton*, supra, on the ground that the statute with which the former case dealt attempted to alter property rights because and by virtue of the married couple reestablishing domicile in California. The new statute, on the other hand, only came into force when the party or parties file a petition for dissolution in a California court.

## d. The Concept of Quasi-Community Property

Wisconsin and UMPA use the quasi-community property concept as a major transitional provision for domiciliaries who were married and owned property on the effective date of the community property law. Wisconsin uses the concept of deferred marital property, which is known as property that would have been marital property if it had been acquired after the determination date.

Quasi-community property statutes, where enacted, can apply in divorce actions to property acquired during marriage. They can also apply in death situations. In the latter, the concept applies only to the decedent's property that would have been community property had it been acquired in the new domicile. The surviving spouse's property is not treated as quasi-community property.

## e. Emigration from a Community Property State

Some of the community property states have attempted to adjust for those who emigrate from a separate property state. But, practically speaking, separate property states do not make a similar adjustment to accommodate the interests of those who emigrate from a community property state.

Community property remains community property when a married person changes domicile to a separate property state. The problem of adapting a separate property system to community property is similar to converting meters into inches without using fractions or decimals: The result is only approximate. Thus, the typical, and most correct, separate property state treatment of existing community property is to consider it as a form of the common law tenancy in common, giving equal shares to each party. This eliminates some of the attributes of community property such as management and control rights and duties, just as whole number usage eliminates fractions or decimals in a metric conversion.

The Uniform Disposition of Community Property Rights at Death Act has been enacted by Colorado, Hawaii, Kentucky, Michigan and Oregon.

As discussed above, a party may ignore community property aspects of the case. But whereas a party is free to ignore whether they are adversely affected (or not) by the strategies they undertake, an attorney is not. An attorney who does not pursue zealously the client's right to community property may face both professional discipline and malpractice claims.

Whenever spouses from a community property state migrate to a non-community property state, those spouses bring with them the protections of the community property system under which they acquired property during their marriage. If their marriage ends, their (non-community property system) attorneys too often neglect the community property ramifications of their client's divorce or estate. By ignoring the community property era of a marriage's existence, attorneys in non-community property states overlook (or even abandon) the significant advantages that their clients (and their families) gained while domiciled under their former community property regime. Such neglect exposes these attorneys to malpractice liability.

## D.   THE INTERNAL REVENUE SERVICE

The Internal Revenue Service maintains an intranet site and a manual to assist I.R.S. employees with community property issues.

## E.   A CONCLUDING THOUGHT

The joke among lawyers who are unfamiliar with intimate partnership law is that community property is easy, just divide in half.

The joke underimagined the risk of dismissing community property as an area of law unworthy of social or philosophical analysis. A community property system is a default property dissolution system, it is true. And it is also a powerful financial tool for intimate partners who want to manage and plan for their own and their family's future. But the whole of a community property system is far greater than the sum of its parts.

Ultimately, a community property system is a public institution for assigning property rights during marriage. Fairness, choice, agreement, financial accountability, financial disclosure, stewardship— these are principles that any community property system develops to cast light on legal issues that can arise between intimate partners. The time has come to embrace these principles in the context of marriage and intimate partnership more generally. My hope is that this Nutshell is one small step in that direction.

# INDEX

**References are to Pages**

**ACQUISITION**
Generally, 3–5
Community Property, 5–11
Onerous and Lucrative, 8
Systems, Differences, 14

**ALASKA**
Community Property Option, 3, 5, 101, 114, 128–130
History, 26

**AMERICAN VERSUS CIVIL LAW APPROACH**
Generally, 20
*See* Apportionment
Credit Acquisitions, 292
Rents, Issues, and Profits, Separate Property, 163, 174

**ANCESTRAL PROPERTY**
California, 561
Washington, 575

**APPORTIONMENT**
Generally, 10, 281
American Rule Jurisdictions, 21, 124, 166–167, 174
Credit Acquisitions, 292, 296
Rents, Issues, and Profits, Separate Property, 20, 174
Bank Accounts, Commingled, 296
Credit Acquisitions, Commingled, 296
Pro Tanto Ownership vs. Reimbursement, 287–290
Reimbursement vs. Pro Tanto Ownership, 287–290
Deferred Work Compensation, Commingled, 209
Separate Property Business, 321
Separate Property Rents, Issues, and Profits, 174–175
State Constitutions, and, 621

**ARIZONA**
Bank Accounts, 114, 334, 340
  UMPAA, 114
Community Property Statutes, 132
Conflict of Laws,134
Credit Acquisitions, 336
  Civil Law Approach, 292
Dissolution, 520
Division of Property, 135
Divorce. *See* Dissolution
Domestic Violence, 193
Gift of Community Property Earnings, 387
History, 20
Intestacy Statutes, 557
Joint Form Titles,
  Community Property with the Right of Survivorship, 256
  Joint Tenancy, 112, 133, 256, 261
  Timing, Dissolution vs. Death, 263, 265
    *See* Reimbursement, General Statute
Liabilities, 457
Management and Control, 408
Personal Injury Recovery, 193
Premarital Agreements, 49
Premarital Debts, 444
Probate, 136, 557
Putative Spouse, 595
Quasi-Community Property, 134
Separate Property
  Rents, Issues, and Profits, from, 163, 174
  Statute Defining, 192
Separate Property Business Rents, Issues, and Profits, 335
Separation, After Date of, 193
Spousal Support, Statute, 527
Termination at Death, 261
Transmutations, 52
  Inception of Title Rule, and, 52
  Interspousal Gifts, 54
Treaty of Guadalupe Hidalgo, 22
Work Benefits, 339

**ATTORNEY FEES PAID**
Impairment of Community Property Interest, and, 197

**BANK ACCOUNTS**
California, CAMPAL, 118, 140, 340
Commingled, Tracing to and Through, 296
Disputed Accounts, 297
Nonmarried Cohabitants, and, 597
Special Presumptions for Sums on Deposit in, 114
Specialized Records, 296
UMPAA, 296

**BORROWED FUNDS**
Community Purpose Test, Rebuttal for, 377
Lender's Intent Test, 316, 319
Time Acquired, 316, 319

**CALIFORNIA**
American Rule of Apportionment, 172
Ancestral Property, 561
Bank Accounts. *See* CAMPAL
   *Estate of Murphy*, 344
   Forensic Records, and *See v. See*, 342
   *Hicks-Mix*, 343
   *See v. See*, 340
   Specialized Records, Tracing, 341
     *See* Statutory Presumptions
CAMPAL, 118, 140, 340
Commingled Funds. *See* Bank Accounts
Community Property Statutes, 137
Constitution, State, 194
Credit Acquisitions, 346
   American Rule, Origin of, 21, 317
   *IRMO Aufmuth,* 347
   *IRMO Marsden*, 224, 348
   *IRMO Moore,* Formula, 223, 350
   *IRMO Walrath*, 352
   Lender's Intent Test, 316
   Marital Appreciation Apportionment, *Marsden*, 224
   Total Appreciation Apportionment of, *Moore*, 223
   *Vieux v. Vieux*, 317

Date of Separation,
   Defined, 194
   Earnings and Accumulations, Character of, 171, 195
Dissolution, 521
Divorce. *See* Dissolution
Domestic Violence Prevention Act, 412
Earnings Shield, Statute, 445
Exhaustion Method Accounting. *See* Bank Accounts
Family Expense Presumption. *See* Bank Accounts
Fiduciary Duties, 412
General Presumption,
   After the Death of a Former Spouse, When Applicable, 140
   Implied from Community Property Statute, 139, 153
*Hicks-Mix. See* Bank Accounts
Historical Forms of Community Property, 188
History, 21
Impairment to Community Property, 414
Intestacy Statutes, 562
Joint Tenancy, 140
   *See* Statutory Presumptions
Judicial Council Forms, 142
Liabilities, 409, 461
Life Insurance, 354
Management and Control,
     Generally, 409
   Equal, 410
   Exclusive, 411
   Fiduciary Duties, 412
   Impairment Claims, 414
   Joint, 410
   Life Insurance Proceeds, Death, 414
   Primary, 410
Marriage Formalities, 595
     *See* Putative Spouse
     *See* Registered Domestic Partners
   Void Marriage, 595
   Voidable Marriage, 596
Married Woman's Separate Property Presumption, 121
*Marvin v. Marvin. See* Nonmarital Cohabitants
Nonmarital Cohabitants, 597

Personal Injury Recoveries,
    Assignment to Injured Spouse, Statute, 141, 525
    Community Property, For Claim During Marriage, 141
        *See* Separate Property
Premarital Agreements, 55
Putative Spouse, 528, 596
Quasi-Community Property, 138, 523, 561
Quasi-Marital Property, 139, 559, 596
Registered Domestic Partners, 598
Reimbursement,
    Education and Training, Direct Expenses of, 526
    General Statute, 263
Retroactive Applications, 264
Revocable Trust Character, 123
*See v. See. See* Bank Accounts
Separate Property,
    Personal Injury Recoveries, Before or After Marriage, 196
    Personal Injury Recoveries, From Other Spouse, 196
    Rents, Issues, and Profits, from, 194
    Statute Defining, 194
Separate Property Business Rents, Issues, and Profits, 344
    *Pereira v. Pereira*, Excess Profits, 309, 345
    *Van Camp v. Van Camp*, Net Labor Reimbursement, 311, 346
Separation, After Date of, 194
Spousal Support, Statute, 354, 528
Statutory Presumptions, 140
    Joint Title Forms, Dissolution Only, 140
    Retroactive Application, 264
    Sums on Deposit in a Demand Deposit Account, 140
Third Party Protection, 125
Transmutations, 65
    Confidential Relationship, 65
    Exemptions, Interspousal Gifts, 66
    Express Declarations, 64
    Presumption of Undue Influence, 65
Treaty of Guadalupe Hidalgo, 20
Work Related Benefits, 353

**CHARACTERIZATION**
    Generally, 3–10, 11, 101

After Date of Separation, 170
Bank Accounts, 114, 140
Before Marriage, 167
    *See* Commingling
Community or Separate, 3, 163
Gifts, 172
Personal Injury Recoveries, 177

**CHOICE OF LAW**
Conflict of Laws, 629

**COMMINGLED FUNDS**
*See* Apportionment
*See* Bank Accounts
*See* Commingling

**COMMINGLING**
    Generally, 284
    *See* Apportionment
Tracing, 291

**COMMON LAW MARRIAGE**
*See* Informal Marriage

**COMMUNITY LABOR**
Separate Property Business, and, 304

**COMMUNITY PROPERTY**
Acquired, 7
Apportionment, 10, 281, 284
Definition, 5
Domicile, and, 10
Exemptions, 6
Exercise, 220
Gambling Proceeds, 165, 476
Ganancial (Spanish) System, 15
Historical Forms of, 188
Income Tax Basis of Surviving Spouse, 240
Intestate Succession upon Death, 552
Labor, 104
Management and Control, 385
Map, 5

Marriage, and, 8
Matrimonial Regime, 14
Onerous Acquisition, and, 7
Probate Administration, 547
Property, 6
States, Default and Private Option, 5
Systems,
    Common Threads, 18, 22
    Types of, 14
    Uncommon Threads, 20
Universal (Roman-Dutch) System, 14
Working Definition, 6

**COMMUNITY PROPERTY DEFENSE**
Personal Injury Actions, 180

**COMMUNITY REGIME**
Assets and Liabilities, 433

**CONFLICT OF LAWS**
Choice of Law, 629
Domicile, 630
Forum, 629
Situs, 633

**CONFUSION**
Character Retention, General Rule, 282
Commingling, 282
Doctrine, 282, 290
Tracing, 280
Transmutation by Operation of Law, 50, 290

**CONSTITUTIONS OF STATES**
Contested Areas, 619

**CONVERSION**
Common Law Equitable Claims, 300–304
Community Personal Property, 389
Damages, 302
Nonmutual Gifts, 396
Restatement (Third) of Restitution and Injust Enrichment, 302
Sums on Deposit in a Bank Account, 303

**CREDIT ACQUISITIONS**
Generally, 292, 316
American Rule vs. Civil Law Approach, 292
    *See* Apportionment
Civil Law Approach vs. American Rule, 292
Commingling, General Tracing Analysis, 318
Pro Tanto vs. Equitable Interest, 347

**DEATH**
Family Protections, 549
Spouse as Heir of Community Property, 553
Terminates Community, 12, 543

**DEFERRED COMPENSATION**
Generally, 321
Dissolution, 328
Government Retirement Plans, 330
    *See* Retirement Plans
Severance, Death, Disability, and Retirement Benefits, 323
Tax Protected Accounts, 555
Types, 321

**DISSOLUTION**
Generally, 337
Alimony, 517
Arizona, 520
California, 521
Concealed Assets, 508
Equal vs. Equitable Division, 102, 507
Idaho, 529
Informal Law Divorce, 497, 621
Louisiana, 200, 531
Nevada, 532
New Mexico, 534
Omitted Assets, 348
Retirement and Disability Benefits,
    *See* Deferred Compensation
    *See* Retirement Plans
    *See* Work Related Benefits
Separation, 340
Spousal Support, 517

Texas, 535
Washington, 537
Wisconsin, 538

**DIVORCE**
*See* Dissolution

**DOMESTIC VIOLENCE PREVENTION LEGISLATION**
*See* California
*See* New Mexico

**DOMICILE**
Generally, 103, 104
Conflict of Laws, 630–633
Residence, compared with, 10

**DUE COURSE**
Texas, 627–629

**EFFECTIVE DATE**
Statutes, 623

**EQUAL CONTRIBUTION**
Irrebuttable Presumption, 104

**EXERCISE**
Community Property, 220

**FEDERAL LEGISLATION**
ERISA, 323, 329
Military Retirement, FUSFSPA, 617
REACT, 323

**FEDERAL SUPREMACY**
Generally, 613

**FEDERAL-STATE INTERACTION**
Approach, 614
Federal Constitution Areas, 618
Federal Preemption, 615

**FORMS OF INTIMATE PARTNERSHIP**
*See* Marriage

**FORMULA**
Arizona, Credit Acquisitions, 338
California, *Moore*, 317, 350
California, *Pereira*, 345
California, *Van Camp*, 346
Time Rule, 328

**FORUM**
Choice of Laws, 629

**GAMBLING DEBTS**
New Mexico Statute, 476

**GENERAL PRESUMPTION**
Acquisition During Marriage, Raised by, 105
Possession During Marriage, Raised by, 106

**GRATUITOUS**
Acquisition of Property, 172
   *See* Lucrative

**HISTORY**
Alaska, Private Option, 26
Arizona, 22
California, 22–23
Idaho, 23
Louisiana, 23
Nevada, 24
New Hampshire, Proposal for Private Option, 26
New Mexico, 24–25
Tennessee, Private Option, 26
Texas, 25
Washington, 25
Wisconsin, 26

**HOMESTEAD**
Idaho, 230
Nevada, 230
Texas, 225, 230, 572, 573
Wisconsin, 231

**IDAHO**
Bank Accounts, 258

Common Law Marriages. *See* Informal Marriage
Community Property Statutes, 142
Credit Acquisitions, 360
Dissolution, 529
Divorce. *See* Dissolution
Earnings During Separation. *See* Separation, After Date of, 105
History, 23
Homestead, 230, 529, 531, 563
Informal Divorce, 600
Informal Marriage, 599
Intestacy Statutes, 563
Inventory Recording, 127, 143
Joint Form Titles
    Community Property with the Right of Survivorship, 266
    Joint Tenancy, 236
Liabilities, 466
Life Insurance Character, 229
Management and Control, 414
Marriage Settlement Agreements, 42
Personal Injury Recovery, 198
Premarital Agreements, 67
Probate Code, 563
Putative Spouse Doctrine, Limited Application, 600
Rents, Issues, and Profits,
    Civil Law Approach, 124, 142, 415, 198
    Separate Property Business, from, 358
    Transmutation of, 468
Revocable Trust Character, 123, 143
Separate Property, Statute Defining, 197
Separation, After Date of, 198
Transmutations, 68
Work Related Benefits, 361

**IMMIGRATION BETWEEN STATES**
From a Community Property State, 637
To a Community Property State, 634

**INCEPTION OF TITLE RULE**
    Generally, 21, 189–190, 283
Apportionment, 10, 292
Credit Acquisitions,

American Rule, 288
Approach, 318
Civil Law, 287
Specialized Financial Records, and, 342
Title vs. Expectancy, 295

**INDEPENDENT EXECUTOR**
Operates Without Probate Court Supervision, 548
Texas, 572

**INFORMAL DIVORCE**
No State Permits, 497, 621

**INFORMAL MARRIAGE**
Common Law Marriage, cf., 8
Idaho, 599
Nonmarital Cohabitancy, cf., 584, 607
Putative Marriage, cf., 585
Texas, 20, 427, 606–607

**INTERSPOUSAL IMMUNITY**
Community Property Issues, 178

**INTESTACY STATUTES**
Arizona, 557
California, 561
Idaho, 563
Louisiana, 564
Nevada, 569
New Mexico, 570
Texas, 572
Washington, 574
Wisconsin, 577

**INTESTATE SUCCESSION**
Decedent's Community Property, 553

**INVENTORY**
Idaho, 127, 143
Nevada, 81, 127, 152, 204
Premarital Property, 127

**IRONIES**
Community Property Defense, 180

**JOINT TENANCY**
Generally, 225
Arizona, 256
Bank Accounts, 252
*See* UMPAA
California, 261
Common Law Origin, 226, 231
Compared with Other Joint Title Forms, 236
Convenience Account, 251
Dissolution, 237, 255
Express Statement to Create, 226
Idaho, 265
Louisiana, 266
Nevada, 266
New Mexico, 267
Nominal Title, 251
Safe Deposit Box, 254
Safe Deposit Box, California Limitation on, 265
Severance, 238
Special Presumptions, 246
Succession upon Death, 237
Tax Consequences for Surviving Spouse, 240
Texas, 270
U.S. Savings Bonds, 613
Washington, 273
Wisconsin, 278

**LAWFUL MARRIAGE**
Generally, 583

**LEGITIME**
Louisiana, 553, 564

**LIABILITIES**
Generally, 433, 436
Arizona, 457
California, 461
Community Debts, 439

*See* Gambling Debts
Idaho, 466
Louisiana, 470
Nevada, 473
New Mexico, 474
Premarital Obligations, 443
Texas, 479
Types, 435
Washington, 481
Wisconsin, 488

**LIFE INSURANCE**
Character, 324
Term Life Insurance, 324
   Last Premium Rule, 324
   Risk-Payment Theory, 362
Whole Life, Savings Component, 284

**LOUISIANA**
Alimony, *Pendete Lite*, 75
Bank Accounts, 363
Civil Law, 15, 23
   Patrimony, Concept of, 144
Community Property Statutes, 143
Covenant Marriage, 532, 601
Credit Acquisitions, 364
Declaration of Separate Property, 128
Divorce. *See* Termination
Fruits and Revenues, 124, 143, 147, 149, 174, 200
   Minerals, cf., 148
General Presumptions, 106, 144
Gifts, 146, 172, 201
History, 23
Intestacy Statutes, 564
Joint Tenancy, 144, 266
Legitime, 553, 564
   *See* Probate, Forced Heirship
Liabilities, 470
Life Insurance, 366
Lucrative vs. Onerous Title, 78, 172
Management and Control, 415

Matrimonial Agreements, 71
Matrimonial Regime, 14
Minerals, Leases and Extracted Products, 148
Nonmarried Cohabitants, 587
Onerous vs. Lucrative Title, 78
Personal Injury Recovery, 202
Premarital Agreements. *See* Matrimonial Contracts
Probate, 564
    Forced Heirship, 553, 565
        *See* Legitime
    Marital Portion, 566
Putative Spouse, 602
Rents, Issues, and Profits,
    Civil Law Approach, 124
    Separate Property, from, 147
    Separate Property Business, from, 364
Separate Property, Statute Defining, 199
Separation, After Date of, 170
Termination, 200, 531
Transgender, Statute Specific to, 601
Transmutations, 44
Usufruct, 150, 167, 174
Work Related Benefits, 366

**LUCRATIVE**
Acquisition by Gift, 172
Onerous, compared with, 8, 78

**MANAGEMENT AND CONTROL**
    Generally, 385
Arizona, 408
California, 390, 409
Community Property,
    Business, 409
    Commingled Property, 390
    Personal Property, 389
    Real Property, 389
Dual Management. *See* Texas
Equal Management, 385
Exclusive Management. *See* California
Fiduciary Duties. *See* California, Management and Control

Gifts, 396
Idaho, 276
Joint Management. *See* California
Louisiana, 417
Male Management, Obsolete Standard, 391
Nevada, 418
New Mexico, 421
Partnership Fiduciary Standard, 391
Primary Management. *See* California
Texas, 423
Third Parties, Protection of, 124
Washington, 426
Wisconsin, 428

**MARITAL PROPERTY**
Wisconsin Usage, 6

**MARRIAGE**
Covenant Marriage,
   Arizona, 520
   Louisiana, 531
Equitable Relationship Doctrine, 610
Lawful, 8, 583
Nonmarried Cohabitants, cf., 500
Putative Spouse, 9, 584
Registered Domestic Partners, 8, 587, 621
Valid Marriage, 8, 583
Void, 9, 139, 497, 501
Voidable, 9, 139, 497, 501

**MARSHALING ASSETS FOR CREDITORS**
Order of Availability, 435, 438
Tort Liability of One Spouse Alone, 484

**METAPHORS**
Inches to Centimeters Conversion, 637
Texas Two-Step, 88
Two-Dollar Bankruptcy, 443

**MINERAL LEASES AND PRODUCTS**
Louisiana, 148
Texas, 155

**MODEL MARITAL PROPERTY ACT (MMPA)**
Uniform Act, 17

**MORTGAGED ASSETS**
*See* Credit Acquisitions

**NECESSARY PARTIES**
Community Property Litigation, 178

**NEVADA**
Bank Accounts, 367
Community Property Statutes, 151
Constitution, 203
Credit Acquisitions, 368
Dissolution, 532
Divorce. *See* Dissolution
General Presumption, 152
History, 24
Homestead, 267
Intestacy Statutes, 569
Inventory, 152, 204
Joint Tenancy, 266
Liabilities, 473
Life Insurance Character, 240
Management and Control, 418
Personal Injury Recovery, 204
Premarital Agreements, 78
Premarital Property Inventory, 127
Putative Spouse, 605
Registered Domestic Partners, 605
Rents, Issues, and Profits, 367, 622
Separate Property,
    American Rule, 622
    Statute Defining, 302
    Tracing, from, 367
Separate Property Business Rents, Issues, and Profits, 367
Separation, After Date of, 302
Spousal Immunity Abolished, 193
Transmutations, 79
Treaty of Guadalupe Hidalgo, 22
Work Related Benefits, 369

**NEW MEXICO**
Bank Accounts, 118, 369
   *See* UMPAA
Community Property Statutes, 152
Credit Acquisitions, 370
Dissolution, 534
Divorce. *See* Dissolution
Family Violence Protection Act, 207
Gambling Debts, Statute Specific to, 476
General Presumption, Statute, 153
History, 24
Intestacy Statutes, 570
Joint Tenancy, 153, 267
   Probate, Statutory Presumption, 244, 267
Liabilities, 474
Life Insurance Character, 242
Management and Control, 421
   Written Agreement for Sole Control, 85
Married Woman's Separate Property Presumption, 122
Personal Injury Recovery, 208
Premarital Agreements, 83
Putative Spouse, 605
Rents, Issues, and Profits, 124, 208
Separate Property,
   Statute Defining, 206
   Tracing, from, 124, 208
Separate Property Business Rents, Issues, and Profits, 369
Separation, After Date of, 207
Transmutations, 84
Treaty of Guadalupe Hidalgo, 22
Work Related Benefits, 371

**NOMINAL TITLE**
Joint Tenancy, 251

**NONMARRIED COHABITANTS**
Defined, 587
Equitable Relationship Doctrine, 610
*Marvin* Claim, 597

**ONEROUS**
Acquisition of Property, 7
Lucrative, compared with, 8

***PEREIRA* APPROACH**
Excess Profits Are Community Property, 309
Formula, 310
*Van Camp*, compared with, 307

**PERSONAL INJURY RECOVERY**
Generally, 177
Elements of, 185

**PREDETERMINATION DATE PROPERTY**
Wisconsin, 189, 215, 218

**PREMARITAL AGREEMENTS**
California, CPAA, 33, 55
Non-UPAA States, 34
Uniform Premartial Agreement Act (UPAA), 33
UPAA, Adopted, 33
Wisconsin, STMPCA, 96

**PREMARITAL PROPERTY**
Inventory, 127

**PRESUMPTIONS**
General Presumption, 105
  Acquisition During Marriage, 103
  Possession During Marriage, 106
Nevada Premarital Inventory, 81
Premarital Property Inventory, 127
Special Statutory Presumptions
  Joint Form Titles, 111
  Sums on Deposit in a Bank Account, 114

**PRIVILEGES AND IMMUNITIES**
Migration to Community Property State, 634

**PROBATE ADMINISTRATION**
Generally, 543
Augmented Estate, UPC, 552
Community Property Variations, 545

Forced Election, Family Protections and, 549
Individual Retirement Account Assets, 555

**PROBATE ESTATE**
Order of Payment, 543

**PUERTO RICO**
Community Property System, 3
Conjugal Partnership, 131
Liquidation of, 132

**PUTATIVE SPOUSE DOCTRINE**
　Generally, 9, 584
Annulment vs. Dissolution, 501
Arizona, 595
California, 139, 528, 596
Dissolution vs. Annulment, 605
Idaho, 600
Louisiana, 602
Nevada, 605
New Mexico, 605
Property Division, and, 584
Texas, 606
Washington, 610
Wisconsin, 610

**QUASI-COMMUNITY PROPERTY**
　Generally, 636
California, 138, 523, 561

**QUASI-MARITAL PROPERTY**
California, 139, 559, 596

**RECORDING OF INVENTORY**
Nevada, 152, 204
Texas, 158

**REGISTERED DOMESTIC PARTNERS**
　Generally, 8
California, Nevada, and Washington, 621
Wisconsin, 610

**REIMBURSEMENT**
Apportionment, compared with, 287
Education and Training, Direct Expenses of, 526
General Statute, California, 263

**RENTS, ISSUES, AND PROFITS**
Generally, 123
Appreciation, compared with, 123
Character, 124, 167
Jurisdictional Split, 124
Tracing, 124
Usufruct, 15, 167, 174
*See* Louisiana

**RETIREMENT PLANS**
*See* Deferred Compensation
Time Rule, 328

**RETROACTIVE APPLICATIONS**
*See* California
Retroactivity, 264, 623

**RIGHT OF SURVIVORSHIP**
Arizona, 236
California, 231, 236
Chart of Joint Form Titles, 225
Community Property, 229
Idaho, Nevada, Texas, 230
Nevada Right of Survivorship, 153
New Mexico, 153
Texas. *See* Homestead
Wisconsin, Family Protection Survivorship Marital Property, 231

**SAFE DEPOSIT BOX**
Generally, 254–255
California Limitation, 265
Signature Card, 234

**SAME-SEX MARRIAGE**
Bans on Same-Sex Marriage Nullified, 619–621
Louisiana, 601
Texas, 606

Wisconsin, 610
Federal Benefits, 620
*Obergefell v. Hodges*, 8
*Windsor v. U.S.*, 620

**SEPARATE PROPERTY**
Acquired Before Marriage, 167
Acquired by Gift, 172
After Date of Separation, 82, 170
Arizona, 192
Business Rents, Issues, and Profits, Jurisdictional Split, 174
California, 194
Gambling Debts and Winnings. *See* Gambling Debts
Idaho, 197
Louisiana, 199
Nevada, 302
New Mexico, 206
Texas, 208
Washington, 212
Wisconsin, 215

**SEPARATE PROPERTY DECLARATION**
Louisiana, 363

**SITUS**
Realty, 633

**STATE CONSTITUTIONS**
Contested Areas, 619
Protection of Community Property System, 21
Right to Own Separate Property During Marriage, 168, 515, 621
Tracing, 21, 167, 291–292

**STEPPED-UP BASIS**
Community Property, 241
Separate Property, 241

**SUCCESSION UPON DEATH**
*See* Intestate Succession

**TENANCY BY THE ENTIRETY**
Right of Survivorship, 227

**TENNESSEE**
Community Property Option, 101, 131
History, 26

**TERMINATION OF THE COMMUNITY**
    Generally, 498
Arizona, 520, 557
California, 521, 558
Conflict of Laws, 515
Elections, 549
Idaho, 529, 563
Intestacy, 552
Louisiana, 531, 564
Nevada, 532, 569
New Mexico, 534, 570
Probate Administration, 547
Separation, 516
Texas, 535, 572
Washington, 537, 574
Wisconsin, 538, 577

**TEXAS**
Bank Accounts, 371
Civil Law, 89
Common Law Marriage. *See* Informal Marriage
Community Property Statutes, 154
Constitution, State, 25, 87, 208, 622
Credit Acquisitions, 372
Dissolution, 535
Divorce. *See* Dissolution
Due Course, 627
General Presumptions, 106, 154
History, 25
Homestead, 155, 225, 228, 230, 236, 255, 270, 572–573
Independent Executor, 548
Informal Marriage, 8, 497, 606
    Nonmarried Cohabitants, compared with, 607
Intestacy Statutes, 572
Joint Tenancy, 270
    Two-Step, 88, 272
Liabilities, 479

Management and Control, Dual, 423
Minerals, Leases and Extracted Products, 155
Nonmarried Cohabitants, 609
   Informal Marriage, compared with, 607
Personal Injury Recovery, 211
Premarital Agreements, 87
Probate Code, 572
Putative Spouse, 608
Rents, Issues, and Profits,
   American Rule, Statutory Option, 89
   Civil Law Approach, Default, 124, 155, 175, 209, 623
   Separate Property Business, from, 372
Separate Property,
   Inventory, Recording of, 158
   Statute Defining, 208
Separate Property Business. *See* Rents, Issues, and Profits
Third Party Protections, 157
Transmutations, 88
Work Related Benefits, 374

**THIRD PARTIES**
Statutes Protecting, 124

**TRACING**
      Generally, 166, 171
      *See* Apportionment
Commingled Bank Account, 175

**TRANSGENDER RIGHTS**
Equal Protection, Need for, 601, 606

**TRANSMUTATIONS**
   Generally, 30
Any Unfair Advantage, and, 32
Arizona, 52
By Operation of Law, 50, 290
California, 40
California Formalities, 40
Changing Character of Property, 81
Commingling, 34
Confusion, Doctrine of, 41, 282, 290

Express Declaration, 40
Fiduciary Duty, 32, 40, 179
Gifts Between Spouses, 34
Idaho, 68
Louisiana, 43, 44
Nevada, 79
New Mexico, 84
Presumption of Undue Influence, 65
Recording of Realty, 33
Texas, 49–51, 158
Texas Grant Deed, 31
Washington, 51
Wisconsin, 52

**TREATY OF GUADALUPE HIDALGO**
Generally, 22

**UNIFORM MARITAL PROPERTY ACT (UMPA 1983)**
Similarity to Community Property, 17

**UNIFORM MARRIAGE AND DIVORCE ACT (UMDA)**
States Enacting, 17, 35

**UNIFORM MULTIPLE-PERSON ACCOUNTS ACT (UMPAA 1989)**
California, 340
Community Property Presumption, Special, 115–121
Community Property States Adopting, 114

**UNIFORM PREMARITAL AGREEMENT ACT (UPAA 1983)**
Adoption by Commissioners, 29
California, CPAA, 33, 55
Consideration Not Required, 29
Disclosure, 34
Formalities, 33–35
States Adopting, 20, 33–34
Test of Unconscionability, 29
Unjust Enrichment, and, 32
Voluntariness, and, 28, 34

**UNIFORM PREMARITAL AND MARITAL AGREEMENT ACT (UMPAA 2012)**
Generally, 36–38
Community Property States Adopting, 114

**UNIFORM PROBATE CODE (UPC)**
Generally, 545

**UNILATERAL STATEMENT**
Wisconsin, 219

**USUFRUCT**
Civil Law Concept, 150
Louisiana, 148, 167, 174
Outright Ownership, compared with, 156
Rents, Issues, and Profits, 15, 124
Wisconsin, 219

***VAN CAMP* APPROACH**
Formula, 311
*Pereira*, compared with, 307
Profits Remain Separate, 311

**VESTED RIGHTS**
Generally, 625

**WASHINGTON**
Ancestral Property, 575
Bank Accounts, 375
Community Property Agreement, 274
Community Property Statutes, 158
Credit Acquisitions, 377
Dissolution, 537
Divorce. *See* Dissolution
Equitable Relationship Doctrine. *See* Nonmarried Cohabitants
Estate Tax, Stand-Alone, 577
History, 25
Intestacy Statutes, 574
Joint Tenancy, 273
Liabilities, 481
Life Insurance Character,
    Risk-Payment Theory, 362

Management and Control, 426
Nonmarried Cohabitants, 587
  Equitable Relationship Doctrine, 610
Personal Injury Recovery, 214
Premarital Agreements, 90
  Substantive Fairness Requirement, 31
Putative Spouse, 587
Registered Domestic Partners, 609
Separate Property,
  American Rule, 212
  Separate Property Business, 375
  Tracing, from, 212
Separate Property Business Rents, Issues, and Profits, 375
Separation, After Date of, 213
Spousal Immunity Abolished, 178
Transmutations, 91
Work Related Benefits, 379

**WEDDING GIFTS**
  Generally, 172
Acquired, When, 172
Arizona, 173
California, 173
Donor's Intent, 173
Louisiana, 172
Texas, 173
Wisconsin, 173

**WISCONSIN**
Bank Accounts. *See* Commingled Property
Commingled Property, 380
Community Property Statutes,
  Determination Date, 218
  Marital Property, 158
  Rents, Issues, and Profits, 174, 218
Concealed Property, 541
Determination Date, 218
Dissolution, 538
Divorce. *See* Dissolution
Gifts, 173, 399, 430
History, 26

Homestead,
    Family Protection Survivorship Marital Property, 231
Intestacy Statutes, 577
Joint Tenancy, 159, 161, 278
Liabilities, 488
Management and Control,
    Community Property Business, 387
    Credit, Joinder Required, 430
    Good Faith Standard, 428
    Impairment Claim, 429
    Marital Property, 158
    Partnership Fiduciary Standard, 390
    Rents, Issues, and Profits, 174, 218
Marital Property Agreement, 216
Marital Property Presumption, 160
Personal Injury Recovery, 219
Predetermination Date Property, 189, 215, 218
Premarital Agreements, 94
    STMPCA, 96
    Substantive Fairness Requirement, 31
Probate, 578
Putative Spouse, 611
Rents, Issues, and Profits, 163
Revocable Trust Character, 123
Separate Property, 215
    Individual Property, 215
    Predetermination Date Property, 189, 218
Separate Property Agreements, 91
Third Party Protection, Real Property, 91, 93
Transmutations, 94
Unclassified Property, 189
Unilateral Statement, 219
Usufruct, 219
Variations from UMPA, 218
Work Related Benefits, 381